THE GREAT AMERICAN BLOW-UP

Puffery in Advertising and Selling

THE GREAT AMERICAN BLOW-UP

Puffery in Advertising and Selling

IVAN L. PRESTON

The University of Wisconsin Press

Published 1975
The University of Wisconsin Press
Box 1379, Madison, Wisconsin 53701

The University of Wisconsin Press, Ltd.
70 Great Russell Street, London

First printing

Printed in the United States of America

For LC CIP information see the colophon

ISBN 0-299-06730-0

To all my girls

Robbie, Micaela, Julie, and Terry

Contents

Foreword   ix

Acknowledgments   xv

1   I'm the Greatest, Yes Sirree, That's All You'll Ever Hear from Me!   3

2   Falsity without Deception: As Possible As the Law Says, but Not As Probable   6

3   Puffery: Used Because It Works, Legalized Because It Doesn't   16

4   The Roots of Sellerism   30

5   Warranty: How Much Promise Do You Find in a Promise?   58

6   Misrepresentation: How Much Lying Do You Find in a Falsehood?   81

7   Opinion and Value Statements and Puffery: Avoiding Fact and Keeping Sellerism Alive   90

8   Factual Puffery: Fiercely Sellerist, but Now Extinct   120

9   The Federal Trade Commission: Accelerating the Consumerist Trend   130

10   Reasonable Consumer or Ignorant Consumer? How the FTC Decided   162

11   The FTC and Puffery: Some Wins and Some Losses in the Fight for Consumerism   175

12   Some Additional Kinds of Puffery: Expanding the Definition   192

13   The Ballooning of Obvious   195

14 Wishing in the Market: Puffing the Social and
   Psychological Aspects of Products   210

15 Still More Kinds of Puffery, but Controlled:
   Literally Misdescriptive Names and Mock-ups   218

16 And It's Not Trivial   245

17 Puff, Your Magic's Draggin'   273

Notes   301

Table of Cases   346

Index   354

Foreword

PATRIOTISM HAS been said to be the last refuge of a scoundrel; when all else fails to justify reprehensible conduct, a malefactor may attempt to cloak his acts by symbolically wrapping himself in the American flag or by using a phrase such as "national security," which serves as its verbal equivalent.

Those who assert unjustifiable claims usually possess a high, if not arrogant, opinion of their own competence and a low opinion of the general public, which is frequently thought to be not only pliable but unworthy of candor. One thinks of former President Nixon's statement that the American people are like children. People who are child-like are not dealt with in the same fashion as fellow adults; instead, they are spoon-fed whatever is deemed appropriate "at that point in time." If the action is unsuccessful, the spoon-feeders rarely conceive of their own low estimate of the public's worth or their own actions as being the cause of failure, but attempt to find some scapegoat on which to hang the blame.

What has this to do with advertising and *The Great American Blow-Up?*

One whose advertising has been challenged as false, misleading, or unfair finds it readily possible to argue that it is unpatriotic to question such advertising. A frequent last refuge of the advertising scoundrel is to assert that the material questioned in the advertising was mere permissible "puffing," and, consequently, it would not be in accordance with the American legal system or the workings of a free enterprise economic system to hold the representations of the advertisement to literal standards of truth, accuracy, and fairness. These assertions are based on a belief that the consuming public is unworthy of total candor and honesty in advertising.

At this stage, some may ask, "what is puffing?" The

detailed answer to that question is in this book, not in the foreword (turn to the first paragraphs of the text for a dramatic demonstration of the art). It may be said here, however, that puffing refers to advertising statements which are not illegal though they cannot be proven to be true. The principal law regulating most advertising in the United States is Section 5 of the Federal Trade Commission Act, which states that "unfair or deceptive acts or practices . . . are hereby declared unlawful." What is unfair or deceptive is for the FTC, and for the courts which review its actions, to determine.

While the proverbial innocent from another planet might consider any statement which is not literally true, or which could not be documented, to be subject to classification as "unfair" or "deceptive," many direct and indirect representations that products are superior have nevertheless been held to be "permissible puffing" even though the statements may not be literally true or subject to proof. There is a long and interesting history which led to this development of the law. Professor Preston traces this history and raises questions as to the applicability of the principles to the commercial world of today.

As a result of these precedents, when an advertiser today is challenged by the FTC and it appears unlikely that the literal truth of the advertising claim in question can be utilized as a defense, it is perhaps natural for an advertiser to assert that the questioned claim was not illegal, but permissible puffing.

I learned this first-hand during the three and one-half years (May 1970 to November 1973) I spent in charge of the unit of the FTC which was responsible for prosecuting false advertising cases. When I had occasion to address a group of business lawyers or advertising people during that time, I was invariably asked to give an example of a representation which *I personally* felt would pass the scrutiny of the FTC and be classed as permissible puffing. The only satisfactory example I felt free to cite came from a 1971 *New York Times* article by Phil Dougherty which described the FTC of that era as being a new, power-laden, enriched, energy-packed agency which scared advertisers twelve ways. Although this example rarely satisfied my questioners, I was unable to provide them with examples acceptable to me from the world of marketing rather than from the realm of journalism or the arts.

In point of fact, the FTC has not been very active in attacking puffing head-on, but, as Professor Preston relates, has generally accepted the historic precedents authorizing puffing. Nevertheless, the advertising community was gravely concerned during the early 1970s that steps to limit or abolish puffing might be undertaken by the Commission. At the Commission's special general hearings on modern advertising practices, representatives of the advertising community defended puffing as unpersuasive to consumers, generally meaningless, and unworthy of government attention. This raised the natural question of "If it's so meaningless, why waste so much precious money to produce it?" At best, this might be answered by assertions that only that which the FTC considers to be puffing is safe from attack.

Indeed, advertisers and their lawyers frequently have attacked FTC programs which result in more careful scrutiny of objectively verifiable claims on the grounds that tight regulation by the FTC will only drive them away from specific representations and into more puffing. This, they assert, is contrary to the announced beliefs of past and present FTC officials (such as myself) that the purpose of advertising in our economic system is to inform the public about the availability, characteristics, and material facts of the products advertised for sale.

While I find their argument specious on several grounds, it should be sufficient for our purposes here to note that advertisers are driven to puffing by strict application of standards to other kinds of advertising only so long as the realm of puffing remains a sanctuary from legal action. Were puffing to be attacked successfully by the FTC, more informational advertising would inevitably result. Perhaps advertisers have not concerned themselves with the possibility because they consider puffing too sacred and ancient a citadel to be assaulted successfully, even in an alleged age of consumerism.

In April 1971 I was one of a number of representatives of government and industry participating in a business-government interface program sponsored by American University. At that conference, I made some remarks on the developing definition of "unfair acts or practices" under Section 5 of the Federal Trade Commission Act. At that time, the business community was still arguing that "unfair" acts were limited to acts which were unfair to competitors and that there could be no such thing as an unfair act which was unfair only to consumers. I felt the law was otherwise and was pleased when the Supreme Court subsequently ruled that a practice which was unfair only to consumers was an illegal act under Section 5.*

Although I was more the advocate of unwelcome views than the herald of bad news, the response to my remarks at the conference was similar to that accorded the ancient bearers of bad tidings. *Advertising Age,* a trade journal of much less conservative views than the majority of the business press, denounced me editorially as a wild man and seemed to imply that I was somewhat to the left of Lenin.†

Being no virgin to criticism, I was not dismayed by the reaction. I found it interesting, however, that the strongest concern of individual business representatives arose from some remarks I made that regulation of those advertising practices which were unfair to consumers as well as those which were deceptive could result in a significant reduction in what has long been considered to be permissible puffing. Although I had suggested in the speech that such

---

*FTC v. Sperry & Hutchinson Co., 405 U.S. 233 (1972). See *Wisconsin Law Review* 1071 and 1097 (1972).

†In case anyone wonders, this is not an accurate assessment of my political views.

practices as the utilization of representations playing upon the fears and anxieties of consumers or the use of special media techniques to convey an unreasonable sense of involvement with a product were areas to which an expanded definition of fairness could be applied, the major concern of many listeners was with puffing rather than with these possible extensions of the law.

How did puffing obtain this exalted position? Professor Preston relates the history of this phenomenon and suggests some modern ways to treat it. He mounts a frontal assault on the given wisdom that puffing cannot be deceptive. The major barrier which Professor Preston faces, in my estimation, is the entrenched belief that puffing is not only too ancient and honorable to attack but, further, that it is not worth serious time and attention by those concerned with the advertising process. I do not think it should be assumed, prior to study of the matter, that puffing is necessarily trivial. True, some individual "puffing" cases may well be too trivial to be worth utilization of the scant resources of the FTC or other advertising watchdogs, but that is frequently the case also with questionable advertising which does not involve puffing. A more significant question is what result would obtain if puffing were treated differently than it is today. Would humor in advertising be eliminated or sharply reduced?* Would product advertising be reduced to tombstone, "compliments of a friend" messages? Would the economy suffer a setback if it became difficult or impossible to assert differences between products which, for practical purposes, differed only in the brand labels placed on them? Would the country be heading pell mell for socialism?

Perhaps these questions seem ridiculous to some. Yet such assertions have been seriously made (and, in some instances, seriously weighed by those who regulate advertising) in response to virtually every significant change

---

*Professor Preston proposes a treatment of humorous exaggeration which would render this objection largely moot.

made or proposed in regulating advertising over the last decade. Surely the questions would be raised again were a serious government scrutiny of puffing to be undertaken. Yet other questions could be as easily raised. Would successful assaults on puffing force advertising to become more informative and more meaningful? Would reduced reliance on puffing result in stronger efforts to compete on some basis other than advertising (such as price) in industries where products were little differentiated? Is it really un-American to question puffing in advertising?

Even more basic, perhaps, is the question of whether there is any justification to assume that puffing, by definition, cannot be misleading. If the FTC and the courts were to question this assumption, as this book urges them to do, there would be a great change in advertising discernible to every American consumer.

Whatever your answers to the questions above, I suggest you keep them in mind as you turn to Professor Preston's history and analysis of the great American advertising citadel—puffing.

Gerald J. Thain

Washington, D.C.
August 1974

Mr. Thain joined the faculty of the Law School, University of Wisconsin—Madison, in the fall of 1974. He has served as an attorney with the Federal Trade Commission and as director of its Division of National Advertising, Bureau of Consumer Protection.

Acknowledgments

I AM indebted first of all to the Law School of the University of Wisconsin—Madison for the use of its library facilities. Professor Maurice Leon and his staff have been generous with their time and have provided valuable advice. The Graduate School of the University of Wisconsin has helped in an equally important way by supplying summer research grants.

A number of experts have aided and encouraged me in preparing this manuscript. The comments of Professors David Fellman of the University of Wisconsin, Dwight L. Teeter of the University of Kentucky, and Donald M. Gillmor of the University of Minnesota have sharpened my writing. The tolerance for a nonlawyer shown by Professors J. Willard Hurst and Robert H. Skilton of the Law School at Wisconsin has helped much in motivating me to continue with this task. I am also grateful for the advice and support of David W. Neeb, assistant attorney general, State of Wisconsin, and of Gerald J. Thain, director of the division of national advertising, Federal Trade Commission, and now professor of law at Wisconsin. For the valuable opportunity to participate personally in the activities of the Federal Trade Commission I am grateful to trial attorneys James Carty and Wallace Snyder of the division of national advertising.

My very special thanks go to Professor Ralph H. Johnson of Southern Illinois University, whose annotating of cases as my graduate research assistant helped immensely in getting this project underway. Valuable research help also was provided by graduate students Ron and Kathy McHale Svoboda.

Professor Johnson and I co-authored an article in *Journalism Quarterly* which was an early version of a portion of the contents herein. Brief portions of this book also appeared first in articles of mine in *Advertising Age* and *The New York Times,* and I gratefully acknowledge the permission granted by these publications to use the material here. Other portions of the book have been presented as research papers at meetings of the American Council on Consumer Interests and the Law Division of the Association for Education in Journalism.

In the past I never believed the typical acknowledgments (mere puffing, I thought) about how a book couldn't have been written without the help of one's wife. From now on I will. For abiding those missed vacations and other impositions, Robbie and our daughters have earned my grateful thanks and, as consolation, this book's dedication.

I. L. P.

Madison, Wisconsin
July 1974

THE GREAT AMERICAN BLOW-UP

Puffery in Advertising and Selling

1

I'm the Greatest, Yes Sirree, That's All You'll Ever Hear from Me!

THE BOOK you are about to read is a superior piece of work. It demonstrates the sheerest true excellence in its treatment of one of the outstandingly important topics of our time. You will find every moment informative and entertaining to a degree you have never before encountered in the world of fine literature. This much-applauded volume has earned for its author a rightful place as one of the top writers on the contemporary scene.

The paragraph you have just read is the purest baloney, and it is precisely the topic of this book. It is puffery. It is the pretentious opinion of salesmen and advertisers, exaggerating their wares, magnifying value, quality, and attractiveness to the limits of plausibility and beyond. It is false, and I know it is false; I do not believe it. If you had believed it, and had bought this book because you relied upon the belief, you would have gotten less than you had bargained for in the marketplace. You would have been cheated.

And you would have been cheated legally. Puffery lies

to you and it deceives you, but the law says it doesn't. You can't always be "sure if it's Westinghouse," but the law says such statements are permissible. State Farm isn't "all you need to know about insurance," but State Farm may claim so without fear of prosecution. Bayer may not "work wonders," and Avis may not "try harder." There's no guarantee that "if it's Borden's it's got to be good," and the *Chicago Tribune* definitely is not the "world's greatest newspaper." Blatz may not be "Milwaukee's finest beer," Nestlé's may not make "the very best chocolate," and Ford may not give you "better ideas."

Yet none of these sales representations are prohibited. Puffery is not against the law; it is a child of the law. Our government acknowledges that sales puffs are false, but rules incorrectly that they are not deceptive. Puffery affects people's purchasing decisions by burdening them with untrue beliefs, but our regulators say it does no such thing except to the occasional out-of-step individual who acts unreasonably and therefore deserves no protection. The law holds that people who act reasonably will automatically distrust puffery, will neither believe it nor rely upon it, and therefore cannot be deceived by it.

Without a doubt the law just described is about as pure a piece of baloney as puffery itself is. Puffery deceives, and the regulations which have made it legal are thoroughly unjustified. There are many varieties of puffery, and they account for a huge proportion of the claims made by sellers and advertisers in the marketplace. The rules which say these false claims are nondeceptive and therefore legal are based on incorrect assumptions about the facts of human behavior and on incorrect applications of the legal precedents from which they supposedly derive. This book is about the circumstances which have brought such strange regulations into being and have contributed thereby to the unhappiness with which today's consumers view the marketplace. It is the story of legalized lying.

We live in an age when standards in the marketplace are rising. The outright deceits of sellers were once acceptable behavior; today they are not. The consumerism trend has removed most of them. But the job is not yet complete, the movement has not yet succeeded. Puffery is the remaining area which has yet to be mopped up; it is the unwelcome residue of what today's standards are replacing. It is soft-core deception, but it is deception nonetheless. It is the last outpost for the seller who wishes to tell lies.

Puffery is the ever-diminishing corner into which the sellers and advertisers have been painted by consumerism. Its perpetrators have been allowed to stay in that corner by the tolerance of the law for the precedents of the past. Just as military cavalrymen maintained their fondness for horses long after tanks and trucks rendered them obsolete, so have the regulators of the marketplace maintained their acceptance of puffery long after changing social conditions have removed the reasons which created it in the first place. The law has allowed puffery to remain without justification and in defiance of the wishes of the American consumer who wants to deal in the marketplace in peace and in truth.

The message of this book is that the consumerism movement need not stop short of a complete elimination of false representations which deceive. An impression prevails widely that all the forms of puffery have been declared legal for all time, and that nothing can be done to get rid of them. This impression is wrong. The means exist for reversing such rules. These means should be used, and deception should be removed entirely, not just partly, from the marketplace.

2

Falsity without Deception:
As Possible As the Law Says,
but Not As Probable

A LONG, long time ago the law of the marketplace adopted a rule of thumb to help it decide which seller's claims were legal and which were not. The rule brought some very good results, but it also produced a bad effect we have been paying for ever since. The bad effect was puffery. What produced it was the rule that falsity is not always illegal.

To simple souls, what is false should be illegal and what is not false should be legal. The bad would be punished, the good would be spared, and all problems would be solved. But sophisticates know (and the law is most sophisticated on this point) that the problems would not all be solved. Under such a rule some of the bad would be spared, and some of the good would be punished. The proper rule, therefore, is that what is *deceptive* is illegal and what is not deceptive is not illegal. That is the rule which the law has most wisely adopted.[1]

Falsity and deception may seem the same. But they're not; what is deceptive is what is injurious to the consumer. The words and pictures directed by sellers toward the public may be considered by the law to be injurious and

6

therefore illegally deceptive even though not false. Or they may be considered to be noninjurious and therefore legally nondeceptive even though false. A claim that is false, therefore, is not automatically illegal, and a claim that is true is not automatically legal.

All of that is good simply because it is correct. If our society systematically approved all nonfalsity, we would fail to assist those consumers injured by such content. And if we systematically condemned all falsity we would be unfair to those sellers and advertisers who affect no one adversely with such messages. The representation that you'll have a tiger in your tank when you use Esso (now Exxon) gasoline illustrates a kind of falsity which is not deceptive. There's no tiger, but regulators have never found anyone who expected a tiger. There was no disappointment and therefore no injurious deception, even though there was falsity.

On the other hand, in 1971 the Federal Trade Commission found the makers of Hot Wheels and Johnny Lightning toy racers to be deceptive in some nonfalse television representations showing the cars moving at high speeds along their tracks. The racers were photographed from a position so close to the track that they zoomed past in what appeared as an exciting blur on the screen. The photography was true; you can approximate it by moving your hand past your eye at point-blank range. But the children who got the racers for Christmas expected the same effect to occur in their own games, and it did not. The representation was technically accurate, but the FTC thought it would deceive children badly.[2]

And so we find that regulators were correct when they separated deception and falsity and declared that the law's task was to identify deception separately as an independent feature of the claims sellers make. We know they were right, but we also know from the record of several centuries that the task they established for themselves has been a most difficult one to carry out. It is one thing to say we must identify deception; it is another to do it.

Unfortunately, neither the regulators nor anyone else can always satisfactorily distinguish between those seller's claims which are deceptive and those which are not.

It is far easier to detect falsity than to detect deception. Falsity is objective, which means we can discover it by looking at nonhuman objects. We can check to see whether the product for sale matches the stories told about it. If the toothpaste lacks the ingredient the ad explicitly claims it has, then the ad is false. We must examine the claim carefully and test the toothpaste properly to be sure our decision is accurate, but usually there is no room for doubt that it is.

Deception is different; it is subjective and it leaves considerable room for doubt. It is a property of human beings. We look for it within the mind of the consumer, the person who is considering the object. If the sales message makes the consumer believe the toothpaste contains something it doesn't, then it deceives him. Maybe the message is actually true, but if its result is a false belief that the consumer might reasonably acquire from it, then it is deceptive.

The individual is the sole person who can tell us about any instance of deception or nondeception which occurs within his own mind. He is free to report that he has been deceived or not, whether he was or not, as he sees fit. No outside observer can directly identify the alleged deception's existence or nonexistence. Yet the regulators, who need desperately to know, are always outside observers. They can "know" deception occurred only by using a method which is very arbitrary—they make their most reasonable guess about the matter. They examine all observable aspects of the situation, including the individual's testimony and any evidence which may support or deny that testimony. They then make their own inferences independently, and some of them "see" deception and some of them do not. They then total up their various opinions to see who is in the majority, and that is how they determine whether deception exists legally.[3]

The problem of puffery is precisely of that sort. The question is not whether it is false, which virtually all of it is,[4] but whether it is deceptive and therefore illegal. To that question the law and this book make exactly opposite determinations: the law says puffery is not deceptive,[5] and I say it is. I believe the law has made an improper finding of a lack of deception.

I believe in the existence of falsity without deception and of deception without falsity. I accept these as events which can reasonably happen, and am sure that the law has properly identified many such instances of their occurrence. But with certain types of false representations, which I have combined under the name puffery, I believe the law has been systematically wrong in finding falsity to be nondeceptive. Just as it would be wrong to make the simple-minded assertion that all falsity is automatically deceptive, I feel it is equally wrong to flip completely over to the opposite assertion that certain types of falsity are automatically nondeceptive.

My argument is made in support of the consumer, yet it is ironic to note that sellers and advertisers are constantly engaged in a very similar protest. They, too, insist that the law has made a systematic mistake in determining deception. While I am concerned that much of the falsity the law calls nondeceptive should properly be called deceptive, the industry is concerned that much of the nonfalsity the law calls deceptive should be called nondeceptive. In this way industry, too, is unhappy over the law's decisions about deception, including in recent times the makers of Geritol, Wonder Bread, Un-Burn, Hi-C, Chevron, Zerex, Lysol, Firestone tires, and Ocean Spray cranberries.[6]

The Federal Trade Commission decided in the case of Geritol, for example, that its ads deceptively implied that people never need see a doctor to treat their "tired blood." The ads did not state this explicitly, and Geritol's maker, J. B. Williams Co., denied vehemently that they implied any such thing. Whatever the truth may be, we know that neither the government agency nor the manufacturer nor any other party actually observed any deception or non-deception. Only the consumers, the viewers of the Geritol commercials, could have made such observations.

It's obvious that a person's disposition to "see" deception depends immensely upon his preference for having the message either prohibited or retained in use. That is why persons directly representing consumers or sellers are not allowed to make such decisions officially. But someone must make them, and it is possible that they, whoever they are, will be disposed to favor one side or the other. It is also possible that they will be *suspected* of favoring one side or the other, even if they don't, and if they are suspected of favoritism there is no way for them to prove absolutely that they are not guilty of it.

So invisible and elastic a concept as deception produces many such consequences. One might assume, for instance, that consumers hate deception far more than advertisers do. But advertisers hate deception, too; they absolutely loathe it. They make speeches about how they want to eliminate deception, more impassioned speeches about this than consumers make.[7] The only trouble is, advertisers don't *see* much deception when they look around. When messages are false, advertisers are wonderfully brilliant in explaining such messages as only jokes or little white lies so obvious that no one possibly could be deceived by them. When the messages are not explicitly false, advertisers cannot conceive of them as being deceptive. Advertisers hate deception when they see it. But they don't see it very often.

Consumer spokesmen are equally inventive. When messages are false, these persons are sincerely certain they must be deceptive. If they're false, they say, then the existence of deception follows automatically. And when messages are not explicitly false, consumerists are brilliant in showing how they must nevertheless be deceptive. Consumerists seem anxious to find that deception exists. They want to see it so they can hate it.

It would be most attractive if the law's determinations

did not need to be based on so slippery a concept as deception. Why not go back to falsity; it is so much easier to determine. Besides, falsity is a bad thing, isn't it? People should be kept from communicating false messages! Why don't we just slip back to the old idea that anything that's false is illegal, and anything that's not is not?

We cannot do that, unfortunately, because a concentration on falsity ignores what the law is trying to do. The law regulates the seller's messages in order to prevent the consumer from having to accept, through no fault of his own, less than what he reasonably believed he was bargaining for. The law is not really regulating the message; it is regulating the fate of the consumer.[8] It is not the message sent, but the message received, which determines that fate.

It may be compelling to believe that the message received is equivalent to the message sent, but the regulators know from experience that that is not always so. They have seen many occasions where the buyer was treated unfairly although there was no falsity. And they have seen many situations where all concerned, including the buyer, agree that the buyer was not disadvantaged even though the seller's statements were false. There is no doubt that the troublesome separation of falsity and deception exists precisely because it must.

The regulators have also seen situations where the buyer was disadvantaged and the seller's statements were false, but the buyer's ill luck appeared due to his own carelessness rather than to improper behavior by the seller. Deception, legally, means not just that the buyer was fooled but that the seller's message fooled him.[9] Buyers may fool themselves all day long and the law will not protect them.[10] Determining who is responsible requires another inference, unfortunately, and therefore another bit of arbitrariness. We cannot see who caused the buyer's perception of the message; we can only make a reasonable guess. But it must be done.

Consider the scene at a hardware store where the salesman points to a hoe and says "Would you like to buy this rake?" The buyer accepts the item as a rake and purchases it. Was it the message which produced the buyer's misperception? If so, there was deception in a legal sense. If not, there was no deception even though there was falsity and the buyer was fooled.

Did the seller trick the buyer into relying on the message, or did the buyer fool himself in doing so? Did the buyer examine the hoe and see the truth, did he examine and fail to see, or did he fail to examine at all? If he failed to examine, was it because he neglected his responsibility or because he felt he could rightfully rely on the seller as responsible?

In a given case we may never know the facts, but the law has made a decision as to what it feels the facts must be in cases of this sort. The law says the buyer must have fooled himself because a falsity so obvious to the eye cannot possibly fool anyone exerting the ordinary wakefulness which the law feels he should show. The rule is more than five hundred years old; a judge named Brian proclaimed in England in 1471: "If a man sells me a horse and warrants that he has two eyes, if he has not, I shall not have an action of deceit, as I could know this at the beginning."[11]

Does such a situation truly involve no responsibility for deception on the seller's part? You could dispute the point easily, although you must concede first that the buyer who thought a hoe was a rake was no great help to himself. He might have taken a casual glance at what he was paying his money for! But granting this, you could then argue forcefully that the seller's falsehood was greatly responsible for the buyer's misperception. If the falsehood had not been told, the buyer might not have misperceived. Isn't that enough to make it a case of deception?

The argument seems impeccable, but is destroyed by yet another element of that wretched arbitrariness which plagues these matters. The law decided long ago in such cases that where both buyer and seller bear some responsibility, the seller is not responsible. In baseball, ties favor the runner; in the market, ties favor the seller. There are some legal matters in some states in which a jury may divide responsibility for negligence among the parties, but in sales representations the rule tends to be all or nothing.

This rule of the market was not so arbitrary originally; it was made at a time when society wished to do all it could to foster the development of trade.[12] Today society no longer wishes to support trade to so great an extent, yet the rule still stands. The buyer who is partly responsible is wholly responsible, while the seller not wholly responsible is not responsible at all.

Examine the fate of partly responsible Herbert A. Williams, who bought a car in Milwaukee, Wisconsin, in 1968. The salesman at Rank & Son Buick, Inc., told Williams the car was air-conditioned, and Williams found knobs on the dashboard marked "Air." Several days after purchase he found these knobs gave only ventilation (just what they said: air!). The car was not air-conditioned at all. Williams sued, but the Supreme Court of Wisconsin told him that "one cannot justifiably rely upon obviously false statements."[13] The court found he had been given ample opportunity to examine the car on his own, including one-and-a-half hours when he drove it away from the premises unaccompanied. No great search, the court said, was required to discover the absence of an air-conditioning unit.

True, the purchase was made in March in a wintry climate, eliminating any possibility that an air conditioner would be used for its customary function. It was also true that the jury, in the original trial, had found that Williams had a right to rely on the salesman's claim, which meant it had found he did not know the falseness of the supposedly obvious falsity. But on appeal, since Williams had identified air conditioning as the main reason for buying that particular car, the Supreme Court of Wisconsin considered it doubtful that he had not checked to see whether it was there. It was clear to the court, by the logic of law rather than the evidence of fact, that Williams had made the examination and flunked it. His suit was thrown out.

The regulation of seller's representations, as all other

areas of law, depends on the facts of the individual case. There were additional facts which may have contributed to the seller's victory in this particular case. Williams told the court he had relied not only on the salesman's statements but also upon a *Milwaukee Journal* ad which claimed for the car, "Full power, including FACTORY AIR CONDITIONING." The ad, however, was not proved by Williams's counsel to have appeared any earlier than two days after he signed the purchase contract, thus his alleged reliance upon it was thrown out. No doubt Williams would have been more successful with the court if he had not allowed his testimony to be thus discredited. Without this mixup, the misrepresentation in the ad might have counted more heavily against the seller. But would Williams have been exonerated? We do not know.

How should a typical consumer feel about this case? How should a seller feel? There was a finding that the salesman had lied, intending to defraud. The decision was clearly a case of ruling that the improper behavior of the buyer rendered inconsequential the improper behavior of the seller. Should the seller be excused in that way?

If you are not entirely pleased with this rule about obvious falsity, it may be consoling to know that the Wisconsin court passed it by the slightest majority, 4-3. The dissenting justices said the misrepresentation couldn't have been all that obvious, since the jury found as a fact that it hadn't been known to Williams. Furthermore, said the dissent, the finding of fact was up to the jury, since it had heard all the testimony. The court had the right to overrule the jury on matters of law but not on matters of fact. Therefore, Williams had a right to rely on the salesman because the misrepresentation wasn't obvious.

The dissenters did not go further, as many people might, to argue that the buyer had a right to rely on the misrepresentation even while knowing its falsity, simply because the seller had said it. As long as we are being arbitrary, why not argue that the seller's responsibility renders inconsequential the buyer's, just the opposite of the rule which was applied! Buyers might feel it would be fair to have this rule for awhile, just to balance the books. This is not to say it would be any more equitable, but only to illustrate that the kind of thinking used arbitrarily to benefit sellers might be used just as readily to benefit buyers.

The rule of obvious falsity is only one of many strange rules you will see in this book. If you disliked that one, you'll detest the rest. The reader who cannot accept obvious falsity as nondeceptive will have trouble with what follows, because that rule depicts the clearest separation of falsity and deception to be seen in this narrative.

To find that the clearest is not clear at all is only to illustrate the problems we will examine as we continue. They are all based on the assumption that *some* objective falsity is not subjectively deceptive, and that *some* objective nonfalsity is subjectively deceptive. There is a certain naturalness when a decision finds deception in conjunction with falsity or nondeception in conjunction with nonfalsity. Were all the world's sales messages examined, one of these two results surely would be declared in most cases. But the other possible decisions are terribly troublesome. Falsity is sometimes not deceptive, nonfalsity is sometimes deceptive. The rules providing for this cannot be called bad in the sense that someone could easily write better ones. But they are vulnerable to criticism because they leave us with so much uncertainty as to when deception of the consumer truly occurs. When do we have deception and when not? We often fail to be satisfied with the answers people give to those questions.

My own dissatisfaction is the basic reason I have written this book. I believe there has been a systematic tendency to answer wrongly the question of whether certain types of falsity are deceptive. The law has decided, inaccurately I believe, that certain falsities known as puffery are nondeceptive in the face of strong reasons for believing they are actually deceptive. Let's see what these reasons are.

3

Puffery:
Used Because It Works,
Legalized Because
It Doesn't

THIS BOOK is about the several types of falsity which legally produce no deception. Technically, they are called:

(1) puffery;
(2) obvious falsity;
(3) social-psychological misrepresentations;
(4) literally misdescriptive names; and
(5) mock-ups.

Before I finish I am going to refer to all of these false representations as "puffery," because they all involve claims which puff up the product to be greater than it actually is. But since the law applies that term technically to only one of the types, we will see first what that narrow definition is and then in later chapters expand the idea to include the other types of falsity through which sellers puff their products. Until we reach chapter 12, then, the term *puffery* will be restricted to the technical meaning which lawyers have traditionally given it.

16

By legal definition, puffery is advertising or other sales representations which praise the item to be sold with subjective opinions, superlatives, or exaggerations, vaguely and generally, stating no specific facts.[1] It appears in various verbal and pictorial forms, the best known being slogans which are used repeatedly, sometimes for years, on behalf of a throng of nationally advertised products and services. Perhaps the oldest of these still actively used is P. T. Barnum's "The Greatest Show on Earth." One might call it the king of them all, which would be puffing about puffing.

Puffery technically must consist of claims which involve opinions, superlatives, or exaggerations about product qualities which actually exist. Statements which say something exists when it doesn't at all are not included in puffery,[2] which presumably stops the puffer at a certain point in his expansion of false claims. It may be illusory, however, to believe that this limitation is very great. Subjective opinion about matters of taste, for example, is always classifiable as puffery because any object good enough for a seller to want to sell has at least some degree of beauty, deliciousness, attractiveness, popularity, or whatever, even though not having as much as claimed.

There will always be someone who thinks the circus is the greatest or Blatz is the finest, even if most people wouldn't. That somebody may be only the promoter or seller, but that's somebody. My opening statement about the superiority of this book qualifies as puffery because it is wholly reasonable to expect that some people will find it so. My mother will undoubtedly find this the most exciting volume she has ever read. I imagine a number of my family and friends will display these words upon their coffee tables while most of the world is consigning them to whatever fate they should happen to deserve. But unless the critics should decide in the end that this is the worst book of the year, with no redeeming social value whatever, the law as it now stands will refer to the superiority claim as merely puffery on the grounds that it amounts only to a vague and general blowing up of characteristics which actually exist.

Among the many examples of puffery which abound in the advertising of our day are:

> Blatz is Milwaukee's finest beer[3]
> When you're out of Schlitz you're out of beer
> Andeker—America's greatest
> When you say Budweiser, you've said it all
> King of beers (Budweiser)
> "premium" beer
> Colt 45 Malt Liquor: a completely unique experience
> We try harder (Avis)
> Bayer works wonders
> The wonderful world of Disney
> Nestlé's makes the very best chocolate
> Get the best—get Sealtest
> Kraft—the mayonnaise lover's mayonnaise
> Ford gives you better ideas[4]
> America's most welcome wagons (Ford)
> The Continentals—the final step up (Ford)
> GM—always a step ahead
> Chevrolet—building a better way to see the USA
> Cadillac—the new look of leadership
> Toronado—as unmistakable as the people who drive it
> Toshiba—in touch with tomorrow
> Finest ride GM engineers have ever developed (Oldsmobile)[5]
> Accucolor—brightest, sharpest picture in RCA history[5]
> The biggest breakthrough in color TV (Zenith Chroma-color)
> Old Grand Dad—head of the bourbon family
> Pours more pleasure (J&B Scotch)
> Try something better (J&B Scotch)
> Anything your whiskey can do, Kessler can do smoother
> The world's most popular Christmas club (Canadian Club)

The world's best-dressed whiskey (Canadian Lord Cal-
vert: Christmas wrapping)
You can't get any closer (Norelco)
The perfect gift (Norelco)
Allied Van Lines—We move families, not just furniture
The two greatest ways to eat peanut candy (Mars)
Be careful how you use it (Hai Karate)
Smells so good you won't want to shave it off (Rise)
Come to where the flavor is (Marlboro)
Kent got it all together! All the good things of a Kent
Viceroy gives you all the taste, all the time
Kool—Measurably long . . . immeasurably cool[6]
Gas gives you a better deal (American Gas Association)
Live better electrically (Edison Electric Institute)
The more you know, the more you'll want Delco
North America's number one snowmobile (Ski-Doo)
The world's number one station (KDKA, Pittsburgh)
The American breakfast, no mistake, starts with sugar,
milk, and Kellogg's corn flakes
What's new for tomorrow is at Singer today
Lysol spray does so much more, so more people use it
Our hotels are what you mean by New York (Biltmore,
Commodore, Roosevelt)
Louisville—strategic city of the 70s
Georgia, the unspoiled
For four generations we've been making medicines as if
people's lives depended on them (Eli Lilly)
Breakfast of Champions (Wheaties)
If it's Borden's it's got to be good
With a name like Smucker's, it has to be good
Keebler—uncommonly good
You can trust your car to the man who wears the star
(Texaco)
You expect more from Standard, and you get it
The most long-awaited gasoline development in history
(Chevron F-310)
You can be sure if it's Westinghouse
State Farm is all you need to know about insurance

Like a good neighbor, State Farm is there
The greatest show on earth (Barnum & Bailey)
The greatest cooking discovery since fire (Amana)
The world's greatest newspaper (Chicago Tribune)[7]
The biggest little treat in all the land (Wrigley)
The world's most experienced airline (Pan Am)
Fly the friendly skies of United
Things go better with Coke
It's the real thing (Coke)
Coke has brought more people together than any other
   soft drink
Parker—maker of the world's most wanted pens
Instrument of the immortals (Steinway)
Prudential has the strength of Gibraltar
Perfect rice everytime (Minute Rice)
Buc Wheats—helps you feel like a million bucks
Hush Puppies aren't such a fancy shoe, or a phony
   shoe; they're just dumb
There's a new you coming every day (American Dairy
   Association)
Every body needs milk (American Dairy Association)
Every kid in America loves Jello brand gelatin
Pepto-Bismol, with its famous coating action
Chemical Bank—we do more for your money
Assembles in minutes (various gadgets which usually
   don't)

Other well-known examples of puffery consist entirely of
names:

> Wonder Bread
> Super Shell (gasoline)
> Rapid Shave
> Champion (spark plugs)
> Top Flite (golf balls)
> Easy Off (oven cleaner)
> Lestoil (liquid cleaner)

Now there is a puzzling thing about the examples of

puffery I've just listed. All of them are regarded as legally belonging under the definition of puffery given above.[8] Yet I doubt whether they actually fit that definition. They do, of course, state opinions which vary subjectively from person to person, and with which the individual consumer will not necessarily agree. These opinions are typically superlatives or exaggerations, and they are vague and general in the sense of stating literally no way in which the products are "greatest" or "finest."

But the definition also says that puffery states no specific facts. That is what is puzzling, because I can only believe that a product which is the greatest or finest must be so in some specific way. Isn't some unnamed physical characteristic being claimed, truly or falsely, to be present in greater quality or quantity than in the competitors' brands?

The answer should be "Yes," with all certainty. Those physical characteristics may not be explicitly mentioned, but an implication surely is made that they exist. When Blatz is called Milwaukee's finest beer, does not the claim imply the existence of certain standards of beer production with no less certainty than if they had been explicitly described? They are not identified, but the fact that they exist is fully implied. What else, really, can "finest" mean?

We have already seen that the law's purpose is to regulate subjective deception rather than objective falsity, and the key to the subjectivity of a message is not in what it says to the consumer but in what it *means* to him. It is a part of our nature to draw implications from messages, and to treat these implications as being just as much present therein as if they had been explicitly stated. When I see blinking lights at a train crossing I stop immediately, treating the lights as implying a train no less certainly than if I were seeing the train itself. When I am told that Nestlé's makes the very best chocolate, why would I not with equal certainty take the statement to mean that Nestlé's is judged superior by specific standards which exist in the chocolate business?

Perhaps we shouldn't draw such implications, but the facts show that we do. Students of general semantics[9] have tried valiantly to teach the public the difference between implication and actual statement, arguing that implications are acceptable as no more than tentative guesses about what something means. The blinking lights are not the train, the semanticists tell us, and they make a useful point in doing so. I have seen crossing lights blinking when there was no train. I have seen left turn signals blinking on cars which did not turn left. And in the marketplace, I have seen products called "finest" which were not.

A particularly gross example is an ad which proclaimed "Professional hockey at its best" in describing a game between the Milwaukee Admirals and the Boston Hawks, whoever they are. Those teams do not play in the top professional leagues, and in fact are not even fully professional. Their players are semi-pros who spend their working week at other jobs and can't always play at the scheduled times. They have the thinnest association it is possible to have with truly professional sport. Their games might accurately be called "Professional hockey at its worst." But they call themselves the "best," and no one asks them to stop.

With ads like that running loose, we certainly should restrain ourselves from confusing things questionably implied with things unquestionably observed. But we accept such implications all the time. The very existence of the general semantics movement is evidence that we do. Organized disciplines typically aren't created to urge us against doing what we already don't do. Sophisticated communications campaigns tell us to get cancer check-ups and fasten our seat belts because so many of us don't. And the semanticists tell us not to accept implications as actual statements because so many of us do.

That is why I am puzzled over the definition of puffery. If the examples given of it in the list above state specific facts even by implication, then they cannot legally be puffery at all. Puffery cannot exist under that definition, because all puffs imply facts. But it does exist because the law chooses to ignore any consideration of what it implies. Advertisers insist on defining puffery only by what it literally states. And the law, for reasons I find inexplicable, goes along with this wish. The law says no reasonable person relies on puffery as meaning any specific thing.

To the question of what "finest beer" means, the regulators' answer is that it means nothing; it's meaningless. I could not possibly disagree more. We might concede as a matter strictly of language structure that puffery states nothing, but as a matter of human behavior we can't state that at all. Can we ever believe that something means nothing? "Nothing never happens" is what an anthropologist once said in dismissing such a possibility.[10] Some meaning always happens, and with puffery it will probably work to the consumer's disadvantage. The facts implied by a piece of puffery are almost always false—or at least not known by the speaker to be true, which amounts to falsity in the sense that he knows he has no basis for claiming it.

Only in a tiny minority of cases will a puff imply true facts. Some items for sale are truly the best in objective ways, and a puff which says so must be called accurate. Polaroid may say it gives you pictures faster than any other camera; there is no way its claim of superlativeness is anything but factually true. Other types of true puffs consist of subjective judgments which happen to be agreed upon by all who have judged the matter. Everyone, for example, says that rubber automobile tires give a more comfortable ride than tires of wood or metal. Therefore advertisers may puff rubber tires as the greatest without fear of implying anything false.

But true puffs are a very limited minority. Notice that the tire example involved a product category, rubber tires; it did not involve the various brands of tires. And while the Polaroid example was about a brand, there is only one brand of camera which produces pictures on the spot. Thus neither example involved competing brands, which is the most typical market situation in which heavy advertising and selling are used. Where there are competing brands, only one can be superior, and the puffs of the others must be false. It is likely, in fact, that *all* are false, because there typically is no established objective basis or consensus of subjective judgment available to prove that any single brand is superior.

So there aren't many situations where a puff *can* be true, and when it's true there aren't many situations where the seller wants to use it. When the puff is true it is usually obviously so or widely known to be so, and the seller therefore has no need to make the point. Polaroid wouldn't bother today to tell us its pictures appear sooner than do those of other cameras. It told us that at first, of course, but the fact has long since been deemphasized in its ads. No rubber company would bother to tell us that rubber is superior to metal for making tires. What they do want to tell us is that their own brand of tires is best, which everybody doesn't know and which very likely isn't true.

Any salesman or advertiser who knew or honestly believed his product to be factually superior would surely state the factual basis rather than the puff. Why would Procter & Gamble bother to call Crest toothpaste the "best" when they could truthfully say it had the endorsement of the American Dental Association? Puffery is what you say when you can't say something like that, which is why I feel justified in stating that the facts which puffs imply are virtually always false.

Paging through an issue of *Gourmet,* a great gold mine of puffery, I spotted an ad which stood out from the rest with what it stated explicitly. There were numerous puffs for wine and liquor, but this one was different: "Marquisat. French law recognizes it as better than ordinary Beaujolais."[11]

Marquisat has on its label the words "Beaujolais Villages," the ad explains, which may be used only for wines from officially recognized areas. That designation is a fact emanating from the entire French wine business, not a puff from one vintner alone. When you see puffs instead, and they imply that such a standard has been met, you might most reasonably suppose it has not. If it had been, you would expect the advertiser to say so, as the Marquisat people have done.

Advertisers may deny such falsity charges by saying their puffs are actually unproved or unprovable. But that is a two-edged argument which gives them no advantage. If the consumer cannot prove the claim is false, the advertiser cannot prove it is true. The law holds illegal falsity to exist not only when the speaker specifically knows the falseness but also when he realizes he does not know the truth.[12] If the advertiser cannot show his puffery claim to be true, he may be liable for that reason alone.[13] One of the most potent ways of illustrating this sort of falsity is to find two or more competitors making incompatible claims that the product of each is the finest. When this happens, we can discuss with some certainty the falsity of the group as a whole, even if we cannot prove the falsity of any individual. The group of manufacturers, each of whom surely knows the other's claims, must be collectively insincere in making a set of claims it couldn't possibly believe.

This conscious awareness of conflicting claims is another reason to convince us of the falsity of what puffery implies, when it is taken to imply something. The only thing saving it from liability is the law's insistence that reasonable people do not take it to imply anything.

How can we prove convincingly that puffery does imply facts and thereby affects people's purchasing decisions? There is no value in showing merely that a few persons such as Herbert Williams[14] have believed claims which the law says reasonable people will not believe. Their cases will be thrown out for unreasonableness, whether that is correct or not. Williams may have acted quite sensibly, but the only way to prove it is to show that many people, not just one, would have believed the claim about the air conditioner.[15] The acts of a substantial portion of the public cannot be dismissed as unreasonable, but we must gather evidence about that portion or lose the argument.

There is a lot of authority afoot that says puffery deceives no substantial numbers at all.[16] The law takes this position, and the advertisers are only too willing to agree. "How far down the road toward idiocy," queried the chairman of *Advertising Age*, "do we go to 'protect' the person who would consider such a phrase a guarantee of superiority?"[17]

That is precisely the viewpoint which must be countered in order to drive legalized falsity out of the market. I know of a big, whopping, absolutely conclusive reason for arguing that puffery is believed by a substantial portion of the public, and in my opinion it proves the point beyond any doubt. The reason is that advertisers and salesmen use puffery all the time. It is endemic in American salesmanship, practically the soul and substance of the American way of selling. It is an established contributor to a decades-long success story achieved by professionals far too skilled to retain a practice the public would see instantly as false. Selling goods is one of the most expert acts ever developed on our continent, and experts don't repeat methods which fail!

Why would the salesman have told Herbert Williams the car was air-conditioned if he had not expected Williams might believe it? The court called the claim obviously false, but if buyers always noticed the falsity then why would the salesman have bothered to say it? Why would Blatz advertise its product as Milwaukee's finest beer if the consumer always noticed the "obvious" facts that Blatz offers no proof for the claim, and that other beer producers make claims which contradict it? While advertising's elder spokesmen pontificate from the board rooms that reliance on puffery is restricted to a few idiots, the industry's toilers in the vineyards, the copywriters, keep putting out the puffs on the obvious assumption that they have a wide-ranging effect. The true industry position is indicated by the ads rather than the speeches. The line would not be used if Blatz felt it had no effect.

When law and advertiser disagree over whether these messages work, one should ask who is the greater expert at determining what sells products. The industry's conviction that puffery works is proof enough for me that it does, because I have a great admiration for the expertise of the advertising profession. When experienced professionals commit themselves to the continuing use of such themes, it can only be from the knowledge that they will sell. And if they sell it is because they produce belief and therefore, when false, because they deceive.

There are few admissions of this by industry people; they try to avoid confessing the obvious. Witness the attempt by FTC Commissioner Mary Gardiner Jones to draw such an acknowledgment from an industry spokesman at the Commission's 1971 hearings on the nature of the advertising process.[18] Commissioner Jones suggested that every advertising claim is surely made with the purpose of influencing the consumer's decision. She then added, in the manner of a chess player's gambit, hoping the opponent will bite, the comment, "This would mean there is no such thing as puffery."

In chess the player may safely refuse the gambit, but the advertising executive was in trouble whether he bit or not. Choosing to protest, he cited the "metaphor" (as he called it) of the washing machine growing ten feet tall in the detergent ad, and argued that such representations were not intended to be believed. Commissioner Jones persisted, asking, "How would you expect it to function if not to be believed?" And the reluctant concession, finally, was "I'm sure they intended that metaphor to be translated into some beneficial attribute."

A rare voluntary admission of the same has been made by an advertising agency president, Peter Geer, in a speech titled "Those Fourteen Words."[19] The words are the slogan of one of his agency's clients, Eli Lilly: "For four generations we've been making medicines as if people's lives depended on it." Here is Geer's analysis of the claim's effectiveness: "A naked boast. A simple unproved assertion . . . of the sort that those of us who pride ourselves on being skilled practitioners and accomplished critics of advertising would normally . . . dismiss out of hand as unsubstantiated assertions of superiority, without documentation and without support. . . . Lilly isn't saying anything in these ads that is buttressed by evidence, and yet, these ads attain levels of conviction and believability that the most reasoned persuasion often fails to achieve in advertising."

He was saying that puffery works and he's glad he uses it. Such candor is not frequent in advertising, but one easily imagines that other purveyors of puffery use it only for the same reason. If the advertisers are convinced, by whatever proofs they find acceptable, surely the regulators must seriously consider the same conviction. Contrary to what the law assumes, there seems little reason to deny that puffery actually is believed and relied upon to a substantial extent.

More evidence comes from a market research firm's survey in 1971. R. H. Bruskin Associates[20] asked a sample of citizens whether they felt various advertising claims were "completely true," "partly true," or "not true at all." Puffery was not identified by name, but a number of claims fell into the category and were rated as follows:

(1) "State Farm is all you need to know about life insurance" (22 percent said completely true, 36 percent said partly true);
(2) "The world's most experienced airline" (Pan Am) (23 percent and 47 percent respectively);
(3) "Ford has a better idea" (*sic*) (26 percent and 42 percent);
(4) "You can trust your car to the man who wears the star" (Texaco) (21 percent and 47 percent);
(5) "It's the real thing" (Coca-Cola) (35 percent and 29 percent);
(6) "Perfect rice everytime" (Minute Rice) (43 percent and 30 percent).

And the highest score in the survey went to Alcoa's claim, "Today, aluminum is something else," appraised as completely true by 47 percent and partly true by 36 percent. All those statements were, in Geer's words, not "buttressed by evidence," yet the results suggest that consumers regard them as facts, and so rely on them.

This survey evidence, plus advertisers' evident commitment to a wide use of puffery, shows we are dealing with an extensive phenomenon. Advertisers do not develop techniques which persuade only a few people; that is not how mass communication works. Techniques must be successful with vast audiences or be discarded. Puffery's continued existence in mass media shows that advertisers think it effective with a substantial portion of the public in obtaining reliance and altering purchase decisions.

Why does the law believe differently? Why does it ignore the evidence we have seen and rule arbitrarily that people who act with reasonable sense and care in the marketplace will not be affected by puffery? Why does it argue that this sort of falsity is not deceptive? In what follows, we will try to explain why this strange occurrence has taken place.

4

The Roots
of Sellerism

THE KEY to puffery's legal acceptability is that its roots lie in yesterday's sellerism, not in today's consumerism. I am using the term *sellerism* to indicate the law's former tendency to favor the seller considerably more than the buyer in the rules governing sales messages. *Consumerism,* of course, indicates the law's tendency to favor the buyer relatively more in those rules today than it did under sellerism.

We will see in this chapter that favoring sellers was culturally desirable in the early United States and that laws naturally developed to reflect that desire. We will also see that the balance of power has trended more recently to favor consumer interests and that many of the sellerist laws have been changed accordingly. It is too early to tell whether consumerism will turn the tables so as to favor the buyer far more than the seller, or will try merely to achieve equality of the two in the eyes of the law. It is not even certain whether consumerism will advance the buyer as far as a position of equality. But there is no doubt that it has already acted to eliminate the gross favoritism once shown toward the seller.

I find it reasonable to believe that our society will continue in the near future to favor the advance of consumerism and the retreat of sellerism. I realize there are many citizens who are against the consumerism trend and will work to see it eliminated. But as we will see in what follows, the trend has been operating with great strength for many years despite that sort of opposition. The best guess, therefore, is that the future will maintain the contemporary consumerist thrust.

Given this assumption, it is natural to expect the old sellerist laws to be eliminated from the marketplace and replaced by rules more consistent with today's standards. In numerous instances this has already happened, yet many laws remain unchanged today as remnants of sellerist times. Because they do, the vast movement of sellerism which began so long ago is not yet over. Consumerism predominates, but sellerism is not yet dead. What we have in the 1970s might be called an incomplete consumerism flavored heavily by some stubborn features of a now-incongruous sellerism which refuses to be pushed off the scene. For the time being these features are immovable objects, while consumerism is a resistable force.

The decisions which favor sellers by finding falsity without deception are among these immovable objects. They were central developments of the era of sellerism, and they remain today as loopholes which thwart the move to consumerism toward which reeent law has most generally been directed. They obstinately reflect ancient rather than modern assumptions about how people should and do conduct themselves in the marketplace.

The obstinacy is no accident; it reflects a movement which dominated the first century of the life of the United States and is still deeply rooted in our thoughts and customs. To see why sellerism clings to us today, let us move back in time to the year it was founded. It is 1534, an ancient era in which nothing like the modern marketplace exists. Nothing, that is, but a two-word phrase set down in Latin which points the way to the twentieth century.

Many things which shaped our lives happened in busy 1534. The Protestant Reformation emerged in England with the Act of Supremacy, by which Henry VIII made himself head of the English church. Anne Boleyn maneuvered through the second of four years which led her from Henry's altar to Henry's chopping block. Thomas More was imprisoned, awaiting his own headsman. Francis I burned Protestants, and Calvin fled his French homeland to write his *Institutes* in Switzerland. Charles V, emperor of Germany, hounded by Luther, still reigned. Ivan IV, the Terrible, later czar, was grand duke of Moscow at the age of one. Gustavus I was consolidating the Swedish Reformation with a beneficent autocracy, while the sultan of the Ottomans, Sulieman I, the Magnificent, widened his holdings of European soil. Clement VII died and Paul III was crowned pope; the Jesuits were founded by Ignatius Loyola. Michaelangelo abandoned the Medici tombs and departed Florence forever for Rome. Titian was 57, Palestrina 8. Copernicus had composed his revelation on revolution but would not yet consent to its publication. Rabelais was publishing, but anonymously, his best-known work. In the New World the Incas and Peru were being subdued by Pizarro, while other explorers and conquerors turned their attention to North America.

And in 1534 a compiler of the law named Anthony Fitzherbert wrote about buying a horse, "If he be tame and have ben rydden upon, then caveat emptor."[1] These famous Latin words, translated as "Let the buyer beware," stated the essence of sellerism in law: the buyer must look out for himself. If he looks at his purchase carefully, he will not need the law. If he does not look, the law will not protect him. If he looks but not carefully, the law still will not protect him. The buyer must accept full responsibility for a sales transaction; the seller accepts none. He must rely upon and trust nothing but his own personal inspection of his purchase, ignoring any representations of the seller which he does not confirm for himself. Any buyer who does other than this must suffer all consequences of a purchase which turns out badly.

Thus we discover the beginning of protected lying, of falsity which is legally nondeceptive. Puffery and other falsehoods are permitted today primarily because caveat emptor introduced legalized lying many centuries ago. Puffery of course goes back farther than 1534, no doubt occurring in the conversations of Adam and Eve ("I've found the nicest apple, Adam dear . . ."). But we are concerned with the way it became established in American law as legal even when false (and outlawed, incidentally, in some other countries[2]). In its heyday caveat emptor permitted enormous amounts of outright deliberate lying, the most blatant kinds of which are now prohibited. But the lesser ones which remain, and are the topic of this book, got their immunity from the same source. In this sense we can place the beginning of puffery in the year 1534, with the advent of caveat emptor into the law and sellerism into the marketplace.

How and why did caveat emptor develop? The question presents us with mysteries never fully answered. Throughout the Middle Ages the law of the market leaned severely toward favoring the consumer rather than the seller.[3] Fitzherbert's rule applied at first only under irregular conditions and did not indicate the general tendency nor describe the typical market law of the time. It was set down in its famous phrasing in 1534, but made no significant impact until much later.

That is a point apparently not widely appreciated. Some writers have stated that caveat emptor prevailed throughout the Middle Ages as a heritage derived from ancient Rome. But the Romans, coiners of Latin phrases though they were, did not give it birth. The impression that they did remains widespread despite the efforts of a legal historian, Walton H. Hamilton, who tried manfully to destroy the myth.[4] HIs luck is indicated in an advertisement published in 1971 by Grolier, Inc.: "Remember the

Roman who said 'Caveat emptor'? We don't. But we remember that he said it. . . ."[5]

Despite this advertiser's acknowledged encyclopedic
grasp of history, no Roman said that at all. People have
mistakenly thought so, Hamilton discovered, because the
Romans indeed had no remedy to protect buyers who
bought goods and later found them defective. Yet that
reflected only that they traded little and so had no appreciation for the protection needed in such transactions.[6]
The Romans simply had no law on the matter, whereas
caveat emptor was not the lack of a law but a law specifying a lack of protection.

As Europe progressed into the Middle Ages, trade grew
and laws to control it were fully developed. Life was
regulated strictly, and bad bargains did not go unpunished;
there was no place for the concept of caveat emptor.[7] St.
Thomas Aquinas, speaking for the principal lawmaker of
his time, the church, made clear that sellers were responsible for defects.[8] When a seller made false statements about
his wares, even if innocently, he must make good the loss.
When he knew of a defect, he must reveal it to the buyer.
Buyers, too, had responsibilities; if after purchase they
found they had received more than they anticipated, they
must compensate the seller for the hidden gain. Only in
one respect did Aquinas reflect what later became sellerism; he felt, in keeping with an apparently ancient adage,
that the seller need not reveal any obvious defects
(although, he said, it would be virtuous to do so). This
exception was no great concession to the seller, however,
because "obvious" in Aquinas's day meant really obvious.

Aquinas, incidentally, was the great rationalizer in the
church's reluctant acceptance of the values of trade.[9] As
trade began to appear in the early Middle Ages the church
made clear its condemnation of it, but later was compelled
toward greater indulgence by perceiving the advantages, in
fact necessities, of dealing with merchants. But how could
it do so without upsetting its own clearly stated standards?
Aquinas saved the day by stating a distinction between

rightful and wrongful trade, the one serving the community generally while the other served only the worldly profit motives of the trader. At first only a minor portion of trade was rightful, but once established the concept was enabled to grow until most trade eventually was found to serve God as well as man. Well beyond 1534, however, the church controlled trade strictly and had no room for caveat emptor. "In ecclesiastical polity," Hamilton wrote, "there was no place for the notion that the seller was not responsible for the goodness of his wares."[10]

Secular justice in the Middle Ages was equally authoritarian.[11] Sellerism was not possible within the bounds of the law. The craft guilds and the market towns controlled sellers and craftsmen tightly, treating them virtually as licensed public officials. The guilds obtained monopoly powers as their reward, and contributed a high level of workmanship and honesty as justification for it. They drew up standards of size and quality, and craftsmen who produced articles otherwise were fined, and for multiple violations were thrown out of the trade.[12] The result was tantamount to consumerism, though the aim was not to serve the buyer as such but to serve the entire community.[13] The cheater was held to transgress against everyone, including his fellow workers as well as his customers, a far cry from later assumptions of the "dog-eat-dog" competitive marketplace of nineteenth-century America. Apart from the market towns, the traders in the Middle Ages had their own courts as well, which developed a body of principles called the Law Merchant. Here, too, trust and not distrust was the basis of commercial dealings.[14]

To summarize history at the height of the Middle Ages, there appears to have been no development of the sellerism idea within the many sources of law which might have produced it, including the civil law with its Roman heritage, the law of the guild communities, and the Law Merchant of the traders. Apparently the only place the caveat emptor tradition could have come from was the trade conducted outside the law.[15] Lawful trade was developing in acceptance by the church and in general respectability with the public, but there remained a fringe area of wandering traders, "persons without rank or of mean estate,"[16] who appeared today and were gone tomorrow, and from whom no redress could be had when the defects in the sale were found only tomorrow. Among these were the multitudinous horse traders of whom Fitzherbert spoke. In this outlaw market, which had no formal legal structures but which developed customs of behavior nonetheless, the rule of action readily evolved that one must look out for himself because no one else would.[17] As with the Romans, this was not law but a folkway reflecting the lack of a law. Yet it was apparently from this source that the notion of caveat emptor was incorporated into actual law.

How could a folk custom which disagreed with the law of the land eventually be made a part of that law? It happened because the king and his courts decided to formulate a national law, rejecting various aspects of existing regulations and drawing substitute rules from whichever sources they pleased. Church (canon) law, civil law, and the laws of the guilds and the merchants had been dominant for a long time, but as the Middle Ages waned the growing power of the king gradually "nationalized" their jurisdictions. This was not without protest among Englishmen, Hamilton wrote: "The towns were constantly apprehensive over the prospect of His Majesty's encroachment upon their liberties."[18] But inevitably the legal dominance of the church and of the local and regional secular powers was blotted out by nationalization. None of the laws subordinated in this way included the concept of caveat emptor; only the lawless element of trade was "ruled" by that principle. Yet the king's courts, because they wanted to do everything possible to encourage growth of trade, ignored the precedents of the lawful markets and chose instead a precedent of the lawless ones.

In this way caveat emptor gained official English recognition.[19]

The king's courts did not accomplish this change in the days of Fitzherbert, but they used Fitzherbert as a reason when they did. They also used other sixteenth- and seventeenth-century writings and events which, as did Fitzherbert, reflected no particular support in previous law for caveat emptor, but could later be interpreted as precedents themselves by those who preferred such interpretation.[20] Among them was the celebrated case of the seller who lied about something called a bezar-stone.

A bezar-stone was a funny thing indeed, but before identifying it we must describe what steps an astute seller might take, as one did in the bezar-stone case, to invoke the principle of caveat emptor. We have said that under that rule a buyer had to rely solely on his own inspection of the object he bought, and otherwise had no protection against eventual discovery of a defect in the object's quality. Technically, however, the caveat emptor rule never pronounced such a responsibility unqualifiedly, saying it would apply in 100 percent of cases. Certainly it could not apply where inspection by the buyer was impossible, as when the goods were in a ship at sea or when the seller intervened deliberately to keep the buyer away from them, as in refusing to reveal their location.[21] A buyer truly unable to inspect had no trouble getting legal support if he relied on a seller's claim which turned out to be false.

Nor did caveat emptor apply 100 percent of the time for the buyer who *could* inspect his purchase. It applied in all cases where a pair of stated conditions both were absent, but not where one or both were present. If the seller made a misrepresentation about the goods which constituted (1) warranty, and/or (2) fraudulent misrepresentation (fraud), then caveat emptor would not apply.[22]

A *warranty*[23] is a seller's factual statement which the law regards as a promise that must be kept. To be a warranty a statement must have a certain style of wording, and when a false claim has that style it is a warranty whether or not the seller knows it is false. He may be entirely innocent of its falsity, but is responsible for it if it is a warranty.

A *fraudulent misrepresentation*[24] is a false statement which is consciously known to be false by its speaker (the seller, usually, although buyers make false claims in trade, also). When that conscious knowledge exists and can be proved, the misrepresentation is fraudulent without regard to the style in which it is worded. It may not be worded as a warranty, but the seller is responsible for it because he knew he was lying in stating it.

To sum up, the buyer had two methods under caveat emptor by which he could take the seller to court for a false claim, showing that it was worded as a warranty and/or that it was known to be false by the seller.

These two possibilities appear superficially to uphold the rights of the consumer, because they supply ways for him to protect himself against the seller. But in reality they came to operate in the king's common law as aspects of sellerism by becoming easy for the seller to avoid. He was entitled legally to lie so long as he escaped warranty and fraud charges. As we will see below, he soon learned that such escape was relatively easy to manage. The cases which established caveat emptor were those in which both warranty and fraud were found to be absent. And the cases which established an extreme sellerism were those such as the bezar-stone incident which made it extremely easy for the seller to arrange for such absences.

Rules which are on the books but can rarely be applied give only the appearance but not the real substance of regulation. Warranty and fraud were of that sort, being strictly burdens to the buyer, compared to the previous provisions which outlawed false claims in no uncertain terms. The seller in the early Middle Ages was wholly responsible for the goods, whether he manufactured them or obtained them from someone else. To Aquinas conscious falsity was sin as well as fraud, but even innocent falsity (which was neither) obligated the seller to make good the buyer's loss.[25] The same held true in the civil law (the heritage of Rome) and the law of the merchants; the seller was responsible for his claims, and was responsible beyond any claims for all qualities which buyers might reasonably expect in the goods. The idea was nonexistent that the buyer had to prove fraud or warranty in order to confer liability on the seller for misrepresentations.

Yet eventually the rules developed that those steps must be taken. Existing records do not tell us exactly when and how it happened. English common law's earliest recorded treatment of fraudulent misrepresentation (then called deceit) in sales appeared in a case from the year 1367 in which a person took some "beeves" from their owner and sold them "as if they had been his own." He did not say the cattle were his, but was found to know he was not the owner, and the act of selling was itself the representation held deceitful.[26] The record of the case is very slim, and it is possible to conjecture that the court did not mean to rule that a misrepresentation must be known false by its misrepresentor in order to be illegal. Perhaps the court meant merely that the falsity of the seller's act was sufficient to make it illegal.

But by happenstance the falsity was about ownership, and we might imagine that anyone who possessed something but had not purchased it could hardly help but know consciously that he did not own it. He might be innocently ignorant of defects in its quality, but could not be ignorant as to whether he owned it. Accordingly, and I am speculating, the court might well have thrown in the remark that the falsity was conscious only because it seemed obvious and added to the case against the seller, without meaning at all to say that a finding of conscious falsity was necessary generally in order to render a seller responsible.

Whether or not this speculation is correct, we know that the fraud requirement crept into the king's common law at some date by some sort of event, very possibly accidental, because it was not present in the laws which preceded it. And we know that it favored the seller considerably because there were many cases in which a statement's falsity was evident but the seller's conscious knowledge of it could not be proved. The buyer might know that the seller was deliberately lying, but be unable to collect the evidence needed to press the charge.

A case from 1585 called *Dale's Case* [27] shows us how effectively this inability could work against an unfortunate buyer. The seller had sold "certain goods" to the buyer, not owning them and not saying he owned them. The true owner showed up, and the buyer was forced to return the goods to him. The seller's falsity was just as evident as in the 1367 case, and the buyer brought suit accordingly. But his case failed because his counsel made the technical error of failing to *allege* to the court that the seller *knew* of his falsity. According to procedure, the court was not empowered to investigate a charge not specifically alleged before it.

One of the three justices, Anderson, disagreed on the grounds of the 1367 case that conscious falsity should be assumed by the court whether alleged or not, because its existence was obvious. He therefore favored a decision in favor of the aggrieved buyer who would otherwise lose both the goods and the money paid for them. Anderson's viewpoint produced a divided court on the question of what the seller had known to be true, but all three justices agreed that conscious knowledge of falsity must be shown in order to find legal misrepresentation. This appears to have been the earliest case to make that point clearly.[28]

The reader perhaps should imagine a case of his own in order to appreciate the strong degree of sellerism which the fraud requirement produced. Suppose a seller has falsely described a product to you, and you have made the purchase on the basis of those claims. You discover the defects later, but the seller refuses to return your money or replace the product. You take him to court, and the judge asks you whether you can prove the seller knew his falsehoods were false. You state you are certain he did, but you acknowledge there is no way you can prove it. The judge concludes that the seller has committed only innocent and not fraudulent misrepresentation. The seller goes free and you are stuck. In the 1970s there are ways by which you may charge nonfraudulent misrepresentation with liability,[29] but in the sixteenth-century it was fraud or nothing at all.

As misrepresentation became a seller's tool, so did warranty. We do not know precisely when the notion developed that an object sold would be held legally guaranteed by the seller only when he made a statement of warranty to that effect. The laws in England prior to the king's common law had bound the seller automatically to guarantee what he sold, statement or not. Warranties might be demanded and supplied to clarify the terms of a sale, but they were not necessary in order to hold a seller liable.

Nonetheless, English court records show a man found liable in 1383 for falsely warranting the quality of a horse,[30] and this first-recorded mention of warranty apparently indicated the start of a custom in which the seller's explicit warranty would be the only means to create a seller's guarantee. Other cases which undoubtedly contributed to this development are lost in the obscurity which veils ancient events. Eventually we find Fitzherbert, in the same year that he mentioned caveat emptor, writing that: "It behooveth that he [the seller] warrant it [the wine] to be good, and the horse to be sound, otherwise the action will not lie. For if he sell the wine or horse without such warranty, it is at the other's peril, and his [the buyer's] eyes and his taste ought to be his judges in that case."[31]

To say a warranty was *necessary* for the buyer to avoid "peril" was a big move in the direction of sellerism. And the next development, that only certain types of seller's statements would constitute warranties, was even more so. Preceding laws had held that no special wording was necessary to make a seller's claim a warranty. "Between a simple word and an oath God draws no distinction," Aquinas had said.[32] But now it turned out that the "simple word" was no warranty unless it indicated by its wording that the seller intended it to be.

This extremely sellerist point, which practically eliminated the buyer's access to warranty protection, was developed primarily in the bezar-stone case. As we look at that famous case of 1603, known in the records as *Chandelor v. Lopus*,[33] we will return to consider fraud as well as warranty, because the case had the coincidental effect of showing how the luckless buyer under caveat emptor could be denied both of those supposed protections at the same time.

The issue in *Chandelor v. Lopus* was whether Chandelor, a jeweler, should be held liable for selling to Lopus an object described inaccurately as a bezar-stone. Since that ancient curiosity is not for sale in our modern stores, we must begin by describing it. The *Oxford Dictionary*[34] has identified the "stone" as a "calculus or concretion" formed of concentric layers and found in the stomachs of animals, chiefly ruminants (cud-chewers), including in particular the "wild goat of Persia." The term "bezar" (also called "bezor," "bezer," and "bezoar") comes from a Persian word meaning "counter-poison" or "antidote." Whatever freed the body of a particular ailment was said to be the "bezar of that ailment." The stone's owner applied it to the diseased part of the body to obtain the cure.[35]

Lopus apparently tried this without success. We know, at any rate, that he discovered his prize to be no bezar-stone. We also know that in subsequent court appearances he was told emphatically that Chandelor had not *warranted* the object to be a bezar-stone. Chandelor had only *said* it was, you see, and that was not enough. The court declared that "the bare affirmation that it was a bezar-stone, without warranting it to be so, is no cause of action."

What a wondrous decision, to say that a statement of fact need not be made as a statement of fact. The seller may make the statement with utter disregard for its truth, because it is merely a claim but not a warranty. The seller may have his cake and eat it, too; he offers the statement as true, but only the buyer is responsible if it is false. The buyer is persuaded because he receives a promise, then finds that the promise unfulfilled was never a promise at all—only a claim.

The difference between affirmation and warranty gave caveat emptor a force it could not otherwise have had. If every seller's claim were a warranty, caveat emptor would have had a much narrower scope. It would have applied only to the extent that the seller could keep quiet about the particular features of an object. Sellers, of course, could keep silent where the features were hidden aspects which buyers would not know about nor think to inquire about, or when buyers were reluctant to press a point. But once asked for information, the seller would hardly want to decline, since such action could warn the buyer of trouble.

But the separation of affirmation and warranty granted the seller a far greater immunity from responsibility. Rather than being trapped by requests for information, he could issue all sorts of statements in the guise of being informative, the while carefully avoiding terms such as "warrant," "promise," or "guarantee" which were the only actions that could compel him to be really informative. The buyer of course had the opportunity to ask the seller to warrant his claims, but as with the unfortunate Lopus the request often was not made.

Buyers probably were reluctant to ask, with a formal request seeming socially improper because it implies that one does not trust the seller. One may not, indeed, but there is embarrassment in making the confrontation openly of a person who has just "affirmed" that something is so. Undoubtedly buyers had strong tendencies to trust, or at least to avoid showing distrust, despite the law's assumption that all persons engaging in trade were automatically distrustful. Sellers, knowing full well that the presumed distrust was only a theory not always practiced, were swift to turn the situation to profit.

An even greater factor probably was that many buyers failed to realize an affirmation was not a warranty. Persons such as Lopus may have distrusted sellers thoroughly, yet thought the seller's claim would make him legally responsible. We can hear Lopus protesting: "But he said it was a bezar-stone. He didn't say 'I think it's one, but I'm not sure.' He said it absolutely was one. What more could he say?"

We agree that Chandelor could hardly have said more. But the court decided he did not specifically designate the statement as being a promise he was willing to back up. Failure to designate indicated he was unwilling to back it up, therefore he was not required to do so!

And so the principle of warranty evolved from a principle of action for buyers into a principle of action for sellers. In original form it was intended to offer buyers the possibility of holding sellers responsible for product claims. In brief logical form the rule stated "If warranty, then protection." Sellers, however, were not slow in grasping the significance of the corollary proposition, "If no warranty, then no protection," which was eventually made law as well. This latter proposition, which offered guidance to sellers rather than to buyers, stated the true essence of the caveat emptor principle as it came to be famous. Its results were of course predictable: if buyers were legally required to distrust what the seller said, it was natural for sellers to expand the practice of making statements which were not to be trusted. It is no surprise, then, to find a contemporary dictionary defining caveat emptor by its negative rather than positive form: "ca·ve·at emp·tor (kā′vē at′ emp′tôr . . .). the principle that the seller cannot be held responsible for the quality of his product unless guaranteed in a warranty."[36]

With the seller-favoring nature of this rule due largely to the affirmation-warranty distinction, and this distinction due greatly to the decision made in *Chandelor v.*

Lopus, we might wonder why such a questionable decision was made by the English court. Possibly it went as it did because of the peculiar nature of those strange objects called bezar-stones. Could the judges perhaps have meant only that an affirmation should not in fairness be regarded as a warranty about something so subjective as that, without intending to rule more broadly that affirmations about *just any* sort of object shall never be warranties? This possibility, as posed by a legal writer named Grant Gilmore,[37] is based on the reasoning that most objects of trade possess solidly tangible features, but the characteristics of the bezar-stone depended to a great extent on the user's state of mind as well as its objective qualities.

If one believed in it, this product of a cud-chewing animal might act more as a bezar-stone than if one did not. We might think of it as an early example of the placebos which doctors use today, pills which contain no medicine but work because patients think they do. The bezar-stone was apparently believed in by substantial numbers of people, so we might wonder whether Lopus gave it a good try. Did he apply his stone to the right place and rub, press or scratch hard enough, and exhibit sufficient faith in his cure to make it work? We shall never know whether he did, nor what disease he had, nor whether his stone might have been the bezar, after all, of some different ailment.

And if it was difficult for Lopus to determine all this, it must have been even more difficult for Chandelor to know with certainty that it was actually a bezar-stone. Perhaps the judges, though they might have been stern in punishing Chandelor had he misrepresented something simple to assess, such as a horse, were less willing to condemn him for a wrong assertion about something which might really have been a bezar-stone had Lopus only thought so strongly enough! Perhaps they thought that under such conditions Chandelor could not reasonably have warranted the stone, and so protected him by declaring that such affirmation was not a warranty.

If this speculation of Gilmore's is correct, then the

intended meaning was obscured in the reporting of the case in the permanent court records. We do not know this, of course, but court reporting in 1603 was not reliable and such incidents were so frequent that we are safe in assuming it might have happened.

There were other accidents, too, in the story of *Chandelor v. Lopus,* which would have altered the case's outcome had they not occurred. Perhaps before describing them I should say that I will be identifying numerous accidental happenings in this book, so many that it may appear that the law of the marketplace developed as it did almost entirely by chance. I do not know the degree to which other areas of the law have been marked by fortuitous events, but it certainly appears that the developments examined here have a full share of such happenings.

I will interpret these accidents as significant, because a principal purpose of this look at history is to determine whether sellerism is as strongly rooted in law as advertisers tend to believe, or whether it has a relatively weak foundation which would tend to justify the efforts of those who would replace it with consumerism. The many accidents contributing to the development of sellerism naturally force me toward the latter belief.

This does not mean, however, that I think the circumstances which produce particular cases are the sole events which determine the law. Accidents may produce a decision such as *Chandelor,* but more critical to long-term legal development is whether or not that decision is used as a precedent for making numerous later decisions. If it is so used, and such use is obviously deliberate and no accident, then the accidental nature of the original precedent becomes less significant.

Probably more critical than what the precedents are, or how solidly they are established, is the matter of *how the court wants to rule.* It is typical to find precedents available to support either side of a case, which gives the court the opportunity to choose those which suit its predilections. A law text such as William L. Prosser's treatise on

torts[38] reveals topic after topic where a long list of decisions made in one direction is followed by another list
made oppositely. In United States law this occurs often
because there are fifty independent states, with a large
number of them accepting a certain rule and another large
number rejecting it. The only circumstance in which this
cannot happen occurs when the highest court of the land
resolves the issue and imposes its ruling on all lower
jurisdictions. But in the law of the marketplace there are
many issues never taken to the highest court and therefore
never decided conclusively.

The critical thing about *Chandelor v. Lopus,* therefore,
was not that it happened accidentally but that the English
courts *wanted* to rule in favor of sellers.[39] They therefore
found the case a convenient one to cite. Had *Chandelor*
never existed the task would have been harder, but the
courts still would have based their decisions on whatever
precedents or arguments they could scrape up in favor of
sellers. This explains why many of the cases we will see
below have cited precedents which seem scarcely appropriate for the role, or offered arguments whose logic seems
severely strained in reaching the decisions they supposedly
compel. Had the courts wanted instead to favor buyers
they would merely have ignored the sellerist cases and used
other cases which have in fact been the ones ignored all
these years. So in emphasizing the accidentalness of many
decisions I am not implying that sellerism wouldn't have
happened if the accidents hadn't.

But the accidents have another sort of significance
because of the current trend toward replacing sellerism
with consumerism. As the switchover from favoring sellers
occurs today, the old precedents of sellerism are being
swept away. And they can be swept away much more
readily when found to have been questionably established
in the first place. Advocates of sellerism in contemporary
times argue that caveat emptor and other rules cannot be
rejected because the heritage which produced them has
been consecrated for all time as a creed of human conduct.

Many cases examined in this book suggest such argument is foolish in the light of what has actually happened.

Let's return now to see what accidents befell the infamous case of *Chandelor v. Lopus.* But for inadvertent misfortune, the court probably would have found Chandelor liable for fraudulent misrepresentation. The misfortune came in the original court case brought by Lopus. The case called *Chandelor v. Lopus* which we have already described was an appeal of that first case by Chandelor before the Court of the Exchequer. The original case was held before the King's Bench,[40] and Lopus was awarded a judgment therein on the grounds that Chandelor was deceitful in representing the bezar-stone. But the case contained a lucky charm for Chandelor, not a bezar but a charm to cure ailments of a legal sort. It was the fact that Lopus's suit had failed to *allege* that Chandelor's deceit was fraudulent (conscious, deliberate). Misrepresentation, as established in the earlier *Dale's Case,* was not illegal when done innocently, only when done fraudulently. And if fraud was to be charged against the defendant, the rules required that it must be charged specifically, which was not done. Perhaps poor Lopus had the same lawyer as did the buyer-plaintiff in *Dale's Case;* it was the same mistake that enabled the defendant there to escape.

In his Exchequer appeal (*Chandelor v. Lopus*) Chandelor was successful in urging this technicality. All the judges but one refused to consider a matter called to the court's attention improperly. The dissenter was Anderson, the same who dissented on a similar point in *Dale's Case* eighteen years earlier. In both cases Anderson thought a fraudulent misrepresentation had happened and so should be held liable, procedural details aside. But he was outvoted, and Chandelor escaped action on the misrepresentation charge. This being done, the court considered the question of warranty, which it would otherwise have ignored. There would have been no need to find Chandelor liable on both fraud and warranty counts, so if the fraud charge had stuck the court would have spent no time pondering whether Chandelor warranted or explaining why it thought he hadn't. But luck brought the warranty issue to bear, and, as we have seen, Chandelor escaped action on this charge, too.

He escaped for the moment only, because Lopus initiated the third court case in the series, this time charging specifically that Chandelor misrepresented knowingly. Again ill fortune played its role, as this suit was omitted entirely from the customary publication of court records. In 1618 a casual mention was recorded in another case to the effect that Lopus had won;[41] perhaps we should assume from this that he did, but we will never know for certain. In 1894 the missing case was discovered in manuscript and finally printed. But it did not resolve the doubt, as the apparently incomplete report ended with the judges adjourning while still divided.[42]

The result of all these events was to immortalize Chandelor's apparent victory in *Chandelor v. Lopus* rather than the final decision, whatever it was. Without these errors there would have been no legitimizing of the difference between warranty and affirmation. Had Lopus alleged deliberate misrepresentation in the original King's Bench case, or had the final case been adequately reported, the warranty aspect of the sale would have been little noted. And had the object of sale not been a bezar-stone, perhaps Chandelor's affirmation would have been a warranty after all.

But the accidents happened, and caveat emptor was on its way. The buyer's loss of warranty protection because affirmations were not warranties was the key to the subsequent fantastic growth of sellerism. The fraud rule contributed, too, but solid warranty protection for buyers would have made fraud protection largely irrelevant. If all sellers' claims were warranties, making sellers liable for falsity whether they knew it or not, buyers would have found little disadvantage in the fact that they could not prove fraud. For this reason the rise of caveat emptor may be equated primarily with the extremely sellerist interpretation of the rule of warranty, as developed in the case of *Chandelor v. Lopus.*

We emphasize again that such developments did not produce a full-blown caveat emptor in the seventeenth century but rather served as enabling conditions when society eventually demanded it. Fitzherbert's rule was in contrast to typical market operations of his day, and the judgment against Lopus occurred similarly in a context of no general inclinations toward sellerism. But, as Hamilton states, "The words were there, ready to bear the ideas of a later age."[43]

When it appeared, the later age brought many events alien to the Middle Ages.[44] Power in human affairs was transferred in great quantity to industrialists and traders, who used it to escape the authoritarian rule of church and king. In the lands of the Reformation, religion became less authoritarian anyway, and in fact developed the helpful dogma that business and trade were God's work after all rather than the devil's. From Protestantism and the philosophers came the notion of individualism, stating that each human being was capable of reasoning and of looking out for himself. From the economists came the notion of laissez-faire, which held that merchants and their customers would arrive at fair and proper bargains through the automatic process of competition, without need for regulation. All of these developments led during the seventeenth and eighteenth centuries to the significant notions that seller and buyer were equal in the marketplace, and that none of their interactions therefore need be, or should be, guaranteed.

How anyone could claim that seller and buyer truly were equal seems amazing in the light of other events occurring at the same time! The growth of trade exposed buyers to a considerable reduction in their trading competence at the exact time that the theory which argued the opposite was developing. In earlier days goods had been familiar and buyers no doubt were as competent as sellers in assessing them. There was no need to ask the seller to describe the goods because the buyer was fully aware of their characteristics and able to examine them personally. There was little opportunity for the seller to engage actively in "selling" (that is, "persuading"). He could only present the object and hope it would withstand the examination it would surely get. Nor could he escape an examination of his own reputation as well; sellers in early times were well known personally in the communities where they dealt.

But times changed. New objects appeared, from strange places, offered by strange sellers. Old objects appeared from a greater variety of outlets, bearing new and unfamiliar distinctions in features and quality. Goods began to be manufactured, produced by technical processes not generally understood by the populace. The chance that the buyer could match the seller's understanding of the object simply by examining it became more and more remote. The buyer's equality of competence dwindled as he became less able to assess the quality of the goods or even simply to identify them.

That equality still existed between buyers and sellers under such conditions has been argued nonetheless on the grounds that the growth of trade produced many sellers who had not manufactured their goods personally, and who thus knew no more about them than the buyers. It is true enough that a class of persons was developing whose business was trade alone, but even so we should suspect that these sellers knew facts about their wares which the buyers could not know. The idea of true equality of seller and buyer in an age of professional selling seems thoroughly unnatural.

The very name of the rule suggests that people tacitly realized no true equality was involved. Why not have called it, given equality, caveat venditor as much as caveat emptor? Under equality the buyer would gain the better bargain as often as the seller, thus the rule might most properly have been worded, "Let *both* parties to the bargain beware." I cannot imagine a judge or any observer

pronouncing the seller and buyer equal and then asserting
as the logical outcome of such situation that it was the
buyer who was to be wary.

I can't imagine it; it just happened! Those who benefited from the new alignments of power decreed that
equality existed and caveat emptor applied; that was that.
Particularly in America did this occur, in the new lands
with the vast frontiers where growth and development were
to be valued above all else. "All purchasers, in presumption
of law, are deemed competent judges of what they are
about to buy," argued counsel for a seller defendant in a
New York case of 1804.[45] "If they will purchase without
attention to circumstances, the maxim of caveat emptor
ought to apply." The court agreed; case dismissed. But not
before one of the judges sermonized that caveat emptor
was a rule of fine moral standing, having the useful social
function of causing buyers to be at their best: "I see no
injustice or inconvenience resulting from this doctrine, but
on the contrary, think it best calculated to excite that
caution and attention which all prudent men ought to
observe in making their contracts."

This stressing of the opportunity for moral disciplining
was a rationalization thrown in by a court desirous of
bolstering the affairs of business, and was, as Hamilton
suggests, a notion new and American in origin: "Not until
the nineteenth century, did judges discover that caveat
emptor sharpened wits, taught self-reliance, made a man—
an economic man—out of the buyer, and served well its
two masters, business and justice."[46]

No one said anything about this applying to the seller,
too, who happened to be just as much in the dark about
the truth as the buyer was. The case in question was *Seixas
and Seixas v. Woods*,[47] in which Woods had sold to the
plaintiffs a shipment of "peachum wood" identified falsely
as "brazilletto," "the former worth hardly anything, the
latter of considerable value." Woods had acted as agent for
a distant merchant; all he knew was that the invoice
described the cargo as brazilletto. He advertised it as such,

and when the Seixases bought it he showed them the invoice and made out the bill for brazilletto. Upon discovery of the inaccuracy he refused to receive the wood back and return the payment. The resulting suit brought judgment against him, but review by the New York Supreme Court brought a reversal on the grounds that no warranty existed and that the misrepresentation was not fraudulent because Woods was fooled just as the Seixases were fooled, or at least there was no proof otherwise.

The court was exceedingly firm in holding that caveat emptor should be applied in the absence of warranty and fraud. Justice James Kent cited the precedent of *Chandelor v. Lopus,* and noted that "there is no instance in the English law of a contrary rule being laid down." He acknowledged that he might alternately have followed the civil law of Roman heritage, which had preceded the king's common law and was much different: "The civil law . . . is more rigorous towards the seller, and makes him responsible in every case for a latent defect. . . . By the civil law, says Lord Coke, every man is bound to warrant the thing that he selleth, albeit there be no express warranty; but the common law bindeth him not, unless there be a warranty in deed, or law."[48]

Here was a chance for the newly developing American law to reject the king's law that embraced caveat emptor and adopt another heritage which had no place for that rule. The American nation had recently relieved itself of the yoke of English control and was free to follow its own lights as it had in many other areas. But Kent thought the English in this instance had made the correct decision: "The rule of the common law has been well and elegantly vindicated by Fonblanque, as most happily reconciling the claims of convenience with the duties of good faith. It requires the purchaser to apply his attention to those particulars which may be supposed within the reach of his observation and judgment."

Was the identification of "brazilletto" really within the reach of the Seixases' observation and judgment? Were all purchasers, as Woods's counsel claimed, truly "competent judges of what they were about to buy"? Surely they were not always, and the law's automatic presumption that they were seems enormously unreasonable. It seems unreasonable particularly when applied to cases in which the buyer's usual level of competence was reduced by the distraction caused by the seller's false claim. Yet the New York court was firm on the point that the Seixases' opportunity to examine the goods made it incumbent upon them to be responsible for what they bought.

Nothing was said about the value of equally prudent behavior by the seller. Charging a buyer with responsibility might seem more palatable if the seller were held equally responsible, but he was not. One might draw a contrast with twentieth-century negligence cases in which the law of some states permits a finding of a certain percentage of negligence by each party. The arrangement seems appropriate for *Seixas,* since both sides were ignorant of the error being made. But the law controlling their transaction gave all-or-nothing, and when both were negligent the seller won all.

These questions about the presumed equality of buyers seem vital, but in 1804 they were thoroughly ignored. Caveat emptor rolled on to a high point in 1870 when Justice Davis, speaking for the U.S. Supreme Court, stated that "no principle of the common law has been better established, or more often affirmed. . . ."[49]

Well established it was, yet the arbitrariness reeks. Events were not fitted to the law, rather the law was fitted to the events desired by those who felt any trade was better than no trade at all: "Trade is beginning to grow, and beginning to appear desirable. Actions against sellers will embarrass trade, and be bad policy. They would increase the risks of trading to an unforeseeable extent, and so discourage enterprise in trade."[50] The solution, therefore, was to adopt standards in the market which would never be accepted in other areas of human endeavor. The difference was never so well illustrated as by a court case in which a defendant tried to excuse his shabby deeds by holding the rule of caveat emptor against the plaintiff, only to be told that the events of the case had occurred away from the marketplace and caveat emptor did not apply.[51]

The year was 1885, and the court's opinion was given by Oliver Wendell Holmes, who we will see later was instrumental in establishing puffery's legal status. In this case before the Supreme Judicial Court of Massachusetts Holmes considered the situation of some persons who, due to legal obligations they had failed to meet, had some property including eight fishing traps "attached" by a deputy sheriff.

Or so the deputy said, though it later turned out his statement was false. "Attaching" means taking under control, and the owners of the traps, who had left them spread in a field for drying, were told by the deputy that if they "meddled with them it would be at their peril." The traps were perishable, subject to destruction by freezing to the ground in winter ice and snow. The owners, therefore, periodically begged the deputy to take proper care of them. They were never touched, however, and subsequently suffered damage which ruined them entirely.

It later developed that to attach the traps validly, the deputy would have had to take them into his actual physical possession. On these grounds he denied responsibility for the damage done, claiming he had not legally made the attachment and so could not be held liable. The owners, nonetheless, went to court on the grounds of the deputy's representation to them prior to the time of damage that he had in fact attached the traps. The owners declared they were justified in relying on the claim of attachment and were not obliged to check further with legal authorities to verify its truth.

The deputy's defense was to rely on caveat emptor, by which he argued that the owners were obligated to check the truth for themselves and not to rely on his statement. Had the owners ascertained the legal requirements for attaching goods, they would have realized the traps were not legally attached. The deputy had not warranted his statement, nor did it amount to fraudulent misrepresentation because the falsity was "obvious" (meaning the owners would have discovered it had they examined the law). Given this, the deputy argued, the owners were fully responsible through their failure to exercise the ordinary care expected of them.

Not so, decided Holmes. The deputy's defense, he said, was based on cases "concerning the manifest quality of goods offered for sale." But this was not a matter of the marketplace; it was not a transaction between buyer and seller, nor a transaction which the owners of the traps entered into voluntarily. Beyond the marketplace, one cannot require persons to distrust representations simply because they themselves may possess the ability and opportunity to obtain an independent verification: "The standard of good faith required in sales is somewhat low, not only out of allowance for the weakness of human nature, but because it is not desirable to interfere too much for the purpose of helping men in their voluntary transactions more than they help themselves."

Aside from sales, the rule was different. The deputy sheriff was held responsible and required to pay the owners $3,298.07 in damages. Thus do we see the difference it makes in law for a person to be dealing in the marketplace rather than in other human affairs. If the deputy had told his lies in a selling transaction, he would have gone free. *The standard of good faith required in sales is somewhat low!* Indeed it was, and in America has always been.

Yet in the twentieth century caveat emptor has lost its original strength, as we will see in the subsequent chapters which discuss what elements of it are now eliminated and what elements still remain. Chapter 5 will examine the warranty rule, detailing its rise as a tool of sellerism from the seeds of *Chandelor v. Lopus* and later its fall as sellerism gave way to consumerism. Chapter 6 will describe the parallel story of misrepresentation, again indicating in modern times a long slide from the heights of sellerism. Chapter 8 will discuss a particularly blatant form of protected lying which is no longer protected. In these three chapters we will see the trend toward rejection of caveat emptor and the imposition of liability upon the seller and manufacturer for the claims they make and for the goods they sell. Chapters 9 and 10 will provide further elements of the same story by describing how the Federal Trade Commission has replaced sellerism with consumerism.

In the remaining chapters, however, we will see the story of those remnants of caveat emptor and sellerism which persist in the law today. They are, of course, the several varieties of puffery, of false claims which may deceive the consumer but which the law by its sellerist traditions still describes as being nondeceptive. It is often written today that caveat emptor is dead.[52] The intention of this book is to show that it is not. The standard of faith required in sales may be considerably improved by consumerism's many developments, but it is still much lower than we would like it to be.

5

Warranty: How Much Promise Do You Find in a Promise?

IN DESCRIBING the development of caveat emptor we have seen how the warranty concept, a most powerful tool of consumerism, was created and almost immediately de-fanged so that it would hardly ever apply. In this chapter we will follow the sellerist interpretations of warranty from English into American law, seeing how they eventually changed so that the advantages which warranty gave the consumer in theory might be realized in practice. There is still trouble today in getting solid protection for consumers under warranty, but the trend away from sellerism is obvious and will probably become stronger as time passes. The methods used to deny enforcement of seller's claims as warranties will die, but they will die hard. The ghost of the bezar-stone still haunts the land.

The trail of warranty is strewn with ironies and accidents, only the first of which occurred with Lopus's magic cud. Very likely *Chandelor v. Lopus*[1] should have been repudiated and forgotten relatively soon, but some further zany incidents helped keep the 1603 decision alive as what jurists call a "leading case." One of these events occurred after England's Lord Holt made two consumerist rulings in 1689 and 1700 which administered an early coup de grace to the idea that affirmations were not warranties. Or would have done so, had they not been distorted by untimely luck so that they appeared to support the *Chandelor* doctrine rather than to oppose it.

The first Holt case was *Crosse v. Gardner*,[2] in which a seller sold two oxen belonging to another but which he affirmed were his own. In opposition to the theory of *Chandelor*, Holt ruled that the bare statement of ownership amounted to a warranty that the seller had legal title to the oxen. Since the warranty was breached, the buyer was entitled to recover from the seller for the loss suffered when the oxen had to be returned to the true owner. Holt's reasoning was the essence of simplicity: the buyer had no way of knowing who owned the goods, thus he deserved warranty protection. This was what Anderson had said in *Dale's Case* in 1585,[3] but it took a century for the viewpoint to win a court majority.

Holt did not use the term *warranty* in *Crosse v. Gardner*, but his intent to invoke this concept was made clear in the related decision of 1700, *Medina v. Stoughton*.[4] This time a seller sold lottery tickets as his own when they were not, and Holt judged that "where one having the possession of any personal chattel sells it, the bare affirming it to be his amounts to a warranty."

Holt's decisions didn't directly reject *Chandelor*, because *Chandelor* was concerned with the quality of goods rather than their ownership. While a buyer couldn't determine ownership by examining the oxen, he *could* check their quality. Therefore Holt's reasoning about the buyer's lack of opportunity to know the truth was not particularly applicable to seller's affirmations about quality. But Holt's cases were significant, nonetheless, because they established that "mere" affirmations amounted to warranties in *some* cases, thereby shattering the implication from *Chandelor* that they could *never* amount to warranties. This small exception paved the way for the eventual discrediting of the bezar-stone case and the establishment of the opposite idea that affirmations would *always* amount to warranties.[5]

But the course of events was tortuous. A funny thing happened to Lord Holt's idea when it was quoted by Justice Buller in an important English case called *Pasley v. Freeman.*[6] Buller stated that: "It was rightly held by Holt, C.J., in [*Crosse* and *Medina*] that an affirmation at the time of a sale is a warranty, provided it appear on evidence to have been so intended."

The final phrase of Buller's statement ("provided . . .") was nowhere stated by Holt in the two cases! But *Pasley* emerged as a landmark case in the law of misrepresentation, and when it became famous for that reason the interpretation of Holt by Buller became much quoted in certain critical cases, turning the treatment of warranty away from Holt's consumerist reasoning and back toward that of *Chandelor.*[7] Holt had wanted affirmations (of ownership, at least) to be regarded legally as warranties whether the seller intended them to be so or not, but Buller conveyed a precisely opposite impression. We do not know why so eminent a jurist made such an error; we know only that the error was a serious one.

In 1804 Buller's mistake was incorporated into *Seixas and Seixas v. Woods,*[8] which became America's leading case in establishing caveat emptor and the warranty rule as law. The seller Woods, as we saw in chapter 4, described the wood as brazilletto, and counsel for the buyers argued that he therefore had warranted it so. "If the facts in the case do not amount to a warranty, it will hardly be possible to create one," they argued. But the court disagreed: "Kent, J.: . . . The mentioning of the wood as brazilletto wood, in the bill of parcels, and in the advertisements some days previous to the sale, did not amount to a warranty to the plaintiffs. To make an affirmation at the time of the sale, a warranty, it must appear by evidence to be so intended (Buller, J. . . .). . . ."

Seixas was decided in New York, a major industrial state whose legal pronouncements weighed heavily upon the courts of other states. The principle that not all claims should be warranties was welcomed by a large number of them. These other courts, however, were not compelled to agree with New York, and in 1816 *Bradford v. Manly*[9] emerged as the first American case to condemn *Chandelor* and rule that something less than a specifically worded promise about the nature of goods should legally be a warranty. The buyer Bradford had purchased two casks of cloves from Manly after examining a sample. But he found the cloves delivered to him to be inferior in quality. A jury upheld his suit because "the purchase was made upon the confidence that the whole quantity was represented by the sample." On appeal the seller Manly argued that an express statement of warranty was necessary and there was none, citing *Chandelor* and *Seixas* among his authorities.

This brought a direct confrontation in which the old cases lost. Chief Justice Parker of Massachusetts held that "a sale by sample is tantamount to an express warranty." He argued from a viewpoint of plain fairness, asking "For what purpose is a sample exhibited, unless it is intended as a representation of the thing sold?" No one, he said, would expect a seller to offer an explicit statement of warranty along with his sample, because "What would an honorable merchant say, if, when he took from a mass of sugar or coffee a small parcel, and offered to sell by it, the man who was dealing with him should ask him if it was a fair sample, and call upon him to warrant it so?" A buyer, rather than asking this, should understand the proferred sample to amount to an express warranty that the articles of sale will be similar. And the law, said Parker, should understand that, too.

Parker appears in this ruling to have grasped the true state of a typical buyer's mind, a mind which was reluctant to openly accuse a seller of not speaking the truth. The *Chandelor* ruling required a doubting buyer to say to the seller, in effect, "You have stated such-and-such, but are you willing to state it again in a way that will make you legally liable for it?" Such statement has the effect of implying "I suspect you're not telling me the truth," a charge most people want to avoid making routinely. Parker's alternative was that the seller's original statement would be legally liable as a guarantee and therefore the buyer would be excused from the obligation to request it specifically. Parker's thinking was consistent with Lord Holt's argument that a buyer should have warranty protection for a seller's claim when he cannot personally check it out. The buyer Bradford could check the cloves' quality by examining the sample, and he did. But he could not check in any other way. There was no way he could have determined that the cloves he would get apart from the sample would be of inferior quality.

Parker also stated that *Chandelor* "would not now be received as law in England," and, he added, "certainly not in our country," a pointed rejection of *Seixas.* He added that in a case at nisi prius of "two or three years ago" he had ruled in favor of a buyer who purchased a commodity on the basis of a newspaper advertisement offering "Carraccas cocoa." He had interpreted the ad as an express warranty that the commodity would be Carraccas cocoa, a decision directly opposed to the ruling about the advertisement for brazilletto.

But the shadow of the bezar-stone was long and would remain for some time on both sides of the ocean. A classic English illustration of its effects came when a seller gave a buyer the following receipt:[10] "Received of Mr. Budd 10£ for a grey four year old colt, warranted sound in every respect." Finding the horse to be only three, the buyer sued for breach of warranty. But the court decided it was quite significant that part of the statement came before and part came after the word "warranted." The judge said: "I should say that . . . the intention of the parties was to confine the warranty to soundness, and that the preceding statement was matter of description only. And the difference is most essential . . . ."

One wonders whether both parties intended to confine the warranty to soundness, and whether both parties agreed that mere "matter of description only" need be subject to no standards of truth. The age of the colt was important to the buyer for breeding reasons, and while he may not have told this to the seller we can scarcely imagine that he openly disclaimed the importance of age, either. Most surely he thought he was adequately covered by the wording and was furious on finding that he wasn't.

On the other side of the Atlantic, in prominent cases of 1831 and 1839, the Supreme Court of Pennsylvania first repudiated *Chandelor,* then reversed itself and decided to retain the bezar-stone principle. In the 1831 case[11] the court agreed with *Bradford v. Manly* that "a sample, or description in a sale note, advertisement, bill of parcels, or invoice, is equivalent to an express warranty that the goods are what they are described." Chief Justice Gibson dissented strongly to the decision, and with a change in the court's make-up his Chandelorian viewpoint eventually prevailed in the 1839 case, *McFarland v. Newman.*[12] A jury had found that McFarland made a "positive averment" that the horse he was selling was sound except for a temporary display of ordinary distemper. The disease being actually permanent, the jury returned a verdict for the buyer.

On appeal, Gibson obtained the majority support he lacked in 1831 and reversed the rule with the ringing declaration that "the naked averment of a fact is neither a warranty itself nor evidence of it." His view, despite being called "a singular atrophy of legal development" by one writer,[13] became so dominant in Pennsylvania law that it remained long after the eventual revoking of the position in other states. The difference was so great that in his famous treatise on sales law Samuel Williston found it necessary to discuss Pennsylvania in a separate section, apart from other U.S. law.[14]

Elsewhere in the United States courts began relenting in the middle 1800s on their long-standing denial of warranty protection where sellers merely "affirmed" that a fact was so. Typical of this trend were cases which repudiated the *Seixas* decision right in its home state of New York. James Kent's influential *Commentaries on American Law* observed in 1867 that there was doubt that *Seixas* had been properly decided.[15] Kent himself was no longer alive, but it is ironic that the expression of doubt written into the fifth edition of the *Commentaries* by the editor, George Comstock, was published under the name of the original author. We recall that Kent had decided with the majority in *Seixas!* His concurring opinion had vigorously defended *Chandelor* and similar precedents, but now the writer in charge of updating his work was having second thoughts upon reading cases such as *Bradford v. Manly*.

This revised judgment was made law in New York in *Hawkins v. Pemberton* of 1872.[16] The seller of a product represented falsely as blue vitriol brought suit against the buyers for refusing to pay the purchase price following receipt of the goods. The seller claimed breach of contract, the buyers countered with breach of warranty. The record established the problem in this now-familiar way: "Did the plaintiff [seller] warrant the article to be blue vitriol? It is unquestioned that . . . he represented it to be blue vitriol." The old rule was at stake, and it lost when the court decided: "It is not true, as sometimes stated, that the representation, in order to constitute a warranty, must have been intended by the vendor . . . as a warranty. . . . The vendor will not be permitted to say that he did not intend what his language clearly and explicitly declares. . . . He is responsible for the language he uses, and cannot escape liability by claiming that he did not intend to convey the impression which his language was calculated to produce . . . ."

From a 1970s viewpoint one cannot help but feel that the sweet breath of common sense at last had cleared the air. Of course one shouldn't be allowed to claim that he didn't mean to imply what his language clearly was calculated to imply—what could be more fair! As in *Bradford*, and harking back to *Dale's Case*, the decision was made precisely on the grounds of sheer fairness, with the comment added that the doctrine of *Chandelor* had been exploded. As for *Seixas*, the *Hawkins* court declared that old case "thoroughly overturned" and said it "can no longer be regarded as authority for the precise point decided" because "the law was not properly applied to the facts . . . ."[17]

Except for independent Pennsylvania, the *Hawkins* turnabout typified the development of United States law in the late 1800s toward making affirmations of fact equivalent to warranties. The trend was solidified by the drafting of the Uniform Sales Act early in the new century. Until that time, warranty law had been a matter of common law, which in modern terminology is the law developed through the opinions of judges in court cases, in response to specific suits brought before them. It is contrasted with statute law, which is that enacted by legislatures in response to general needs. The Uniform Sales Act[18] was a model statute drawn with the hope of standardizing sales law in all of the states. The success of any model statute depends upon the number of adoptions, and during the period 1907–42 versions of the act were passed by thirty-four states, plus Alaska, Hawaii, and the District of Columbia. Here is what it said about warranty:

§12: Definition of Express Warranty.—Any affirmation of fact or any promise by the seller relating to the goods is an express warranty if the natural tendency of such affirmation or promise is to induce the buyer to purchase the goods, and if the buyer purchases the goods relying thereon . . . .

Passage of the act, and of a corresponding Sale of Goods Act which preceded it in England,[19] assured that the warranty principle would contribute genuinely to consumerism in the twentieth century. There continued, however, to be cases which through ignorance or stubbornness harked back to the sellerist interpretation of old. In 1913

England's House of Lords dredged up Buller's quotation of Holt to the effect that any warranty must be so intended by the seller.[20] This was so obvious a mistake it might have been easily corrected but for the nasty complication of the House of Lords being forbidden to overrule its own decisions. And in Pennsylvania, the court managed several times to ignore the Uniform Sales Act and rely upon Gibson's decision about the "naked averment of a fact."[21] In 1965, a cool fifty years after the state's passage of the act, a U.S. Court of Appeals had to remind a Pennsylvania judge he had gone against his own state's law by instructing a jury to find no express warranty unless the seller actually intended to be bound by his statement.[22]

Too, a number of states never adopted the Uniform Sales Act. But this was corrected when the act was supplanted by the Uniform Commercial Code, adopted in all fifty states and the District of Columbia beginning in 1954 (Pennsylvania) and ending in 1968 (Mississippi). The code's section 2-313 defined warranties much as section 12 of the Uniform Sales Act had, and its unanimous adoption finally brought the ancient bezar-stone interpretation to an end.[23]

While defining any factual affirmation as a warranty has been a big help to consumers, this step alone does not represent the full extent to which warranty developments have aided modern consumerism. We cannot see it all until we describe *implied* warranties, which are entirely distinct from the warranties discussed so far. Warranties consisting of statements actually expressed by the seller are known technically as *express* warranties, while implied warranties are those held to exist legally without being expressed. They apply automatically, and without the seller necessarily consenting, whenever a sale of goods is transacted.

Implied warranties are the very antithesis of caveat emptor. At its sellerist height the Latin phrase not only excused the seller from responsibility for his false representations which were neither warranty nor fraud, but also excused him without qualification from responsibility for

any characteristics of the goods he made no representations about at all. The buyer was obligated to inspect all
nonrepresented matters himself, and to rely wholly upon
that inspection, with no legal recourse. The seller had zero
accountability with respect to his silence.

The implied warranty exactly reversed that situation,
making the seller wholly accountable. There is no surprise
that such a concept was slow to develop, considering the
resistance shown against express warranties. Anyone arguing that an affirmation should not be a warranty would
argue all the more against something less than an affirmation. If sellers found express warranties annoying, they
would be absolutely appalled over the idea of implied
ones. The very idea was contradictory to sellerism.

The more implied warranties there are, the less the
buyer need check the goods himself to fulfill his legal
obligation. If there were implied warranties covering every
characteristic of the goods sold, and every aspect of the
selling transaction, there would be no more caveat emptor.
No such extreme has yet occurred, but the trend over time
has been to recognize implied warranties more and more.
The general concept and a small number of applications
are firmly established today.[24]

In the days of sellerism the implied warranty concept
was largely nonexistent. One exception, deriving from
ancient statute, was an implied warranty of the pureness of
food and drink imposed on persons selling those articles in
public places ("common victualers").[25] This rule reflected
the tendency of the early Middle Ages, as we saw in
chapter 4, to make sellers wholly responsible for the quality of their wares. It was one of few such rules to be
retained when the king's common law was established.
Another early development was that the law of ownership
(title) evolved quickly toward an implied warranty. We
have already examined the *express* warranty of ownership,
in which a seller's statement of ownership was regarded as
a warranty even though he did not indicate intent to
warrant.[26] The *implied* warranty of ownership went a step

further, holding ownership to be warranted by the act of the sale even though the seller said nothing on the subject.

Such an implied warranty had not existed in the 1367 case in which the person selling "beeves" as his own was cited for deceit (fraudulent misrepresentation).[27] Without the deceit charge he would have gone free. Nor did an implied warranty apply in *Dale's Case* of 1585,[28] although the dissenting Justice Anderson had favored such a concept. "It shall be intended," he stated, "that he that sold had knowledge whether they were his goods or not." He did not persuade his colleagues to adopt this liberal interpretation, but Sir William Blackstone agreed about two hundred years later, in 1771, that: "In contracts for sales, it is understood that the seller undertakes that the thing sold is his own."[29]

That seems a more reasonable law than in *Dale's Case,* where the majority of judges excused the seller with the lame reason that "it may be, the defendant [seller] did know no otherwise but that they were his own goods." Admittedly no proof had been offered that the seller knew the truth about ownership, but the implied warranty concept eventually adopted was based on the reasoning that the seller *ought* to know and therefore was responsible for knowing even in the rare case when he might not. In America the implied warranty of ownership (title) was made standard by the Uniform Sales Act[30] and the Uniform Commercial Code.[31]

Except for pure food and ownership, early English law resisted implied warranties. The American states followed suit, particularly New York and Pennsylvania, which supported continuance of the *Chandelor* and *Seixas* doctrines about express warranties. Pennsylvania's Chief Justice Gibson admitted in *McFarland v. Newman* that the implied warranty of title existed, but declared haughtily that "caveat emptor disposes of all beside." In the long run Gibson was proved wrong as the development of other implied warranties moved the law instead toward disposing of caveat emptor. There emerged two implied warranties of the quality of goods, one guaranteeing their "merchantability" and the other their "fitness for a particular purpose."

Merchantability means a product shall be fit for the uses to which it is ordinarily put, which are not necessarily all the uses to which buyers may put it. The buyer of dress shoes may benefit from the merchantability warranty if he wants them for ordinary walking or social purposes, but not if he wants them for mountain climbing. For the latter intention, however, he may invoke the implied warranty of fitness for a particular purpose, which means a thing will be fit for the purpose he specifies.

The merchantability warranty, where enacted, applies automatically to all transactions of sellers established in the community as merchants of that item. The fitness warranty is not similarly automatic but applies when the buyer makes the particular purpose known to the seller and the seller understands that the buyer is relying upon his judgment in the matter. Generally this understanding requires a specific message from buyer to seller, although sometimes the seller is presumed to know it through his knowledge of usage in the community.

The two implied warranties do not guarantee all aspects of quality which may be disputed; in fact, they do not at all guarantee what the buyer may regard as "good" quality. They guarantee only the minimum goodness needed for the object to carry out its ordinary or particular purposes.

Merchantability was poorly treated when the earliest attempts were made to introduce it to English law.[32] In *Parkinson v. Lee* of 1802,[33] a buyer had purchased grain from an agent of a grower who watered it to increase its weight and enhance its price. There was a similarity to the *Seixas* case, because the suit was brought against the agent, who had no knowledge of the deed. But there were important differences from *Seixas:* the problem with the hops was a hidden defect which led to rot but was impossible to detect at time of sale, whereas the identity of the peachum wood was detectable on the spot by anyone with the proper expertise. Another difference was that no representation was made that the grain was unwatered, whereas in *Seixas* the express claim was made that the wood was brazilletto.

The buyer Parkinson's dilemma was precisely that which seemed most unfair under caveat emptor. The seller made no representations and therefore had zero responsibility, yet there was no conceivable opportunity for Parkinson to discover the hidden defect no matter how hard and long he examined it. To remedy this unfairness his counsel argued for "an implied warranty ... that the commodity should be in a merchantable condition at the time of the sale." The request seems heartily sensible, but what makes sense in the twentieth century made something less than that before. One justice in the court agreed that there had been some legal thinking about implied warranties, but there was no acceptance of them, he said.[34] Parkinson's suit therefore was doomed: "Lawrence, J.: ... He exercised his own judgment upon it; and knowing, as he must have known, as a dealer in the commodity, that it was subject to the latent defect which afterwards appeared, he bought it at his own risk. Grose, J.: ... If he doubt the goodness, or do not choose to incur any risk of a latent defect, he may refuse to purchase without [express] warranty."

Suppose a merchant today said these things to a customer who had bought a television only to see the picture tube blow out on the first day. "You should have known," said the dealer, "that it was subject to the latent defect which afterwards appeared." Picture tubes, after all, are going to go bad sometime, which means they *could* go bad on the first day. The ordinary purchaser can't determine the date any better than Parkinson could tell the hops were watered, but he knows it could happen and so should know enough to demand an express warranty against the event. Outside of that he must take the television entirely at his own risk, or not buy it at all.

A seller who debated that position would have on his side some reasonable arguments. He would point out that buyers always have the opportunity to request an express warranty. The seller is bound to fill the request or else suffer loss of credibility for not doing so. The debate opponent might retort that the consumer, although knowing of prominent components such as the picture tube, couldn't reasonably know all the things which could go wrong with a television and therefore couldn't ask for express warranties covering them all. To this the seller could respond that the consumer could ask for an express warranty of general soundness or of merchantability (which would be an express warranty if explicitly stated by the seller). All of these points would score heavily for the seller's argument.

Despite these possibilities, the law has taken consumer protection the big step further which implied warranties represent. The basis for doing so is the considerable difference between what consumers might reasonably do and what they actually do. Despite the seller's argument that they should, consumers just don't ask for express warranties. They typically don't know how to protect themselves in this way, or if they know they often forget or decline to make the effort. They thus suffer losses for which the seller is, ethically at least, responsible. The purpose of implied warranties, then, is to bring legal obligations into line with ethical obligations by making the seller liable for goods which fail to serve the consumer in their ordinary or particular uses.

All of this thinking came too late to help Parkinson, but in 1815 the seeds of the merchantability warranty were established in England in *Gardiner v. Gray*.[35] The object of sale was described as "12 bags of waste silk" in a sale note written when the bargain was made, before delivery. On delivery the goods were found to be "of a quality not saleable under the denomination of 'waste silk,'" despite the seller's contention that such materials were customarily described by that name. The buyer charged in court that the description constituted a guarantee that the goods would be merchantable as "waste silk" and not merely describable as such. The court agreed, Lord Ellenborough's opinion stating that: "The intention of both parties must be taken to be that it shall be saleable in the market under the denomination mentioned in the contract between them. The purchaser cannot be supposed to buy goods to lay them on a dunghill."

Lord Ellenborough had been one of the justices in *Parkinson,* and his ruling seems as though it would apply to that case, too. The difference the court noticed, however, was that Gardiner had bought his silk on the basis of the description only, whereas Parkinson had examined some of his hops before purchase. It is hard to imagine what difference a chance to examine could make for a defect impossible to see, but the court thought it made Parkinson negligent in a way Gardiner was not. A person who examined his purchase was held responsible at law for knowing everything there was to know about it, whether possible to know or not![36]

There is apparently no leading case in which merchantability was introduced to America,[37] but the concept was established here in the nineteenth century and has been enshrined in the Uniform Sales Act[38] and the Uniform Commercial Code.[39]

The implied warranty of fitness for a particular purpose began in the 1800s with several English cases[40] and was established in American law by *Kellogg Bridge Company v. Hamilton* of 1884.[41] Hamilton was a subcontractor to Kellogg Bridge, which had driven some foundation piles in the early phases of a bridge-building job. When Hamilton came on the scene to erect the bridge he found the piles insufficient. He suffered losses through delays and extra work and sued for damages. Kellogg Bridge obviously knew the specific purpose for which the piles were to be used, and the trial judge instructed the jury that an implied warranty existed that the work was suitable and proper for that purpose. Kellogg Bridge appealed to the U.S. Supreme

Court that there was no such warranty, but the Court found there was and confirmed the judgment for Hamilton.

Although *Parkinson* involved merchantability and *Kellogg Bridge* the fitness warranty, they both involved the problem of latent defects. An excerpt from the latter decision shows us what a remarkably different attitude had developed toward such defects over the eighty-two-year span: "While Hamilton must be charged with knowledge of all defects apparent or discernible upon inspection, he could not justly be charged with knowledge of latent defects which no inspection or examination, at or before the sale, could possibly have disclosed. . . . The buyer did not, because in the nature of things he could not, rely on his own judgment . . . . He must be deemed to have relied on the judgment of the company . . . ."

The Supreme Court said *Kellogg* was different from *Parkinson* because it involved dealing directly with the manufacturer, who should have known of the piles' unfitness for their designated purpose. *Parkinson* had involved an agent who was conceded no chance of knowing. Yet it is hard to believe that the *Kellogg* result stemmed solely from that fact. The wording of the two cases suggests that a much greater sympathy for the buyer had developed by 1884. Hamilton was not told brusquely to go get an express warranty if he was worried about hidden defects. He was told his reliance on the piles' fitness was justified because the fitness qualities were hidden and he was left with no reasonable choice but to rely.

The implied warranty of fitness for a particular purpose eventually was codified into the Uniform Sales Act[42] and the Uniform Commercial Code.[43] There is no question under the now-applicable UCC that both of the implied warranties of quality apply for defects which an inspection could not reasonably be expected to reveal, whether the buyer has the "opportunity" to inspect or not.[44]

For features of the goods which an inspection might

reasonably reveal, application of the two implied warranties cannot always be assumed. The Uniform Sales Act was interpreted in courts to mean that when the buyer had the opportunity to examine, whether he did or not, he was held responsible for whatever the inspection ought to have revealed.[45] Thus the implied warranties were not in effect with regard to those inspectable features of the goods. This seriously crimped the help given buyers by implied warranties, but the point was changed when the UCC superseded the USA. If the buyer inspects the goods today, he is responsible for whatever the inspection ought to reveal, and the implied warranties are negated for those features. But if he has the opportunity to inspect but does not use it, he is now held to forfeit the implied warranties only where he specifically refuses a demand by the seller that he inspect. If the seller does not insist, it is not considered that the buyer has refused. In this way it is relatively less likely today that the once-formidable inspection obligation will interfere with the buyer's chance to employ the implied warranties.[46]

In addition the UCC provides that the buyer's refusal to inspect or unsuccessful inspection will not negate the implied warranties if the seller has stated the content of such warranties expressly and the buyer has indicated his reliance on those words rather than on his examination. In such instance the seller's words are said to transform the implied warranties into express warranties, which will not today be overruled by the buyer's inspection obligation.[47] This is a real breakthrough for the buyer, because a seller will scarcely care to deny upon express request that his goods are merchantable.

The availability of implied warranties and the liberalization of the definition of express warranties have made major contributions in converting sellerism to consumerism. But we cannot leave the topic before considering two related matters which have been given strong consumerist interpretations in the twentieth century. One of them concerns the reach of a warranty, involving whether a manufacturer's warranty extends only to the retailer or whether it operates as well for those to whom the retailer sells. Early sellerist interpretations held that the warranty stopped with the retailer, and the ultimate customer enjoyed only those warranties given by the latter. The theory was that two separate sales occurred, and the conditions of one transaction should not be imposed on another (there must be privity of contract, in legal parlance).[48]

More recently the law has acted to extend manufacturer's warranties to consumers. In particular, the rule has developed that statements made by the manufacturer directly to the public, as in mass media advertisements, amount to express warranties directly to the buyer. The theory is that when the sales messages are aimed beyond the dealer, it is only fair that the warranty protection should be extended as well. This consumerist interpretation is owing largely to *Baxter v. Ford Motor* of 1932. [49]

Baxter purchased a car from a local dealer from whom he also received advertising materials distributed by Ford to aid dealers in making sales. The printed matter said Ford's Triplex Shatter-Proof Glass Windshield was "so made that it will not fly or shatter under the hardest impact. . . . It eliminates the dangers of flying glass." The statements proved false when a pebble from a passing car struck Baxter's windshield, throwing glass which blinded his left eye and damaged his right. Sued, Ford contended no warranties existed without privity of contract. It did not deny its advertising representations were express warranties, but argued from established precedents that they extended no further than the dealer. The Washington state court decided that the old understandings must be revised: "Radio, billboards, and the products of the printing press have become the means of creating a large part of the demand . . . . It would be unjust to recognize a rule that would permit manufacturers of goods to create a demand for their products by representing that they possess qualities which they, in fact, do not possess, and then, because there is no privity of contract existing between the consumer and the manufacturer, deny the consumer the right to recover if damages result from the absence of those qualities, when such absence is not readily noticeable."

The *Baxter* reasoning was widely adopted in other states, and decisions to the contrary since that time have been rare.[50] In addition, since 1960 the implied warranty of merchantability has also been held to pass from the manufacturer directly to the ultimate purchaser. In *Henningsen v. Bloomfield Motors*,[51] another injury case, there was no express warranty attributed to the manufacturer, but the court held that: "under modern marketing conditions, when a manufacturer puts a new automobile into the stream of trade and promotes its purchase to the public, an implied warranty that it is reasonably suitable for use as such accompanies it into the hands of the ultimate purchaser . . . ." *Henningsen* also extended the coverage of the warranty beyond the buyer to his wife, who was the one injured: "It is our opinion that an implied warranty of merchantability . . . extends to the purchaser of the car, members of his family, and to other persons occupying it or using it with his consent. It would be wholly opposed to reality to say that use by such persons is not within the anticipation of such a warranty . . . ."

With cases such as these,[52] there no longer appears to be much threat to warranty protection from the fact that the manufacturer does not sell directly to the consumer.

A second and more serious threat to protection is the tendency for manufacturers and sellers to disclaim warranties they have made. They do this by placing "not warranted" on labels or inserting in contracts such statements as "all warranties express or implied are hereby disclaimed." A warranty appearing in a contract may include a statement that it is offered "in lieu of all other warranties express or implied." This threatens to eliminate the warranty status of advertisements, salesmen's statements, or other representations made to the buyer prior to presentation of the written contract.

Such representations then would have no more status as warranties than did Chandelor's or Woods's "affirmations" about bezar-stones and brazilletto. And the disclaimers threaten the implied warranties, too, which would throw consumer protection back to the state the unfortunate Parkinson knew.

There is not much the consumer can do about a disclaimer's sheer presence. He can hope it will be invalidated if he sees fit to challenge it later, but he probably can't negotiate successfully to have it removed. In theory, the buyer presumably might dicker with the seller over warranty provisions when working out a deal. In practice, however, there is usually less to it than that. Here is what a Federal Trade Commission report stated about the automobile market: "Automobile sales normally involve the unilaterial imposition of terms by the seller. It is unrealistic to view an automobile warranty as a voluntary contract between two bargaining parties. The purchaser of an automobile has no true bargaining power beyond the power to haggle over price."[53]

What happens if people *do* haggle over warranties, or refuse to sign unless the disclaimer is removed? Chances are they will get nowhere, because the dealer has no authority to commit the manufacturer to a change of terms. If the dealer grants the request he will have to take responsibility himself, with no help from the manufacturer. So probably he will remain stubborn. He will not be worried by the buyer threatening to go to another seller, because the persuasive power of the dealers' association makes him confident that his competitors will be equally firm.

Disclaiming, for all of that, is not entirely bad. It is necessary to trade in the sense that many transactions can be made on no other reasonable basis. This is particularly true in the second-hand market. An auto dealer might decline a trade-in if he had to repair it and sell it with a warranty. The person who exchanges the car is benefited because it has trade-in value only if the dealer can sell it "as is." And those buyers are benefited who can afford cars only at the low prices which such practices make possible.

But disclaiming may be unconscionable where the seller does not reasonably require it, and especially where the buyer may reasonably expect warranties to exist. This occurs when items are presumed to be new or when the buyer is not aware of the disclaimer in advance, as when he does not see it until the contract-signing moment that invariably comes after his decision. The disclaimer becomes part of the bargain although not part of the decision; that is where its use may be regarded as an unreasonable attempt to defeat the effects of a warranty. Under such conditions the court in *Henningsen* struck down the manufacturer's disclaimer because it amounted to a "studied effort to frustrate the protection afforded by an implied warranty of merchantability."

But too often disclaimers of warranty have remained in force. Both the Uniform Sales Act and the Uniform Commercial Code have included provisions permitting them. Their widespread use could reverse the effects of the consumerist developments in warranty law, and there is alarm among those who do not want to see that happen. [54] Even here, however, the trend of the law is favorable to the buyer; the UCC imposes tighter regulations than the USA did. Wording which attempts to disclaim express warranties is described by the UCC as "repugnant" to the essence of the bargain between buyer and seller,[55] and disclaimers of implied warranties are sanctioned only when presented so that the buyer is not unduly surprised by their presence.[56] In addition, writes an expert on warranty law, "The courts have displayed no very favorable attitude toward disclaimers, construing them away, or finding that they were not adequately brought home to the plaintiff."[57]

A problem remaining with disclaimers is that the consumer who sees them in print may still accept them at face value rather than bring the challenges which are likely to defeat them. But at least disclaimers *are* susceptible to defeat under existing law.

The warranty law we have examined is used primarily in suits brought against sellers by individual consumers. As such it is not directly relevant to the operation of the Federal Trade Commission, which is the primary legal vehicle today for consumer protection. In warranty cases it is only the breaching which is unlawful, not the representation as such. A warranty which is offered but never accepted by a consumer cannot be prosecuted under warranty law. The Federal Trade Commission, using procedures we will examine in chapter 9, operates by prohibiting sales claims on the basis of their capacity to deceive, without having to show that consumers have accepted them and been subsequently deceived and injured. This means the FTC can achieve its purposes without going to the trouble of proving breach.

This does not rule the FTC out of acting against warranties, because it can find warranty representations deceptive as such and therefore can rule against them as deceptions rather than strictly as warranties. An automobile dealer, for example, may advertise an unconditional guarantee and then later offer the buyer a contract to sign which contains a narrowly limited warranty or even an "as is" provision. This makes the advertised statement a deceptive misrepresentation which the Commission may act against. Its *Guides Against Deceptive Advertising of Guarantees* state that "any guarantee in advertising shall clearly and conspicuously disclose the nature and extent of the guarantee."[58]

The FTC's capabilities, however, are limited because it cannot act on behalf of individual consumers, its legal role being only preventive and not remedial. It cannot recover a purchase price nor compensate for damages to an individual. Suits to obtain these remedies must be brought by the individual himself, and that is the special value of warranty law.

Nor do modern developments in misrepresentation

law, which we will see in chapter 6, eliminate the importance of warranty regulations. Misrepresentation complaints also may be brought by individuals, but in many cases it is easier for the buyer to prove the existence of a warranty than of a liable misrepresentation. A statement can be judged a warranty on the basis of its wording alone, while the liability of a misrepresentation depends on various complicated assessments of the seller's culpability in making it and the buyer's right to rely on it.

For all of these reasons the consumerist developments in warranty law have been most useful in easing the burden of caveat emptor for twentieth-century consumers. To summarize, we have examined a trend which has changed the probability from low to high that a seller's statement will be deemed a warranty. Under the extreme sellerist interpretations, implied warranties did not exist, and seller's statements were called express warranties only when it appeared certain that the sellers intended them to be so. Statements which did constitute warranties might be denied to the consumer anyway by the privity argument or by disclaimers. But today, under consumerist interpretations of the law, implied warranties compel the seller to observe certain responsibilities toward the consumer, and it is highly likely as well that the protection of an express warranty will be available for any advertising or sales representation which constitutes a fact or a promise about the goods for sale.

6

Misrepresentation: How Much Lying Do You Find in a Falsehood?

AS WITH warranty law, the probability that misrepresentation law will operate to the consumer's advantage has increased dramatically since the time such rules were formulated in early English courts. A misrepresentation at the time of *Chandelor v. Lopus*[1] was most difficult to prove liable. Today it is relatively easy. In this chapter we describe how the rule was changed so that liability might be imposed on the seller without requiring the buyer to prove fraud.

We have noted in chapter 4 the development of the sellerist idea that a representation must be not only false but that the seller must commit fraud in stating it. He must be shown, that is, to have been consciously aware of the falsity and to have used it with the deliberate intent of deceiving the buyer. Such fraudulent misrepresentation was unlawful; all other misrepresentations were not. (Misrepresentations may be made by buyers, too, to the detriment of sellers. But seller's representations in the marketplace far outnumber those made by buyers. Therefore this discussion is devoted principally to situations in which sellers make representations and buyers receive them.)

The consequences to buyers of the fraud requirement are not hard to imagine. Misrepresentations made by sellers in true innocence might damage buyers, but the seller shares no responsibility for that damage. Even worse, responsibility falls wholly on the buyers for all consciously deliberate falsities by sellers which cannot be proved in court to be such. Fraud in the legal sense occurs only when the buyer proves it. Obviously there are sales occurring all the time in which fraud occurs but the buyer cannot produce the level of proof required in a court of law. Such a rule virtually constitutes an invitation to sellers to commit legalized lying.

The first breaching of the fraud barrier came in a case of 1663 which was most uncharacteristic of its time in being so generous to a buyer. In *Ekins v. Tresham*[2] the buyer Ekins bought a building because the seller told him the rent paid by the tenants was 42£. When after purchase the rent turned out to be considerably less, 32£, Ekins claimed fraud and won his case even though he was unable to prove that Tresham knew of the falsity. The court took the initiative of assuming by sheer logic that the seller must have known the true amount of rent he was receiving. This thinking was similar to the decisions of Lord Holt[3] that a person could not help knowing whether he held legal ownership to goods.

But it was reasoning which failed to impress most courts in the seventeenth and eighteenth centuries.[4] The necessity to prove fraud in cases other than ownership and rent claims was solidly affirmed, particularly in the influential case of *Pasley v. Freeman* of 1789.[5] "The fraud must be proved," Justice Buller declared. "The assertion alone will not maintain the action; but the plaintiff must go on to prove that it was false, and that the defendant knew it to be so." This position was adopted in American law in *Seixas and Seixas v. Woods* in 1804.[6]

Yet in 1801 there occurred an English case in which

the fraud barrier was ever so slightly pierced. In *Haycraft v. Creasey*,[7] Creasey falsely represented to Haycraft that a Miss Robertson might safely be extended credit. The truth was that the lady was not a good risk; she defaulted to Haycraft's loss, and it was learned after the fact that various persons had reason to think she might do exactly that. But the evidence also suggested that Creasey had been duped. He did not know these reasons, and did not know his statements were false. It looked like another case where the person who spread the false facts was to go free because he did so innocently, and the sole liability would fall on the unfortunate recipient of the claim.

But Haycraft decided to pursue what seemed a likely angle. He charged that Creasey had been most definite in his assertion, saying "I can positively assure you of my own knowledge that you may credit Miss Robertson to any amount with perfect safety." To this Haycraft's brother had responded, "I hope you do not inform me this upon bare hearsay; but you do know the fact yourself." To which Creasey answered, "Friend Haycraft, I know that your brother may trust Miss Robertson with perfect safety, to any amount."

In contrast to these positive statements, the evidence showed that Creasey had no reason to know, and knew he did not. He did not know the statement about Miss Robertson was false, but he also didn't know it was true. In other words, there were two falsehoods stated by Creasey; the first was that Miss Robertson was a good credit risk, the second was that he knew this to be a fact. He may not have known of the first falsity, but Haycraft argued before the court that he surely knew the second and was guilty of fraudulent misrepresentation for that reason.

The court's ruling was decided on a point irrelevant to this argument, and it went against Haycraft. But all the court members said they were sympathetic to the notion that proof of fraud might be shown by a speaker's insincerity of belief as well as by the narrower grounds of conscious knowledge of falsity.[8] Their declaration technically was dictum, an aside rather than a binding legal ruling, since the case was not decided on that particular point. But the point at least appeared in the record, and in 1843 was made law in *Taylor v. Ashton.*[9] From that time on it was clear in England, and recognized as well in America,[10] that fraudulent behavior included making a claim insincerely, not knowing its truth, as well as making it when knowing its falsity.

Still, the definition of fraud went no further than that point for many years. No matter how damaging a misrepresentation might be, it would not be fraudulent if made without knowledge of falsity. Some statements occasionally would be so ridiculously or obviously false that a court would not accept the speaker's claim that they were made honestly.[11] But if a defense of honest belief could not be overthrown, a misrepresentation could not be found fraudulent and therefore could not be found unlawful.

Some legal experts, however, were considering ways to change this rule as the nineteenth century progressed. They were toying with the notion that the speaker might sometimes be *negligent* even though not fraudulent, which means he ought to have been consciously aware of the falsity of which he was not aware. He did not know, nor did he know that he didn't know, but he ought to have known. This might typically occur with the representations of a technical expert, who by dint of his training should be expected to know the truth or to know when he didn't know. A layman who commented with honest falsity on the same matters could not be called negligent in doing so. But the man who represented himself as an expert should be called negligent if his normal expertise failed him, even though he was completely honest in what he falsely claimed.

An 1867 case, *Western Bank of Scotland v. Addie,*[12] reflected the negligence view when the judge told the jury it might find fraud (deceit) if the defendants made statements they did not believe *or statements they had no reasonable ground to believe.* It was a strongly consumerist ruling, because it greatly increased the probability of finding sellers legally responsible for misrepresentations which injured buyers.

But negligent misrepresentation received a sharp setback in a landmark English case which is now infamous for having failed to accept the principle. In *Derry v. Peek* of 1889,[13] the court found the directors of a tramway corporation had honestly and sincerely, though falsely, published in a business prospectus that their company had the right to operate its trams with steam. The General Tramway Act of 1870 had provided that tramway carriages be run only by animal power unless their operators obtained a special act of Parliament authorizing alternate power. The company duly obtained an act authorizing steam power, though under condition that the Board of Trade must consent. On publishing the prospectus the company had not received that consent, though getting it was universally regarded as a "rubber-stamping" procedure. Therefore the court found it reasonable to conclude that the directors honestly believed they had obtained the right to steam, and were honestly shocked when the Board of Trade declined consent. The charge of fraud against them was ruled not established.[14]

In announcing this decision Lord Herschell rejected the precedent from *Western Bank* for finding fraud when someone stated what he ought not to have believed. No previous case, he said, had given grounds for so defining fraud. All the valid precedents declared that fraud could not exist where there was honest belief, no matter how foolish a belief it might be: "A man who forms his belief carelessly, or is unreasonably credulous, may be blameworthy when he makes a representation on which another is to act, but he is not, in my opinion, fraudulent in the sense in which that word was used in all the [prior] cases . . . ."[15]

The climate of opinion following *Derry* leaned toward the feeling that the persons damaged deserved relief. The legal writer Williston wrote much later that decisions in which conscious dishonesty had to be proved in order to find unlawful misrepresentation "represented a distinctly lower standard of morality and justice than the contrary decisions."[16] Prosser, another well-known legal interpreter, called *Derry* a "storm center" which in the twentieth century has been "condemned as a backward step in the law," to the extent that a substantial minority of American courts now refuse to follow it.[17]

The problem with which Lord Herschell grappled in *Derry* was whether to incorporate negligence into the meaning of fraud. Fraud meant conscious awareness of falsity or insincere belief, and negligent behavior, even when "blameworthy" as Herschell implied, simply didn't amount to that in his opinion. He felt the judge in *Western Bank* was incorrect in trying to assimilate negligence into fraud, even though justice apparently was well served in that case and would have been, too, by a similar ruling in *Derry*. Perhaps Herschell would have ruled differently if the *Derry* suit had been brought on negligence grounds rather than fraud, but it was brought for fraud and had to be adjudged on that basis. In England his position remained firm until 1963; negligent misrepresentation was not fraud and was not illegal. After that time, though still kept distinct from fraud, it was made subject to a separate legal action.[18]

American courts have shown a strong tendency to observe English rulings, and quite a few of them accepted *Derry v. Peek,* originally at least, as the model for their own decisions.[19] That is the reason so many English cases are cited here in what is intended to be a story about American law. In the field of sales regulation American law appears to derive from British law as though the two were not separate at all. That is not true in all legal fields, by any means. The student of seditious libel, for instance, will notice differences so vast that indeed the English stance helped prompt the colonies to revolt. But for misrepresentation and other topics relating to sales messages, it appears that American jurists have held a great affinity for their English brethren.

Derry was a controversial case, however, and not all American courts agreed to it; some broke away. Negligent misrepresentation was recognized as liable here as early as 1898, and other American courts from the same early date ruled that fraud existed for misrepresentations which were not strictly fraudulent but could be called negligent.[20] Whatever the method, American law has generally determined today that a seller's negligent as well as fraudulent conduct may be grounds for ruling his misrepresentations liable.

Can the law go even further and declare misrepresentations liable which are neither fraudulent nor negligent but entirely innocent? This would be the most extreme consumerist ruling possible; it would mark a complete reversal of earlier attitudes by transferring to the seller all responsibility for misrepresentation. The buyer would have to prove nothing more than that the misrepresentation was made and that he relied upon it to his detriment. Would the law be willing to take this step? The reader who thinks back to the previous chapter will realize that many innocent misrepresentations by sellers are indeed liable—they are called *warranties!* We have already seen, in other words, the story of how the law came to hold sellers responsible for their innocent misrepresentations.

This question occurs, however: if many seller's misrepresentations are liable as warranties when innocent, what advantage does the consumer find in bringing suit against fraudulent or negligent misrepresentations, which are more difficult to prove? In a great many cases in the 1970s, in fact, there is no longer any reason for a consumer to employ misrepresentation law because warranty law can be applied simultaneously with greater ease and often can be applied where misrepresentation law cannot. Why discuss the latter, then?

One reason we have told the story of misrepresentation law here is because it contributed greatly to consumerism in the days before warranty law was adopted universally in the United States. With the Uniform Sales Act never adopted by all states, and the Uniform Commercial Code adopted by the fiftieth state only in 1968,[21] warranties have been available to all United States citizens for only a short time. More important, however, there are still conditions today under which warranties do not aid buyers. One occurs in the minority of cases where privity of contract still assists sellers.[22] Another is in the cases where disclaimers of warranty are used successfully.[23] Still another occurs because warranties apply only to the sale of "goods"—that is, to what the law calls tangible chattels.[24] Automobiles and houses are examples of goods, being physical objects, while stock certificates or building leases are not. False claims concerning such intangibles must still be charged under misrepresentation law, where developments have now moved in some cases to allowing a buyer to recover for entirely innocent misrepresentation (called "strict liability").[25] In this way misrepresentation law still plays a role in consumer protection where warranty law cannot.

Another reason for continuing to value misrepresentation law today is that warranty law has not moved as far in a consumerist direction to protect against opinion statements which imply false facts. We will take up the topic of opinion claims in the next chapter, and say here only that misrepresentation law today may guard the consumer against false opinions under certain conditions where warranty law will not.[26]

The misrepresentation concept is not technically relevant to the operations of the Federal Trade Commission, which offers (along with the state agencies modeled after it) the most significant degree of consumer protection in America today. To prohibit sales messages the Commission need show only their capacity to deceive,[27] whereas suits by individuals charging misrepresentation must show specific damage incurred as a result of relying upon the falsity.[28] However, the FTC's concept of "deception" certainly was founded in the earlier common law concept of misrepresentation. It seems fair to say, too, that FTC's liberal and consumer-favoring definitions of deception owe their existence to the trends we have described here in misrepresentation law, which have given consumers considerably more legal protection than they once had.

7

Opinion and Value Statements and Puffery: Avoiding Fact and Keeping Sellerism Alive

THE CONSUMER gains achieved by the changes in warranty and misrepresentation law are solid indeed. But they are severely blunted by an important qualification we have not yet examined. I am sorry that so many qualifying details are necessary to this story, but there is simply no other way to tell it. A person can take a legal rule and state it easily enough, but when he wants to put it into practice he must cope with dozens of restrictions and reservations carried to a degree which befuddles the mind (Rule A applies except in Situation B except not where Aspect C exists, but all of the above is only for D types of people, and so forth).

People need lawyers to guide them through such mazes—and please remember that I am not a lawyer and am not attempting to write like one. My role as a journalist rather than lawyer gives me certain advantages; it means I can choose the details I think are useful in telling the general story of sellerism and consumerism and can skip those details which are peripheral to that narrative yet would have to be mastered by anyone conducting an actual legal case. I have not, to give one example among many, discussed the question of when a statement by a seller is actually represented to the buyer. Suppose a storekeeper had a sales message on the back of his front door, and the evidence indicated the door was normally opened inward during business hours so that the message was not seen. Let us suppose a warranty case is brought, in which a customer claims he saw the message and was damaged by relying on it. The seller, we'll imagine further, claims in rebuttal that the message was not really conveyed to the public, and calls the buyer unjustified in stating that it was. In such a situation, it's possible that the question of whether the message was a bona fide warranty would be completely obscured by the issue of whether it was represented to the buyer in the first place.

Such issues are important in this book if the court rulings concerning them once favored one party to a transaction but now favor the other. Where such a trend is evident I have tried to include the issue in my story. But where it is not, I have not. I have not attempted to pursue those details which will not add significantly to the broad story of the trend from sellerism to consumerism. This is not a law textbook in which all the necessary details for case action are described, and I can positively warrant that point to you.

So if you're stirred by the contents of this book to charge somebody with illegal behavior, or to refrain from doing so, I'll be pleased to know I had some influence on your actions. But before you climb those marble court-house steps make sure you get proper counsel. And if your case comes out differently from what I've suggested it would, don't blame me. The cases I'm describing here are those which the expert authors of law review articles and legal summaries have felt indicated the general trends, but there have always been cases which go against those trends or are decided on grounds other than those represented by the trends.

How Opinion Statements Gained Special Treatment

Now that I've given my caveat reader, let's look at one of the most essential qualifications to the rules we've seen on warranty and misrepresentation. It is that they apply to *factual* representations only.[1] They do not apply to statements of *opinion* or *value,* of which puffery claims are a subcategory. There are different rules for these supposedly nonfactual statements, and these different rules restrict the seller less and so protect the consumer less. They have lagged in following the trend away from sellerism which we have traced in the previous two chapters. These rules are a sore spot, a principal reason for the fact that the consumerism movement today is far from complete.

The traditional reason for distinguishing opinion statements from factual statements is that they are nonfactual and therefore cannot be true nor false nor harm a person who relies on them. I have already explained that I think this reason is nonsensical, and I have given some evidence for why I think that.[2] There seems to be no reason remaining today to doubt that opinion statements *do* have factual implications and may therefore be false in what they imply.

To see why the factual nature of opinions should ever have been denied, we will return again to the early days of English common law. We will see that this early law considered the literal content of representations only and attributed no importance to what they implied. The literal content of an opinion statement is of course not factual—I have no intention of arguing that it is. It is only what an opinion *implies* about the goods that is factual, and implications admittedly are much more difficult to deal with.

But the recognition of the process of implication is so well established today that it is difficult to see why the law has clung to the old assumption that seller's opinions have nothing to do with facts. The precedents of sellerism apparently have such strength that they continue to survive in the face of opposing evidence. We are going to take a long look at those precedents to see why they have such great staying power.

The exemption of opinion and value statements, thus of puffery, began over three centuries ago.[3] *Harvey v. Young,* an English case of 1602,[4] involved a seller's false statement that a "term for years" (an archaic phrase meaning an estate held for a specified number of years) "was worth 150 pounds to be sold." The buyer paid that much for it, but later could not get even one hundred pounds. He went to court seeking recovery, but was thwarted to find the seller's liability denied because the claim "did not prove any fraud; for it was but the defendant's bare assertion that the term was worth so much, and it was the plaintiff's folly to give credit to such assertion."

The court may or may not have approved the seller's conduct in stating the falsity; it didn't say. But it found no illegal behavior to be involved. It was a straight case of caveat emptor, calling the buyer negligent in the absence of warranty or fraud for relying on the seller's claim rather than examining the quality of the "term" for himself.

Why was fraud not found in the claim? The scanty report[5] added only that if the seller had warranted the value the result would have been otherwise, "for the warranty given by the defendant is a matter to induce confidence and trust in the plaintiff." Apparently, then, a "bare assertion" without warranty was *not* sufficient to induce confidence and trust (in modern terms, to permit justifiable reliance by the buyer). But the point was not elaborated, and we will never know with certainty what was meant. Perhaps the court's intention was to say that the bare assertion was not to be relied upon because it was a statement of value and not of fact. We know at least that courts in later decisions chose to interpret *Harvey v. Young* in that way.

Another early English precedent was *Baily v. Merrell* of 1615.[6] Baily agreed to transport Merrell's load of wood for a payment of 2s. 8d. per hundred pounds. Lacking scales, he accepted Merrell's statement that the wood weighed eight hundred pounds. The true weight was two thousand pounds, as Baily discovered only when the burden made two of his horses collapse and die. The court told this feckless unfortunate it was his own folly to overload the horses when he could have avoided the disaster by his own initiative. The case was similar to *Harvey* in rejecting reliance on a "bare assertion." But it made fully clear, as *Harvey* did not, that the recipient of the misrepresentation was capable of checking its truth for himself. It also made clear that the rule applied even though the seller committed fraud, the fraud being innocuous because the buyer might readily (the court said) have perceived it.[7]

The next important precedent was *Ekins v. Tresham* of 1663, already discussed in the chapter on misrepresentation law.[8] The defendant had falsely claimed the rent paid by tenants of the building he was selling was forty-two pounds rather than the true figure of thirty-two pounds. Hauled into court, he argued that no fraud (deceit) was involved in such a statement. He cited *Harvey v. Young* in saying so. The court voiced its approval of the principle of *Harvey*, giving it support which led to its eventual widespread acceptance. It also offered an explanation of the principle as follows: "An action will not lie for saying, that a thing is of greater value than it is . . . because value consists in judgment and estimation, wherein men many times differ."

The court then interpreted the Harvey rule further by telling why it could not, after all, be applied to the rent statement. Rent was different because it could not be confirmed independently by the buyer, the decision said, thereby implying that the court felt a statement of value *could* be confirmed independently. A companion report of the same case stated the distinction similarly, saying that rent involved "certain" rather than "uncertain" amounts of money.[9] The term *fact* was not used in contrast to the term *value*, but the implication in modern terms was that the rent figure was an actual fact about the property while the value figure was not. Therefore the seller could be found liable for misrepresenting rent even though not for speaking dishonestly about value. The case also implied that a person's evaluation of a thing can be made by no one but himself; reliance on another to make that judgment was negligence, through which the buyer brought full responsibility upon himself.

The three cases we have examined may have been merely straws in the wind before 1789. The law of fraud was a liquid thing, undergoing the zigs and zags of tentative development. But in 1789 several of the strands were pulled together by the scholarship and authority of the court in *Pasley v. Freeman*,[10] which became the leading English case on fraud and the model for its treatment in the new American republic. It also became the first case to describe as "opinion" the kind of statements now called that. The plaintiffs in the case, planning to do business with a man called Falch, had relied to their detriment upon misrepresentations by Freeman commending Falch's credit rating. The court found Freeman's statements to be fraudulent, and also found the plaintiffs had "no means of knowing the state of Falch's credit but by an application to his neighbors." Since it was one of those neighbors who misled them, the ruling was made as in the rent case (*Ekins*) that the plaintiffs lacked the means to investigate the truth independently. They could not have known the truth about the fraudulent statement and therefore were entitled to recover for the damages caused by their reliance on it.

One of the four justices, Grose, dissented. He claimed the statements about Falch's credit were not fraudulent and the plaintiffs did not lack the means to know their truth. He agreed the claims were false, but pressed the point that not all false statements were fraudulent. To illustrate, he cited *Harvey*, *Leakins*, and *Baily* as typical of cases "where the affirmation is (what is called in some of the books) a nude assertion; such as the party deceived may exercise his own judgment upon; as where it is a matter of opinion, where he might make inquiries into the truth of the assertion, and it becomes his own fault from laches [negligence] that he is deceived."

Another justice, Buller, although holding with the majority that Freeman's statements did not fit this category, agreed that the type of assertion Grose had described was not fraudulent. Such an assertion, Buller said, "was of mere matter of judgment and opinion; of a matter of which the defendant had no particular knowledge, but of which men will be of many minds, and which is often governed by whim and caprice. Judgment or opinion, in such cases, implies no knowledge."

Evaluation requires knowledge, of course, but Buller apparently meant there was nothing the seller could know which the buyer could not. The temper of the times ruled out any acknowledgment that a seller might have some "particular knowledge" which the buyer did not, or that there was any chance lacking that the buyer "might make inquiries." The difficulty the buyer might have in obtaining equivalent knowledge was not recognized. Stressed was possibility, not probability; the possibility of obtaining equivalent knowledge satisfied the law, and the low probability of actually doing so was ignored.

From what we have described of their judgments so far, it appears that the justices in *Pasley* believed opinion or value statements would not typically be spoken fraudulently. The court in *Harvey* had expressly said the false claim proved no fraud, and the *Ekins* decision supported this by defining value as a subjective rather than objective element. Justice Grose's statement, however, included some additional comments which suggested rather confusingly that opinion statements would be legally *nonfraudulent even when spoken with conscious intent to deceive.*

That was a startlingly new development. Opinion statements were already less liable than factual ones to charges of fraud because conscious knowledge of falsity was difficult to charge against the maker of statements which presumably could be neither true nor false. But a speaker would certainly *sometimes* be aware of the falsity of his opinions, as when he exaggerated them grossly, and so the chance of charging fraud undoubtedly made sellers wary about using opinion or value claims recklessly.

To go further, however, to the extreme of entirely removing the possibility of charging fraud would be a wildly sellerist action, placing opinion statements far apart from factual statements in degree of liability. With fraud no longer a factor the seller would be permitted, as long as the buyer could examine the object of sale independently, to make opinion and value claims with utter abandon, damn the torpedos! The ratio of opinion statements to factual statements would rise, and would probably become the majority type of seller's claim.

Come to think of it, doesn't that sound like a description of today's advertising? I don't mean that contemporary ads represent the height of fraudulent selling, because the consumerist trend in the twentieth century has pared that activity down a good bit. But today's salesmanship is the way it is largely because of the release of opinion statements from the fraud rule, a release which was generated largely by the famous case of *Pasley v. Freeman.*

How did it happen? If conscious intent to deceive would normally produce a finding of fraud, how could Justice Grose hint otherwise? He did so by citing as a precedent *Baily v. Merrell,* a case which expressly condoned fraudulent misrepresentations. The finding in *Baily* had been that someone who could check a truth which was "readily apparent" was responsible for doing so even in the face of receiving a fraudulent claim about it.

We will never know why Grose thought *Baily* was relevant to the question of opinion statements. The misrepresentation which harmed Baily was a claim that a load of wood weighed a certain amount. It was a statement of fact, not of value. It does not seem to have been appropriately lumped together with the other cases which Grose used to illustrate "nude assertions." While claims concerning monetary value, as in *Harvey,* may vary among people and represent subjective judgment and no particular knowledge, the weight of wood is an objective amount which cannot vary from person to person. An *estimation* of weight may vary among people, but one figure must be objectively correct and the others wrong. A false claim of weight clearly is factual and involves particular knowledge. Yet Grose lumped such claims together with "nude assertions," a mistake which invited later observers to see his statement as implying that opinion statements can be spoken with fraudulent intent and yet not amount to fraud.

Justice Buller must have grasped this unlikely suggestion from Grose's words, since in his recorded opinion he objected strongly to the idea. He pointed out that *Harvey* did not condone fraud; neither did *Ekins.* If a statement was spoken fraudulently it could not possibly be a mere "bare naked lie," Buller said. But Buller did not choose specifically to refute the use of *Baily* as a precedent; he made no mention of the case. The other two justices mentioned *Baily* approvingly without commenting on the point in question. Thus the set of statements by the four justices in *Pasley* tended to leave the impression that *Baily* was a good precedent for determining the law of opinion statements.

Exaggerating this accident was the fact that Grose, in his interpretation of the opinion rule, cited not just one but two precedents which dealt with facts rather than opinions. Along with *Baily* he cited a rule from *Rolle's Abridgement*[11] that a seller's claim was not legal fraud when it stated falsely the amount of money the seller had been offered for the goods. The amount some previous potential buyer had offered the seller is certainly related to value, but is itself an objective figure. And a claim that the offer was made is a statement of fact, involving particular knowledge. A rule covering such statements appears inap-

propriate as a precedent for the handling of opinion and
value statements. Yet with Grose's help the *Rolle's
Abridgement* rule was allowed to lend weight to the idea
that opinion and value statements should be treated much
more loosely than factual statements. In the future these
two accidental precedents, and *Pasley* itself, were to be
cited in several crucial cases. Without their help, the most
extreme sellerist interpretations of the opinion rule, which
legalized a great deal of lying, may never have been established.

A typical reflection of the ideas which passed from
Pasley into later English law may be seen in this statement
in 1810 by Lord Ellenborough of the misrepresentation
rule: "A seller is unquestionably liable to an action of
deceit, if he fraudulently misrepresent the quality of the
thing sold to be other than it is in some particulars, which
the buyer has not equal means with himself of knowing; or
if he do so, in such a manner as to induce the buyer to
forbear making the inquiries which . . . he would otherwise
have made."[12]

To see what this rule meant for opinion statements, we
must turn it around: A seller is not liable to an action of
deceit if he fraudulently misrepresent the quality of the
thing sold to be other than it is in some particulars which
the buyer has equal means of knowing . . . [and, presumably, with opinion statements he always has equal
means of knowing] .

The Ellenborough pronouncement shows how greatly
influential the *Pasley* interpretation was in determining
how opinion and value statements would be handled.
When the seller made such statements he could do so as
fraudulently as he pleased, and the law did not object. In
America the *Pasley* influence was evident in the first case
to mention the opinion rule, Justice Kent citing Justice
Buller as authority on the topic.[13] Other early American
cases also mentioned the matter peripherally[14] but the
first case to establish the opinion exemption specifically
here was *Davis v. Meeker* of 1810.[15]

Meeker, who had sold Davis a wagon, was accused of

falsely and fraudulently claiming that "he had been frequently offered, by different persons, 50 dollars for the
wagon." Finding this later to be untrue, Davis sued and
won a jury verdict, which implies that the jury felt Meeker
had been aware of his falsity. But in reversing on appeal
the court appears to have ruled that the deception was
exempt from liability even though consciously false. It did
not say so explicitly,[16] but other rulings appeared eventually which quite directly stated that opinion statements
should be excused even when consciously false.

The first of these strongly sellerist rulings about opinion statements came in 1843 in Massachusetts, beginning a
long and liberal interpretation which made that state the
great American hotbed of the great American blow-up. In
Medbury v. Watson[17] the court described *Pasley* as "the
leading case, in modern times, on the subject of false
affirmations made with intent to deceive," and then used
the authority of *Pasley* to declare: "Hubbard, J.: . . . 'But
in actions on the case for deceit, founded upon false
affirmations, there has always existed the exception, that
naked assertions, though known to be false, are not the
ground of action, as between vendor and vendee . . . .
[S]uch assertions, though known by him to be false, and
though uttered with a view to deceive, are not actionable.
They are the mere affirmations of the vendor, on which
the vendee cannot safely place confidence, and will not
excuse his neglect in not examining for himself.' "[18]

In interpreting *Pasley*, Justice Hubbard obviously relied upon the dissenting opinion of Grose more than upon
the majority opinions. Buller had objected to conscious
falsity, while Grose relied heavily on cases which explicitly
condoned such behavior. Hubbard made it clear that an
American court now condoned conscious falsity, too.

Hubbard also made it clear that he recognized none of
the confusion inherent in the *Pasley* decision. His un-
troubled vision was accepted wholeheartedly in later cases,
including one which blithely reinterpreted the *Harvey* case
to suit modern needs. In *Veasey v. Doton* of 1862,[19]

another Massachusetts case, the jury found the defendant to have known his representation was false. Yet the appeals court reversed the finding of liability and said the case was "not distinguishable from *Harvey* . . . ." We recall that in *Harvey* the finding of fraud would have brought liability whereas in *Veasey* it did not. If that didn't make *Harvey* "distinguishable," nothing could. Massachusetts apparently was most reluctant to let history interfere with its widening of the opinion rule.

Undoubtedly the reader wants to know just *why* some of these decisions were made. I have been much aware that this narration is long on the facts of what happened, and short on the explanation behind them. Much of the reason for this is that I can only reflect the contents of the decisions printed in the historical records. When precedents are misinterpreted or distorted it isn't likely that the judge writing the decision would explain why he did so. Undoubtedly judges often think a certain precedent was intended to be interpreted flexibly, or that the facts of the particular case somehow merit such interpretation. But the tendency usually is to write the decision so as to imply that the precedent is perfectly and straightforwardly applicable to the role it is being made to perform.

Surely the principal reason for the decisions we have seen was not the state of the precedents but the prevailing social atmosphere. Precedents only provide the excuse, strong or feeble, for doing what the court thinks society demands at the given time. And what society, or at least its most powerful elements, demanded in early America was sellerism. To me the trend is best summed up in Hamilton's statement that caveat emptor served well its two masters, business and justice.[20] That is a barbed statement, possibly unfair if interpreted to imply a lack of ethics on the part of the law in nineteenth-century America. What Hamilton meant, however, was that the law was faithfully supporting the prevailing social ethic of the time. That ethic was that business could do no wrong.

After *Medbury v. Watson* the rules for opinion and

value statements might seem to have been stretched about as far as they could go toward favoring sellers. But the philosophy of "anything goes" was still impeded by the requirement that the buyer must be capable of checking the seller's claim for himself. Falsity, even fraudulent falsity, in nonfactual statements was perfectly acceptable up to that point, but not beyond. Do you think the full-blooded sellerists felt hampered by that? Maybe they did, because it wasn't long before another Massachusetts case got rid of that "impediment" and settled everybody down to an even greater degree of good old-fashioned lying. In *Brown v. Castles* of 1853 the court added the following twist to the rule that deliberate misrepresentations beyond the observation of the recipient amounted to fraud. The rule, it said, was inapplicable under certain conditions because it "is not applied to statements made by sellers, concerning the value of the thing sold, former offers for it, &c., it always having been understood, the world over, that such statements are to be distrusted. Multa fidem promissa levant [Many promises lessen confidence] ."[21]

All buyers know to distrust these kinds of statements! Therefore there is no harm if the seller is deliberately false in speaking them, and it also doesn't matter (this is what goes beyond the earlier law) that the buyer has no chance to check them himself. He would never *want* to check such claims himself because he rejects them automatically to begin with. Nothing is needed in law to protect the buyer because he protects himself. Holy sellerism!

All of that may be quite logical and a reasonable extension of the rules as long as you accept the beginning premise. You have to believe that no buyer would trust a seller's claim about something's quality or value. If you can accept that, you can believe everything else. But can you accept it? I certainly cannot. I don't think that many people, in the last century or in this one, automatically distrusted such claims. Nor should they have—some such claims were true, after all. Why would people be accustomed to automatic distrust when some of the sellers they dealt with were honest? The rule, of course, is utterly foolish if the basic premise is wrong. It would mean that anyone who trusted a seller's false value claims would be told that such claims are not fraudulent *because nobody trusts them.* How is that for logic!

There is an extenuating circumstance, actually, which makes the *Brown v. Castles* rule seem a bit less foolish. What the judge probably meant was that all those people who *act reasonably and sensibly* would automatically distrust opinion statements. A few people who behaved unreasonably might trust them, but such people would be negligent under the law and therefore not eligible for its protection. Remember Baily, who let his horses die from an overload? Such people are beyond the law's cognizance, so when the judge said it's always understood that such statements are to be distrusted he meant it's understood by all those persons whom the law considers itself obligated to protect.

That logic may be a bit better, but it's still not without its problems. How does the law determine what is reasonable behavior and what is unreasonable? How did it decide that it's reasonable to automatically distrust opinion statements which you can't check personally? Prior to that time the law itself said no such thing. It said that if the buyer can't check personally, then fraudulent behavior was punishable. That meant the buyer was invited legally to trust the seller (not in the sense that the seller would necessarily be honest, but that the buyer at least would be protected if he were not).

But the court in *Brown v. Castles* decided that false opinions which can't be checked independently by the buyer should be immune from punishment even though stated fraudulently, because a reasonable person wouldn't believe such statements anyway. The matter clearly is open to differences of opinion, of which mine is that a large proportion of the public has always been inclined to trust or at least not to automatically distrust such statements. I am certain it is too large a group to call them all unreasonable.

The concept of reasonableness I have been describing

was later identified in the common law as the "reasonable man standard." I'm going to defer further discussion of it to chapter 10. This standard was not mentioned in *Brown v. Castles,* but it's likely that the court was implying the existence of such a notion. The words of the case taken literally, however, stated that absolutely all persons (not just reasonable ones) distrust statements of a thing's value.

The point was to be repeated eloquently in later cases. Look at these words from an 1887 Massachusetts case: "The law recognizes the fact that men will naturally over-state the value and qualities of the articles which they have to sell. All men know this, and a buyer has no right to rely on such statements."[22] Two years later the same Massa-chusetts court, ever a friend to the seller, made the point again in *Deming v. Darling.*[23] Deming had purchased a railroad bond on representations that the railroad was good security and the bond was the very best and safest, an "A No. 1" bond. It wasn't, and Deming took the matter to court. The defendant's counsel requested the trial judge to instruct the jury that the statements were expressions of opinion no one might rightfully rely on. Such instruction would have been in line with precedents such as *Medbury v. Watson,* but the judge chose to ignore that line of thinking. He instructed the jury that the representations "so far as they were expressions of opinion, if made in good faith . . . would not support an action of deceit." In other words, the trial judge thought opinion statements made in bad faith should be called fraudulent.

The jury found Darling liable accordingly, but appeal to the Supreme Judicial Court of Massachusetts brought a reversal stated by Justice Oliver Wendell Holmes: "The language of some cases certainly seems to suggest that bad faith might make a seller liable for what are known as 'seller's statements' . . . Pike v. Fay, 101 Mass. 134. But this is a mistake. It is settled that the law does not exact good faith from a seller in those vague commendations of his wares which manifestly are open to differences of opinion . . . and as to which 'it has always been under-

stood, the world over, that such statements are to be
distrusted,' (Brown v. Castles . . .) . . . ."

Holmes was undoubtedly the most famous of puffery's
judicial godfathers, these words having been oft-quoted for
their emphasis and eloquence. He added some explanation
for why he thought the rule was a good one: "The rule of
law is hardly to be regretted, when it is considered how
easily and insensibly words of hope or expectation are
converted by an interested memory into statements of
quality and value, when the expectation has been disappointed."

Another eloquent figure was the famous Judge
Learned Hand of the Second Circuit Court of Appeals,
who offered in 1918 a similar defense of the idea that
"everyone" knows enough to distrust opinion statements:
"There are some kinds of talk which no man takes seriously, and if he does he suffers from his credulity . . . .
Neither party usually believes what the seller says about
his opinions, and each knows it. Such statements, like the
claims of campaign managers before election, are rather
designed to allay the suspicion which would attend their
absence than to be understood as having any relationship
to objective truth."[24]

With statements such as these the rule from *Brown v.
Castles* was virtually carved into stone. There was no doubt
in the law's mind that "all" people, at least all reasonable
ones, put no reliance whatever into statements of opinion
or value. Perhaps they could investigate the truth, but they
were thought to distrust seller's opinions and puffs whether they could investigate or not.

The result is a rationale for puffery today which actually
flaunts the original reason for excusing false opinions. When
the exemption from liability originated it was based on the
premise that the individual could examine for himself; it did
not apply where he could not. But the rule today is based not
on the individual's opportunity to examine for himself,
but on his supposedly natural tendency to disbelieve automatically if he is a reasonable person.

The latter is a significantly different type of proposition. Rather than being based on a norm, on something which people *should* do, it is based upon a fact about what they presumably *do* do. Any such rule stands in a precarious position to the extent that what it claims about people's behavior may be incorrect. Where reasonable people rely upon puffery and are deceived by it, it would be absurd to call their action unjustified on the reasoning that they wouldn't have done that in the first place. Another measure of the rule's absurdity is that it calls for the consumer to distrust automatically items of puffery which may in fact be true. Investigation, when possible, would enable a person to separate the true puffs from the false ones, but automatic distrust prevents him from ever making such a reasonable discrimination.

But we have seen what happened. Returning to our historical survey, the matter of opinion statements reached the U.S. Supreme Court in 1881,[25] and the Court supported the opinion rule: "The law does not fasten responsibility upon one for expressions of opinion as to matters in their nature contingent and uncertain. Such opinions will probably be as variant as the individuals who give them utterance."

The case involved a property which was thought potentially fruitful for quarrying, but which had not been developed: "No one could know its actual value until further development was made. Until then, any estimate must have been entirely speculative and conjectural. It would depend as much, perhaps, upon the temperament and expectations of the party making it, as upon any knowledge of facts."

That is different from any other case we have discussed, because *both* buyer and seller were unable to examine the property and determine what quantity of valuable stone or ore might exist beneath its surface. The case didn't get into the matter of conscious falsity; the seller couldn't have known what was true or false. But the case, as far as it went, put the Supreme Court's seal on the sellerist interpretations of opinion statements.[26]

In 1902 the topic again reached the Supreme Court,[27] and again the matter of bad faith was not involved. The postmaster of Nevada, Missouri, named McAnnulty, had refused to deliver mail to a local organization called the American School of Magnetic Healing. The School was founded on the "proposition that the mind of the human race is largely responsible for its ills, and is a perceptible factor in the . . . remedying thereof. . . . The human race does possess the innate power, through proper exercise of the faculty of the brain and mind, to largely control and remedy the ills that humanity is heir to . . . ."

The School had been turning a good profit up to the day when its mail, including a large volume of money orders, began to be stamped "fraudulent" on McAnnulty's orders. It was returned to its senders under a statute forbidding "obtaining money through the mails by means of false or fraudulent pretenses, representations, or promises." The Supreme Court ordered restoration of delivery, however, saying: "We may not believe in the efficacy of the treatment to the extent claimed by complainants, and we may have no sympathy with them in such claims, and yet their effectiveness is but matter of opinion in any court. . . . Unless the question may be reduced to one of fact as distinguished from mere opinion, we think these statutes cannot be invoked . . . ."

In 1916 in *U.S. v. New South Farm*[28] the Supreme Court again considered the mail statute after a district court had held that the false representations it denounced should not include "mere puffing or exaggeration" of qualities or value. The Court tended to agree, saying "Mere puffing, indeed, might not be within its meaning." But the particular case went beyond puffing, the Court said, because when the seller "assigns to the article qualities which it does not possess, does not simply magnify in opinion the advantages it has but invents advantages and falsely asserts their existence, he transcends the limits of 'puffing' and engages in false representations and pretenses."

In making clear what puffery was not, the Court recognized its status as a type of claim not subject to charges of fraud. In later years the Federal Trade Commission has used the *New South Farm* definition in its own determinations about puffery.

We have now described the way in which opinion, value, and puffery statements have been established in American common law. More cases might be cited, but we have chronicled those which make the principal points. Warranty law runs parallel; the cases seen in chapter 5 which provided that affirmations shall be warranties never deviated from the requirement that they should be affirmations of fact. The Uniform Commercial Code specifies today, "An affirmation merely of the value of the goods or a statement purporting to be merely the seller's opinion or commendation of the goods does not create a warranty."[29]

In chapter 11 we will describe the rulings made on opinion statements by the Federal Trade Commission. Enacted by statute, the Commission need not follow the rules developed in the common law of misrepresentation. But basically its decisions today are parallel to what is described in this chapter.

How Opinion Statements Have Been Restricted

Before finishing this chapter's description, however, we must look at the restrictions imposed by the common law upon opinion statements. The impression given thus far is of a rampant sellerism, but in truth the immunity of opinion statements from liability has been curtailed in certain ways which reflect the modern consumerist trend.

The principal method by which opinion statements have been made liable has been by asserting what the early cases denied—that the statement amounts to a misrepresentation of fact. The old cases said an opinion statement literally states no facts, and that was the end of that. The newer cases recognize that opinion statements imply facts and therefore may be liable on that basis. If the seller can be held to have misrepresented a fact by implication while making a statement of opinion, he can be held liable even though the opinion per se may appear superficially to be innocent of falsity.[30]

The question of what particular facts an opinion may imply is extremely difficult. But the conviction developed rather early that any opinion statement implies at least one. It implies—what could be simpler!—that the speaker believes his opinion. As an American case said as early as 1827, "The affirmation of belief is an affirmation of fact, that is, of the fact of belief."[31] Other courts did not leap to accept this reasoning at that early date, but recognition came when England's Lord Bowen stated in 1885 that "the state of a man's mind is as much a fact as the state of his digestion. It is true that it is very difficult to prove what the state of a man's mind at a particular time is, but if it can be ascertained it is as much a fact as anything else."[32]

The viewpoint that an opinion could be related to no fact was accordingly disposed of.[33] Furthermore, via another statement of Lord Bowen, it became accepted that there could be implied facts about the *object* of one's opinion. In *Smith v. Land and House* of 1884,[34] the sellers of a property asserted they had a desirable tenant, whereas in truth the tenant paid his rent late, irregularly, and often only under pressure. When the buyers sued against the falsehood, the defense argued it was just "one of the flourishing descriptions which auctioneers insert and which do not amount to a statement of any specific fact." Replied Bowen: "It is often fallaciously assumed that a statement of opinion cannot involve the statement of a fact. . . . But if the facts are not equally known to both sides, then a statement of opinion by the one who knows the facts best involves very often a statement of a material fact, for he impliedly states that he knows facts which justify his opinion."

To say the tenant was desirable, Bowen concluded, "amounts at least to an assertion that nothing has occurred in the relations between the landlords and the tenant which can be considered to make the tenant an unsatisfactory one. That is an assertion of a specific fact." This type of ruling entered American law in a number of cases beginning in 1886.[35] Their impact has been distilled in a summarization of the law called the *Restatement of Torts*, authored by legal experts under sponsorship of the American Law Institute:

§539: A statement of opinion as to facts not disclosed and not otherwise known to the recipient may, where it is reasonable to do so, be interpreted by him as an implied statement (a) that the facts known to the maker are not incompatible with his opinion; or (b) that he knows facts sufficient to justify him in forming it. . .[36]

Further restrictions on opinion statements are described in another section of the *Restatement:*

§542: The recipient of a fraudulent misrepresentation which is one only as to the maker's opinion is not justified in relying upon it in a transaction with the maker, unless the fact to which the opinion relates is material, and the maker

(a) purports to have special knowledge of the matter which the recipient does not have, or

(b) stands in a fiduciary or other similar relation of trust and confidence to the recipient, or

(c) has successfully endeavored to secure the confidence of the recipient, or

(d) has some other special reason to expect that the recipient will rely on his opinion.[37]

The rule stated in clause (a) of section 542 specifies that a presumed expert may not throw his opinions around carelessly the way other people may. This rule is owed principally to *Picard v. McCormick* of 1862,[38] which involved false statements "by a jeweler to an unskilled purchaser of the value of articles which none but an expert could reasonably be supposed to understand." The court found the jeweler deliberately took advantage of the buyer by claiming that watches and other jewelry were worth far more than what a knowledgeable person would believe.

Contrary to other cases we have seen, the court in this instance did not worry about whether the buyer might have inspected for himself. Rather, it emphasized that reliance on the seller's claims was reasonable due to the seller's position. If false claims of value were usually deemed innocent, the court said, it was "only because [they] can rarely be supposed to have induced a purchase without negligence . . . . It is undoubtedly true that value is usually a mere matter of opinion, and that a purchaser must expect that a vendor will seek to enhance his wares, and must disregard statements of their value."

But this case was different, the court stated, because:

Frauds are easily committed by dishonest dealers . . . and can not be detected in many cases except by persons of experience. . . . We are aware of no rule which determines arbitrarily that any class of fraudulent misrepresentations can be exempted from the consequences attached to others. Where a purchaser, without negligence, has been induced by the arts of a cheating seller to rely upon material statements which are knowingly false . . . it can make no difference in what respect he has been deceived, if the deceit was material and relied on. . . . We think it can not be laid down as a matter of law that value is never a material fact . . . .

We can see what a difference the *Picard* decision made by comparing it to the case of that other nasty jeweler, Chandelor. The court in 1603 never considered that Chandelor was more expert than Lopus in assessing bezar-stones. In those days everyone was presumed an expert on all commodities; the concept of special knowledge didn't exist. The law was concerned that a buyer should have equal means to know, but his access to the sale object was considered sufficient to cover that point. It took until 1862, 259 years, for the law to figure out that there might be more to expertise than simply having the jewel in front of your eyes.[39]

The other clauses of section 542 represent similar legal situations in which the modern view is to restrain people from throwing opinions around wildly. Clause (b) also involves special knowledge, with the added factor of a close personal relationship. It refers to the actions of trustees, bank officials, real estate agents, attorneys, priests, physicians, and family members, all of whom might take advantage of a person's trust to persuade him against making inquiries which could reveal falsities.[40] Most trade transactions today, of course, are not conducted between buyers and sellers who have a close personal relationship.

Clause (d) is for miscellaneous conditions where a sentor stresses rapport with a person due to common membership in a church or other organization, or the fact that they come from the same area.[41] It is based on a case in which a seller gained a buyer's willingness to forego checking a purchase and rely solely on his claims by stating he was an Irish Catholic like herself and she could therefore trust him.[42]

Clause (d) is for miscellaneous conditions where a person might be induced to forbear inquiry through lack of intelligence, illiteracy, or unusual gullibility.[43] It is aimed at representations which involve a deliberate attempt to take advantage of such characteristics. Much selling, of course, is done by mass methods aimed at more than one person simultaneously, and most sellers, when they meet individual buyers, would not be likely to know them personally well enough to know of cases of unusual gullibility. But if the seller does personally learn of a buyer's gullible behavior and deliberately takes advantage of it by stating false opinions, he may be held responsible for a fraudulent opinion.

In these ways, the indiscriminate use of opinion statements has been curtailed, and we may easily get the impression from the rules just examined that opinion statements are quite readily associated with facts today and thereby given no freer rein than factual statements.

Reconciling Some Contrasting Rules

Let's think a bit about what we've seen in the two preceding sections of this chapter. Don't the cases we saw in the first section, which gave sellers the right to a rather wild-eyed and reckless use of opinion statements, seem to be contradicted by the rules seen in the second section which appear to curtail the use of such claims?

There was the rule cited in the first section, for instance, that all buyers realize they have no right to rely on the overstatements of value and quality which sellers will make quite naturally. How can this rule be reconciled with the one in the second section that says we may rely on the seller's statement when he has special expertise? Most sellers have expertise, after all, so wouldn't that rule largely eliminate the other rule? Or if the first rule were insisted upon, wouldn't it obliterate the expertise rule? The two could hardly exist together, because application of one would tend to squash the meaningfulness of the other. What's going on here, anyhow?

The answer is that *puffery* is going on. There is one important characteristic of the rules in the second section which I have not yet mentioned. It is that they do not apply to puffery! They apply to all opinion statements except puffery, but most opinion statements made by sellers constitute puffery. Outside the marketplace puffery is not recognized, therefore the restrictions specified in the second section apply generally in those other areas. But in the marketplace they apply only to that small proportion of seller's opinion statements which cannot be called puffery.

There are certain seller's opinion statements which must properly be called *opinions-as-to-fact* rather than opinions about subjective value or quality.[44] The opinion-as-to-fact is not puffery because it involves the uncertain representation of an objective fact (as in "I think this table is made of pine wood") rather than a representation of a subjective feeling (as in "I think this table is worth $100"). Any opinion-as-to-fact, made by a seller or by anyone else, is as illegal as a factual statement if it misrepresents.

But most seller's opinion statements are not opinions-as-to-fact. Imagine an ad saying "We believe this table is made of pine wood." Most seller's opinions are puffs about value or quality, and this means the restrictions the law places on opinion statements simply do not apply very often to the claims sellers make. The result is that the marketplace, as we've seen earlier, has a set of rules essentially different from those applied to other human affairs. And it means, to resolve the conflict between the two above sections, that opinion statements in the marketplace are handled mostly by the rules of the first section and allowed to ignore the rules of the second section.

The following shows how the law creates a separate standard for the marketplace, keeping substantial vestiges of caveat emptor alive. It is what the authors of the *Restatement of Torts* have added as "official comment" in explanation of section 542, clause (a):

Comment on Clause (a): f. . . . The ordinary purchaser of jewelry cannot be expected to know the quality or value of the gems shown him by a jeweler. He must rely and is therefore justified in relying upon the jeweler's statement that a diamond is of the first water and, after making allowance for the natural tendency of a vendor to puff his wares, he is justified in relying upon the jeweler's statement of the value of the gem.[45]

Consider the difference this qualification makes. If your lawyer offers you his opinion that one way of writing your will is better than another, you have a right to rely on his opinion because of his special knowledge. But if a jeweler tells you a diamond is worth so much or has certain superior qualities, you may rely on his opinion only to the extent of assuming it will not go beyond the "natural tendency" to puff. Don't be misled, therefore, by what *Picard v. McCormick* said about relying on the jeweler because he's an expert. You may do that, yes, but only to a restricted degree.

Imagine you go to a jeweler and listen to his opinion about a diamond. Recalling the rule, you remind yourself that you must ignore that part of his opinion which is the puff, but you may rely on that part which is not the puff. How can you be expected to do that? Suppose, for example, that the diamond was known in the jewelry industry, by a consensus of experts, to be worth $100. Suppose, too, that the jeweler tells you it is worth $150. How are you to determine how much of that opinion is acceptable puffing and how much is not? Would it be only puffing if the jeweler said it was worth $125, but more than puffing to state any higher price?

What sort of protection is offered to buyers by a rule which outlaws not exaggeration but merely too much exaggeration? Doesn't section 542 amount, really, to a great big sellout to puffery? Notice how it places legal puffing ahead of illegal fraud—that is, the first part of the exaggeration is the puffing part which the buyer is told he must accept as legal. To get any protection, the buyer must show that the exaggeration has gone further than that, which must be a very difficult thing to do.

Here is more of the "official comment" upon section 542 which the authors of the *Restatement of Torts* have supplied:

d. . . .Thus the purchaser of an ordinary commodity is not justified in relying upon the vendor's opinion of its quality or worth. . . .

e. This is true particularly of loose general statements made by sellers in commending their wares, which are commonly known as "puffing," or "sales talk." It is common knowledge, and may always be assumed, that any seller will express a favorable opinion concerning what he has to sell; and when he praises it in general terms, without specific content or reference to facts, buyers are expected to and do understand that they are not entitled to rely literally upon the words . . . .

Comment on Clause (c): . . . the rule does not apply to one who has by ordinary marketing methods or by the propriety of his past dealings secured the confidence of a prospective purchaser.

No question remains that the handling of opinion statements gives little comfort to consumers. Though the law reflected in section 542 is instrumental in controlling misrepresentations elsewhere, for consumers it is nothing more than a concession to the traditional sellerist use of false opinions and puffs. It mirrors perfectly the Massachusetts cases of the nineteenth century. Caveat emptor may be dead in some senses, but in the land of opinions it thrives as strongly as ever in the twentieth century.

The same status quo attitude is evident in the interpretation of section 539 of the *Restatement,* which states that opinions may be held fraudulent by their associations with incompatible facts. Again, it is illusory to believe that this means what it seems to say in regard to marketplace transactions. We recall that in *Smith v. Land and House* the seller was not allowed to get away with "one of the flourishing descriptions which auctioneers insert" because he knew something which contradicted it. But before we assume that buyers are protected from all such flourishes, let us consider the "official comment" to section 539:

c. The habit of vendors to exaggerate the advantages of the bargain which they are seeking to make is a well recognized fact. An intending purchaser may not be justified in relying upon his vendor's statement of the value, quality, or other advantages of a thing which he is intending to sell as carrying with it any assurance that the thing is such as to justify a reasonable man in praising it so highly. However, a purchaser is justified in assuming that even his vendor's opinion has some basis in fact, and therefore in believing that the vendor knows of nothing which makes his opinion fantastic.

So there we are! In the marketplace the buyer is not justified, as he would be elsewhere, in believing that the facts known by the seller are compatible with the opinion. The buyer must understand that they *may be incompatible,* and that the only prohibition is that they may not be *fantastically* incompatible. Apparently the flourish in *Land and House* was fantastically incompatible, but that does not mean all such flourishes are. The uncertainty created is similar to saying that the puffery may exaggerate some, but not too much. The jeweler's claim that a $100 diamond is worth $125 is incompatible with the facts, but perhaps not unreasonably so. Possibly a claim that the diamond is worth $150 would be fantastically incompatible. Again, how do we determine such things?

What about the point that every opinion statement implies the fact that the speaker sincerely believes it? No doubt a true-blue sellerist would say it wouldn't be fantastically incompatible for a seller to say his product was worth so much, or was the best or most popular, when he didn't believe it. That would be incompatible only to an ordinary degree. So much for sincere belief in the marketplace.

All of these developments sadly recall the comment of Oliver Wendell Holmes, "The standard of good faith required in sales is somewhat low."[46] No better commentary can be made on the state of good faith in buying and selling than to compare the light touch of sections 539 and 542 upon the marketplace against the more solid impact these rules have upon other dealings. Why should not the correct rules for the market be the same as those applied elsewhere—being, in other words, what is literally cited in sections 539 and 542, omitting the added comments. Most puffery, after all, comes to us from manufacturers or sellers who purport to: (1) have special knowledge which we do not (see clause [a] of section 542); (2) stand in a relationship of trust and confidence to us (clause [b]); (3) have successfully endeavored to secure our confidence (clause [c]); and (4) have a special reason, since their continued use of puffery indicates they think it has been relied upon by a gullible public in the past, to expect we will rely on it again (clause [d]).

Certainly all of these specified circumstances might reasonably be applied to the marketplace. I would like to emphasize especially the condition cited in clause (a) about the representor having special knowledge. The ancient assumption of caveat emptor, exemplified in *Seixas & Seixas v. Woods*,[47] was that the buyer and seller had equal knowledge. Can anyone imagine today that the manufacturer of a television set or headache remedy or detergent knows no more about his product than the typical citizen who may use it? Under today's market conditions the very notion of making or selling a product implies special knowledge because it *requires* special knowledge. There is no reason why a double standard should exist to excuse misrepresentations just because they are made in commerce.

Similar remarks apply to the rule stated in section 539. There is no reason why knowledge of incompatible facts should be excusable for sellers when it is not excusable for other people who misrepresent opinions. I once said as much in a newspaper article,[48] and got a complaint from an advertiser I mentioned, John Galbreath & Co., Realtors, who couldn't believe their ad could have been associated in any way with incompatible false facts. The ad's headline quoted an official of General Refractories Company as saying, "Moving to the U.S. Steel Building has really helped us attract and hold good people." I observed that substantiation for the claim was not provided in the ad and would be difficult to obtain because attracting and retaining employees depends on so many factors that the effects of any one may be impossible to isolate.

I acknowledged in the article my acceptance of the claim that General Refractories had a lower employee turnover in its new location, and also the supposition that a new modern office building could contribute to such success. But I also pointed out that the move to the new building in Pittsburgh had been made all the way from Philadelphia, which meant there were many other changes which could have affected employee turnover. My conclusion was that there was no way the advertiser could have known the U.S. Steel Building itself was responsible for the difference. Furthermore, the advertiser must have known he didn't really know, and that was a fact incompatible with the claim.

A letter protesting my comments came from a Galbreath official,[49] expressing his opinion that the ad was not in any way false puffery. The ad and similar ones, he said, were "in no way intended to be anything other than statements of truth expressed by the particular parties in reflection of their personal experiences, attitudes and feelings." But then he added the following illuminating statement: "We did not ask that the parties interviewed substantiate their comments and we would certainly not question the integrity of anyone of them with respect to observations freely offered."[50] He didn't know whether the claims were true, in other words, which is exactly what I had said in my article. The gentleman precisely verified my point that a fact incompatible to the puff existed.

What his letter really reflected, of course, was his utter amazement that the puffing claim could be called false on the basis of what was to him a trivial fact. I am sympathetic to his viewpoint in the sense that I understand full well that commercial operations have been conducted for years according to the custom that such things don't matter. I accept his protest as a quite genuine feeling of outrage against my criticism of habits which have been traditional in industry. It's not the only such protest which advertisers have lodged. The over-the-counter drug advertisers were reported to have "bristled with indignation" over FTC's proposed guidelines which would require them to identify a product's "miracle ingredient."[51] What could be more appropriate than having to tell the public what the ingredients are in the products they're trying to sell? But the companies had been hiding the facts for so long that they simply didn't find it fair to be asked to stop.

Why shouldn't they be asked to stop? Why should the standard of honesty required in sales remain so low? Sellers with their puffery statements should be asked to make the same accountability for incompatible facts that is required in transactions elsewhere. This would not really be a new rule, but merely removal of questionable immunity from an existing rule.

It was 1885 when Justice Holmes made his comparison of market dealings to other human affairs. Unless changes are made, we can be sure that in the area of opinion statements, at least, it still applies.

8

Factual Puffery:
Fiercely Sellerist,
but Now Extinct

THIS CHAPTER is a short digression about a kind of puffery which has been thoroughly and completely crushed and is no more.

As described up to this point puffery has been a type of opinion statement, and there is nothing which the law calls puffery today which may be anything else but a kind of subjective opinion claim. But in times past there were many sales puffs (usually called, in the nineteenth century, "seller's talk" or "dealer's talk"[1]) which quite literally and openly stated false facts. They were of explicit factual form yet were immune from liability as misrepresentations even when the seller stated them fraudulently and the buyer had no chance to check them independently. This breached the general rule for handling falsity and represented probably the most extreme sellerist treatment of sales misrepresentations the marketplace has ever seen.

Since these factual statements are not part of what we mean by puffery today, one authoritative source says we should no longer use the term as a description of contemporary seller's representations: "The use of the word 'puffing' seems inadvisable, because it may suggest too broad an exemption if it is taken to imply that the common law concept of puffing is applicable to FTC proceedings. The term, which grew up in an era of caveat emptor, reflects the view that the buyer should expect a considerable amount of actual lying by sellers eager to dispose of their products."[2]

The terms *puffing* and *puffery* are widely understood today, however, by legal authorities, advertising people, and consumerists to refer to claims which are of opinion form and associated with facts only by implication. It would not seem wise, therefore, to abandon the accustomed name.

But to clear up any possible misunderstanding, this chapter discusses the factual puffery which once existed in order to show what forms it took and particularly in order to emphasize that it no longer possesses legal status. Today's puffery may be bad, but it is not that bad. Many aspects of sellerism still linger, but factual puffery is one which is dead and gone.

There were two types of this extinct puffery, the first of which began with a judgment made in 1598, best known for its citation in 1668 in *Rolle's Abridgement of the Leading Cases and Theories of the Common Law.* We may call it the *Rol. Ab.* rule:

If a man, having a term for years, offers to sell it to another, and says that a stranger would give him 20£ for it; by means of which assertion the other buys it, when in truth he was never offered 20£ for the term; though he be deceived in the value, yet in truth no action on the case lies. M. 40 and 41 Eliz. B. R. adjudged.[3]

Note that the claim the seller made was related to the term's value, but was a statement of a factual event rather than an estimation, judgment, or opinion. What the "stranger" thought the term was worth was his own opinion, but the event of his offering such amount was a factual event which either truly did or did not happen. Why such a claim was excused from liability when false we do not know. Perhaps it was considered so closely related to a value statement that it should be treated as one, but that is only a guess. There is no primary record of the 1598 court hearing, and Rolle's abridged discussion contains no more than what I have quoted.

But rules which courts welcome do not go long without rationales, as we saw in chapter 7 with *Harvey v. Young.* The process of constructing an acceptable explanation of the *Rol. Ab.* rule began with *Leakins v. Clissel,*[4] the alternate report of *Ekins v. Tresham,*[5] the case in which the seller of a building lied about the rent tenants were paying him. The published record of *Leakins* shows the court mentioning that the *Rol. Ab.* rule involved statements about things of "uncertain" value.[6]

Such explanation should not have been an auspicious start on building a rationale, because the price offered by a third party surely was a *certain* figure, as was the statement of rent. Yet the *Leakins* court regarded it as an *uncertain* figure, lumping it together in that respect with the value statement from *Harvey.*

The version of the case called *Ekins v. Tresham* did not mention the *Rol. Ab.* rule, but it contrasted rent and value statements on the grounds that rent could not be investigated independently but value could. If statements of price offered were lumped together with value statements, this meant the court was saying that false statements about price offered could be investigated independently and therefore were legally acceptable, while false statements about rent could not be investigated independently and therefore were not legally acceptable.

In other words, the court said it was not okay to tell the lie that "The rent paid by the tenants of this building is 42£." Yet it was okay to tell the lie, "Someone else has offered me 20£ for this term." No explanation or reasoning was given for the difference, and I can think of none which I would accept. Perhaps price offered was considered so relevant to value that it might as well be a value statement. But lawyers and judges are generally so picky about fine distinctions that I find it hard to believe they would have failed to notice this one.

Overall, then, the *Ekins-Leakins* case (I wonder what his name really was! And Tresham-Clissel, too!) would not seem to have contributed much to explaining why the law should accept the *Rol. Ab.* rule that a false statement about price offered was legal. But in *Pasley v. Freeman*,[7] Justice Grose accepted the rule as equivalent to the cases we have seen in chapter 7 about "nude assertions" which amounted to opinion about which anyone concerned presumably could make his own inquiries. Rent could not be investigated independently, nor ownership, nor the claims in *Pasley* about Falch's credit—all these types of statements had to be taken on faith by the recipient, who was therefore justified in relying on them. But a seller's claim of price offered by a third party was supposedly something the buyer could check for himself!

One supposes that the buyer in many instances couldn't even locate the third party to ask him about his prior offer. Perhaps the seller wouldn't tell the buyer where he could look for that person, or even reveal his name. Yet according to Justice Grose the claim of what the third party had done was readily open to determination by the buyer.[8]

The widespread influence of *Pasley* was reflected in *Vernon v. Keys,* an English case of 1810[9] which developed further the rationale for exempting statements of price offered from liability. The case was unusual because it was the prospective buyer of a property who made a misrepresentation to the seller, thereby taking advantage for himself of the rules of sellerism (which of course virtually always operated to favor sellers). The buyer Keys reported untruthfully that his partners in the purchase "would not consent" for him to pay more than a specified amount. He would not tell the seller Vernon the names of these partners, thus Vernon had no chance to check the claim. But after sale at the "consent" amount Vernon learned of the falsity and brought suit.

Vernon's counsel urged the court to accept as a precedent the rule from *Ekins* that a person would be liable for misrepresenting something which the other person could not determine for himself. Lord Ellenborough's decision stated that the court agreed with that rule in principle. But Keys's counsel offered as a precedent the *Rol. Ab.* rule,[10] and the court accepted it in place of the *Ekins* rule and announced its decision for Keys.[11]

In the decision Ellenborough showed some tendency to retain the fiction from *Pasley* that a statement of price offered could be readily confirmed by the recipient. But rather than rely entirely on that explanation he provided a further rationale that such statements are "gratis dictum," not material to the recipient's assessment of value: "It appears to be a false representation in a matter merely gratis dictum [loose talk] by the bidder, in respect to which the bidder was under no legal pledge or obligation to the seller for the precise accuracy and correctness of his statement, and upon which, therefore, it was the seller's own indiscretion to rely; and for the consequences of which reliance, therefore, he can maintain no action."[12]

This new argument was significant because it explained how statements of price offered could be treated differently from statements about rent and ownership and Falch's credit. The latter were regarded as material to the recipient's evaluation, but price offered was gratis dictum—not material. Of course I don't see why a statement about price offered shouldn't be material, too. I'm sure my own evaluation of a property would depend on someone else's evaluation; subjective judgment often is based in part on the objective fact of someone else's subjective judgment. So there is no certainty that Ellenborough added any real sophistication to the *Rol. Ab.* rule, but there's no doubt he lent it the weight of his great authority.

The matter of price offered first appeared in America in 1810, but was not recognized as such at that time. In

Davis v. Meeker[13] the seller was accused of claiming falsely that "he had been frequently offered, by different persons, 50 dollars for the wagon." But in rejecting the charge of deceit the court referred loosely to "the assertion of the defendant that it was worth more than its real value," thus failing to distinguish between a statement evaluating the wagon and a statement citing a previous offer for it.

But the *Rol. Ab.* rule[14] was considered explicitly in *Medbury v. Watson* of 1843,[15] where it was not only accepted but surprisingly expanded to involve statements not only of price offered but also of price paid by the seller when he had been the buyer. There was no precedent for expanding the rule in that way, nor did any rationale appear for doing so. A statement of the price someone has offered might conceivably be defended as hypothetical in the sense that it was merely suggestive of the price the person would pay when he actually paid. But a claim of the price the seller himself once paid reports a decision definitely carried out, hypothetical in no way. Nonetheless, counsel for the seller who lied about what he had paid in *Medbury v. Watson* argued: "Former cost is no test of present marketable value, nor is supposed to be, by any man of common discernment. Nor do false affirmations as to such cost, or as to former offers, render the affirmant liable to an action. 1 Rol. Abr. 101. Yelv. . . . [Harvey v. Young]. Davis v. Meeker . . . Cross v. Peters, 1 Greenl. 389. Vernon v. Keyes . . . Baily v. Merrell . . . The People v. Williams, 4 Hill, 1. 1 Cowen's Treatise, (2d ed.) 316."

None of the cases cited by counsel discussed statements of what a seller once paid,[16] but the court accepted the argument that price paid was one of those claims which were strictly nonmaterial to the buyer's own evaluation.[17] This statement by the *Medbury* court was dictum (an aside, with the decision depending on another factor),[18] but the principle thus introduced remained in Massachusetts law for more than one hundred years. Another dictum was offered in *Brown v. Castles*,[19] and

the rule was made law in the state in *Hemmer v. Cooper*.[20]
It spread widely into the law of other states.

One of the most influential cases outside Massachusetts
was *Holbrook v. Connor* of 1872, in Maine,[21] in which the
court agreed with Lord Ellenborough that a claim of price
paid was not material to the buyer's evaluation: "It gives
no light whatever as to any inherent fixed quality, or
description which goes to make up the value, and, in this
respect, is not distinguishable from an offer made, except
that it is even more unreliable, as an indication of value."

In another Maine case two years later statements of
price paid or offered were called nonliable because they
were "only 'dealer's talk.' "[22] The court's use of that
phrase, a forerunner to the modern term "puffery," very
likely was what started people thinking of such factual
statements as belonging to the category of puffery. They
were treated as though they were opinions, and in a few
cases were accidentally identified as opinion, an error
apparently stemming from the *Holbrook* decision in which
the court said a claim of price paid was an *unreliable*
indication of the seller's opinion of value.[23]

But *Holbrook,* although it helped confuse the *Rol. Ab.*
rule with puffery, also contributed to the rule's eventual
downfall. The rule was then at the peak of its acceptance,
but there were two dissenters on the seven-man *Holbrook*
court who said the Ellenborough idea of nonmateriality
was nonsense: "While misrepresentation of the cost of
property does not ordinarily increase its value, it is a
material fact, and naturally calculated to mislead the purchaser by its tending to enhance its value, and give it an
attractiveness and firmness beyond that given by the force
of mere opinion."

The two dissenters also jumped on the notion that
price paid or offered was something the buyer could check
for himself: "The vendee [buyer], by the exercise of
common prudence, may ascertain the truth of a representation of value, and save himself from loss. Not so with
a representation of cost. This is not an opinion but a fact,

specially confined to the knowledge of the owner and his vendor; and they may sustain such confidential relations toward each other, that no prudence can discover the falsity of the representation."

These devastatingly sensible points made little immediate impact, yet by 1900 they had won the day nearly everywhere but Massachusetts. Williston cites a number of cases in which Ellenborough's rationale about nonmateriality was utterly discredited.[24] One was an 1893 New York case, *Fairchild v. McMahon:*[25] "The representation was with respect to a fact which might, in the ordinary course of business, influence the action and control the judgment of the purchaser . . . and so we think that a false statement with respect to the price paid . . . constitutes a sufficient basis for a finding of fraud."[26]

Williston added: "Some early cases in Massachusetts and Maine treated statements of cost as similar to statements of value . . . but this doctrine has been discredited by the cases cited . . . ; and although followed in a few jurisdictions must be regarded as erroneous."[27]

In holdout Massachusetts the denial that statements of price paid or offered were material lasted until the late date of 1952, when it was finally laid to rest by *Kabatchnik v. Hanover-Elm.*[28] The defendants had falsely represented an offer to buy, and the court agonized that the long line of precedents in its own state was not in harmony with those elsewhere. Finally it decided: "The time has come, we think, to depart from the rule . . . . Not only is it opposed to the weight of authority but it is difficult to justify on principles of ethics and justice. Moreover, several exceptions have been grafted upon the rule . . . . The reason given for the exception in *Brown v. Castles* [reflecting *Ekins v. Tresham*, actually] is that the amount of the rent lies 'in the private knowledge of the landlord and tenant' . . . . But similar reasons can be urged with respect to representations concerning the purchase price or an offer from a third person."

Thus was correction made after so many years to the

confusion caused by the early English cases. The *Restatement of Torts'* summary of today's law states, "Normally the price realized at a private sale of the article in question, or an offer made for it, is a fact which is properly taken into account in determining the value of the article." The comment adds that such statements are important primarily as opinion if the person receiving them has knowledge of the transaction and the persons involved. But if the opportunity to know does not exist, the buyer may rely on the claims as material facts.[29]

So ended the tenacious heritage of the rule from *Rolle's Abridgement.*

The second kind of now-extinct factual puffery had a shorter history, beginning later and ending sooner than the *Rol. Ab.* type. It was best exemplified by *Kimball v. Bangs* of 1887,[30] yet another of the many nineteenth-century cases from the state which gave puffery its most fertile soil. The plaintiff Kimball had invested in an attachment which converted wood stoves to oil, relying on the defendant's false claims that successful experiments had been made with the apparatus, that it produced no dirt, smell, or smoke, that it burned a year without requiring repair or renewal, and that its fuel requirements were not more than stated amounts. The court rejected the suit because: "We are of opinion that all the representations alleged in the declaration which are material fall within what is known as 'dealer's talk' . . . . The representations . . . are all, in their nature, statements of opinions as to the value and utility of the invention. . . . Such representations must in most cases be matter of opinion, expectations, and probability."[31]

The ruling was based on a few cases such as *Hunter v. McLaughlin,*[32] in which an excavating machine was represented falsely as able to cut ditches and deposit earth outside the ditch. The machine had never been constructed; the claims were based solely on a model and letters patent. For that reason the seller's claim for its success was called only an opinion that the machine would perform accordingly when constructed.

But in *Kimball* the oil converter was already constructed and operated, and the claims were clearly false facts, not conjectures or predictions. The application of *Hunter* should not have been appropriate.[33] Yet *Kimball* became the precedent for a general rule that misrepresentations of the operation of inventions were dealer's talk "although put in the form of the statement of a past fact."[34]

Kimball was never explicitly rejected, but subsequent cases showed a reluctance to apply the rule and it faded away.[35]

There remain in the law today no statements identified as puffery which literally state false facts.

9

The Federal Trade Commission: Accelerating the Consumerist Trend

OF THE steps we have seen taken toward consumerism in this volume, none have gone as far as the actions of the Federal Trade Commission. Its role has been so significant in modern times that many persons may think the trend toward favoring buyers was begun in that agency. But the Commission was only created in 1914;[1] it did not begin the consumerism trend. What it did was to adopt the movement and extend it to lengths probably not achievable by any other type of regulatory method.

The first action the FTC took in this direction was to decide whether seller's misrepresentations were part of its business at all.[2] The decision was not obvious, because the Commission had been originated for the express purpose of more adequately enforcing the nation's faltering antitrust laws. Its basic mandate was stated in section 5 of the FTC Act: "Unfair methods of competition in commerce are hereby declared unlawful."[3] This implied the protection of consumers against sellers, but only indirectly by protecting sellers against sellers. The specific purpose was not to control sellers' public messages, but to aid competition by prohibiting the build-up of monopolies and other restraints of trade.

The earliest Commissioners, however, exercised their imagination and decided that a seller would compete unfairly and restrain the trade of his fellow sellers if he made misrepresentations to consumers. False claims, after all, would attract business the seller would not have gotten otherwise, business taken from competitors who did not use those claims. To cheat consumers thus meant to cheat competitors, and by that logic the FTC Act permitted the Commission to stop sellers from cheating consumers. From its early years on a large number of the FTC's cases involved advertising and sales practices,[4] making it seem almost as though deception of the public was the Commissioners' principal interest. In prosecuting such cases, however, they were required always to say they were moving against a seller's unfair acts toward other sellers, because that was the only type of business practice they officially had the right to call illegal.

Sellers naturally were incensed over this bold acquisition of power. A new federal agency was hard enough on business when it merely instituted more efficient handling of traditional types of cases. But inventing new kinds of unfairness as well was, well, just unfair! Sears, Roebuck & Co. was one of the earliest to suffer the indignity, and it went to court to object.[5] Caught advertising falsely that its competitors were cheating the public, Sears did not deny doing so but told the court the practice hadn't been illegal prior to the FTC Act. The phrase "unfair acts of competition" was nowhere defined, Sears said, nor had any list of unfair methods been compiled. Therefore, it petitioned the court, the "vague" phrase must be held "void for indefiniteness" unless understood to mean no more than what was unfair under common law before 1914.

The court admitted the vagueness of "unfair acts of competition," but wasn't impressed with Sears's argument that what had been legal before must still be legal now.

Congress, it said, had specifically intended that the FTC define what was unlawful. The critical phrase had been left deliberately vague in order to leave such judgments entirely to the Commissioners. The failure to provide a list left the FTC "free to condemn new and ingenious ways [of unfair competition] that were unknown when the statutes were enacted." Because the FTC had defined Sears's operations to constitute such new ways, the court upheld the decision and declared that the Commissioners were obligated to "stop all those trade practices that have a capacity or tendency to injure competitors directly or through deception of purchasers, quite irrespective of whether the specific practices in question have yet been denounced in common law cases."

The idea of giving the FTC so liberal a privilege was questioned the first time a Commission decision was appealed to the Supreme Court. In *FTC v. Gratz* of 1920,[6] the high tribunal declared it was the job of the courts, not the Commission, to define "unfair methods of competition." The decision was made over the strong dissent of Justice Louis Brandeis, who reiterated that Congress had designated such determinations to be the Commission's right. Brandeis's point later prevailed, and in any event the *Gratz* case was not concerned with advertising and so did not specifically rule the FTC out of that field.

But a weak point remaining for the Commission was an assumption it adopted that injury to consumers was sufficient evidence of injury to competitors. The *Sears* decision had implied to the Commissioners that they need not bother in their prosecutions to collect any evidence nor even state their expert opinion that injury to competitors was actually a factor. Very possibly they took occasional advantage of this situation in the ensuing years by acting to protect consumers without even *caring* whether injury to competitors was truly a factor.

In 1931 the Supreme Court clamped down,[7] saying that cases concerning advertising were not sufficient unless injury to competitors was shown specifically. This decision pulled the FTC away from direct consumer protection momentarily, but in 1938 the Wheeler-Lea Amendments to the FTC Act[8] expanded section 5 to read: "Unfair methods of competition in commerce, and unfair or deceptive acts or practices in commerce, are hereby declared unlawful." From that time onward the FTC was expressly in the business of regulating seller's misrepresentations.

As such, the Commission has been a formidable supporter of the consumer interest. Prior to its existence, legal help for consumers was restricted largely to court suits instituted by individual citizens. Criminal charges against sellers could be brought by public authorities, but the requirements of proof of criminal action were so great, and the penalties likewise so great, that such suits were rare. Suits could be brought by competitors against each other, but this offered no consistent aid to the consumer cause. The individual's protection was left pretty much up to himself, and while the chance of success was much improved by the early twentieth century, there were still many reasons, cost most of all, which would prompt individuals not to bother going to court.

The FTC changed this situation by attacking misrepresentations on *behalf* of the consuming public, without the public having to take any active role and often *before* any damages occurred. Consumers not only got help without initiating it, and often before realizing they needed it, but each FTC action represented thousands, perhaps millions, of affected consumers at one time. Suits under common law must be carried out on behalf of specific individuals, usually a single person, and when successful they benefit no one else. But the FTC can relieve a problem for the entire public in one action. Unfortunately it cannot recover damages for anyone; the Commission does not remedy the wrongs a practice has caused but only prevents the practice from continuing. But there is no doubt that its prohibitions represent a mammoth contribution to consumer protection.

The agency's right to regulate what sellers say was only

one of the consumerist surprises it pulled off. Its method of regulating misrepresentations was from the beginning as unique as its decision that such things were within its jurisdiction. Just as it superseded the common law by redefining unfair methods of competition, it also superseded those precedents by redefining what it means to misrepresent unlawfully. The common law of misrepresentation provided many pitfalls for buyers, because many factors had to exist before a misrepresentation could be defined as illegal.[9] The buyer might fail to show that he had: (1) been an actual recipient of the misrepresentation; (2) understood the misrepresentation to convey (literally or by implication) a fact; (3) relied upon the supposed truth of the misrepresentation (not just have heard it stated); (4) been justified in relying; (5) been damaged; and (6) been damaged *by* reliance on the misrepresentation. And of course the buyer might fail to show that the seller had consciously used the falsity to deceive (this being mandatory in most misrepresentation cases in the year the FTC was created, 1914, because the ideas of liability for negligent or innocent misrepresentation were only weakly established then—and warranty law was not well established).

In total, the common law made it necessary for the buyer to prove he had been damaged specifically because of his justified reliance upon the seller's intentionally deceptive representation which was heard and understood as a factual assertion. All of these requirements were deemed necessary to assure that a misrepresentation be remedied only if shown to have *caused* the damages for which redress was being demanded.

There was fairness in that arrangement, because it provided that the seller not be punished unless his personal responsibility was established. But it is also fair to say that consumer protection might amount to more than that. Where a consumer was damaged but could not implicate the seller upon all the necessary points, the consumer would go remediless in a situation where the responsibility might fairly lie at least partly with the seller. An advanced form of consumer protection would try to do something about this, and would also try to aid the consumer where the seller was entirely faultless in what the consumer suffered. The ultimate in regulatory policy would be to try to keep damages from happening in the first place, regardless of fault or lack of fault.

That was the breach into which the FTC stepped. It took upon itself the privilege of calling misrepresentations unlawful when they were not proved to have been actually received by, understood to represent facts by, relied upon as true by, or been damaging to, any consumers—or to have been consciously intended to deceive by the seller. None of these things were retained as necessary by the FTC—its cases sought to show only that a sales misrepresentation, in the Commissioners' opinion, *possessed the capacity to deceive.*

Now that is a truly different approach! The message may have deceived no one; it may merely appear to have had the potential for doing so. The idea was outlandish, it destroyed precedents, it did things never done before. But it was confirmed, the *Sears* decision saying, "The legislative intent is apparent. The commissioners are not required to aver and prove that any competitor has been damaged or that any purchaser has been deceived."[10]

Probably the biggest of the legal requirements thus discarded was that of finding fraud, of proving that the seller consciously intended his falsehood to deceive. The absence of this requirement (and of negligence, too) meant that entirely innocent representations might be held unlawful, and innocent sellers thereby penalized. That was the biggest break from previous law, and the biggest target at which industry directed its objections.

But in writing the FTC Act Congress had cleverly subverted these objections in advance by reducing the penalty against the seller at the same time it reduced the requirements for determining liability. Commission procedure made it easier than ever before to act against misrepresentations, but also made the penalty for unlawful misrepresentation the lightest it had ever been by aiming the legal action away from the seller and toward the message. Common law prosecuted the seller; the FTC prosecuted his message. The penalty was that the seller must stop the message; that's all. The seller technically was not adjudged guilty of anything; he was simply told to cease and desist what he was doing.[11] If he didn't stop he could later be judged guilty of violating a direct order, but otherwise the FTC did not convict him, nor fine him, nor send him to jail, nor punish him in any of the ways traditionally associated with legal offenses.[12]

Of course the seller might feel that stopping his ad was an action against himself as well as against his ad. It curtailed his behavior; it made him stop doing something he wanted to do. There was the chance, too, that the order to cease his sales messages might be interpreted by the public as a finding of guilt, with consequent loss of credibility and good will, and loss of sales as well. Still, technically, the FTC in its normal actions does not find sellers guilty nor punish them in any legal sense.

There have been objections by consumerists that these procedures are not strict enough with wrong-doers.[13] Deliberate crooks get off with no punishment, true enough, yet there are two sides to the story. There have been gains to the consumer because a Commission which does not punish severely has not been hesitant to act. Many times messages which *might* be harmful have been taken out of circulation, whereas if it were necessary to prove beyond doubt that they were harmful many of them would not have been prohibited. The difference in strategy is one of prevention rather than punishment and remedy. The goal is to give maximum aid to consumers at the sacrifice of less than maximum punishment to offenders, rather than the opposite. Increasing the punishment would only result in fewer convictions and more deceptive messages continuing to run unimpeded.

The reader may wonder how this can be stated with

such certainty. How do we know the FTC strategy is the best, particularly in view of the complaints consumerists have made against it? Isn't there some chance that greater penalties would amount to greater deterrents? Why not get the most consumer protection simultaneously with the most punishment to offenders by easing the requirements for guilt without easing the punishment?

It happens that that's been tried, and it didn't work very well. In 1911 a law called the Printers' Ink Model Statute was proposed by the trade magazine of that name to the various states and was eventually adopted by all but three. It prohibited as a misdemeanor any advertising which was "untrue, deceptive, or misleading."[14] The requirements for unlawfulness were similar to those later used by the FTC; in particular, conscious intent to deceive did not have to be proved. The penalty, however, was more severe because a misdemeanor is a criminal act—not a serious one, but criminal nonetheless. As such it was not only more severe than the FTC sanction, but also more so than the common law interpretation of misrepresentation as a civil act. A civil wrong is not regarded as a crime, and is subject only to restoration of damages—no fines, no jail.

The Printers' Ink statute has resulted in few convictions and the removal of little advertising.[15] The reason undoubtedly was the imposition of the criminal penalty without having to prove fraudulent intent. Common law developments in 1911 were not yet close to relieving a plaintiff of having to prove intent to deceive, particularly in criminal cases. Many legal observers felt the requirement was so traditional it could not be omitted. Eight of the states which adopted the statute did so only after amending it to require proof of a knowing falsehood or a conscious intent to deceive. Eight others amended it to require proof that the advertiser ought to have known of the falsity, a matter of negligent rather than fraudulent behavior.[16]

Printers' Ink objected to these alterations, since they ruined the intended strategy of making illegality easier to

demonstrate.[17] A majority of the states agreed with the
magazine that dropping the fraud requirement was consti-
tutional, and they obtained confirmation of this in at least
one instance. In Ohio the point was challenged, and the
court ruled in the statute's favor: "The act was intended
for the protection of the public; it was not enacted because of any assumption of turpitude on the part of the
seller."[18] The primary purpose, in other words, was not to
punish the seller but to get the undesirable advertising out
of circulation. But while the rule would fail this purpose
when it included the fraud requirement, it also failed when
it dispensed with it. A criminal conviction tended to
charge the seller with turpitude in the public eye whether
the prosecutor intended it or not. Charging the seller with
a crime was really more serious in the absence of a fraud
charge than it was with it, so prosecutors just didn't do it.
The Printers' Ink Model Statute was a noteworthy experiment, but it was not a success.

The trouble seems simple by hindsight: *Printers' Ink*
was on target in desiring to attack the advertisement rather
than the advertiser, but it misfired when it chose to do so
by calling the advertiser a misdemeanant. That is why we
can be relatively certain that the FTC is correct in its
procedure of attacking the advertisement simply by stopping it and otherwise leaving the advertiser alone. Crooks
go free, of course, but under FTC rules it is far more likely
than ever before that a seller's misrepresentation will be
declared unlawful. By this test the FTC Act has been
successful indeed.

But the Commission did not gain its privileges without
challenge. The advertisers may have appreciated the reduced level of penalty, but they did not appreciate the
reduced requirements for determining liability. They
fought all the steps the FTC took to eliminate what had
been customary at common law. They fought them, and
they lost. Most significant was the matter of no longer
having to prove intent to deceive. The privilege was implied in the *Sears* decision,[19] but was not made clear until

1934. In *FTC v. Algoma*,[20] the Supreme Court told several companies who wished to continue using a name found misleading that they were "not relieved by innocence of motive from a duty to conform. Competition may be unfair within the meaning of this statute and within the scope of the discretionary powers conferred on the Commission, though the practice condemned does not amount to fraud as understood in courts of law. Indeed there is a kind of fraud, as courts of equity have long perceived, in clinging to a benefit which is the product of misrepresentation, however innocently made."

Thus ended fraud, although an occasional advertiser thereafter had to be reminded of the fact. Not only was fraud unnecessary to prove, but proof of its absence, unlike the result of *Derry v. Peek*,[21] no longer automatically excused an advertiser. In *Moretrench v. FTC* of 1942,[22] the appeals court agreed that the FTC's finding of unlawful misrepresentation in an ad was appropriate even though the statements were conceded to have been made in good faith.

In addition to removing fraud, FTC procedure also removed the need to show that any consumers had read, heard, or seen the misrepresentation, relied on it, been deceived by it, been damaged by it, or even that they had been exposed to it. All that was necessary was for the five Commissioners to conclude by a majority vote that a representation had the capacity to deceive a substantial segment of the population.[23]

The original version of the FTC Act had not designated this severely reduced level of proof specifically, though as the *Sears* decision said the legislative intent was apparent.[24] In 1938 the wording was made explicit when the Wheeler-Lea Amendments[25] prescribed in section 12 that the dissemination of "any false advertisement" for food, drugs, medical devices or cosmetics should be included among the unfair or deceptive practices prohibited under section 5. The use of the term "false advertisement" rather than "deceptive advertisement" may appear to blur the distinction described earlier between falsity and deception, but the amendments added in section 15 a definition of "false advertisement" as one which was "misleading in a material respect" ("material" being interpreted to mean "affecting a purchasing decision"). The ads which the amendments prohibited, therefore, were the same as those the Commission had been acting against already—those having the capacity to mislead in a way affecting the consumer's purchasing decision. They were deceptive ads rather than literally false ones.

The broad separation thus produced between deception and falsity gave the law a substantial and hotly disputed turn toward consumerism. At common law a representation typically escaped liability if shown to have some relationship with truth. But the FTC now began determining that deception could exist with factual statements even when they were in some technical sense true. *DDD Corp. v. FTC* of 1942,[26] involved a product called D.D.D. Prescription, the "Original Formula of Doctor Dennis," touted in ads as just the thing "for quick relief from the itching of eczema, blotches, pimples, athlete's foot, scales, rashes, and other externally caused skin eruptions." FTC issued a cease and desist order contending that this quoted line impliedly represented D.D.D. as a remedy, notwithstanding its use only of the word "relief." The potential for deception was presumed to lie in the common confusion between a relief, which merely alleviates symptoms, and a remedy, which alleviates their cause.

D.D.D. rejoined that the statement nowhere said "remedy," and that it referred to relief only from the *itching* of eczema, etc., and not to actual relief from the eczema, etc. The appeals court agreed that "there is merit in petitioner's contention that this and similar statements, when carefully scrutinized, may thus be construed." But the court then criticized the "weakness of this position," which "lies in the fact that such representations are made to the public, who, we assume, are not, as a whole, experts in grammatical construction. Their education in parsing a sentence has either been neglected or forgotten. We agree with the Commission that this statement is deceptive.''

The case legitimized the notion that deception might occur apart from clear and evident falsity; the deceptive statement might be literally and technically true. It also confirmed FTC's lack of requirement to show actual deception; the Commission's findings were not consumer responses, but primarily the ads themselves, supported by testimony of expert medical witnesses.

The notion that literal truth may be deceptive is an idea of consequence because it opens the way for prosecution of many claims which cannot be touched in any other way. When the FTC leaps upon one of these "untouchables," the advertising industry screams bloody murder because it has been using that type of claim for years without concern for liability. In the 1970s an absolute furor has developed over the idea that an ad, when it truthfully claims a brand has ingredient "X," may be falsely implying to the public that ingredient "X" is present in that one brand alone.

The fight against these allegedly deceptive "uniqueness claims" began in 1971 with a group of George Washington University law school students who called themselves Students Against Misleading Enterprises (so as to be known by the acronym SAME).[27] They filed a petition asking the FTC to rule that the various brands of aspirin, bleach, and other product categories in which all the brands were chemically similar be required to carry a statement disclosing that fact. Deception is inherent in the advertising of such brands, they said, particularly in view of the price differentials gained by those with heavy advertising. Bayer, they said, sells more than 50 percent of the aspirin sold, despite its high price, and the same is true of Clorox in the bleach market.

Ralph Nader soon entered the fray with a letter to the FTC[28] arguing that ads for Wonder Bread attempted to make consumers think the brand is more nutritious than other enriched breads containing essentially the same ingredients. Wonder, he said, should be made to admit the sameness in order to avoid deceiving the public. Convinced, the FTC entered a complaint[29] in which it agreed that any existing differences were not significant. It called Wonder a "standard enriched bread" which contained nutrients at about the same levels as other enriched breads. Therefore, the complaint said, Wonder Bread should make no "uniqueness claims" unless its specific differences were listed and accompanied by a statement that competing breads were in all other respects the same.

Wonder Bread's maker, ITT-Continental Baking Co., sent its president, M. Cabell Woodward, to the Commission to protest, "No one is saying that our advertising isn't true, but that there's an alleged implication in it of nutritional sameness. We say it's not there. We haven't said other brands don't have similar qualities."[30] Nonetheless, the FTC entered an order in 1973 which restricted the company's opportunities to differentiate Wonder Bread from its competitors.[31]

Another type of situation in which the FTC has begun finding deception without literal falsity has emerged in the case of Un-Burn ointment.[32] Claims for Un-Burn's effectiveness, a Commission complaint stated, implied falsely to the public that laboratory tests had been conducted by the company to prove that effectiveness. The complaint did not call the effectiveness claims false, but said rather that the maker, Pfizer Chemical Co., did not know with sufficient certainty whether they were true. Pfizer protested that there was every reason to believe the claims were true even though specific tests had not been made, and that the public, in any event, did not take the ads to imply anything about what testing had been done.

Pfizer won the case when the Commission finally conceded the ingredients in Un-Burn were old ones proven effective long ago. The particular formulation called Un-Burn was new, and never tested as such, but the components had been tested sufficiently in previous formulations to satisfy technical experts that they would be effective in

Un-Burn. The FTC, nonetheless, won the general point of view it introduced in the case: it stated that from then on any claim of effectiveness would imply that the advertiser had substantiation in hand to prove the claim was true.

The Wonder Bread and Un-Burn cases have made clear that the FTC will go to broad lengths to distinguish deception from falsity and find the former in the absence of the latter. Another way it has developed this privilege has been in calling entire ads deceptive for what they omit even though no individual statements therein are deceptive. Permission to do this was incorporated into the FTC Act by the Wheeler-Lea Amendments, section 15,[33] and was confirmed in *Aronberg v. FTC* of 1942,[34] another case involving the term *relief.* The Commission felt that ads for a product promising relief of delayed menstruation were deceptive in failing to reveal the presence of dangerous drugs in quantities sufficient to endanger health. The appeals court agreed, specifying, "The ultimate impression upon the mind of the reader arises from the sum total of not only what is said but also of all that is reasonably implied."

The impression users might get, "because of ignorance, alarm, or desire for quick relief," was that the medicine would be perfectly safe not only in recommended doses but also in larger or more frequent doses. Nothing was said specifically which would prompt the consumer to think that—but he might think it nonetheless, the FTC said.

The rule behind the *Aronberg* decision was restricted to ads for food, drugs, medical devices, and cosmetics, but the FTC has applied it to other products simply by construing the principle into its interpretation of section 5. This produced probably its most outstanding instance of determining deception on the basis of a message's net impression, the 1950 case of *Lorillard v. FTC.*[35]

What Lorillard did was quote statements out of context so as to convey precisely the opposite of what a *Reader's Digest* article had said about Old Gold cigarettes. "Old Golds found lowest in nicotine, Old Golds found lowest in throat-irritating tars and resins," the ads claimed. In contrast, the story had actually explained that the smoker "need no longer worry as to which cigarette can most effectively nail down his coffin. For one nail is just as good as another. Says the laboratory report: 'The differences between brands are, practically speaking, small, and no single brand is so superior to its competitors as to justify its selection on the ground that it is less harmful.' How small the variations are may be seen from the data tabulated on page 7."

The court record went on to explain that "the table referred to in the article was inserted for the express purpose of showing the insignificance of the difference in the nicotine and tar content of the smoke from the various brands of cigarettes."

But Lorillard, the court said, "proceeded to advertise this difference as though it had received a citation for public service instead of a castigation from the *Reader's Digest*." Here is some more of what Chief Judge Parker of the Fourth Circuit Court of Appeals thought about the case:

The company relies upon the truth of the advertisements complained of, saying that they merely state what had been truthfully stated in an article in the *Reader's Digest*. An examination of the advertisements, however, shows a perversion of the meaning of the *Reader's Digest* article which does little credit to the company's advertising department—a perversion which results in the use of the truth in such a way as to cause the reader to believe the exact opposite of what was intended by the writer . . . .

To tell less than the whole truth is a well known method of deception; and he who deceives by resorting to such method cannot excuse the deception by relying upon the truthfulness per se of the partial truth by which it has been accomplished.

In determining whether or not advertising is false or misleading within the meaning of the statute, regard must be had, not to fine spun distinctions and argument that may be made in excuse, but to the effect which it might reasonably be expected to have upon the general public.[36]

I have quoted from *Lorillard* at length to emphasize that this kind of legal response simply was not established before the FTC accomplished the trick. The confirmation by the appellate court promoted a conception of justice which may seem obvious today, but which took the FTC a lot of straining to achieve.

Another area opened up for prosecution was that of situations containing no message at all. The Commission was upheld by the appeals court in *Haskelite v. FTC* of 1942[37] in its decision that a failure to reveal a fact relevant to the consumer's purchasing decision could be called a deceptive nondisclosure. Haskelite was a maker of buffet or lap trays composed of a hardwood core and surfaced with processed paper simulating walnut and Mexican capomo wood. The FTC ordered the company to print statements on the trays or their cartons disclosing that the surfaces were of paper. Haskelite objected that failure to provide such explanation could not be a deceptive practice because no representation was made at all. How could "nothing" be deceptive? It could, the court said, when it accompanied certain other practices: "The process used by the petitioner to simulate woods does great credit to the ingenuity of the petitioner, and is so skillfully carried out that the physical exhibits shown us in court were distinguishable from the real wooden trays only after the most careful scrutiny. The trays themselves were the best evidence of the possibility of confusion. Without some warning, the trays of themselves are almost certain to deceive the buying public. The Commission has a right to consider this fact."

The Commission, in other words, has the right to *require* certain statements as well as prohibit certain statements. This requirement of "affirmative disclosure" has been used in many cases; Geritol advertising, for example, must state that most cases of tiredness are not due to "iron-poor" blood.[38] Another instance is the FTC settlement with cigarette makers requiring that print advertising display conspicuously the health warning which appears on cigarette packages.[39] In addition to specific cases, the FTC also has written a variety of guides and trade regulation rules which require disclosure by sellers in certain situations. One, for example, requires light bulbs and their wrappers to have figures for brightness and estimated life stated thereon.[40] Another requires octane ratings to be posted on gasoline pumps.[41] These are only a few of the FTC's many disclosure requirements.

Another widening of its privilege to find misrepresentation was accomplished by the Commission when it established that a deception need not deceive the public generally to be unlawful. This extended its reach beyond those cases, *Lorillard* for instance, in which the misrepresentation was such that virtually all seeing it would be misled. In *Siegel*[42] the FTC found deceptive potential in advertisements for coats made of something labeled "Alpacuna," a name inspired by the terms *alpaca* and *vicuna*. Vicuna was the more expensive fiber, and was not contained in "Alpacuna." The FTC ruled "that while in some cases the name might not be understood by prospective purchasers as indicating the presence of vicuna fiber, in a substantial number of other instances it would indicate the presence of such fiber. . . . The Commission therefore finds that the name 'Alpacuna' is misleading and deceptive to a substantial portion of the purchasing public."

In this way the Commission's privilege to find capacity to deceive extended to ads which would harm only a "substantial portion" of the public. The advertiser could no longer defend himself merely by showing that *some* or even *many* persons were undeceived. The Commission's findings in *Seigel* showed that many citizens understood the truth accurately, but this was no longer significant when another portion was misled.

In all of the ways described, the FTC has been highly successful in finding new ways to define unlawful misrepresentations. Perhaps it has been too successful, seeing deception in too many places. When a decision process is subjective mistakes may occur, and the Commission has not been immune. Perhaps its most famous "goof" was prohibiting Clairol from saying it will "color hair permanently."[43] In other cases, the Commission has said it would prosecute a certain alleged deception but then has withdrawn when more careful review suggested the deception didn't exist.[44]

Those who criticize such errors point out that the FTC's real criterion for unlawful misrepresentation, no matter how much explanatory logic it attaches to its decisions, is fundamentally the staff's and the Commissioners' subjective conviction (or plain gut feeling!) that an ad has the capacity to deceive. Recent research findings, *Advertising Age* said in 1972, "may be casting doubt on the long-standing legal doctrine that members of the FTC are qualified to determine on the basis of their own impressions the probable impact of an ad on a consumer."[45] People in official capacities need to know, not guess, and their own best judgment, although sincere and carefully considered, is often just a guess. Suggestions have been made about habits of data-gathering which the FTC might develop,[46] but generally the old ways of making decisions have continued.

I ran into this situation personally when an FTC attorney asked me to participate as an "expert witness" in a case alleging misrepresentation in ads for Sunoco gasoline.[47] He showed me the ads, and I said, well, I thought they could deceive people. But that, I added, was just my own opinion; why did he think I would be an *expert* on the matter? He said it was because I had a Ph.D. and held a reputable university position in advertising and mass communications. I said, "What the hell's *that* got to do with it? It says something about my knowledge of ads generally, but not about the Sunoco ads in particular." The attorney answered that that's what they mean by an expert witness in FTC procedures. If the Commission can trot more "experts" onto the witness stand than the other side does, why, it'll help them win!

I'd heard somewhere of the legal concept called "de-

ciding a case on its merits," and the thought occurred to
me that this deal looked like something else. I realize now
that that wasn't quite fair, because the procedures used
involve a careful weighing of the evidence, with a pretty
good eye on what the witness says as well as on who he is.
But the problem is that very few witnesses can say anything solidly conclusive on the fundamental point of what
the consuming public actually perceived the advertisement
to be saying. They haven't asked the public what it
thought the ad meant, so they fall back on what they
think it would think.

That's where credentials come in, because when somebody testifies he thinks the public would think such-and-
such when he really doesn't know, then you can bet his
degrees, position, reputation, and related qualifications are
going to have a lot to do with whether the Commission
officials believe him. It's an adversary proceeding, which
means there'll be somebody testifying for the other side
about what *he* thinks the public will think. Witnesses for
both sides, naturally, will think the public thought things
favorable to their side's position. The Commissioners have
to straighten out that tangle of weeds in the best way
possible, and when the time comes to do so they may
discover that examining their experts' professional qualifications is in fact the best way possible.

In cases where experts disagree, the FTC today has the
right to decide which expert's opinion to accept. I am
referring here to objective opinion-as-to-fact, not to subjective opinion such as puffery. Some early court appeals
denied the Commission the right to choose among conflicting opinions-as-to-fact. In *L. B. Silver v. FTC* of 1923,[48]
an appeal was brought after the Commission told a breeder
to stop claiming his hogs were separate and distinct from
another breed. The FTC had obtained expert testimony
that the breeds were not distinct, but the court of appeals
pointed out that other experts felt differently: "There is
practically no substantial conflict in the evidence tending
to establish the facts from which these breeders and ex-

perts reach different conclusions. . . . Each of the individual members of these groups . . . though differing in opinion based on the same state of facts, appears to be entirely honest, sincere, and equally firm in the belief that his conclusion is the right one."[49]

Since the breeder's opinion was as valid as anybody's, the FTC was refused the right to prohibit it. The implications of the case were ominous; they implied that any conflicts in testimony would negate all testimony. All a company needed to do, under this rule, to protect itself against misrepresentation charges would be to place someone on the stand who would testify it was not a misrepresentation.

A similar rebuff occurred when the Commission charged that Marmola, a remedy for obesity, was neither safe nor scientific as claimed. The appeals court[50] said determinations of both these points were matters of expert opinion rather than fact, "determined by the particular expert's conceptions of science and of safety." Since the evidence showed the experts could not agree, the FTC was not permitted to call the claims false. The case went to the Supreme Court, which did not reverse the ruling.[51]

But the Commission worked up an alternate strategy which produced a new and successful cease and desist order against Marmola.[52] It specified some alleged misrepresentations of Marmola which it said were more "direct and specific" than the ones it had mentioned earlier. And it worked hard to introduce and establish the expertise of its witnesses as being the best available. No one could deny that conflicts of opinion still remained, but the Commissioners' summation observed that "the medical testimony offered in support of the complaint far outweighs that offered in behalf of the respondent . . . . Without intending to detract from respondents' expert witnesses . . . the expert witnesses who testified in behalf of the complaint, taken as a group, are more outstanding professionally and their opinions entitled to more credit . . . ."

See what I mean about citing credentials! The procedure worked marvelously, the Supreme Court noting on the next round of appeals, "This time the Commission found with meticulous particularity that Raladam [the manufacturer] had made many misleading and deceptive statements . . . ."[53]

Eventually the FTC gained even greater leverage in the use of expert witnesses. Cases occurred in which the appeals court showed a willingness, contrary to the attitude in the *Silver* and *Raladam* appeals, to accept without independent assessment the Commission's own decisions where a conflict of experts occurred.[54] The Commission was required to have substantial evidence for the decisions it made, but where such substantial evidence existed on both sides the courts fell into the practice of more or less automatically accepting the Commission's choice. Not surprisingly, the Commission invariably chose in favor of those experts who felt the alleged misrepresentations did in fact misrepresent. In this way it acted to prohibit those claims which had substantial opposition from experts, whether or not they had substantial support from experts as well. Substantial support was not enough, in other words, to make a claim acceptable in the marketplace; what was necessary would be better characterized as a preponderance of support.[55]

With these precedents, there was no doubt that the FTC could bolster its position in the Sunoco case by bringing someone such as myself to Washington to give my "expert" opinion. Every Ph.D. added to the line-up would make the evidence more substantial! Even if the Sunoco attorneys did the same thing, the Commission's attorneys could argue that its string of experts was just a little more expert. The whole set-up was fine and dandy from the Commission's point of view, but I didn't like it very much. It would be much more satisfactory, I thought, if someone went out to the public and asked people what they thought about the Sunoco ads! Each individual consumer was a separate expert on what the ads mean to consumers, and I was only one among many. Why not get the responses of many! They couldn't all come to testify, of course, but they could "appear," in effect, if someone obtained their responses and presented a tabulation of the total as evidence.

So I said to the attorney, "Look, why don't you let me do a little survey? Perhaps it isn't customary," I said, "but it won't cost much if I use the college students who reside in plentiful numbers at my university. I know they would not constitute a representative sample of the entire United States population, but their responses should provide some insight into how the public sees the Sunoco ads. If I get some data about these actual perceptions, I can come to Washington and give you substantially more than just my own opinion on what the Sunoco ads mean to people." The attorney agreed, and I did the survey and presented it as evidence in the FTC's case against Sunoco.[56] I'm going to describe that survey here to show what kind of information it's possible to obtain about what a message implies to people over and above what it literally states.

I went to three University of Wisconsin classrooms and showed a total of 303 students a sixty-second television commercial. An automobile is seen in the ad fueled with Sunoco gasoline and then driven, pulling an empty U-Haul trailer, up a ramp specially constructed over the seats in the Los Angeles Coliseum.[57] The Sunoco gasoline pump, capable of dispensing eight blends of gasoline having different octane levels, is shown and discussed. Finally, the run up the ramp is shown a second time. During all this a voice is announcing:

"We're at the famous Los Angeles Coliseum. We're going to drive a car pulling this trailer from the field to the top of the stands to demonstrate an unusual gasoline. A gasoline that will help this car's engine put out every bit of power it has. Okay, Bill, up you go. What makes this gasoline unusual? It's blended with the action of Sunoco 260—the highest octane gasoline at any station anywhere. With 260 action the car and trailer go up the ramp just like that. You can get the same 260 action at Sunoco. The custom blending pump blends just the right amount of 260 into every gallon of premium, middle premiums, even regular. Watch again as Sunoco regular delivers in this car. Let Sunoco with 260 action deliver in your car. Get Sunoco 260 action. Action to be used, not abused."

The students sat in their customary classroom seats and saw the commercial run two times. They then turned to a questionnaire sheet which read as follows:

This is a test to determine how well an advertiser's message comes through to you. The statements below refer to the Sunoco commercial you have seen. Each statement represents something which may or may not have been stated or implied in the ad. None of the statements are exact quotes from the ad, but some of them are accurate re-statements of the ad's content and some are not.

If you think the statement is an accurate re-statement or paraphrase of what the advertisement stated or implied, either in words or in the described action, put the letter "A" for "accurate" beside it.

If you think the statement is *not* an accurate re-statement or paraphrase of the content of the advertisement, put the letter "I" for "inaccurate" beside it.

Don't concern yourself with whether or not you believe or accept what you think the ad says or implies. We are interested *not* in what you think is true or what you would like to be true, but only what the advertiser appears to be telling you.

1. _____ Sunoco 260 is the highest octane gasoline at any station anywhere.
2. _____ We're demonstrating an ordinary gasoline here.
3. _____ Sunoco 260 action is action to be used, not abused.
4. _____ We're going to drive a car pulling a loaded trailer to the top of the Los Angeles Coliseum.
5. _____ You can get the power supplied by Sunoco 260 action only by buying Sunoco gasolines.

6. _____ When your gasoline is blended with the action of Sunoco 260 you will get all the benefits of using the highest octane gasoline at any station anywhere.

7. _____ You're seeing a stunt which a car can perform only if it is powered by Sunoco 260 action.

8. _____ Gasolines blended with the action of Sunoco 260 are unusual because they provide more power than you would get with other gasolines.

9. _____ This demonstration shows that gasolines with 260 action are unusual.

10. _____ Having 260 action means that you have the highest octane gasoline available at any station anywhere.

11. _____ You're seeing here the performance of a car using Sunoco 260.

Be sure to place "A" or "I" beside all statements.

NAME _____

That is the method I used to find out what the Sunoco commercial meant to a group of persons. What do you think it meant? Why don't you try the questions yourself before reading on, in order to determine your own perceptions. See which statements you think were accurate indications of what the commercial stated or implied. If you want to determine your feelings independently of the university students' responses, do so before reading the following paragraphs.

Now to explain the results. A little information behind the commercial will be helpful, because a key characteristic of many sales messages alleged to misrepresent is that important facts are not mentioned (which, in fairness, is not unlawfully deceptive per se). The typical service station has two or three gasolines, each distributed to the customer through a distinctive pump which draws from its own separate underground storage tank. At the time of the "Coliseum" commercial, Sunoco stations were different; they had only one kind of pump, and it supplied all eight of Sunoco's gasolines. There were two underground storage tanks, both linked to the special blending pump. One tank contained 190, the lowest octane Sunoco offered, while the other contained 260, the highest octane it offered.

When the Sunoco pump dispensed 190, it drew gasoline solely from the 190 storage tank; the same was true for pumping 260. But when any of the intermediate gasolines were required (200, which was regular; 210, 220, 230, which were middle premiums; 240, which was premium; or 250, a super premium), the correct blend was obtained by pumping from both the 190 and 260 storage tanks. The proportion was varied; for 200 the gasoline was drawn mostly from the 190 tank, while for 250 it came mostly from the 260 tank. The consequent blends resulted in levels of octane ranked according to the numbers used. The numbers 190, 200, 210, etc., were not octane levels but were trade names which accurately indicated the relative octane levels.

A consequence of this system was that seven of the eight available gasolines, all but 190, utilized to some degree the gasoline drawn from the 260 tank. Even regular (200), as the ad pointed out, contained some 260. Sunoco gave a name to this feature of utilizing gasoline from the 260 tank; they called it "260 action." Your choice of Sunoco gasoline had 260 action if it contained, at least in part, Sunoco 260.

At that time the "Coliseum" commercial ran on television, 260 was the highest octane gasoline a motorist could buy. But what did it mean to say that a blend which was only partly 260 had "260 action"? I shared the FTC's suspicion that people might take it to mean more than it actually should, and more than was literally stated in the ad. I felt people might confuse 260 action with 260 so as to think that 260 action would provide them with the benefits obtainable from 260. 260 was truly unique, but the blends which promised "260 action" contained reduced levels of octane which were not unique to Sunoco but obtainable from many competitors.

If "260 action" could be used to describe these blends, it was also true that "190 action" would describe them just as accurately. They all contained some 190 as well as some 260. Sunoco would never want to use the term "190 action," of course, but an accurate description of its products could be made only if both terms were used. Using only one of the terms without the other was inaccurate and, I thought, deceptive.

I chose the eleven statements in the questionnaire to help me test this supposition, and also to test the charges which the FTC had made against the company. In the chart below, these statements are described in various ways. The first column tells whether they were actually true or false, in my judgment. The second tells whether they were literally stated in the ad, or literally denied, or neither. The third column explains how a person ought to respond to the questionnaire *if* he were responding exclusively on the basis of the ad's literal content. If the ad literally stated the statement, he should respond "A" for "accurate"; if the ad did not literally state it, he should respond "I" for "inaccurate." The fourth column states the percentage of the 303 university students who actually responded "A" for "accurate."

The critical figures in the chart are those which show how many people responded "A" where the correct response would be "I" if one were responding to literal content alone. The instructions for the survey had not asked the students to respond with respect to literal content only. They asked them to respond with "A" if they thought the ad literally stated the given content but also if they thought the ad *implied* that content. Therefore if the students responded "A" where the ad didn't literally state the given content, it must have been because they thought the ad implied it. The results indicate the latter is what happened for statements 4 through 11. All of these statements were false and were not literally claimed in the ad, but substantial numbers of students saw the ad implying such beliefs.

Statement	True-false	Literal treatment	Response predicted on basis of literal treatment	Percentage of "A" response
1	True	Literally stated	A	80
2	True	Literally denied	I	10
3	True	Literally stated	A	95
4	False	Literally denied	I	41
5	False	Neither literally stated nor literally denied	I	78
6	False	Neither literally stated nor literally denied	I	61
7	False	Neither literally stated nor literally denied	I	48
8	False	Neither literally stated nor literally denied	I	79
9	False	Neither literally stated nor literally denied	I	71
10	False	Neither literally stated nor literally denied	I	68
11	False	Literally denied	I	92

Now let's look at the misrepresentations which the FTC alleged were contained in Sunoco's advertising.[58] I have listed these alleged misrepresentations below, with an indication in parentheses of the survey statements which related to the point:

(1) Gasolines which have 260 action give the user the octane benefits of 260 (statements 1, 6, 10—also 5, 8, 9).

(2) 260 action provides the maximum available engine power and performance, and therefore more than competing gasolines (statements 5, 7, 8).

(3) The demonstration of engine power shown (i.e., the steep climb to the top of the Coliseum) constituted actual proof that 260 action outdoes competing gasolines in providing engine power and performance (statements 7, 9).

The students' responses to the questionnaire suggested to me that the alleged misrepresentations actually occurred in their minds. Probably the key alleged misrepresentation was the first of the three mentioned, relating to the confusion which the FTC thought would occur between "260" and "260 action." To explain how such confusion could have occurred, we may observe that most of the students acquired the correct belief about 260—80 percent of them responded to statement 1 with "A" for "accurate." But then they attributed that belief incorrectly to the gasolines blended with 260—68 percent of them thought that statement 10, which the reader should compare with statement 1, was also "accurate." The same result is shown by statement 6 (61 percent said "accurate"), and by several other statements. There seems little doubt that the persons participating in my survey saw the ad as saying that "260 action" gasolines give the user the octane benefits of 260.

In addition, the results for statement 11 strongly suggest some confusion in understanding the ad. This statement was specifically denied in the ad by the representation that the car was using Sunoco regular, yet 92 percent of the students took the ad to be saying that the car was using 260. Perhaps they noticed the line about using regular, but believed the ad was saying this was tantamount to using 260. Confusion between 260 and 260 action could have been so well established earlier in the ad that it affected people's understanding of the statement that regular gasoline was being used.

It's my own personal conviction that the Sunoco advertising people deliberately intended to produce confusion between 260 and 260 action. My survey questions provided no direct evidence on the point, nor do FTC procedures, as we've seen earlier, need to get into the question of whether the advertiser intended to deceive. But I believe the phrase "260 action" is inherently likely to be misleading because it so obviously refers to 260 and yet was used to describe gasolines which did not have the qualities of 260. I think it is what advertising people call a "weasel," a false suggestion intended to convey more than it can truthfully mean.[59] Even if the phrase were first conceived in pure innocence, it seems unlikely to me that anyone could look at it and not recognize the confusion it could produce when used as it was in "Coliseum."

I feel I'm supported in this opinion by the existence of a falsity which was explicitly stated in the Sunoco ads. It was the claim that the ad will "demonstrate an unusual gasoline," which certainly must have been false since the car was using regular, which was not unusual in its octane level. Ninety percent of the students in my survey recognized the claim of unusualness (i.e., only 10 percent specified "A" for statement 2), and the only way the demonstrated gasoline could have been perceived as unusual would be if they had perceived Sunoco regular to be unusual in its octane level because it was blended with 260. In other words, the explicitly false statement could be accepted by the viewer *only* if the implied falsity about 260 action was accepted first. That's why I feel the writers of the commercial probably intended for that implied falsity to be accepted.

I hope my survey helps explain the difference it can make to get actual evidence of how people perceive and misperceive. It enabled me to represent 304 experts rather than just one. It gave me something more to take to Washington than just my own gut feeling about how the Sunoco ad worked.[60] Opinions stated by so-called "experts" aren't nearly as good because different experts have different gut feelings. The only real expert on what the ad is saying to any individual is the individual himself. You can't ask the advertiser, because he knows deep down that his ad just couldn't have deceived. You can't ask the critic because he knows just as deeply that it couldn't have done otherwise. You never saw anybody so stubborn about giving up a belief as when you ask one of these people to change their minds.

I saw this happen exquisitely at a State of Wisconsin hearing in 1973 on proposed rules to prohibit deceptive price comparisons.[61] Under attack was the type of ad or sales tag which says "Now $10, was $15," when it never was $15. The state was contemplating a rule to disallow such price comparisons unless true, and unless the higher price had been in effect for at least two weeks out of the previous ninety days. The purpose of the latter requirement was to make sure the object had been at the earlier figure for some honest period of time. Otherwise anybody could circumvent the rule's intent by listing the higher price for about ten minutes last November sometime and then making an essentially phony claim about the new low, low figure.

In the hearing a lawyer for a retailers' association asked what this rule would do to a grocer who put strawberries on sale for 69c per pound in the morning and then marked them down to 59c in the afternoon so as to move them off the shelf while they were still fresh. That couldn't possibly be deceptive, could it, he asked me after I testified in favor of the rule. I said I thought it could, and you should have seen the industry representatives jump. It was like Oliver Twist asking for more porridge. To a man they couldn't believe it.

When you tell industry people a sales message might be deceptive they always interpret you to be charging the seller with intent to deceive. They don't know or in the heat of the moment they forget that the ancient concept of fraud is not part of the legal definition of deception as the FTC and other regulatory agencies use the term today. When I said the strawberry ad might deceive I wasn't saying anything about the grocer at all; I was saying only that the buyer might misunderstand and make his purchase on the basis of the misunderstanding. If so, it might be reasonable to help the buyer in this situation even though the actions of a perfectly innocent seller would be impeded. That's straight from the philosophy of conducting regulatory activities with a preventive rather than remedial purpose.

Obviously the strawberry situation couldn't create much deception, which is precisely why that crafty lawyer used it as an example. He didn't see how anyone could question it. The reason I questioned it was not because I thought there'd be deception, but because I thought there *could* be. But why should we have sat there in a hearing room far from any strawberries and tried to figure out the answer by logic? Didn't that go out with metaphysics? The thing to do would be to go get actual public responses to the situation. Somebody should put a sign over the berries saying 69c with a line drawn through it and saying 59c below that. They should put the sign up and then ask people who come along to say what it means to them.

I suspect that a variety of responses would occur; that is, different people would think the sign meant different things. If it meant different things it's likely some of them would be meanings different from what the storekeeper meant the sign to mean. If we saw that happening we'd suspect there was deception, and if we didn't we'd conclude there wasn't. Maybe every customer who came along would understand perfectly that the berries were marked down because they couldn't be kept fresh much longer. Whatever the result, if we did the experiment we would know what the message meant to the consumer rather than just guessing about it.

There's always the critic of the FTC who'll say that if the concept of deception produces so many problems we ought to go back to falsity as a criterion. But there's no going back when the regulatory purpose is to protect the consumer. The giant strides made by the FTC may have resulted at times in seeing misrepresentation where it did not occur, but they undoubtedly also have resulted in properly identifying a much greater proportion than ever before of the misrepresentations which actually occur. There has been a net gain, in other words, of correct over incorrect identifications. In this way the FTC has added considerably to the movement away from sellerism and toward consumerism.

The FTC has contributed to consumerism not only by its widened definitions of deception but also by its new actions against deceptions. Its traditional action has been a cease and desist order, which will fine the advertiser for continuing his misrepresentation but does not punish him for having committed it up to that time. But in the 1970s the Commission has added the concept of corrective ads, requiring selected offenders to include in their coming year's advertising the acknowledgment that their previous claims were found deceptive.[62] Another new development is the substantiation program, which requires companies to document the truth of the claims they have been making.[63] The FTC also has participated with the Federal Communications Commission in encouraging the use of counter ads, which involve free broadcast time for proponents of opposing viewpoints after an advertiser has taken a stand on a controversial issue.[64] These and other developments are very significant in describing the Commission's increased consumerist activity, but I will not elaborate on them in this book. They involve methods of *dealing* with deception rather than of defining it, and therefore are outside the topic I have set here.

In the two subsequent chapters I want to add two more dimensions to the FTC's approach to deceptive seller's messages. The first concerns whether the whole public or only a portion of the public deserves legal protection. The second is about the FTC's dealings with opinion statements and puffery.

10

Reasonable Consumer
or Ignorant Consumer?
How the FTC Decided

IS THE Federal Trade Commission obligated to protect only reasonable, sensible, intelligent consumers who conduct themselves carefully in the marketplace? Or must it also protect ignorant consumers who conduct themselves carelessly?

Since its origin in 1914 the Commission has varied its answer to these questions. It has committed itself at all times to prohibit seller's claims which would deceive reasonable people, but has undergone changes of direction on whether to ban claims which would deceive only ignorant people. At times it has acted on behalf of the latter by invoking the "ignorant man standard."[1] At other times it has been ordered by courts to ignore these people and invoke the "reasonable man standard." In still other cases it has chosen to protect certain ignorant persons but not others.

The significance of the issue is that the FTC will rule against the fewest types of seller's claims under the reasonable man standard, and against the most under the ignorant man standard. The latter guideline therefore means, in the eyes of many, the greatest protection for the consuming public. Consumerists may feel, in fact, that such a standard should be mandatory on the grounds that a flat prohibition is needed against all seller's deceptions which would deceive anyone at all.

The FTC, however, works under a constraint which makes it necessary to temper its allegiance to the ignorant man standard. The constraint is that the Commission may proceed legally only in response to substantial public interest.[2] Over the years the Commissioners have been sensitive to the argument that there is no public interest in prohibiting messages which would deceive only a small number of terribly careless, stupid, or naive people. To explain the compelling nature of this argument, I would like to describe a deception of that sort.

In my hometown of Pittsburgh, Pennsylvania, there appears each Christmastime a brand of beer called Olde Frothingslosh. This quaint item is nothing but Pittsburgh Brewing Company's regular Iron City Beer in its holiday costume, decked out with a specially designed label to provide a few laughs. The label identifies the product as "the pale stale ale for the pale stale male," and there is similar wit appended, all strictly nonsense. One of the best is a line saying that Olde Frothingslosh is the only beer in which the foam is on the bottom.

My old friend at Pittsburgh Brewing, John deCoux, the ad manager there, once told me about a woman who bought some Olde Frothingslosh to amuse friends at a party, and was embarrassed to find the claim was nothing but a *big lie:* the foam was right up there on top where it was on every other brand of beer she'd ever seen! She wanted her money back from the beer distributor (another quaint Pennsylvania custom), but he told her Hell, no, so she went to her lawyer with the intention of bringing suit. The story (and it's true) ended right there; the lawyer told her to forget it. She would have had less chance than poor Herbert Williams,[3] because air conditioners have been known to exist on automobiles but nobody in earth's history ever saw a beer with the foam on the bottom. The reasonable man (woman! person!) standard would be applied to her suit, her reliance on the belief about the foam would be judged unreasonable, and that would be the end of that.

Had the ignorant man standard applied she would possibly have succeeded, which illustrates the difference the choice of standards makes. It also illustrates the essential weakness (in conjunction with definite strengths) possessed by a legal standard which sets out to protect everybody from everything. Many of the prohibitions it produces would eliminate only infinitesimal amounts of deception.

There are other reasons, too, for the FTC's cautious attitude toward the ignorant man standard. One problem is that the Commission does not have the resources to prosecute all cases,[4] therefore those which are investigated might better be ones which endanger greater numbers of people. Another problem is that an extreme concern for the ignorant could lead to repression of much communication content useful to consumers, and could lead as well to possible violation of the First Amendment's freedom of speech guarantee.[5]

Probably the most important objection to the ignorant man standard is that the reasonable man standard was traditional in the common law which preceded the development of the FTC in 1914. The common law held that to avoid being negligent a person must act as a reasonable person would act under like circumstances.[6] Mention of the reasonable or prudent person first appeared in an English case of 1837[7] and has been in widespread use since.

I have described the concept of negligence in discussing misrepresentation law,[8] but am using it here in a different sense. The earlier use involved whether the seller (defendant) was negligent: did he state a misrepresentation which he didn't know but ought to have known was false, and

which deceived and damaged the recipient (plaintiff)?
Here, however, the question is whether something called
contributory negligence may be charged against the plaintiff, the person deceived. He brings a suit against the
deceiver, and the rules require him to assert and show that
he relied upon the misrepresentation, and that the damages
suffered were a result of such reliance. In addition, he
must show that his reliance was justified—that is, his reliance must pass the test of the conduct of a reasonable
person. He may not claim to have relied on a statement
which sensible and prudent people would recognize as
preposterous. If he does, he is guilty of contributory
negligence which the deceiver may use as a defense which
can result in having the suit dismissed.[9]

This rule usually does not apply in the case of a
fraudulent misrepresentation, where the deceiver consciously knows it was false and intentionally seeks to
deceive with it. If that is shown, the person deceived is
entitled to rely without having to justify his reliance as
reasonable.[10] But an exception to the exception comes
with puffery and the other false but legally nondeceptive
claims which are the topic of this book. The law states that
people know and understand they are not to rely on such
misrepresentations, even when stated fraudulently.[11]
Therefore with these kinds of statements the reasonable
man standard, when it is the prevailing standard, applies.

At the time the FTC was created, the only specific law
on these matters was the common law just described. The
FTC Act said nothing explicitly about what persons the
Commission was authorized to protect; it said only that
proceedings must "be in the interest of the public."[12] The
most obvious way of pursuing this mandate would have
been to follow the common law precedents and embrace
the reasonable man standard. Instead, the FTC did the
unexpected and flaunted the reasonable man standard in
many of its early cases. Neither that concept nor a replacement standard were discussed explicitly, but numerous
cases show that the Commission was applying an ignorant

man standard or a close approximation of it. In 1919 it ordered a manufacturer to stop advertising that its automobile batteries would "last forever."[13] One might assume that no reasonable person even in that year would have relied upon the claim literally, especially when the same ads offered a service by which "the purchaser pays 50 cents per month and is entitled to a new battery as soon as the old one is worn out." The FTC saw the latter phrase, however, as confirming the falsity and deceptiveness rather than the sheer frivolousness of "last forever." The case indicates the Commission was developing a deliberate policy of stopping deceptions which would deceive only a minority.[14]

This switch to the ignorant man standard appeared questionable legally; precedent did not support it. But before we describe the eventual court considerations of this matter, we should acknowledge that there was much argument against the reasonable man standard in common sense if not in law. The legal conception of the buyer who failed to be reasonable in the marketplace was that of a person who made a stupid purchase through his own fault—he should have known better.[15] It was this conception with which common sense could disagree. Some so-called stupid choices may be made not through carelessness but through the impossibility of obtaining and assessing information even when great caution and intelligence are applied. The world of goods and services was once simple, but has become terribly technical. Many poor choices are made by persons who *couldn't* know better.

These problems might have been incorporated into the reasonable man standard by adjusting that standard to the realities of the market. Consider a store scene in which a product is available at six cans for a dollar while one can is sixteen cents. In considering whether a reasonable person would be deceived, the law might have taken into account that many people are slow at arithmetic, and that the bustle of a market and the need to make many other choices in the same few minutes render it unlikely they would fully use the mathematical capacity they possess. The competence assumed of a "reasonable person" might have been reduced accordingly, and the traditional standard, altered in this way, might still have been applied.

What actually occurred in legal actions was something bordering on the opposite. The reasonable person came to be regarded as a *better* than average person, as someone who was never negligent and who therefore was entirely fictitious outside the courtroom.[16] He was "an ideal creature . . . . The factor controlling the judgment of [his] conduct is not what *is*, but *what ought to be.*"[17] The law, apparently, had created an unreasonable conception of the reasonable person.

It was this problem the FTC sought to correct. We do not know, because the point was not discussed as such, whether the Commission regarded its new conception as a move to the ignorant man standard or as a redefinition of the reasonable man standard by the method described above. But the practical effect was the same either way— the Commission moved toward protecting the public from deceptions which regulators previously had ignored because they did not harm the fictitiously reasonable person.

Considerations of the reasonable and ignorant man standards eventually were made explicit through the intervention of appeals court decisions into FTC affairs. In *John C. Winston* of 1924,[18] the Commission outlawed a sales method which offered an encyclopedia "free" provided a purchaser paid $49 for two supplementary updating services. The seller appealed and won a reversal on the grounds that no deception was involved: "It is conceivable that a very stupid person might be misled by this method of selling books, yet measured by ordinary standards of trade and by ordinary standards of the intelligence of traders, we cannot discover that it amounts to an unfair method of competition . . . ."[19]

The FTC did not adopt the reasonable man standard as a result of this ruling; its subsequent activities reflected instead a posture of resistance.[20] When it stubbornly invoked a similar restraint against a different encyclopedia company, Standard Education Society, in 1931,[21] it was again reversed by an appeals court.[22] Circuit Judge Learned Hand was most adamant in declaring that "a community which sells for profit must not be ridden on so short a rein that it can only move at a walk. We cannot take seriously the suggestion that a man who is buying a set of books and a ten year's 'extension service,' will be fatuous enough to be misled by the mere statement that the first are given away, and that he is paying only for the second. Nor can we conceive how he could be damaged were he to suppose that that was true. Such trivial niceties are too impalpable for practical affairs, they are will-o'-the-wisps which divert attention from substantial evils."

This time, however, the FTC took the case to the Supreme Court, where a new justice delivering his first opinion told Learned Hand that the encyclopedia decision *was* a substantial evil. Hugo Black's opinion in *FTC v. Standard Education* of 1937[23] restored the Commission's use of the ignorant man standard: "The fact that a false statement may be obviously false to those who are trained and experienced does not change its character, nor take away its power to deceive others less experienced. There is no duty resting upon a citizen to suspect the honesty of those with whom he transacts business. Laws are made to protect the trusting as well as the suspicious. The best element of business has long since decided that honesty should govern competitive enterprises, and that the rule of caveat emptor should not be relied upon to reward fraud and deception."

Though Black mentioned the name of neither standard, his words suggest he was rejecting the reasonable man standard rather than proposing merely to adjust it. Black's words, above all, led to the concept of an "ignorant man standard" for the FTC in place of what went before.

Just how *Standard Education* was supported by precedent is a curious question. Justice Black's opinion cited none. It affirmed that the sales method not merely had deceptive capacity but clearly deceived many persons, and it also stated that the deception was committed knowingly and deliberately.[24] This suggests that the Supreme Court was invoking the common law notion that the reasonable man standard should not apply in case of deliberate deception. Something left unclarified, however, is what significance such a ruling should have for an agency such as the FTC which routinely did not make findings of deliberate deception. Deliberate intent to deceive undoubtedly occurs in many cases where no one can prove it. The whole advantage of FTC procedure, in comparison with what went before, was that it could rule seller's messages out of the marketplace *without* bothering with the traditional requirement of proving intent. What was the advantage, then, of obtaining the right to use the ignorant man standard only in conjunction with proving intent to deceive?

The result, strangely, was that the FTC, on the basis of *Standard Education*, began applying the ignorant man standard liberally without regard for determining intent, and in some cases without regard for the fact that intent to deceive was almost surely absent. The appeals courts, also via *Standard Education*, approved this procedure. The trend was thoroughly questionable but was pursued decisively, particularly by the Second Circuit Court of Appeals, the court which *Standard Education* had reversed. In *General Motors v. FTC* of 1940,[25] a case involving a "6% time payment plan" which actually charged 11.5 percent interest, the Second Circuit's Judge Augustus Hand concluded: "It may be that there was no intention to mislead and that only the careless or the incompetent could have been misled. But if the Commission, having discretion to deal with these matters, thinks it best to insist upon a form of advertising clear enough so that, in the words of the prophet Isaiah, 'wayfaring men, though fools, shall not err therein,' it is not for the courts to revise their judgment."

The influence of the *Standard Education* reversal was

unmistakable on the one Hand—and on the other Hand as well. When Judge Learned Hand considered an appeal to the Second Circuit of the Commission's finding of deception in an admittedly untrue claim that "one Moretrench wellpoint is as good as any five others,"[26] he said: "It is extremely hard to believe that any buyers of such machinery could be misled by anything which was patently no more than the exuberant enthusiasm of a satisfied customer, but in such matters we understand that we are to insist upon the most literal truthfulness. Federal Trade Commission v. Standard Education Society . . . ."

Turning to another literally untrue Moretrench claim, that its product had an advantage to which "contractors all over the world testify," Hand stated: "It is again hard to imagine how anyone reading it could have understood it as more than puffing; yet for the reasons we have just given, if the Commission saw fit to take notice of it, we may not interfere."

It was clear that the Second Circuit's Hands were tied. Substitution of the ignorant man standard for the reasonable man standard proceeded in additional Second Circuit cases,[27] and in others as well.[28] Under these liberal interpretations the FTC appeared during most of the 1940s to be knocking down right and left every advertising claim it thought had the slightest chance of deceiving even the most ignorant person. There was a good bit of unchecked exuberance in this spree, including the action against Charles of the Ritz's use of "Rejuvenescence" as a name for its face cream.[29] The FTC outlawed the term on the grounds that it referred literally to the restoration of youth and the appearance of youth. The company protested that it was merely a "boastful and fanciful word" used nondeceptively, but the Second Circuit agreed with the Commission. I find it amusing that Charles of the Ritz has been using the trade name "Revenescence" ever since, avoiding the literal meaning but apparently retaining some of the persuasive value it once received from "Rejuvenescence."

The Second Circuit's thoughtfulness toward the ignorant man reached an extreme when it agreed with the FTC in forbidding Clairol to say that its dye will "color hair permanently."[30] The FTC thought the public would take that as a claim that all the hair a person grows for the rest of her life will emerge in the Clairol color. That expectation was based on the testimony of a single witness who said she thought somebody might think that—although she added that *she* wouldn't.

On Clairol's appeal one judge of the Second Circuit, Clark, agreed fully with the FTC: "Petitioner's [Clairol's] actual defense is that no one should be fooled—a defense repudiated every time it has been offered on appellate review, so far as I know, since it is well settled that the Commission does not act for the sophisticated alone."

The majority of judges, Swan and Augustus Hand, disagreed with this reasoning. They said they couldn't imagine *anybody* believing the Clairol claim: "There is no dispute that it imparts a permanent coloration to the hair to which it is applied, but the commission found that it has 'no effect upon new hair,' and hence concluded that the representation as to permanence was misleading. It seems scarcely possible that any user of the preparation could be so credulous as to suppose that hair not yet grown out would be colored by an application of the preparation to the head. But the commission has construed the advertisement as so representing it . . . ."

Nonetheless, the majority said, they had to support the FTC position no matter what they personally thought: "Since the Act is for the protection of the trusting as well as the suspicious, as stated in Federal Trade Commission v. Standard Education Society . . . we think the order must be sustained on this point."

In basing the decision on *Standard Education*, the Second Circuit offered no judgment that the Clairol claim was used with intent to deceive, and made no acknowledgment that *Standard Education* might have been intended by the Supreme Court to apply only where such intent was

evident. The inclination to apply the ignorant man standard appears to have overridden any other consideration.
We may speculate that if the Olde Frothingslosh matter
had been appealed to the Second Circuit in the same year
as the Clairol case, 1944, the purchaser might have re-
covered damages because the beer's foam wasn't on the
bottom!

This chapter thus far has discussed the development of
a strong emphasis on the ignorant man standard. The next
task is to describe how this emphasis came to be diluted, a
matter which involved additional curious events. One of
the arbitrary facts of life in American law is that the
various circuit courts of appeal are sometimes inconsistent
in their rulings. They need not take each other's decisions
into account, so a case may be decided differently in one
than in another. The Second Circuit was the one reversed
by *Standard Education,* and we have seen that this court in
subsequent cases applied the ignorant man standard assidu-
ously. This included the prohibition of puffery in *Moretrench,* even though puffery had traditionally been called
nondeceptive. With its long-standing immunity, puffery
might have been expected to resist the courts even if
nothing else did, but under the ignorant man standard the
Second Circuit moved to eliminate this kind of falsity
along with everything else.

But the time came, in 1946, when a puffery case was
appealed to the Seventh Circuit rather than the Second,
and the difference was significant. *Carlay*[31] involved a
claim that Ayds candy mints make weight-reducing easy,
which the FTC said was false. On appeal the Seventh
Circuit,[32] which had tended earlier to object to the ignorant man standard,[33] decided, "What was said was clearly
justifiable . . . under those cases recognizing that such
words as 'easy,' 'perfect,' 'amazing,' 'prime,' 'wonderful,'
'excellent,' are regarded in law as mere puffing or dealer's
talk upon which no charge of misrepresentation can be
based." The court cited previous non-FTC cases which
allowed puffery,[34] and completely ignored the cases stem-

ming from Justice Black and the Second Circuit, which would have supported the FTC's outlawing of "easy."

As a result the FTC had a contradiction on its hands. The Second Circuit told it to protect the ignorant man; the Seventh Circuit told it to permit puffery which could deceive the ignorant man. The contradiction might have been resolved by the Supreme Court, but was never considered there. The FTC's resolution was to allow puffery thereafter, which tended to dilute the ignorant man standard.

The trend away from the extreme ignorant man standard had begun, but only slightly. Cases followed in which the FTC retained a strong protective stance on behalf of ignorant consumers.[35] But in 1963 the Commission finally commented that the standard could be carried too far. *Heinz W. Kirchner*[36] was a case about an inflatable device to help a person stay afloat and learn to swim. Called Swim-Ezy, it was worn under the swimming suit and advertised as being invisible. It was not invisible, but the FTC found it to be "inconspicuous," and ruled that that was all the claim of invisibility would mean to the public: "The possibility that some person might believe Swim-Ezy is, not merely inconspicuous, but wholly invisible or bodiless, seems to us too far-fetched to warrant intervention."

What about the few persons who would accept this "far-fetched" belief? The Commission made clear it no longer intended to protect such ignorant persons:

True . . . the Commission's responsibility is to prevent deception of the gullible and credulous, as well as the cautious and knowledgeable. . . . This principle loses its validity, however, if it is applied uncritically or pushed to an absurd extreme. An advertiser cannot be charged with liability in respect of every conceivable misconception, however outlandish, to which his representations might be subject among the foolish or feeble-minded. . . . A representation does not become "false and deceptive" merely because it will be unreasonably misunderstood by an insignificant and unrepresentative segment of the class of persons to whom the representation is addressed.

That is the position the FTC has followed since. It holds no longer to the strict ignorant man standard by which it would protect everyone from everything which may deceive them.[37] It would reject consideration, for example, of the Olde Frothingslosh claim which apparently fooled only one stray individual. Perhaps we may call the new stance a modified ignorant man standard which protects only those cases of foolishness which are committed by significant numbers of people.

Some readers may protest that any behaviors which are customary for a substantial portion of the population shouldn't be called "ignorant." They might rather call the new stance a modified reasonable man standard in which what is reasonable has been equated more closely than before with what is average or typical.[38] Whatever the name, however, the FTC's present position appears to remain closer to the spirit and practice of the strict ignorant man standard of the 1940s than to the reasonable man standard of tradition.[39]

11

The FTC and Puffery:
Some Wins and Some Losses
in the Fight for
Consumerism

THE FEDERAL Trade Commission's encounter with puffery is a story of an original firm resistance against sellerist tradition, which softened into a court-enforced return to the past and then semi-toughened into a stance of renewed but modified resistance which prevails today.[1]

Early Resistance

The earliest FTC cases showed a strong tendency to reject the notion that sellers might puff with immunity. It was not an explicit rejection, but rather the omission of acceptance in situations where prevailing common law precedents would have made acceptance seem normal. It was silence with a definite loudness to it.

In the 1919 case, for example, of the automobile batteries said to "last forever,"[2] the decision against the advertiser simply ignored the possible defense that the phrase might be merely opinion. The claim was factual in a way, yet traditionally its maker would have enjoyed the

175

defense that he was only puffing the claim that his batteries would last a long time. He would probably have succeeded with such excuse under common law but the tradition-scorning FTC would have none of it.

There were several such early cases where the puffery defense was conspicuous by its absence.[3] One involved a maker of electric belts and insoles who advertised "so as to mislead the general public into the belief that [the] articles possess wonderful curative values."[4] The apparatus made no "real" medical contribution, so the ad was outlawed. But might there have been a psychological "placebo" effect? The possibility had been implicit for years in decisions permitting puffery. It is recognized today in ads for the well-known tonic (patent medicine!) called Geritol, which, according to the confident TV personality, "is one of the good things I do for myself." But the FTC in 1920 had no patience with such arguments. There was no room for the subjective viewpoint, no speculation about the "eye of the beholder."

That policy was maintained despite common law cases which continued and encouraged puffery. Using the flamboyant phrases quoted in chapter 7, in 1918 Judge Learned Hand excused a seller of a patented vacuum cleaner for claims which "even though consciously false, were not of a kind to be taken literally by the buyer."[5] The claims were that the product was excellent, had the most economical operation and greatest efficiency of any vacuum cleaner, was easily operated, would give perfect satisfaction, would last a lifetime (maybe using the batteries that "last forever"?), and so on. The evidence showed that the company which bought the rights to the cleaner on the basis of these claims found it to have no value and no marketability whatsoever.

Thus the advertising for the electric belt, which might have comforted users who believed it would, was outlawed by the FTC, while the "consciously false" commendations for a vacuum cleaner which had no chance of working, even for believers, was legally sanctioned by a tradition-serving court. Clearly a new direction was under way in the new agency.

But the FTC eventually collided with the common law precedents when certain de-puffed sellers asked the courts for review and relief. The first jolt came when the Commission charged Ostermoor & Company in 1926[6] with unlawfully illustrating the insides of a mattress expanding to a height of thirty-five inches when its outside bindings were cut away. Such expansion presumably indicated the powerful support features of the product, impressive if true. But on actual test Ostermoor mattresses expanded only three to six inches, and the FTC thought the exaggeration in the illustrations implied a "resiliency or elasticity far beyond the fact."

The cease and desist order was dissented to by Commissioner William E. Humphreys, who said it "allows no room whatever for exaggeration. It eliminates the thrilling and time sacred art of 'puffing.'" Obviously hearing a different drummer than previous commissioners, Humphreys added that the enforcement of this "rule of exactness" would destroy half the magazine advertising in America. The appeals court supported Humphreys's position and threw out the order, saying that "the slightest pictorial exaggeration of the qualities of an article cannot be deemed . . . a misrepresentation . . . . The time-honored custom of at least merely slight puffing . . . has not come under a legal ban."[7]

The Commission, though reversed, proved unrepenting—perhaps because a technicality made the *Ostermoor* ruling ambiguous. The FTC's charge of deception assumed that the illustration showed the mattress interior freed of its bindings after first having been compressed as it would be in the finished product. But the appeals court ruled that the illustration showed the mattress material during construction, prior to being compressed for fitting inside the finished mattress. Its thickness prior to compression would naturally be greater than the expansion possible after compression and release. The court, in other words, thought the illustration depicted a much less severe exaggeration than the FTC had indicated. This aspect of the decision may have encouraged the Commissioners to think of the court's reversal as due primarily to inadequate identification of the alleged misrepresentation rather than to the traditional immunity granted to puffery. By adopting such a rationalization the Commission could recognize the court's reversal without having to admit that the court was trying to force it to recognize and permit puffery.

The FTC went ahead with its attacks. In 1934 it took Fairyfoot Products[8] to task for its bunion plaster advertising and successfully weathered a challenge that the claims were only puffs.[9] Fairyfoot said its product would stop pain instantly, dissolve and remove bunions, return a deformed foot to its original shape, and perform other convenient miracles. The company defended these claims as "largely" justified by the facts and said that "where exaggeration appeared it was only such 'puffing' of the article as is not violative of the law." The FTC saw it another way, as did the appeals court, the latter stating: "Just where lies the line between 'puffing,' which is not unlawful and unwarranted, and misleading misrepresentations in advertising, is often very difficult of ascertainment. But in our judgment this case does not present such embarrassment, since the advertising here condemned is well beyond any 'puffing' indulgence."

In 1939 the Commission was not equally successful in charging that Kidder Oil Company[10] had advertised its motor oil in a misleading way. As in *Ostermoor*, the cease and desist order was overturned on appeal.[11] The appeals court agreed with FTC that there was some exaggeration in Kidder's description of its product as a "perfect" lubrication which would enable a car to operate an "amazing distance" without oil. But the court said: "Such terms are largely a matter of personal opinion. What might be an 'amazing distance' to one person might cause no surprise to another. So far as we know, there is nothing 'perfect' in this world, but still it is a common term, which undoubtedly means nothing more than that the product is good or of high quality. . . . We are of the opinion that [these claims] are nothing more than a form of 'puffing' not calculated to deceive."

The court's rejection of the *Kidder* case was certainly in keeping with the intentions of one of the authors of the 1938 Wheeler-Lea Amendments to the FTC Act.[12] Although the amendments generally strengthened the Commission in opposing deceptive advertising, U.S. Senator Burton K. Wheeler had not intended for puffery to be involved. He explained his position in the following debate on the Senate floor:[13]

Mr. Copeland (New York): "I remember that years ago, when I was a medical student doing graduate work in Germany, I used to see the sign, 'Das beste in der Welt,' 'the best in the world.' Suppose a manufacturer of rayon in Cleveland, Ohio, should advertise, 'My rayon is the best in the world. It is superior to any other rayon.' What could the Federal Trade Commission do about that?"

Mr. Wheeler (Montana): "It could do nothing about it."

Mr. Copeland: "Why not?"

Mr. Wheeler: "If he said in his advertisement that it was the best in the world, and he was honestly of the opinion that it was the best in the world, the Federal Trade Commission could ordinarily not do anything about it, because it would be difficult for the Commission to convince the Supreme Court that 'seller's puff' was an unfair practice. The object of the proposed legislation is not to stop the issuing of exaggerated opinions with reference to one's own articles."

Mr. Copeland: "The Senator means 'trade puffing'?"

Mr. Wheeler: "Yes; trade puffing. What the Commission has tried to do is to stop the issuing of a definite statement with reference to a fact which was not true. There is a vast difference between a statement of a concrete fact with reference to some article and the mere puffing of one's own goods."

Mr. Copeland: "There may be, but I fail to see it."

Mr. Wheeler: "The law recognizes a vast difference . . . ."

But Wheeler's comments made no apparent impression on the FTC. In 1939 it brought a complaint against puffery representations by the Moretrench Corporation,[14] and survived the company's court appeal through the fortuitous intervention of the ignorant man standard.[15] The judge who wrote the *Moretrench* decision, Learned Hand of the Second Circuit, had been reversed earlier in *Standard Education* by the Supreme Court's decision calling for application of the ignorant man standard.[16] That standard clearly implied a prohibition of puffery, because puffery possesses the capacity to deceive those who would take it literally, which the ignorant and careless members of the population surely would do. Therefore Hand had little choice in *Moretrench* but to support a complete shackling of puffery. "We understand that we are to insist upon the most literal truthfulness," he said.

As other cases followed (see chapter 10), it seemed that the substitution of the ignorant man standard for the reasonable man standard would wipe out puffery for good. In *Gulf Oil v. FTC* of 1945,[17] the court interwove two of the well-known quotations about protecting ignorant men and fools into its finding that Gulf's puffery defense could not be accepted. The die appeared cast and puffery appeared doomed.[18]

Return to Tradition

But surprises were in store for the Commission in cases it brought against Bristol-Myers in 1942, attacking such phrasing as "Ipana for the Smile of Beauty," and against Carlay Company in 1943. The latter case involved the criticism described in chapter 10 against calling a weight-reducing plan "easy." The *Carlay* cease and desist order of 1944 was reversed on appeal in 1946,[19] decisively forcing the Commission to permit a free flow of puffery despite a commitment otherwise to invoke the ignorant man standard.[20]

This unseemly contradiction posed a strange problem for the FTC in deciding the Ipana case. Maintaining the ignorant man standard would leave no room for puffery, while maintaining puffery would substantially deteriorate the ignorant man standard. The pending complaint against Ipana loomed as the "playoff" to determine which standard would win.

The Ipana decision (*Bristol-Myers*) was not handed down until 1949,[21] seven years after issuance of the complaint. The *complaint* is the FTC's initial announcement that it has reason to suspect a violation and is therefore undertaking an investigation. Complaints are made with the confident presumption that the facts will fulfill the suspicion, but the Commission does not commit itself to the proposed actions until it issues its "findings as to the facts," its "conclusions," and its "order to cease and desist."

In *Bristol-Myers* the time required to reach these latter stages was unusually long, allowing for the intervention of events which changed the Commission's feelings about the charge. The 1942 complaint had called false and misleading the phrase "Smile of Beauty," seeing it as an implied claim that Ipana's "use will result in the user possessing a beautiful smile and increased popularity." Against this implication the Commission had argued, in passionate protection of the ignorant man, and perhaps somewhat witlessly,

In truth and in fact, the smile is a change in facial expression, the most notable components of which are a brightening of the eyes and an upward curving of the corners of the mouth. It does not necessarily involve a display of teeth or gums. A smile not otherwise pleasing will not be rendered so by the possession of good teeth. Beautiful teeth will not insure a beautiful smile or social popularity. The beauty of human teeth depends primarily upon their conformation, color, arrangement in the mouth and other natural physical features, and teeth which do not possess these natural qualities will not be rendered beautiful by the use of Ipana tooth paste.

In other words, the Commission had seen "Smile of Beauty" as a claim that Ipana will straighten out your crooked teeth. To me it's remindful of a Katy Winters commercial for Secret deodorant in which Katy tells a friend about the product, and the friend happens to wear glasses. But after she starts using Secret it apparently improves her vision so much that by the end of the commercial she doesn't need to wear glasses anymore.

I don't know whether ignorant persons would believe that, or would believe the implication about the crooked teeth. But in 1942 it was a fact, prompted by Black's decision in *Standard Education* and by Hand's opinion in *Moretrench,* among other cases, that protection of the ignorant man was a primary criterion for FTC decisions. By 1949, however, the *Carlay* case had intervened to force the Commission to acknowledge puffery. Its response to this new pressure was to abandon the ignorant man standard where puffery was involved and conclude that Ipana's "Smile of Beauty" could not be attacked. The "findings as to the facts" declared, "The reference to beautification of the smile was mere puffery, unlikely, because of its generality and widely variant meanings, to deceive anyone factually. As used in the advertising, the expression 'brighten and whiten the teeth,' according to the opinion evidence, means simply cleaning the teeth, and the record shows that while the use of Ipana will not alter the shape . . . of the teeth, it will assist in the cleaning of them."

Perhaps the flatfootedness of the complaint's remarks about the anatomy of the human smile prompted some realization of the absurdity of aiding just *every* ignorant man. In any event, the *Carlay* policy had won,[22] and the ignorant man standard was eroded to the extent of its application to puffery. FTC policy now stated, in effect, that ignorant consumers might be fooled by almost anything, but they wouldn't be fooled by puffery.

From *Bristol-Myers* onward the FTC adapted itself to the realities of puffery and gave the concept full consideration. In several cases, aspects of the original complaints were discarded on the grounds that only puffery was involved. Mushroom growing, for example, was permitted to be called an "easy" occupation. The Commission said it

realized the task was difficult work, yet accepted the claim
because many people might find it easy compared to other
occupations.[23] An insurance plan was allowed to imply
that it provided "adequate insurance" because what was
adequate differs from person to person.[24] A brand of
sewing machine was allowed to be described as "almost
human and gives the housewife a tailor's skill." It might be
over-generous to designate the reference to "tailor's skill"
as puffery, the Commission observed, but it extended the
generosity nonetheless.[25] A shoe company was allowed to
represent that its special innersole will assure comfort and
perfect fit, although this would not be so for all individuals. The Commission's grounds were that the innersole
would provide an advantage which would not be present in
its absence.[26] The case, *Tanners Shoe,* invoked the Supreme Court's explanation from *New South Farm* of
1916,[27] that the distinction between puffing and falsity
was the difference between exaggerating qualities a thing
possesses as compared to asserting qualities it does not
possess at all.[28]

A Renewed but Modified Resistance

Still, the FTC did not acquiesce entirely on the subject
of puffery. Steelco Stainless Steel, Inc., claimed its statements were only puffery even though clearly of factual
form. The company had made disparaging claims that food
handled in aluminum utensils would cause cancer, stomach
trouble, anemia, blood poisoning, and other ailments. The
FTC said it was not impressed with the "suggestion that
representations relied upon can be excused on the basis
that they are only 'puffing' . . . . Statements made for the
purpose of deceiving prospective purchasers and particularly those designed to consummate the sale of products
by fright cannot properly be characterized as mere 'puffing.' "[29]

More significantly, the Commission several times rejected or ignored the defense of a claim as puffery even

when its literal form was that of opinion. The claim was described instead as misrepresenting a fact by implication. A medicine called N.H.A. Complex was said to "make one well and keep one well," a phrase perhaps innocent in itself but prohibited because the nostrum was advertised as preventing and curing a remarkable variety of diseases upon which it had no effect.[30] In *Tanners Shoe*,[31] although one instance of puffery was permitted, the manufacturer was denied the right to claim that his shoe "provides support where it is needed most." The latter phrase, said the Commission, carried an orthopedic or health connotation, which made a difference. Nor was puffery seen in claims by another shoe manufacturer that its insert would give "increased foot health and comfort," provide "more normal foot action," make "foot pains disappear as if by magic," and so on.[32]

Reweaving was not allowed to be called "easy to learn" when it was felt likely that no one would find it easy.[33] The Commission still regarded "easy" as a flexible term, harking back to when Ayds candy mints were permitted by the appeals court to be called an easy way to diet. But the flexibility with Ayds was that some people might truly find the task easy even though others would not. In contrast, the Commission thought that *no one* would find reweaving easy, therefore the term was not merely an exaggeration of a true quality but a false fact misrepresenting the absence of a quality.

In these and other cases a new strategy of resistance against puffery was created to replace the earlier one which had failed. The original means of resistance had been to call puffery unlawful misrepresentation, but after *Carlay* the Commission was forced to recognize that the common law precedents for such messages would prevail. The new strategy was to admit that puffery existed as a legal oasis for the seller, but to argue that a particular sales claim was fact instead. In other words, the FTC no longer denied the overall category, but sought instead to deny acceptance into the category to certain false representations.

A strong application of this strategy occurred in 1958

when the Commission ruled out a representation which
traditionally had been called puffery. *Liggett & Myers*[34]
involved an advertiser's attempt to hide behind the puffery
rule in defending his use of the word "milder" in describing Chesterfield cigarettes. When the FTC attorneys for-
mally presented their complaint, the Commission's hearing
examiner indicated his sympathies lay with the advertiser:
"For more than 20 years the term 'mild' . . . has been in
wide use by cigarette manufacturers in advertising . . . . The
present case appears to be the first in which the use of the
word has been challenged. This would indicate that
through the years the Commission has regarded the term as
harmless or innocuous, as merely a laudatory or 'puffing'
term noting high quality or pleasant sensory reaction, not
as a term relating to the amount or degree of irritation
produced in the nose, throat or accessory organs."

Many such preliminary decisions are allowed to stand
as FTC rulings, but this one was not. Previous Commissioners may have responded as the examiner[35] said they
did, but the present Commissioners now decided "milder"
was a false representation of fact. In the twinkling of an
eye a long-term item of puffery disappeared.

The new resistance was extended with three cases
which soon followed. In *Lifetime*[36] claims of "first class
craftsmanship and materials" were prohibited although
defended by a maker of building materials as "a customary
claim of American suppliers and artisans and . . . no more
than puffing." The Commission ruled that the business was
one in which grade and quality distinctions were commonly made and depended upon and were of prime importance to prospective purchasers. In *Dannon*[37] a claim
that yogurt was "nature's perfect food" was called misrepresentation of a material fact rather than puffing. The
same era also featured the case of *Colgate*,[38] the famous
sandpaper caper.

Colgate is best known for the use of a mock-up in
television filming, a topic whose details we will save for
chapter 15. Describing it briefly here, the advertiser said
sandpaper really could be shaved after soaking with Rapid

Shave shaving cream, but claimed the event could be depicted accurately on the screen only by faking the scene with a piece of plexiglas on which large grains of sand had been sprinkled, loose. This "mock-up" was necessary, the argument went, in order to demonstrate to the viewer something which the product actually could perform. The FTC thought the mock-up was not necessary and therefore illegal.

A separate line of defense offered by Colgate was that no reasonable viewers would have regarded the demonstration as serious; they would have seen it only as puffing. This argument was fairly ridiculous; the lawyers who devised it must have realized that were it true it would have been unnecessary for Colgate to use the mock-up in the first place. There would be no need to convince the viewer he was actually seeing something if he wouldn't have taken it seriously anyway. But lawyers will be lawyers! Probably they were not surprised to find the mock-up defense to be their strongest (though not strong enough) argument, while the counterfeit angle about puffery was disposed of in nothing flat: "The argument that respondents [Colgate] only indulged in a little harmless puffing is obviously out of place. They represented, unqualifiedly, that 'Rapid Shave' will dramatically facilitate the shaving of sandpaper and that they were demonstrating this fact before a television audience to prove it. Both of these were factual representations; neither is true."

Though Colgate was only puffing with its puffery defense, the argument gave the FTC the opportunity to comment on its new strategy of resistance. From an earlier FTC era Colgate had cited *Ostermoor, Kidder,* and *Carlay* as precedents,[39] to which the Commission answered that in the present era the precedents which ruled *against* puffery were more significant than those which favored it. The latter, it said, were now "inconsistent with the prevalent judicial and administrative policy of restricting, rather than expanding, so-called puffing."

Many more cases might be cited to illustrate FTC's renewed policy of restricting puffery by refusing to admit various seller's claims into the category.[40] One of the most recent is a settlement concerning the nutritional values of Carnation Instant Breakfast,[41] the ads having claimed that Carnation was equivalent to a pictured breakfast of bacon, toast, eggs, and juice. FTC insisted upon a revised illustration containing fewer eggs. "That may seem like a very small change," a spokesman said, "but it accomplishes what the commission considers proper: it prevents the advertiser from using a visual which exaggerates the true quantity of major nutrients in the product."

In addition to cases against individual advertisers, a relatively new FTC strategy against puffery involves writing rules to apply to an entire industry. Rather than condemning the puffery line, the strategy requires affirmative disclosure of the facts the puff implies. Light bulb makers, for instance, were found to use fact-related puffs such as "long life," "extended life," "better light," and "stays brighter longer." The nature of light bulbs makes it possible that one hundred-watt bulb may burn brighter than another, but only at the expense of living a shorter life. The maker naturally advertises the gain in brightness without mentioning the loss in shortened life, and his competitor of course advertises longer life without mentioning the lesser brightness. Rather than outlawing the terms, the Commission required that they be accompanied by disclosures of light output in lumens and expected hours of life along with the customary disclosure of wattage. The manufacturers may still communicate their vague phrases, but the consumer now can check the precise facts behind them.[42] In this way puffery remains, but lacks the potential it formerly had for implying certain false facts.

In summary, we have seen in this section the story of a considerable effort by the FTC to renew its original resistance against puffery.

Assessment of FTC Policy

What does the resistance described above really indicate about the way the FTC regards puffery? Has the

Commission truly acted to eliminate it, or does it still support the basic idea that this seller's privilege cannot be called deceptive? Has it said only that certain statements don't belong in that sanctuary, while continuing to protect the sacredness of the sanctuary?

The answer is that the Commission's primary action toward puffery has been to protect its use. It has continually asserted the basic privilege of the salesman to puff his wares, and in doing so has reflected a stance unchanged since *Carlay*. It's true, of course, that the privilege means little to sellers who cannot avail themselves of it, and the recent resistance has reduced the number who can. If this indirect action were carried to the extreme of saying that no statements belonged to the puffery category, the privilege then would mean nothing at all. It would be like a law permitting hippopotamuses to drive on the left side of the road, the effect being mooted by the fact that hippos rarely drive at all.

FTC Commissioner Mary Gardiner Jones has said in similar vein that there can be no ad claims which really can be called puffs: "In face of the huge dollar outlays expended by industry for its advertising campaigns, it is difficult to take seriously their arguments that any segment of their messages should be regarded as so unimportant and with so little effect on their audience as to justify being called mere puffing . . . ."[43]

Miss Jones, whose term ended in 1973, raised virtually no support for this point among her fellow Commissioners. But in theory it is entirely possible that the FTC could eliminate from the puffery category almost every one of the claims called that today. They could do so by saying that each instance of puffery implies a fact falsely and so deceives. The implied fact would be that there is, and that the seller knows there is, some puff-related aspect of quality in which the product objectively and factually excels its competitors. With most puffery there is no such aspect, and the seller knows there is not or at least knows he does not know.

My point, bluntly, is that virtually all puffery is false by implication and the FTC could prohibit it, *but the FTC doesn't prohibit it.* The Commission's actions may amount to "restricting rather than expanding" puffery, but there is no serious hint that the restrictions will become severe or that the basic concept of puffery will be effectively eliminated.[44] Fundamentally, the Commission is still reflecting the intervention of the courts of appeal in the *Ostermoor, Kidder,* and *Carlay* cases, which themselves reflected the ancient seller's privilege to flaunt opinions, going back to *Harvey v. Young* in 1602.[45]

A further conclusion about the FTC's permissiveness-with-exceptions policy toward puffery is that its inconsistencies are unfair to some and confusing to all. The exceptions are formulated like other FTC rulings on a case-by-case or industry-by-industry approach, with results such as the Tire Advertising and Labeling Guides which outlaw words such as "premium" in tire advertising for the following reasons: "The consumer does not understand the significance of the absence of acceptable grading or quality standards and is likely to assume that the expressions 'line,' 'level,' and 'premium' connote valid criteria. Since the consumer is likely to misinterpret the meaning of such terminology, he may be deceived into purchasing an inferior product because it has been given such designation."[46]

The reasons make sense, but why are they not used also to prohibit the phrase "premium beer"? Certainly that is a phrase which the consumer would take to "connote valid criteria." We know that the consumer often pays an (objectively) premium price for a (subjectively) premium beer. Since American advertising instills in the public the idea that we get what we pay for, why wouldn't the criterion of higher price deceive us when we get nothing more for the price in buying so-called premium beer?

Perhaps America's beer drinkers know all about the word "premium" and are fooled by it not at all. Perhaps! But there is no record that the FTC knows this, nor any record that it is true. Nor do we know anything about people's perceptions of "premium" as applied to products other than beer or tires. But if the FTC outlaws "premium" for one product and not for others, it could inadvertently give the impression that those uses not outlawed are not deceptive.

Uneven application of this sort is all too typical. Philco-Ford said in 1972 it had promised the FTC six years earlier to stop promoting its room air conditioners as "noiseless." It was now angry that the FTC had let others—for example, Remington Rand's "noiseless" typewriters—continue using the term without challenge. The word was only puffery, Philco-Ford said, meaning "operating with a quality of sound that is not unpleasant." Therefore it now regretted its earlier willingness to drop the usage. The FTC, it said, seemed to be playing favorites. [47]

Has the Commission played favorites elsewhere, for example in the action against the eggs in the Carnation ad? The action undoubtedly reflected the hard line developing in the 1970s against nutrition claims, but it did not necessarily reflect a policy against exaggerations per se. The prevailing practice still is that some exaggerations will be removed, and some will not. A general policy would be preferred, but does not exist.

When decisions are made piecemeal, no one knows whether a claim called puffery today may be called fact tomorrow. In two cases the FTC has changed its mind bewilderingly on this dimension, first converting a traditional puffing item to fact and then changing it back to puffery again. In 1970 it brought a series of charges against Hi-C fruit drink, one being that the product's name deceptively implied a false claim of high vitamin content. [48] Elimination of such a puffing name would be unusual considering the existence of Easy-Off oven cleaner, Topflite golf balls, and many others. But it would be justified if the name deceptively misrepresented a fact. For a reason not clearly explained, however, the FTC later dropped the demand that the name Hi-C be eliminated. [49]

Also in 1970 the Commission brought a complaint against Chevron gasoline, including a charge of deception in the claim that the additive F-310 made Chevron "the most long awaited gasoline development in history." [50] Again the charge was unusual because the claim was so classic an example of legally acceptable puffery. And again the FTC later dropped the charge against the phrase.[51]

Such actions indicate that the FTC's moves against puffery are strictly spot exceptions to the general policy which permits such false representations to exist. If there is one thing we can say to sum up the handling of seller's puffs, it is that the Commission still primarily admits them to the marketplace on the grounds that they are not deceptive.

12

Some Additional Kinds
of Puffery:
Expanding the Definition

THE STORY of puffery cannot be complete without a look at some other false but legally nondeceptive seller's statements which have strikingly similar sellerist effects. Puffery, technically speaking, may do no more than exaggerate in expressions of opinion and value those features which are truly present in the object for sale.[1] But there are other false seller's claims which amount to "puffing" even though they state or imply facts about characteristics which are wholly absent. These statements may also be called puffery in the sense that they blow up the features or value of the object to seem more extensive or greater than they actually are.

To avoid confusing the reader who may encounter these topics elsewhere, I have used the word "puffery" up to this point in its narrow legal meaning only. But in any practical sense it is most appropriate to think of puffery as comprising the wider field of all false but legally nondeceptive seller's claims. These claims differ in various ways, but they have attained their legal status for roughly the same reasons and their notoriety for roughly the same problems as we have seen for puffery. The reasoning applied to one is applicable to all, and the decisions made for one could easily be reflected in decisions made for the others. All such false representations may deceive, I feel, but the law says they do not. Let's identify them.

One we have already mentioned briefly is the obvious lie, such as the claim about air conditioning on Herbert Williams' car.[2] By using it, the salesman puffed up the automobile to be worth more in Williams's estimation than it would otherwise have been. The presence of the air conditioner was not exaggerated as a matter of subjective opinion, but was falsified as a matter of objective fact. It is permissible to "puff" something which is entirely absent, the law says, in cases where the absence is obvious. Whether the air conditioner's absence was truly obvious may be argued, but no one would question the general possibility that obviously false claims might be made. A car, for example, might be described as in good condition when it had no tires, or no steering wheel. As with puffery, the law calls such falsity nondeceptive because the buyer will neither believe it nor rely on it. The buyer is held responsible for what he presumably knows, and therefore is not permitted to rely on any statement which contradicts what he presumably knows.

Another type of falsity the law says is nondeceptive associates the product with sociological or psychological values which the product does not literally provide. Ultra-Brite gives your mouth sex appeal! You've come a long way, baby! You meet the nicest people on a Honda! Again, the advertiser is puffing the product's value by assigning it a characteristic it doesn't have at all. You might meet no one at all on your Honda, but the claim is permissible on the same grounds that puffery and obvious lies are—that no one would take it literally.

I feel it's nonsense to make an automatic assumption that any of these kinds of statements are nondeceptive. Whether or not an obviously false lie or a socio-psychological value is accepted or rejected by particular consumers should be a matter of fact determined by observation, not something decided as a matter of law rather than fact. Undoubtedly some of these statements are accepted by some consumers—why else would sellers or advertisers use them? Without question they deceive the public to some significant degree. Yet in reflection of its ancient attitudes the law is reluctant to look and see, choosing often to decide dogmatically that no adverse effects could possibly be happening.

The reason for the law's position on these statements is much the same as already described for puffery. The same social trends, the same attitudes toward sellers and buyers, apply. But the specific rules and precedents have developed separately from puffery and in the following two chapters we will look at the details of these developments.

13

The Ballooning
of Obvious

THE RULE of obvious falsity began in Anglo-American law with this statement by Justice Brian in 1471: "If a man sells me a horse and warrants that he has two eyes, if he has not, I shall not have an action of deceit, as I could know this at the beginning."[1]

Spelled out more precisely later, this meant that caveat emptor would apply without exception in such situations. That is, it would apply even though the seller had made what would ordinarily be a false warranty or fraudulent misrepresentation (deceit). The warranty and misrepresentation rules were voided under such conditions on the grounds that the buyer was not justified in relying on falsities he was assumed to be aware were false.

The reader may feel an instinctive aversion to this rule. When the seller speaks out it seems unbelievable that he not be held responsible for what he says. But the reader may also notice that the rule seems rather limited and incapable of having much effect. It applies to what is obvious to the buyer, and to nothing else. And what's obvious is obvious, isn't it? With falsity of that sort the most likely result, today as five hundred years ago, will be that the buyer will avoid a foolish purchase in the first place. True, some folks will be careless, and when that happens they will find themselves up against what seems a severely unfair law. Still, the rule fundamentally seems limited in its application.

If you can notice something about the product right away, just by being around it briefly, then it's obvious. If you can't do that, then it's not. The regulator who wants to determine which is the case can check the facts for himself, or ask a representative group of consumers for their opinions, and decide accordingly. Mistakes may be made in such decisions, but one supposes that the proper conclusion should almost always emerge.

If that were all that had ever happened with the obvious falsity rule, its story would be easy to tell. But much more has happened; sellerist developments occurred which made the rule much more capable of having an adverse effect on consumers. The law, as typified in the case of Herbert Williams and the air conditioner, developed a tendency to treat obvious falsity as it treated puffery, assuming that certain falsities were obvious (or puffs were automatically distrusted) without checking to make sure of the facts. The obvious falsity rule thus was given a systematic sellerist bias by the tendency of regulators to believe that obviousness existed in many situations where in truth it did not.

Why was this done? As with puffery, the answer lies in the ancient history of the rule. Let us return again to the days when the law favored the seller overwhelmingly, and so decided that many things would be "obvious" legally when they were not factually. As early as the year 1615 this result occurred in that strange case of *Baily v. Merrell*.[2] Merrell, you'll recall from chapter 7, lied to Baily about the weight of the wood piled on the wagon. But when the overload killed Baily's horses he couldn't make his damage suit stick because the court felt the actual weight was apparent enough that he should have known it. The court said its decision was based on Brian's 1471 rule.[3]

Is a load's weight obvious in the same way the existence of a horse's eyes or limbs is obvious? Surely it's not. One of the judges said, in fact, that if Baily doubted the weight he could have weighed the load and found out. If you have to weigh things to determine their weight, it must be because the precise figure isn't obvious. The basic means of determining weight is by using a measurement device which supplements the human faculties. Any observation a person "makes" with such aid should properly be called not obvious if "obvious" is to retain its meaning of being something a person notices and cannot help noticing instantly at sight.

Another judge in the case may have recognized this distinction and sought to reconcile his decision with it. He also voted against Baily, but on the grounds that it should have been easy, presumably without weighing, to see the difference between 800 pounds and 2,000 pounds. The *difference* should have been obvious to Baily even though the precise weight might not be. Under this view, the meaning of "obvious" would still mean really obvious, and the rule of obvious falsity would have been held to a fairly narrow scope.

Whichever may have been the better argument, later courts interpreted *Baily v. Merrell* as sanctioning expansion of the term *obvious* to include much more than just what was instantly noticeable. The rule came to be treated as virtually equivalent to the requirement of inspection under the rule of caveat emptor. That is, it came to apply to anything the buyer might observe either instantly *or by inspection of the object.* A seller's false statement about anything capable of being inspected became an "obvious falsity" and therefore could not legally be relied upon by its recipient.

American law adopted this idea with great vigor, finding it attractively compatible with the rising tide of caveat emptor which marked the nation's early decades. In *Sherwood v. Salmon* of 1805,[4] Sherwood had told Salmon and another man about some land he described as "excellent bottom land," "side-hill fine for pasture land," and "good timber land." It was worth one dollar per acre, he said, except for one tract which was worth two. But he was willing to sell it for twenty-five cents per acre!

The buyers were in Connecticut, and Sherwood's land was in Virginia, a distance of 500 miles, which might be equivalent in the 1970s to 5,000 miles. The purchase was made without a trip to Virginia. When the buyers eventually saw their land they found the descriptions false and the value per acre far less than the twenty-five cents they had paid. They won a suit for misrepresentation, but had to defend themselves in an appeal in which Sherwood's counsel blithely conceded the misrepresentations had been false. "It is agreed," the record stated, "that [Sherwood] falsely and fraudulently misrepresented the quality of the land; that his assertions were untrue, and known by him to be so."

That is not a good way, ordinarily, for lawyers to begin when they are trying to get someone off the hook. But in this case the concession laid the groundwork for Sherwood's winning argument, which was, "The defects complained of must, from the nature of the subject, be visible defects . . . . The rule of caveat emptor relative to visible defects was without exception, if the purchaser has eyes to see, and the subject misrepresented did not require peculiar skill to discern its real condition [citing *Baily v. Merrell*, among other cases] ."

Counsel for the aggrieved buyers protested futilely that the caveat emptor rule ought to be relaxed in this case, because it would have been overly difficult to inspect the land personally before purchase: "Where the quality of the article can be ascertained with *ordinary diligence,* the buyer shall stand by the loss; but to say, that in all events, he is to inform himself, is to place an honest man, in many instances, in the power of a swindler. It is often said, in our books, that courts should, as far as possible, enforce the duties of morality. The principle advanced [on behalf of the seller] seems to be rather a protection to fraud."

A seller, counsel for the buyers added, shouldn't "throw dust in a man's eyes, and then say that he might have seen." The seller had lied, and the buyers were in no good position to know he had, therefore the seller should be liable. If that wasn't a winning argument, what could be? Unfortunately, it wasn't. The court declared that the buyers could have won only by going to Virginia before the purchase; their failure to do so was fatal because "the maxim caveat emptor applies forcibly in this case. The law redresses those only who use due diligence to protect themselves . . . . The purchaser can see, if he will but look . . . . Whatever morality may require, it is too much for commerce to require, that the vendor should see for the purchaser. It is enough for him, in point of law, that he does not conceal the knowledge of secret defects, nor give a warranty, express or implied."

We see again the difference between the law of the market and ordinary morality. The absence of the claimed bottom land and pasture land was *no secret.* If you stood there and *looked,* you could see! It might take some effort to reach the point where you had to stand, but that's what you had to do. "Whether lands be five, or five hundred miles from the purchaser's residence," said the judge, "does not vary the requisition of due diligence, though it may the expense of complying with it."

Was the meaning of "obvious" getting less obvious? In *Baily* the qualities of the object were called obvious even when not seen instantly, but at least the wood was in front of Baily and he was looking at it. But in *Sherwood v. Salmon* the qualities were called obvious even though the purchase was entirely out of sight and though it would take extraordinary diligence to reach the point where it could be seen.

A similar sellerist viewpoint was offered in *Gordon v. Parmelee* of 1861,[5] in which the sellers of a piece of land said it contained fifty acres when the true figure was twenty-eight. This time the buyers were on hand to look before they bought, although they failed to see the truth. When they sued for misrepresentation the court ignored the falsity of the sellers and said—shades of *Baily v. Merrell*—that the buyers had to do more than just drop around for a glance when they purchased land: "They omitted to measure it, or to cause it to be surveyed. By the use of ordinary diligence and attention, they might have ascertained that the statement . . . on which they placed reliance, was false. They cannot now seek a remedy for placing confidence in affirmations which, at the time they were made, they had the means and opportunity to verify or disprove."

Reading between the lines, these cases were establishing more than just a rule about obviously false representations. They were aiming toward a caveat emptor which would exist entirely without exceptions. No matter how much a sellerist device it may have been, caveat emptor had traditionally acknowledged the right of the buyer to be protected against false warranties and fraudulent misrepresentations. But here were attempts to eliminate even that protection and impose what might be called a rule of Super Caveat Emptor. This rule was the most extreme sellerist form ever achieved by the law of sales statements, offering the least protection that could be offered (i.e., none) against the most clearly fraudulent lies that could be told. If the obvious falsity rule may be thought of as Dr. Jekyll, Super Caveat Emptor was the Mr. Hyde which it spawned.

The U.S. Supreme Court never supported the infamous Super Caveat Emptor, but in 1871 it lent its weight to a milder form of the obvious falsity rule in *Slaughter's Administrator v. Gerson.*[6] Slaughter had wanted a boat which drew no more than 3½ feet when fully laden, but the one he purchased from Gerson later grounded in water deeper than that. Slaughter charged that Gerson had claimed the draught was only 3½ feet, although other evidence suggested that Gerson had stated this merely as something asserted by another person and not known to himself personally. Slaughter also claimed he was unable to measure the draught, his counsel arguing, "Unless the sea was calm—which does not appear—it was impossible to make an accurate measurement of the draught of water."

But Slaughter had taken two shipcarpenters to the boat prior to purchase, and one of them reported to him a draught of 4½ feet measured at midships. When this evidence was revealed, it turned the case around. The Supreme Court declared that *even if* Gerson fraudulently misrepresented, he would not be liable because the truth was obvious to Slaughter. The truth was obvious not because Slaughter might determine it but because he *had* determined it, and was therefore bound to rely on it: "The neglect of the purchaser to avail himself, in all such cases, of the means of information, whether attributable to his indolence or credulity, takes from him all just claim for relief."

The Supreme Court thus supported the obvious falsity rule under circumstances where the buyer held the primary responsibility for his own fate. Unfortunately it said nothing about the rule's application where the buyer was more clearly the innocent victim of the seller's false acts. But cases on the point were destined to arrive and to doom the extremist rule of Super Caveat Emptor.

In *Roberts v. French,* an 1891 case[7] very similar to *Gordon v. Parmelee,* the buyer of a piece of land again failed to check false information about its size. But this time the seller had not merely stated the acreage falsely but had assured the buyer that the land had been most carefully and accurately measured. The court felt this made a difference, and ruled for the buyer: "When a man 'conveys the notion of factual admeasurement,' . . . still more when he says that he has measured a line himself and found it so long, his statement has a stronger tendency to induce the buyer to refrain from further inquiry . . . ."

The buyer was not physically restrained, but the court

perceived what would be called today a psychological lack of opportunity to inspect. As a matter of social intercourse one simply cannot examine something for oneself when the action would affront another who claims to have made the examination sufficiently for both. In that situation the correct acreage was not obvious, and the buyer was not held at fault.

The case did not really reduce the scope of the obvious falsity rule; it only kept it from expanding further. The implication remained that measuring land was "obvious" in the sense of being open to ordinary diligence. But as the century mark passed the consumerist thinking which affected so many rules caught up with this one, too. In *Judd v. Walker* of 1908,[8] a court finally decided that determining exact acreage was beyond what should be expected of a buyer who looked at his land before purchase.

Judge Lamm of Missouri was an eloquent man who gave in *Judd* one of the strongest consumer orientations that existed up to that time. To set the stage, he described the rule of obvious falsity as he felt it was meant to be stated, with "obvious" really meaning obvious: "The vendee is held to know what his own eyes would disclose, and knowing, could not be deceived. . . . For instance, if B. wants oats, and A. shows B. an open sack of beans (both . . . knowing beans when the bag is open), and A. tells B. they are oats, B. ought not to complain when he buys the sack because he gets beans. . . . In such case the fraud is made innocuous by the fact that it was patent to the vendee."

Lamm then objected to the idea that measuring land was as easy as looking at beans in a bag. "Such defect," he said, "is not a patent defect to be got at by the use of natural facilities and the exercise of ordinary diligence . . . ." Further, Lamm turned his attention not only to the buyer's capability but also to the seller's culpability, the latter being a rare consideration in the history of the obvious falsity rule. Earlier comments on the rule referred exclusively to the buyer's responsibility, ignoring any obligations the seller might have. Lamm reversed this attitude strongly:

> Due diligence does not require that the vendee should suspect the vendor of lying, nor that the vendee should survey and measure the land to prevent being deceived by the lies of the vendor. . . . If the rule be construed to mean that a vendee must survey the land and measure it . . . and cannot rely on the positive assurance of the vendor as to his knowledge of the number of acres in his own land, then we do not agree to it as good doctrine. . . . It has sometimes been loosely said that the negligence of the vendee will prevent recovery for the fraud of the vendor. . . . That such an act in the vendor should not be actionable because of the mere negligence or inadvertence of the vendee in preventing the fraud ought to be neither good ethics nor good law.

It was time, he added, to question the ancient principle of distrust: "Until there be written into the law some precept or rule to the effect that the heart of man is as prone to wickedness as is the smoke to go upward, and that every one must deal with his fellow man as if he was a thief and a robber, it ought not to be held that trust cannot be put into a positive assurance of a material fact."

Court decisions concerning false representations have rarely been accompanied by so direct an examination of the underlying foundation of the marketplace. The change from sellerism to consumerism meant in its depths, as Lamm recognized, the change from distrust to trust in one's dealings. The law, Lamm was saying, should be written to protect and support those who trusted, rather than maintaining the earlier attitude of protecting those who distrusted. His comments were predictive of the criticisms which eventually emerged of the reasonable man standard.[9] It is probably no great coincidence that they were echoed by Justice Black in *Standard Education* when he said "There is no duty resting upon a citizen to suspect the honesty of those with whom he transacts business."[10]

Judge Lamm's consumerist tendencies have been strongly developed in the present day, particularly in warranty law, where no trace remains of the Super Caveat Emptor notion.[11] Protection is assured against false warranties whose falsity is not patently obvious, and the law has shown in addition a "growing tendency" to retain warranty protection *even when* the falsity is obvious: "There seems no reason if the seller contracts in regard to an obvious defect or if he makes representations upon which the buyer in fact relies, why the seller should escape liability. It can hardly lie in his mouth to say that though he was making false representations or promises to induce the buyer to make the bargain, and the buyer was thereby induced, he should not have been."[12]

In misrepresentation law the consumerist change has not been so great. The obvious falsity rule has been specifically retained, as the *Restatement of Torts* indicates:

§541: REPRESENTATION KNOWN TO BE OR OBVIOUSLY FALSE. The recipient of a fraudulent misrepresentation is not justified in relying upon its truth if he knows that it is false or its falsity is obvious.[13]

The appended comment favors the consumer, however, by declaring falsity to be obvious only where it may be determined by a "cursory inspection" or at a "cursory glance." If it is not instantly obvious in this way, the rule today is as follows:

§540: DUTY TO INVESTIGATE. The recipient in a business transaction of a fraudulent misrepresentation of fact is justified in relying upon its truth, although he might have ascertained the falsity of the representation had he made an investigation.[14]

Section 540 is vastly different from the sellerist adherence to caveat emptor. The difference was reflected in 1936 by one of the authors of the *Restatement*'s original edition, Francis Bohlen, who said: "Had this been stated fifty years ago it would have been regarded as great heresy. I think it represents, however, a view that while starting as an inconspicuous minority is now approaching a majority view."[15]

Since 1936 the majority has increased. The obvious falsity rule now strongly reflects contemporary consumerism. Under sellerism "obvious" was ballooned into meaning anything a person might determine by inspection, but under consumerism this meaning has been contracted to mean only what is instantly noticeable.[16]

In addition, there exists today the opportunity, since the obvious falsity rule is disappearing from warranty law, to make one's case on breach of warranty rather than unlawful misrepresentation. Herbert Williams founded his air conditioner suit on a matter of misrepresentation, and the court's decision noted pointedly, "This is an action brought in fraud and not an action for a breach of warranty."[17] Could Williams have won under warranty law? The court seemed to be suggesting he could.

Still, why didn't Williams win under misrepresentation law? The court decided as a matter of law rather than of fact that the falsity of the salesman's representation was obvious. This extremely sellerist consequence of the obvious falsity rule happened as late as 1969 because the outmoded precedents of the past are not yet obliterated from judicial thinking. The memory of Baily and his unweighed load of wood still looms.[18]

Because it does, the obvious falsity rule joins the puffery rule in postponing the disappearance of sellerism. Just as the law may decide without checking that the public automatically distrusts puffery, it may decide that the falsity of a representation is obvious. Both types of decisions should be regarded as prime candidates for change as the replacement of sellerism by consumerism moves toward its ultimate completion.

We should not conclude the story of obvious falsity without mentioning the Federal Trade Commission. In FTC considerations the common law rule plays no formal role, but the question of whether the public is deceived is always at issue. In some cases it is evident that people will know a falsehood immediately for what it is, Olde Frothingslosh's claims being a good example. Prominent among today's obvious falsities are the spoofs we see regularly in television commercials. The huge and menacing Korean who played Oddjob in the film *Goldfinger,* for example, is seen violently tearing up the neighborhood with every coughing spasm. Then his wife gives him Vicks Formula 44, and he falls into a childlike calm. It's a lie, of course, if you want to be literal about it, but the FTC assumes nobody does. There is always *some* potential for deception in such things, admittedly, but probably only with those stray ignorant persons whom the FTC no longer worries about.

I've enjoyed many spoofs myself because I know what I'm seeing is false, and because I believe the advertiser is not attempting at all to make me think otherwise. Particularly amusing was the Hai Karate aftershave ad where the guy who uses the stuff suddenly must ward off a pride of ferocious women with karate chops and dexterous leaps over furniture. One of the greatest spoofs ever made is the one for Dr. Scholl's foot deodorant in which someone seated in an airliner takes off his shoes and socks and everyone else immediately faints dead away from the odor.

I feel personally that spoofs are all right when it's really obvious that what's being literally stated is ridiculous. A physical event occurs which nobody has ever seen happen and which no one would expect to happen on the basis of anything they *have* seen. Without question this is truly innocent falsity, though I hasten to add that my comment applies to adults only, not to children. With children the obvious may not be obvious, and the FTC has been properly concerned in recent years with the presumably innocent falsities youngsters may be taking literally.[19]

Children aside, the spoof probably should not be the target of those who want to remove falsity from the marketplace. I said at the outset of this book that the goal should be to eliminate all falsity, but I find it necessary to relent on that mission in this one instance. When the seller's misrepresentation not only is obviously false, but is obviously intended to be understood as false, then I see no harm done. I suppose I am opening myself to criticism from those with strong consumerist viewpoints, but I just do not believe that false representations *offered clearly as false* are a proper target for criticism.

In addition, I believe that spoof claims invariably are immaterial. The law says that to be illegal misrepresentations must be material—that is, they must refer to something which actually plays a role in the purchasing decision.[20] The falsehoods about Oddjob's coughing violence or about the passengers keeling over in the airplane are not material because people (apart from the stray ignorant person) simply are not going to purchase the product for the purpose of preventing those "catastrophes" from happening.

Let's acknowledge, however, that the line between spoofs and other sorts of representations is hard to draw. There is a TV demonstration for Bounty towels, for instance, which I am not certain whether to call a spoof. The paper towel is shown being touched to some spilled milk, and the milk races up into the towel with a loud slurping sound. It is a clearly impossible physical event, which points the ad initially toward the spoof category. But the representation is made in a straightforward manner, and this moves it away from the spoof category. It would clearly qualify as a spoof if it showed, for example, a magician pulling a rabbit out of a hat and then doing the trick with the paper towel.

But the ad did not indicate in any such way that the representation was offered as false. It might therefore be taken to represent that the towel has extraordinarily fast action. Such implication would be deceptive even if the Bounty towel *were* extraordinarily fast, because the act seen on the screen falsely overstated the fastness. So was the ad a spoof or not? I don't know. It seems evident from this dilemma that if spoofs are permitted legally they should be admitted only under the strictest guidelines.

Possibly the FTC has commented by analogy on the Bounty ad in its rejection of a commercial for All detergent in which water was shown rising around an actor clad in dirty garments. The water reached the man's chin, then receded quickly to show his clothing free of stains. Noting that the cleaning action was accomplished so quickly, the FTC decided that "even humorous commercials have actionable capacity to deceive where, as here, they depict the product in use and exaggerate the results ostensibly achieved from such use."[21] The theory apparently was that the ad was no spoof because it was an exaggeration of something that could actually happen rather than something impossible to happen. Furthermore, it apparently was not puffery, either, because the exaggeration was just too great.

If this explanation were applicable to All detergent, one would think by analogy it should be applicable to Bounty and to many other ads as well. Such ads, however, generally have not received FTC criticism. As we saw with puffery, the actions on record indicate a case-by-case resolution rather than pursuit of a definite policy.

That the FTC has not made its position clear on spoofs v. nonspoofs was suggested by testimony from hearings it held in 1971. Eugene Case, an advertising executive, described as false an Alka Seltzer commercial depicting "professional pie eaters."[22] The ad showed some fat men taking Alka Seltzer to ease their stomachs after participating in a contest which one of them described as being on the "professional pie-eating circuit." The ad was false, Mr. Case said, because there was no such circuit and no such professionals. He assumed therefore that the ad, though he admired it very much, would be vulnerable to FTC attack.

Mary Gardiner Jones, the Commissioner taking the strongest pro-consumer stance at the time, disagreed with Mr. Case. "I would take very strong umbrage with your implication that we would take that off the air," she said. The only fact she saw implied to the public by the commercial was that the product gives relief from over-eating. Therefore she was concerned only with whether that fact was true, and not at all with the obvious unreality of the professional pie eaters.

Miss Jones did not formulate a rule for identifying spoofs, however, nor has the Commisssion as a whole done so. As a result, the misunderstanding experienced by Mr. Case will probably occur again as advertisers continue their accustomed habits of operating in close proximity to legal borderlines.

Because I hope that such problems are soluble, I cautiously maintain my position that spoofs are an acceptable form of falsity. In keeping with the principal thrust of this book, however, I find it appropriate to insist that any forms of material misrepresentation, if they are not presented to the public specifically as false, no matter how obviously false they may be, should be banned from the marketplace as deceptive.

14

Wishing in the Market: Puffing the Social and Psychological Aspects of Products

THE STORY of the regulation of social and psychological misrepresentations is easy to tell, because there has been virtually no such regulation. These misrepresentations have been declared legally nondeceptive by default rather than by, as with puffery, deliberate rulings. They are no less deceptive and deserving of regulation, and the failure to control them represents another large gap in the growth process of consumerism.

A social or psychological misrepresentation is a claim that a product possesses a feature which in truth exists only in the consumer's social environment or within his own personality or mental state of mind. "The man who knows how to take care of himself uses Vaseline hair tonic." The feature of competence and self-confidence is not truly part of the product, but is associated with the product only in the representation. The message implied to the consumer, however, may be that the feature will accompany the product with such certainty that it can be taken as if it were an actual part of the product.

Such features or values are attached to products in an entirely arbitrary manner. "What sort of man reads Playboy?" "Us Tareyton smokers would rather fight than switch." They are there because the message says they are there, and *only* because the message says they are there. They are different from inherent product features, which are present in an objective sense. An ad stating that Vaseline contains alcohol or that the Volkswagen has an automatic transmission describes an inherent feature—something that is physically there. By contrast, the social misrepresentation describes a feature not of the product at all, but of the consumer's social environment ("Your friends will love you for serving such-and-such . . ."). And the psychological misrepresentation describes a feature of the consumer's own personal nature ("Be the person you've always wanted to be . . .").

Of course the advertising industry does not regard such messages as misrepresentations. It regards them as suggestions about results which can in fact occur for the lucky purchaser. Don't tell the advertiser that "You'll meet the nicest people on a Honda" is false. You might go out on your Honda and meet some fantastic folks! Some people will, and every buyer might. It's one of those projective things you can make seem true by wanting it to be true, by a process of wishful thinking.

Yet I believe the advertisers are lucky they have not been challenged on the question of deceptive content in these claims. Clearly it is false to promise with the product some feature the buyer does not actually get with the product. You might make some friends with your Honda, but it is false to imply you will for sure. All that you actually get are the tangible components of the cycle, the parts made of metal and rubber and leather. The dealer from whom you buy does not physically hand you any social values, nor would he respond favorably if you asked him to guarantee any such thing as part of the product warranty. Social-psychological values are literally not there, and any representation which states or implies that they are is false. If advertisers are ever taken to court on these matters, they will be unwise to deny this falsity. If they can muster a defense, it will have to be based on the idea that such falsity is not deceptive.

One such defense might be to claim that social and psychological misrepresentations are obviously false to any but the stray unreasonable person. Industry people reading this chapter have undoubtedly thought of this point already, and have been screaming to themselves that there's nothing in such claims that would harm anyone, because the public knows how to interpret them. The public knows that what you literally get is only the Honda and not the social values—who would be idiotic enough to think otherwise?

The answer the industry deserves on this point is the same I have given it for puffery:[1] if it is so idiotic, why do you use it? You say it's legal because it's obviously false, but if that is so then what is the point in using it? The truth is that it's not obviously false at all. The absence of social and psychological features is never obvious in the sense of being instantly noticeable. The falsity is a feature of the product in use rather than the product itself, and thus cannot be observed at the place of purchase. You can look at a car and see that there's no steering wheel, but you can't look at a cycle and see that you won't meet the nicest people on it. The absence of the claimed features is not observable by a "cursory inspection" or "cursory glance."

Therein, from the seller's standpoint, lies the magic of such features. The consumer can think they'll be present later even though he doesn't see them at the store. He doesn't expect to see them at the store, therefore their absence at that point does nothing to alarm him that they'll be absent later. That's subtle falsity, not obvious falsity, and accordingly there seems little chance of invoking the obvious falsity rule in its defense.

Another defense of social and psychological misrepresentations might be to claim they are only puffery. As noted earlier, they constitute puffing the product in the broad and generic sense of that term. But the narrow legal definition of puffery restricts it to exaggerated opinions about features and values which are truly present.[2] A puff legally may falsely imply the extent of the product's popularity or superiority or beauty or monetary value, because the product always has some degree of those elements, no matter how little. But while the puff refers to the product's popularity, the social-psychological misrepresentation refers to what the product will do for *yours*. That may be enough to keep such misrepresentations separate from puffery, because they thus attribute features to the product which are not truly present. This difference should be enough to warn the industry of danger in building a defense on the puffery rule.

There's really no good defense, I believe, for an assertion that false social-psychological representations are not deceptive. The only thing that has permitted them to exist as nondeceptive is that they have not been challenged. When the challenge comes, the lack of legal precedents will work against them, since while the law has never condemned such representations it also has never condoned them. They are much more vulnerable than puffery and obvious falsity because the latter at least have the weight of some shaky precedents behind them. Social-psychological misrepresentations have none, thus their only hope is that the issue continues to be ignored.

To have no history of regulation is to have a situation quite different from what we have seen elsewhere in this book. The difference is that social and psychological misrepresentations in any significant volume are a product only of the twentieth century.[3] They were developed because competitors began desiring to differentiate their own brands of goods in order to distinguish them from other brands which were virtually similar in inherent physical characteristics. Before the 1900s the makers or processors of soap, bread, grain, salt, milk, and numerous other commodities had not yet been concerned with this desire.

They had been producing their goods with no thought of making them distinct from the production of their fellow makers. They didn't care, because demand traditionally was greater than supply and everyone was selling all he could make. A man's competitors were not really competing in the sense of threatening to drain off sales he would otherwise get.

Conditions eventually changed. Manufacturing increased to the point where supply overtook demand and passed it. The individual producer became threatened with an absence of markets, and began seriously to compete for those which remained available. As this competition heightened in the late nineteenth century, producers became painfully aware that the nondistinctiveness of their product was a liability. With over-demand it had not mattered, but with over-supply it became crucial.

Yet the ultimate customer did not care. The flour in the bin at the store might come from anywhere; flour was flour. The question the producer began to ask was, "How can I get the public to want mine?" The solution was that he should differentiate his flour as a brand and build a demand for the brand's distinct attributes. If the process worked and people demanded Smith's flour, they could get it only from Smith. There might be a slack demand for flour in general, but the traditional over-demand might be created nonetheless for Smith's brand.

In the twentieth century many markets have changed in this way from selling products to selling brands. The marketer's goal is to make the brand appear to the customer as though it *is* the product. "When you're out of Schlitz you're out of beer" is a perfect modern statement of this purpose. Not all consumers will accept so extreme a suggestion, of course. But when they write "Kleenex" on their shopping list instead of "paper handkerchiefs" they are reflecting the strength with which the change has occurred.

Successful brand distinctions were difficult to achieve in the beginning. The producer could put his own distinctive name on the product easily enough, but efforts to differentiate beyond that point were hampered because his soap or flour or sugar was basically the same in its inherent features as that of his competitors. When he tried to add, augment, or alter inherent characteristics he found that the differences thus produced did not make enough of a difference. And the competitors in any event could generally match him by making the same adjustments.

This is not the place to recount the story of all the steps taken to solve the problems of scarcely differentiable brands. We shall be content to explain that the producers eventually followed the advice of advertising specialists who had perceived that apparent product differences could be achieved in sales messages even when not achievable in the product itself. With this insight, sales communication soon turned to stressing features which were not inherent parts of the brand but could be associated with the brand in the public's mind *as if they were inherent.* Today we have "Gusto" in our Schlitz, "Schweppervescence" in our Schweppes, dumbness in our Hush Puppies, and many other features we didn't have before. We have all these social and psychological features, but we have no law concerning them.

A law review article entitled "Psychological advertising: a new area of FTC regulation"[4] was published recently, and I turned to it with the expectation that someone at last had identified and compiled a list of FTC actions taken toward this sort of advertising. The author, however, had founded this "new area of FTC regulation" on exactly two cases, which is more than none but not enough really to establish a new direction. In both cases, furthermore, the FTC attacked social-psychological misrepresentations only in conjunction with charges against misrepresentations of inherent product features in the same ads.

The Commission filed the two complaints in 1971. In the first, advertisements for Wonder Bread were alleged to make several false nutritional claims and also to falsify the bread's contribution to people's mental and social states.[5] The advertiser, said the FTC, "tends to exploit children's aspirations for rapid and healthy growth" and also their parents' concern for their growth and development. "This part of the complaint," the law review article stated, "is concerned with the psychological effects on both parents and children. It is not concerned with the misrepresentation of the inherent product qualities and is, therefore, a departure from previous FTC policies."[6]

In the other case,[7] ads for a product called Vivarin told women their husbands would be more attracted to them if they used it, apparently implying some sort of sexually based arousal which would renew the lagging instincts of tired old married folks. To quote the ad directly:

"One day it dawned on me that I was boring my husband to death. It was hard for me to admit it—but it was true. . . . Often by the time he came home at night I was feeling dull, tired and drowsy, and so Jim would look at television and, for the most part, act like I wasn't even there. And I wasn't.

I decided that I had to do something. I had seen an advertisement for a tablet called Vivarin. It said that Vivarin was a non-habit forming stimulant tablet that would give me a quick lift. Last week . . . I took a Vivarin tablet . . . just about an hour before Jim came home, and I found time to pretty up a little, too. It worked.

All of a sudden Jim was coming home to a more exciting woman, me. . . . The other day—it wasn't even my birthday—Jim sent me flowers with a note. The note began: 'To my new wife . . . .' "

All very nice, but the contribution of Vivarin was to provide merely the amount of caffeine found in two cups of coffee. No miracle aphrodisiac, just good old caffeine at a premium price!

The major allegation of the FTC's complaint about Vivarin concerned this social-psychological misrepresentation, indicating again a departure from past policy. But the Vivarin ads were also alleged to be deceptive because they did not disclose caffeine to be the critical ingredient. As with Wonder Bread, the Commission did not attack the social-psychological element alone but only in conjunction with misrepresentations about inherent features. This suggests that the former may have been merely thrown in to help prosecute the latter, just to fatten up the case, so to speak. Successful prosecution of such cases would not necessarily indicate that the FTC could effectively prosecute a social-psychological misrepresentation standing alone.

Nor can two cases in any event make much impact on a business which produces hundreds of social-psychological misrepresentations annually. The general conclusion can only be that false social-psychological claims are essentially unregulated at this time.[8] They are a case, again, of the law assuming without checking that the falsity is non-deceptive. And they are a case, again, where reasons exist to think the law is wrong.

15

Still More Kinds of Puffery, but Controlled: Literally Misdescriptive Names and Mock-ups

THUS FAR we have defined the puffery concept to include three kinds of falsity which deceive the public but escape the clutches of the law. This chapter introduces two more kinds of puffing, and describes them as types of falsity which are much less likely to escape.

Literally misdescriptive names and mock-ups are carefully regulated; their deceptive potential has been subjected to legal control rather than to legal indifference. No systematic tendency exists to allow them to continue unchecked. Instead, there has been a systematic effort to eliminate such representations when they deceive and to permit them only when they do not. The handling of these kinds of puffery might be regarded, therefore, as a model for the handling of all categories of false representations.

Literally Misdescriptive Names

This type of puffery consists of names or labels which are literally false in describing the product and which puff up its value in doing so, but which are held by the law to be nondeceptive where the falsity is obvious. Danish pastry need not legally come from Denmark, nor china from China, nor Irish potatoes from Ireland, nor Boston baked beans from Boston. The law says people know the name is merely a label and not a literal claim and therefore are not deceived.[1] People understand that Swiss cheese may come from America, and Idaho potatoes may come from Maine. They know Gouda cheese isn't Dutch, French toast isn't French, permanent waves aren't permanent, and the United States Rubber Company is not a branch of the federal government.

Chances are that most consumers would agree with the law in assuming that these literal misdescriptions are usually recognized as such, and that the public interprets them by secondary meanings which have superseded the literal meanings. Consumers understand that the "Swiss" in Swiss cheese refers to a style (strongly established secondary meaning) rather than a point of origin (traditional primary meaning).

I am certain the law is correct in assuming the existence of such secondary meanings—I have no quarrel to make with such decisions.

But let's try some other names on you. What is your understanding about a substance called Stone China, which is used to make dishware? What do you think is the nature of Plyhide, advertised as follows: "Lounge chairs, upholstered in 'Plyhide'—with that tailored leather look"? What fact do you believe about a product called Six Month Floor Wax? What does "Made in USA" mean when it is stamped on a product? What business do you think the National Laboratories of St. Louis engages in?

These are a little tougher than Danish pastry, aren't they! Stone China is not china but the material known as earthenware or stoneware. Plyhide is vinyl; it contains nothing made of nor associated with leather or other products of animal hides. Six Month Floor Wax will not last six months nor does it have any characteristic or quality describable by the term "six months." "Made in USA" has been stamped on goods made in Japan in a town whose name was changed to Usa. National Laboratories of St. Louis operates and services vending machines and has no connection with any laboratory.

If you didn't know these secondary meanings, then those puffing names have the capacity to deceive you. As a matter of fact, there is reason to believe they *have* deceived people and should rightfully be taken out of the marketplace. Some names, apparently, have effects quite different than "Swiss cheese," and the law ought to be treating them accordingly.

Perhaps as you've been reading this you have thought to yourself: Here we go again, here's another category of false puffery which deceives the public, and again the law says it's nondeceptive and does nothing about it. It's another of the many rip-offs which this book is about. Once more the law shows it can't keep up with the kinds of falsity sellers use.

Not so. With misdescriptive names the law has acted decisively. The FTC has banned the terms Stone China, Plyhide, Six Month Floor Wax, Made in USA (where not true), and National Laboratories of St. Louis.[2] The effect on the public has been considered, and judgments have been rendered that these names are misdescriptive not only literally but also in fact. The secondary meanings the companies claimed were established in the public's eye have been ruled not established.

In these cases the FTC has demonstrated a willingness to act which we have not seen elsewhere. It has refused to permit the development of a category of representations receiving automatic immunity. Puffery, obvious falsity, and social-psychological misrepresentations are such categories; they are like umbrellas under which the seller may run to be safe. But with misdescriptive names the law has allowed no sure immunity. It has taken each case on its own merits. Secondary meanings may be used only when they are established in the public's mind, and the burden is on the user of the name to prove it has been done.

The FTC's right to ban misdescriptive trade names was made secure by the Supreme Court in *FTC v. Winsted* of 1922.[3] The Winsted Hosiery Co. had been selling underwear labeled variously as "Merino," "Natural Merino," "Gray Merino," "Natural Wool," "Gray Wool," "Australian Wool," and "Natural Worsted." All of these labels were found by the FTC to mean to "a substantial part of the consuming public" that the underwear was made entirely of wool, whereas in truth the material used was mostly cotton with a small portion of wool. Winsted protested that the terms were understood within the trade to indicate goods made partly of cotton. The manufacturers and dealers, it said, had created secondary meanings which in their minds fully superseded the original ones. There could be no unfair competition, therefore, if everyone involved knew how the words were being used by everyone else.

But "everyone," said the Supreme Court, consisted not merely of members of the trade but of the consuming public as well. For that public, it observed, the labels using the words "wool" or "worsted" had no trace of any secondary meaning, but only the primary meaning of "all wool." A secondary meaning did exist, the Court found, for the terms containing the word "Merino"; they indicated a wool-cotton combination. But this was found to be "not a meaning so thoroughly established that the description which the label carries has ceased to deceive the public." The public, in other words, was only somewhat aware of the secondary meaning of "Merino," and thus relied generally on the primary meaning which was therefore false and deceptive in its application to Winsted underwear. The result was that the Supreme Court affirmed the FTC's position and outlawed the use of all the disputed terms as descriptions of underwear which was not all wool.

While Winsted's customers were not getting what they thought, a more subtle problem may occur when the consumer gets what he expects but from a source different from the one he thinks is involved. There is surely less harm done by this kind of deception than by the other, but the FTC banned it, too, and was upheld by another ruling of the Supreme Court, *FTC v. Royal Milling Co.* of 1933.[4] The Commission had attacked several companies which had "milling," "mills," or "millers" in their names, although they did not actually mill (i.e., grind into flour) the wheat from which they mixed various blends of flour. The variations of "mill" were found to be commonly understood by dealers and the public to indicate companies which *did* grind wheat into flour. On appeal, the Court agreed a legal remedy was necessary: "If consumers or dealers prefer to purchase a given article because it was made by a particular manufacturer or class of manufacturers, they have a right to do so, and this right cannot be satisfied by imposing upon them an exactly similar article, or one equally as good, but having a different origin.... The result of [the "milling" companies'] acts is that such purchasers are deceived into purchasing an article which they do not wish or intend to buy, and which they might or might not buy if correctly informed as to its origin."

The point was reinforced by the Supreme Court in *FTC v. Algoma* of 1934,[5] in which the Commission sought to prohibit confusion in the lumber industry between the terms "white pine" and "yellow pine." Genuine white pine was adjudged superior to yellow pine, and deemed worthy of being correctly identified. But a practice had developed within a portion of the industry to refer to some yellow pine as "California white pine," resulting in some buyers getting a product other than what they ordered. The Supreme Court emphasized that the confusion thus produced should be prohibited *even if* the yellow pine received were equivalent to the white pine ordered. "The consumer is prejudiced if upon giving an order for one thing, he is supplied with something else."

But the Court also made clear that confusion does not necessarily occur when a name is literally misdescriptive. If "California white pine" had been found to have "two meanings with equal titles to legitimacy" (a secondary one meaning "yellow pine" as well as the literal "white"), then no confusion would have existed. That can happen, the Court said, when "by common acceptation the description, once misused, has acquired a secondary meaning as firmly anchored as the first one."

That has become the FTC's test, and it is clear that many terms pass it and are allowed to remain in use. The secondary meaning of "Danish pastry," for example, is far better established within the United States than the primary meaning. It remains a possibility that the falsity of the original meaning could lower the consumer's regard for the genuine product, pastry really from Denmark, for those consumers who know the term only by its original meaning. They would buy the misdescribed product, be disappointed with it, and avoid buying both it and the genuine product in the future. That would damage the sellers of the genuine product if it happened.

But the evidence suggests it will not happen with any appreciable portion of the public. The sellers of the product in its original version deserve protection if they need it, but usually they don't need it. (An exception has occurred when sellers of a product in its secondary form [i.e., American Danish pastry] have used a label such as "Genuine Danish pastry." The FTC has recognized this as an attempt to falsely reinstate the original meaning in the consumer's mind, and has strictly forbidden such labels when not literally true.[6]

The wide range of misdescriptive names prohibited as deceptive by the FTC will be indicated here by mentioning only a few of the many cases which have been pursued. The "Institute of Hydraulic Jack Repair" was called deceptive because it created the false impression of being a bona fide institution of higher learning.[7] "Madras," unless describing "fine cotton, handloomed and imported from the Madras section of India," may not be used except with a clear and nondeceptive statement of the way the fabric actually resembles India Madras fabric.[8] "Scout," "Eagle Scout," and "Cub Scout" sleeping bags may not be so designated when the manufacturer has obtained no affilia-

tion with nor approval from the Boy Scouts of America.[9]
A cigar maker situated in New Jersey may not misrepresent itself as the "Havana Florida Company."[10] A sweater manufacturer was prohibited from using the term "Kashmoor" for sweaters containing no cashmere unless accompanied by the qualifying phrase "contains no cashmere."[11] Another manufacturer was prohibited without exception from using "Cashmora" on sweaters containing no cashmere, but was allowed to use the label on part-cashmere sweaters if the percentage of cashmere were disclosed.[12] The word "liver" was removed from "Carter's Little Liver Pills" because the pills had no medical effect on that organ.[13] A furniture company was denied the use of "Grand Rapids" in its name because its furniture was not manufactured in Grand Rapids, Michigan.[14] "Virginia" may be used only to describe hams from hogs raised in Virginia and given the specific Virginia curing and processing which imparts a distinctive flavor; it may not be used on hams given Virginia processing but coming from hogs raised outside the state.[15] The United States Testing Co. was banned from implying it had connections with the United States government.[16] The Army and Navy Trading Co. was told to change its name because it did little or no business in goods actually purchased from and manufactured to specifications of the U.S. Army or Navy.[17]

While the above misdescriptive names were in use before being outlawed, others have been restricted from the start to their primary meanings; no secondary meanings have been given any chance to develop. Typical of these are names for European liquor and wine. United States government regulations state that while liquor distilled in America may be called "brandy," no liquor may be called "cognac" or "cognac brandy" unless it is grape brandy distilled in the Cognac region of France.[18] A similar rule applies for Scotch whiskey.[19] Wines called "champagne" must be produced in the Champagne district of France; so-called American champagnes must be labeled "sparkling wine" first, followed by the place of origin (i.e., California) preceding the word "champagne."[20] No wine may be called "port" in America or England unless produced in a small area along the Douro River in northern Portugal and exported through the Portuguese seaport of Porto. In England this rule has no exception, but in America qualifications concerning origin, such as "California Port," may be used.[21] A similar rule applies to sherry, which comes originally from the Spanish town of Jerez de la Frontera.[22] But *Consumer Reports* tested American sherries against the Spanish standard and stated that American producers who can't stand such comparisons ought to drop the name voluntarily rather than complain.[23] It's one thing to get the right to the name, but another thing to live up to it.

Another European name protected under American law is Roquefort cheese, which may be sold by that name if made in only one place: the village of Roquefort, France, population 1,300.[24] A number of localities in France are called Roquefort, but the cheese comes only from the one in the Aveyron section of the south. Blue or bleu cheeses are made in many other places, but no blue cheese may be called "Roquefort" unless aged a minimum of three months in the caves of the Rocher du Cambalou, the mountain on which Roquefort village stands. Production from the caves amounts to only 15,000 tons per year, which explains the high cost of this delicacy.

American restaurant diners may not be aware the real thing is so rare, because they are constantly being offered "Roquefort dressing" on their salads. I have made a personal practice of asking waitresses whether the "Roquefort" is really that, and they invariably report from the kitchen that it's really blue cheese. They are violating the law by using a valuable name falsely, and I believe in most cases they are doing it entirely innocently. Somebody on the premises isn't so innocent, but such parties are careful to position the waitress between themselves and the public. Many pitfalls await the regulator who hopes to achieve vigorous enforcement of misrepresentation law in the area of oral representations.

The precedents are available, however, to restrain the

perpetrators of literally misdescriptive names which deceive. The result is that this type of puffery, unlike the
others we have seen, has been carefully subdivided into
categories of deception and nondeception. We might ask
why the law has discriminated so effectively in this area
while simultaneously making its automatic and nondis-
criminatory assumptions of nondeceptiveness about the
great bulk of puffery, obvious falsity, and social-psychological misrepresentations.

The answer, in part at least, is that the newness of
misdescription law makes a difference. Puffery and obvious falsity are founded in the ancient heritage of caveat
emptor; attempts to change them crash on the reefs of that
still-powerful precedent. But elements of the law created
only in the twentieth century have no such backing. When
misdescription went to the Supreme Court in *Winsted*, the
manufacturer actually cited precedent in reverse, saying
such practices had never before amounted to unfair competition against one's competitors. His argument backfired,[25] but it showed that the issue of misdescriptive
names had not been developed in the pre-FTC days of
common law. Thus there was no chance for the caveat
emptor mentality to play a role in shaping regulation in
that area.

This explanation is cast into question, however, by the
fact that social-psychological misrepresentations are a post-
caveat-emptor phenomenon, too, yet are regulated as they
would have been under that rule. Why has the FTC not
attacked them as it has attacked misdescriptive names? I
believe the answer is related to the relative degree of threat
which sellers perceive in those two kinds of falsity. A
seller's competitors may feel more directly affronted by
his literal misdescriptions than by his social-psychological
misrepresentations, and so be more prone to ask the FTC
to intervene. A company making real china, for example,
might be more threatened by a stoneware company which
utilized the name "Stone China" than by one which made
a false claim about social satisfactions to be achieved. That

is because the social misrepresentation does not so directly negate the quality differential which real china possesses. The "Stone China" claim contradicts the china-stoneware distinction, while the social satisfaction claim, though inconsistent with the distinction, does not contradict it head on.

Whatever the reason, the decisions about literally misdescriptive names have reflected the consumerism trend most thoroughly, and strongly suggest directions the law might take toward controlling the other forms of allegedly nondeceptive falsity. These decisions also suggest, however, the sticky problems which develop when the law tries aggressively to determine the deceptive potential of misrepresentations. Decisions may be made arbitrarily, and perhaps wrongly; there is no way to avoid the possibility of mistakes. The case of the Milan hats demonstrates this instructively.

Korber Hats v. FTC of 1962[26] involved an appeal against an FTC decision that Korber's hemp hats could not be called "Milan" hats because the public understood that term by its primary meaning, that is, hats made in Italy from wheat straw and with a distinctive weave or braid. The use of wheat straw was the most important aspect of this meaning, the FTC thought, which meant that hats of hemp should not be called Milan. But Korber argued that a secondary meaning had been well established to the effect that a Milan hat was known by its weave or braid exclusively, and therefore could be made of hemp as well as wheat straw and could be made outside Italy.

The problem the court of appeals faced was that substantial evidence existed for both meanings. It accepted Korber's claim of the presence of the secondary meaning, but felt such meaning had developed alongside rather than in place of the primary meaning. A considerable portion of the public had the one understanding about "Milan," but a considerable portion also had the other. How does one resolve a situation like that? The solution the court proposed was that Korber could use the term "hemp Milan" or "imitation Milan." It thus could retain use of "Milan," in recognition that its hats matched the secondary meaning, but could use the term only qualifiedly, in recognition that its hats did not match the original meaning. The name "Milan" unqualified would remain reserved for Italian wheat straw hats.

There was sense in the proposal; it may have been the best solution available. Yet one can imagine the dissatisfaction it could produce. Korber Hats would dislike using a qualifying word in front of "Milan." Makers of "genuine" Milan hats would dislike Korber's using the name at all. And since virtually no one, neither public nor trade, would use the term in both meanings, *everyone* would be upset to some degree by official recognition of the meaning they didn't use. The solution made all parties a little unhappy, whereas undivided support of either primary or secondary meaning would have fully satisfied half the people concerned (though making the other half wretched).

What else can be done when both meanings are popular? The Food and Drug Administration, which also plays a role in regulating names, had a similar situation concerning the use of the term "Swiss chocolate."[27] Switzerland's chocolate industry presented survey results which showed that many people interpret "Swiss chocolate" to mean imported from Switzerland. But American companies which widely use the term insist it has gone the way of "Swiss cheese," to mean nowadays only a style. The FDA strongly desires to eliminate deception in this area, but it seems probable that deception will remain for many persons no matter how it rules.

Another case which necessarily left people dissatisfied was *Quaker Oats,*[28] in which the company had marketed "charcoal briquets" made from corncobs. The FTC's complaint charged that consumers thought "charcoal" meant something made from wood, and therefore would be treated unfairly if they got something else. The ads for the product did not identify the source of the charcoal, although they did claim it gave "real Hickory Flavor." But the case was noteworthy for the absence of any indication that consumers would be dissatisfied with corncob charcoal or that such charcoal would function less effectively when used. Apparently for this reason the majority of Commissioners dismissed the complaint. But the two dissenting Commissioners left troubled waters when they denounced the decision as giving no protection to consumers who believed charcoal must be made from wood.

Readers of this book will undoubtedly have their own experiences to relate about the confusion produced by names which don't mean what they literally say. I recall the time I went to a lumberyard to get some boards to make a brick-and-board bookshelf. I already had the bricks, and since I wanted a close match I asked the man for some boards that were twelve inches wide. He brought several from the back room and returned for more, during which time I picked up a loose ruler and discovered the boards were only about 11¼ inches wide.

When the man showed up again I said I wanted boards that were twelve inches wide, and he said "Those are twelve-inch boards." I said they weren't, and he then related that twelve-inch boards weren't really twelve inches wide, but they called them that, anyway. Everybody around lumberyards knows that! And you can't get boards that are actually twelve inches wide, because boards come only in standard sizes—such as twelve-inch! I took that size home because I wanted the bookshelf, and they were the closest I could get.

There is a reason for that literal falsity. Whether it deserves acceptance I don't know, but at least it deserves to be heard. The lumbermen start with raw lumber which they saw to twelve inches, and the planing process then removes more wood to smooth down the surface. That is what gets the width down around 11¼. So there is a reason for referring to the result as a twelve-inch board, and the practice probably wasn't originated with any intention of deceiving or even accidentally misinforming. It began at a time when the customers at sawmills were mostly quite conversant with the nature of the business. They understood what they were going to get. It was only much later that folks began showing up who did not understand.

So there's a reason for what happened, but that doesn't necessarily justify continuing a name which is literally false. It's curious how naming practices just happen to work out so the customer gets less than what is literally stated. The only exception I know is the baker's dozen, and that happened in the guild days before caveat emptor[29] when the law controlling falsity was so strict that bakers packed a thirteenth item for safety. The baker who counted one short by occasional accident would still be supplying twelve and would avoid serious penalties. His "dozen" was thus a literally false name whose falsity favored the buyer in order to protect the seller.

But caveat emptor arrived, and the penalties were systematically weakened or eliminated. So it's no surprise that today's literally false names always favor the seller. McDonald's "quarter-pound hamburger" is a recent case in point. The company advertises the hamburger by that specific name, and a Nassau (N.Y.) County official said it wasn't so. His inspectors checked 150 McDonald's outlets in the county and found the hamburgers averaging 3 7/8 ounces. A spokesman at company headquarters quickly came up with what we might call a "lumberyard explanation." He said McDonald's weighs the hamburgers before they're cooked, and they lose weight during the cooking.

Both the lumbermen and the hamburgermen, forced to work with items which begin at one size and end at another, feel perfectly justified in choosing for a name the size which the customer doesn't get. Everyone, after all, is supposed to know those things, aren't they? As a matter of fact, they're not, said Nassau County, and charged McDonald's on eight counts of false advertising.[30] Shortly thereafter, the company's television commercials for the "quarter-pounder" began including the legend "Pre-cooked weight one-quarter pound" superimposed over the visual representation.

Real problems develop over what people *should* know, as contrasted to what they do know. People probably should know meat loses weight when cooked, but the charge against McDonald's assumed they should not be expected to understand that the weight advertised was the pre-cooked amount. If they thought they would get four ounces of meat, post-cooking, then that is what they ought to get.

Here's another example to test your opinion against. A woman complained to Virginia Knauer that she bought a nine-inch pie and found the true diameter was only 7 3/4 inches. The explanation was that industry practice includes the rim of the pan in determining the stated size![31] Did you know that? *Should* you know that?

The answer lies in the fact of usage. I rather suspect McDonald's usage and the piemaker's usage are by no means widely understood by the public. In the lumber business, on the other hand, literally misdescribed twelve-inch boards have been sold by the millions to buyers who typically know what to expect. This can happen because the misdescribed board is functionally equivalent to the one which the name literally indicates. By contrast, the smaller hamburger or pie is not equivalent.

Let me describe another example where a misdescribed item could not be functionally equivalent. I once had a bathtub installed which was fifty-eight inches long. To put up the shower rod, the plumber attached metal holders on the walls at either end of the tub. The space between the outer reaches of these was fifty-seven inches, to be filled by an expandable rod which would be temporarily compressed to a shorter length, placed between the holders, and allowed to stretch to fifty-eight inches to be suspended firmly in place. To get a rod of the proper size the plumber cut off a portion of a longer one, and inadvertently he cut it so that its fully expanded length was less than fifty-seven inches. It could not be suspended between the holders, and he had to obtain another at his own expense.

This case differs from the twelve-inch boards because there was no reasonable way the plumber could have handed me the ruined shower rod and said "Here's a fifty-eight-inch rod." A rod only slightly shorter was strictly nonequivalent functionally, so misnaming the difference would be unfair. On the other hand, people who use lumber find normally that the 11¼ inch board is functionally the same as one of precisely twelve inches, because they use building methods which allow widths to vary within that range without affecting the finished job. The builder gets exactly what he bargained for because he knows this, and therefore a common usage develops in which the misdescription has no deceptive impact.

It has no deceptive impact on those in the trade, that is. You might feel that my personal situation was different because I was not in the trade, and because I wanted the boards for a purpose which was untypical. My bookshelf plan called for a matching of sizes close enough that the bricks and boards would not be noticeably apart in their dimensions. My situation also was different because I had stated clearly to the man that "I would like some boards which are twelve inches wide." I didn't use the name, "twelve-inch boards"; I used a description which the man incorrectly interpreted as a label. On these grounds I may have had a case if I had bought the boards without discovering the difference. Perhaps someone should take such a case to court, because the public would benefit if sellers ceased referring to twelve-inch boards (and Roquefort dressing) in their representations to the public.

You'll be glad to know, however, that everything turned out just fine with my bookshelf project. When I got home with my boards I found my twelve-inch bricks weren't twelve inches, either!

Mock-ups

Another benign (because tightly regulated) form of false puffery is the mock-up, associated most often with the visual media of TV commercials and photographs. You make a mock-up by artificially altering your product in order to get a good picture of it. TV cameras cannot photograph a dish of ice cream, because it melts almost instantly under the hot studio lights. So technicians substitute mashed potatoes, and in the finished commercial the product looks just like ice cream.

This practice is acceptable legally where you cannot get your picture otherwise. Shampoo or soap suds are used to form the head on beer because natural heads won't stay fluffy long enough. Wine is used for coffee because filming gives coffee a murky color, less attractive than what the naked eye sees. Similar problems of appearance occur with orange juice and iced tea. And while it's not a problem with today's color cameras, blue sheets and towels and shirts were substituted for white in the days of black-and-white TV, because white threw a haze ("halo") over other objects. All such arrangements puff the product falsely and therefore deceive, but the law calls them nondeceptive.[32]

I find it appropriate to agree generally with such rulings, because the values which mock-ups may add deceptively to the product are not especially likely to attract customers. Few people care to eat ice cream under hot studio lights anyway, so implying it can be done adds no particular enticement. Besides, the mock-up contributes in many ways to *removing* deception rather than producing it. It is the only way certain perfectly true and nondeceptive representations about a product's features can be made. It is *technically required falsity*, something which cannot be said for the other types of falsity we have examined.

Still, the existence of mock-ups produces problems for the consumer similar to those produced by other forms of puffery. The custom of altering before photographing has invited abuse by encouraging ad men to devise illustrations in which the consumer perceives the product as having qualities it truthfully lacks. The Aluminum Company of America[33] did this in a TV demonstration which contrasted "New Super-Strength Alcoa Wrap" with a brand of "ordinary" aluminum foil, both wrapped around hams. The foils were said to have been wrapped and unwrapped a number of times, resulting in the "ordinary" foil being wrinkled and torn and its ham being dried out. The Alcoa Wrap had held up perfectly, and the ham inside it was shown to be fresh.

Was anything wrong with this demonstration? Only the fact that the "ordinary" foil was deliberately torn before filming, and the ham it "protected" was already less fresh than the other at the time they were first wrapped. Had a freshness test genuinely been conducted and Alcoa Wrap found superior, the alterations might have been defended as simply the reenacting in a studio of something which truthfully happened elsewhere. It's conceivable that a test couldn't be conducted in a studio and that pictures couldn't be taken in a laboratory, thus necessitating an artificial reconstruction. But in this case there had been no prior test and the mock-up was a construction, not a reconstruction.

In Colgate-Palmolive's "invisible shield" commercial,[34] objects thrown toward the announcer were deflected, just before hitting him, by a sheet of scarcely visible glass. The announcer implied that Colgate Dental Cream's protection was similar in fighting tooth decay. If the toothpaste's effectiveness was precisely similar, meaning that no harmful substances can reach the teeth, then the mock-up would be defensible as a demonstration device, illustrating by analogy a process which could not be illustrated literally. The truth, however, was that the implication was false; the use of Colgate could not guarantee that decay will never happen.

On behalf of Blue Bonnet margarine,[35] TV commercial makers devised something called "Flavor Gems," which were drops of moisture shown glistening on the surface of Blue Bonnet but not on butter nor on another margarine. The Flavor Gems were offered as the reason why Blue Bonnet tasted more like butter than other margarines. They might have illustrated by analogy some characteristic of Blue Bonnet which could not be shown on film otherwise. But in fact these drops of liquid, applied by a prop man and magnified, stood truthfully for nothing but themselves. Even if Blue Bonnet did taste more like butter than other margarines, it could not have been because of the Flavor Gems or anything they stood for.

When Libby-Owens-Ford Glass Company[36] wanted to demonstrate the superiority of its automobile safety glass, it smeared a competing brand with streaks of vaseline to create distortion, then photographed it at oblique camera angles to enhance the effect. The distortionless marvels of the company's own glass were "shown" by taking photographs with the windows rolled down.

Carter Products[37] promoted its Rise shaving cream with a mock-up which was equally fair to poor old Brand X. A man was shown shaving with an "ordinary" lather which dried out quickly after application. He then switched to Rise and demonstrated how it fulfilled its slogan, "Stays Moist and Creamy." Unbeknownst to the TV audience, the substance he used on the first try was not a competing brand nor a shaving cream at all. It was a preparation specially designed to come out of the aerosol can in a big attractive fluff and then disappear almost immediately.

As with literally misdescriptive names, mock-ups which deceive the public have been carefully discriminated by the law from those which do not. There is no sign of any systematic permissiveness which would recognize mock-ups generally as immune from liability. The FTC's actions, in fact, have come closer to blanket condemnation than to blanket immunity. All the commercials just mentioned have been stopped by the Commission, and the industry has been severely warned of the limits beyond which it may not go.

The case most responsible for this legal stance is that of the "great sandpaper shave." Colgate-Palmolive's Rapid Shave shaving cream was shown enabling a blade razor to slice the grains of sand from a piece of sandpaper just as easily as you please. It was "apply . . . soak . . . and off in a stroke," the commercial said, and it was entirely phony, false, and deceptive. Loose grains of sand sprinkled over plexiglas were what was being shaved. The FTC's interest in the commercial developed when numerous complaints arrived from people who said they couldn't shave sandpaper the way they saw in the ad. The Commission agreed it couldn't be done, and accordingly moved against Colgate in 1961.[38] But Colgate turned the matter into one of the most heavily contested advertising cases on record by maintaining that the demonstration constituted a legitimate mock-up.

You *could* shave sandpaper, the company said, if it were a fine grade with quite small grains. But fine sandpaper couldn't be photographed for TV because it would look on the screen like smooth paper, which would cost the demonstration its credibility. Coarse sandpaper would look like sandpaper, all right, but Colgate conceded it couldn't be shaved. The only thing to do therefore, it said, in order to illustrate the legitimate fact of shaving sandpaper, was to do the test with fine sandpaper but illustrate it with a mock-up depicting the coarse variety.

That may have made a satisfactory argument if certain other facts had not also been true. For one thing, sandpaper could be shaved by a blade only after much more prolonged soaking than appeared to be implied by the phrase "apply . . . soak . . . and off in a stroke." At the FTC hearing Colgate's attorneys cited the dictionary meaning of "soak" to be "wet thoroughly, saturate," which they said implied an extensive period of time. But such argument was drastically undercut by the accompanying phrase "off in a stroke" and the fact that shaving followed application of Rapid Shave almost instantly in the commercial. (The speed-up might be defended as another mock-up, necessary when a commercial can take no more than a minute, but such speed-ups today are permitted by the law only when accompanied by phrases such as

"Elapsed time: ten minutes") An even more significant additional feature of the Rapid Shave ad was the implication to the audience that it was seeing an actual demonstration. Ice cream ads utilizing a mashed potato mock-up typically do not emphasize to the viewer that he is actually seeing ice cream. But the Rapid Shave commercial implied not only that the demonstration was true but that it was being seen actually happening.

With this evidence the FTC might have called the mock-up defense improper simply because the mock-up was implying the occurrence of something which had not actually happened. But the Commission, shockingly to the industry, made a ruling far more restrictive than that. *All* mock-ups were unlawful unless disclosed, it declared, because they showed the viewer something which was not so. Undisclosed substitution of plexiglas for sandpaper would be unlawful *even if* the sandpaper could be shaved easily, because the viewer thought he was seeing something which in fact he was not. Let there be, accordingly, no more shampoo heads on glasses of beer, no more colored water substituting for iced tea, no more mock-ups at all. The Commission was calling for utter elimination of this entire category of misrepresentation.

In *Colgate v. FTC* of 1962,[39] the First Circuit Court of Appeals disagreed with this extreme view. What could be wrong with undisclosed mock-ups, it asked, which merely involved the product's appearance, as in the mashed-potatoes-for-ice-cream switch? Moreover, what could be wrong with undisclosed mock-ups which also depicted the product's performance, so long as that performance was accurately shown? Shouldn't the only thing prohibited, the court said, be the mock-up which gives an inaccurate depiction? The Rapid Shave commercial was an example of the latter and thus the court agreed with the FTC on that specific decision. But the court sent back the Commission's cease and desist order for rewriting to correct the points of disagreement about the general rule.

The FTC made an attempt at reformulating the rule,[40]

and the First Circuit again rejected it.[41] The Commission then took its case to the Supreme Court, where the determinative decision about mock-ups finally was made. In *FTC v. Colgate* of 1965,[42] three questions were involved:

(1) Were undisclosed mock-ups of mere appearance acceptable? The FTC had said no; the court of appeals had said yes.

(2) Were undisclosed mock-ups demonstrating true performance acceptable? The FTC had said no; the court of appeals had said yes.

(3) Was the Rapid Shave undisclosed mock-up acceptable? The FTC and the court of appeals both had said no, the court of appeals using the grounds that the mock-up depicted an untrue performance.

The Supreme Court ruled in favor of the appeals court on the first question and in favor of the FTC on the second. On the third, it ruled the Rapid Shave mock-up was unlawful because the commercial had implied the actual seeing of a demonstration and not just because the performance supposedly demonstrated was false. Even if the performance illustrated in the mocked-up demonstration had been true, the Supreme Court said, the undisclosed use of a mock-up would be deceptive because of the audience's belief that it was actually seeing such performance in the commercial.

The operative rule, then, is that undisclosed mock-ups are acceptable only where no value is placed on the idea that the viewer is actually seeing what appears to be shown. If the mocked-up appearance is presented without fanfare, without an accompanying claim that what appears to be so is actually being seen, the mock-up is acceptable for use without disclosure. But if the appearance is presented with fanfare, with the implication that you're seeing something real when you're not, then the mock-up is illegal unless disclosed.

This distinction presumably is clear enough to the

regulators, but I saw an indication that it had not trickled down to the public. Ed McMahon had just finished a Smucker's commercial on a 1966 Tonight Show segment when Johnny Carson asked him "How long will it take to melt?"[43] The commercial was done live in the studio for Smucker's butterscotch topping, which Ed had shown poured over a bowl of ice cream. "It depends on the temperature of the room," said McMahon without spilling the beans. But Carson persisted with, "You made it and you were talking about how wonderful it was. It does look wonderful on television." McMahon finally admitted the "ice cream" was a vegetable spread used for cooking, which prompted Carson to harangue: "There ought to be a certain amount of honesty." He went on to say, "When they show that woman cleaning the floor and say, 'One swipe to it,' did you ever see that floor? It's the filthiest thing you have ever seen and they go right through. . . . They put graphite on the floor, powdered graphite . . . . I don't think that's fair."

Johnny was right in his comments about the graphite, but was unfair to Smucker's when he mixed the two examples together. The floor cleaning portrayed an utterly phony demonstration, while the Smucker's ad merely showed the ice cream without comment. It wasn't even an ice cream ad but a butterscotch topping ad, which removed the mock-up further than usual from illegality. The discrimination between legal and illegal mock-ups apparently still needs to be learned by many laymen.

That the discrimination has been learned by the industry, and has soundly affected its actions, is illustrated by the memory of a friend of mine for a demonstration he rigged up about fifteen years ago. As advertising manager for a chemical company, he had the job of showing the effectiveness of a chemical designed to retain the natural color of meat placed on display in stores. Many meats when sliced and exposed to fluorescent lights will oxidize and take on a gray discoloration after a short period, which ends their sales life well in advance of the time they lose any actual freshness. The chemical, when included in the curing process, slows down this oxidation and retains the meat's natural color. Some consumers may regard that as an undesirable mock-up in itself, but I am inclined to call it OK so long as the meat remains acceptable in other respects.

When my friend went to the photo studio to make a comparison shot, he was dismayed to find the treated meat turning gray, matching the untreated piece, almost immediately under the hot lights. The chemical could keep meat red under store conditions, but not under these. What could he do to get a picture? He could run to the nearest drug store, buy some mercurochrome, and daub it on the chemically treated meat. Without a second thought he did exactly that and got the picture he wanted.

My friend's mock-up was legal at the time he used it, but in retrospect he finds it amazing to recall that the question of legality or illegality never pierced his consciousness in that pre-Rapid Shave age of innocence. Today he would still conjure up such ideas as the mercurochrome gimmick, but he wouldn't act on them without consulting the company's lawyer first. Caution has become the primary rule where mock-ups are concerned. Ad agency creative experts who never talked to lawyers in their life are learning to curb their instincts until the legal beagle says OK.

One agency, doing a cleanser commercial in which a bathtub ring was shown being scrubbed away, grew frustrated over the fact that the ring had to be replaced for each of many re-takes.[44] There was no question the cleanser could do the job, so the producer wondered why a prop man couldn't just whisk a new ring onto the tub each time with some water-soluble spray paint. No, said the lawyer, if we're going to demonstrate removal of a bathtub ring, it's got to be the genuine thing. The public has got to see what we're saying they're seeing. So some poor fellow on the production crew was recruited to take half a dozen baths that day while expensive cameras and cameramen stood around waiting for him to whip up yet another batch of dirty suds. An agency executive later asked an FTC official if all that tub time was necessary, or did he think the agency's lawyer was just running scared. The FTC man said he would have given the same advice the lawyer had.

Another recent victim of mock-up worries is that venerable figurehead of General Mills, the famous Betty Crocker. Mock-ups usually involve pictures of products, but Betty's an exception. Thousands of women yearly write her letters and get answers with her signature affixed. Someone else at General Mills must be the letterwriter, because Betty Crocker is an absolute lie and always has been. She was invented in 1936, and for most of her life the company undoubtedly worried no more about her fictional existence than my friend did about his mercurochrome caper. But the board of directors must have been jolted in the middle of 1973 when they saw a newspaper story headlined "Betty Crocker is a lie—so is Aunt Jemima."[45] The story implied no legal charges against those unreal ladies, but suggested that consumers are wondering these days about practices which never brought a murmur in times past. A spokesman for General Mills thought it was still unimportant, however; he claimed it wasn't the company's fault that women insist on believing in Betty Crocker.

Spurred by such sellerist attitudes, mock-up problems have continued in the 1970s. The rules may be tightened, but some advertisers can't resist the temptation to test their bounds. Campbell Soup Co., for example, put so many marbles into its bowl of vegetable soup that it created a deceptive practice out of something which might have been perfectly legitimate. Campbell's problem was that showing the solid ingredients is vital, but when the soup stands still the solids settle to the bottom of the bowl and the resulting photograph shows nothing but the broth. The solution adopted was to place marbles in the bottom of the bowl before pouring in the soup. This would cause the solid ingredients to poke above the surface where they would appear attractively in the photograph. So far so good—it was a legitimate mock-up because it would show the product only as it really was.

What happened, however, was that the mock-up got out of hand. The executive in charge of marbles put so many of them into the bowl that the photographed soup displayed a far greater proportion of solid ingredients than Campbell's vegetable soup actually has. The result was a 1970 FTC-imposed agreement in which the company consented to avoid such practices in the future.[46]

Another 1970 mock-up case involved a Borden's ad in which Kava instant coffee was "shown" to have far less acidity than other brands.[47] A needle swung far to the left-hand side of a scale to show Kava's low acidity and far to the right to show the others' high acidity. Although the difference was true, the FTC was concerned that the portion of the acidity scale shown on the screen was only a small part of the total scale. It was as if a household thermometer, typically about ten inches high and calibrated from 120 degrees to -50 degrees, was revised to show a range of only 70 to 75 degrees in the same ten inches. On such a thermometer a temperature drop of two or three degrees would look like a mammoth change, but would really be insignificant.

Most citizens would understand, of course, that there was something unusual about such a household thermometer. But the same citizens would not likely know that the top and bottom ends had been chopped off the unfamiliar acidity scale. Therefore, said the FTC, the Kava ad was deceptive because the over-exaggeration of the true difference amounted to misrepresentation. The case demonstrated the relationship of mock-ups and puffery, showing that puffing exaggerations may be made not just with words but also with rigged demonstrations.

In other mock-ups attacked by the FTC, a demonstration showing Black Flag bug killer as superior to Raid was found to have been done by using a strain of roaches which had developed an immunity to one of Raid's critical ingredients. Typical American household roaches do not have such immunity.[48] When Easy-On starch and a competitor were sprinkled onto white shirts and an iron applied, the other starch scorched and Easy-On did not. The reason, the FTC said, was because the iron was superheated, again a situation which does not typically occur.[49] Easy Off's superiority over another window cleaner was "shown" in a demonstration in which the other brand's directions for use were not followed.[50] In "before" and "after" pictures, Sudden Change facial lotion was shown to conceal lines, wrinkles, and puffs and improve overall appearance. In the "after" picture, however, the woman was wearing not only Sudden Change but also eye liner, eye shadow, lipstick, cream and powder, complexion base, and compact powder.[51] Hot Wheels and Johnny Lightning racing cars were "shown" traveling at swift speeds by the use of camera angles which greatly exaggerated actual performance.[52] Dancerina doll appeared in mocked-up ads which "showed" it walking and dancing on its own; in reality the doll could stay up only with human assistance.[53] Mickey Spillane took a shower with Dove soap in a Lifebuoy commercial because he couldn't get the Lifebuoy to lather enough.[54]

As in other areas, the FTC has committed some mistakes on mock-ups. It mistakenly charged Zerex with misrepresentation in a can-stabbing demonstration in which a container of the product was pierced with a sharp instrument. The anti-freeze began to flow out but its sealing qualities quickly closed the hole, just as it would do, the commercial implied, in an automobile radiator. The FTC complained that the pressure and other conditions in the punctured can mock-up were not similar to the conditions inside a radiator and therefore misrepresented Zerex's ability to stop leaks. It's obvious that the conditions were different in some senses, but apparently they were similar by analogy. FTC later withdrew the charge and conceded that the demonstration did not misrepresent Zerex's performance.[55]

To summarize our discussion of mock-ups, we have

found legal attitudes very similar to those applying to literally misdescriptive names. The law has reflected the consumerism movement strongly in handling mock-ups, refusing to permit the widespread development of a category of misrepresentations declared immune from liability on an indiscriminate basis. Advertisers seem to keep on introducing mock-ups which deceive, but the law has shown no systematic tendency to accept them as legal—quite the opposite! One probable reason for this type of handling is that the mock-up is a new phenomenon, occurring in any volume only since television began and thus escaping the sellerist interpretations of the age of caveat emptor.

The handling of mock-ups and literally misdescriptive names shows that the law is fully capable of testing false representations for possible deceptive potential. The fact that it does so vigorously in these areas only serves to highlight the contrasting way in which it glosses over the many cases of puffery, obvious falsity, and social-psychological misrepresentations which deceive. There is no really acceptable reason for taking such differing approaches to the various subcategories of what ought to be a unified law of misrepresentation. If the law can recognize the deception in two kinds of puffery, it can surely recognize the deception in others as well.

16

And It's Not Trivial

THE STORY of puffery in its many forms is now told. I have drawn my conclusion that it is deceptive and have attempted to back up that claim with evidence and reasoning. I have described the law as systematically avoiding the discovery of much of puffery's deception and have indicated that there appears to be no acceptable reason why such discovery should not be made.

A task that remains is to deal with the recalcitrant reader who thinks eliminating deception is not very important. The defenders of sellerism are a tough lot, as anyone must be who founds a career on propping up an outmoded practice whose fate was knelled long ago. They will defend caveat emptor to the end, and their first line of defense, as we saw at the beginning of this book, is the argument that puffery is merely false and not deceptive. I hope we have demolished that argument by this time and have forced the concession that puffery's false representations typically *do* deceive. For sellerism's partisans, however, the loss of one line of defense means only a falling back to the next, which yields a new position: Puffery deceives, but so what?

I must make the grudging concession that this second line of trenches is harder to hurdle than the first. An extreme consumerist viewpoint would attempt to handle it by insisting that unregulated deception is bad per se, but such an argument suffers from its unwillingness to examine puffery's actual effects. To say that deception is bad per se is no less dogmatic than saying that puffery is nondeceptive per se. Thus the consumerist who takes that position is making the same mistake of nondiscrimination which I have accused the law of making. I have said the law should look and see whether puffery deceives, and it is only consistent to say as well that all concerned should look and see whether puffery's deception is important.

Deception under FTC practice is not illegal unless it is material, affecting the consumer's decision,[1] and substantial, affecting many such decisions.[2] Some deception is not material or not substantial, and so is not illegal. A much better consumerist position, therefore, would be to concede that deception comes in varying degrees of importance, and then go on, as I will do here, to argue that most deception is in fact very material and very substantial.

I have found three arguments which appear to support the sellerist counter-position that puffery's deception is neither material nor substantial. One is that nobody talks much in public about puffery, not sellers, not consumers, not consumerists, not regulators. I don't think that really supports the sellerist position more than superficially, but I have to concede it is a fact. Except for myself and Milton Handler and then-FTC Commissioner Mary Gardiner Jones, whose curiosities have done much to provoke my own, no one has found puffery a very compelling topic of public conversation. Something that matters ought normally to be something that's discussed, but puffery has been the recipient instead of a good deal of silence. Contrary to the weather, everybody does it and nobody talks about it.

A second argument that puffery's deception cannot be very great is that it is typically not an absolute deception. By absolute I mean that the consumer is promised some specific thing with utter clarity and finds that expected promise directly negated. Straight literal falsity deceives in this way. For example, the claim "Buttermilk cures cancer" makes a very specific promise, and buttermilk provides absolutely nothing toward fulfilling that promise. Puffery typically deceives to a far lesser degree than that. The puff is taken to mean something less than the literal ultimate, and the puffed product gives sufficient satisfaction that the user never concludes that the vague promise has been denied. No one precisely expects what "You'll meet the nicest people on a Honda" literally promises; nobody but a few wierdos would think that. But the performance of the Honda never specifically contradicts what they think *has* been promised. The effect can always happen tomorrow, after all. Therefore, the argument goes, any deception produced by puffery is really quite innocuous.

This argument is a good one which cannot be ignored. I disagree with the conclusion that the resulting deception is insignificant, but I must concede the point that puffery deceives subtly and results, when believed, in far less harm than literally false representations.

The third argument is that consumers themselves bear great responsibility for any deception associated with puffery. It is their own fault if they are deceived; they deceive themselves. They believe what they want to believe even though they possess the capacity to know better. Deception occurs in conjunction with puffery, but not because of puffery. Therefore any deception associated with puffery cannot be illegal because the puff is not materially related to the harm which occurs. The argument continues, furthermore, that people *want* to be deceived; they deceive themselves not always inadvertently but sometimes purposely.

Again the argument is a good one. I disagree that it is

always true and believe instead that it serves often as a cover-up for damages definitely attributable to puffery. But I cannot dispute the notion that consumers do play a role themselves in producing what are loosely called communication effects.

In a fit of generosity toward the opposing side, I am going to describe an experience from a typical American life, my own, which confirms at least superficially all of these arguments that puffery is pretty innocent stuff. It's the story of my first job, a sales position in which I perpetrated puffery myself rather thoughtlessly, yet consciously. Though suffering some slight twinges from the lies I was telling, I observed with satisfaction that people's objections to them were few and insignificant. I eventually let my mind go to sleep on the point, confident in the realization that I was doing business in the accepted American way. Whether it serves to indict that way of life or not, my story will certainly confirm that the American public has generously taken puffery for granted.

It all happened when I sold hot dogs at Forbes Field in my hometown of Pittsburgh, Pennsylvania. They were called Red Hots—that was the puff. It was one hell of a puff, too, because those vague resemblances to food were about as cooled-off as the Pirates in their horrible Ralph Kiner-and-nobody-else stage. I must have loved baseball to get interested in that team! But I did—I wanted to see the games so badly I was even willing to work for the privilege when necessary.

I'd go out to the ball park with my twin brothers four hours before the game and crawl through the tiny gate off Bouquet Street where the players also entered. (Bending their heads to get in must have put the "Bucs" in the proper frame of mind for the day's losing effort.) We gave our social security numbers to the supervisor and were issued vendor's uniforms, the wrong size of shirt, trousers, and military-like cap, all garish-blue for easy spotting by the patrons. There was nothing to do four hours before the game, but we had to get there because jobs were on a first-come basis. So we explored the stands and learned where to sneak in, which eventually made the vendor's jobs unnecessary. Why work for admission when you can scale the right field wall and hide out in the football press box![3]

Two hours before gametime the gates opened and we vendors were assigned our products: scorecards, ice cream, souvenir bats (on Boys Day only), Red Hots, or soda pop, in severely descending order of attractiveness. The scorecards and ice cream, lightweight and with fast turnover, went to the veteran regulars on the staff. The really favored vendors got to sell scorecards before the game and through about the third inning, after which sales petered out and they switched to ice cream. Those guys carried off twenty or thirty bucks a game on a 10 percent commission basis. One of them lugged his ice cream case around screaming "It'll freeze your teeth and curl your hair, and make you feel like a millionaire." The son-of-a-gun was a millionaire himself compared to me because I never got scorecards or ice cream even once!

It was the seniority that did it, and the Preston brothers couldn't work regularly enough to get that. School was on for the first few weeks of the season, and then our devout mother wouldn't ever let us work on Sundays. Work! She wouldn't even let us go to the game at all. We couldn't even get out to that good old right field wall. I cry for those lost doubleheaders. People didn't just snack at double dips, they ate whole meals there—what a profit you could make!

But for us, no doubleheaders and no seniority. So when we worked we always got stuck with Red Hots or pop, which weighed so much and moved so slowly. The Red Hots had to be laboriously prepared: you put a roll in the napkin, a weiner in the roll, and mustard or catsup or both on the weiner. If you got mustard on the napkin you had to start all over. With the pop you had to stand around reciting what six flavors you had to every idiot who couldn't think to look in the bucket for himself. It slowed you down and kept your mind away from the game. With those items I never made much more than carfare home on the old yellowbird trolley lines.

I got souvenir bats once on Boys Day and cleaned up about nine dollars commission selling those little foot-long replicas for fifty cents each. I was so caught up in making money I even let myself miss some of the action on the field, which was sinfully contrary to my reason for being there in the first place. Most games I never missed a pitch. The fans were screaming for vendors, and I was hiding in the entryway where I could see the whole field but nobody could see me. One time my brothers carried this act to the notable extreme of seating themselves on the third tier, a tiny portion of the grandstand with one exclusive row of boxes sky-high. With so little traffic up there, these jokers figured they could help themselves to comfortable chairs and watch the game in peace and quiet. It was a hot day, so to avoid the supervisor they took off their blue shirts and caps and sat there half-naked, which was normal enough in ball parks although a mite less than chic in the costly sections. They hid their shirts under the seats along with their pop buckets, which soon contained nothing but melted ice and about twenty unsold bottles growing warmer by the minute. The boys enjoyed three glorious innings, but the supervisor spotted them on his first trip up. How many pairs of twins do you see around a ball park?

I began my career by selling pop, too, in those heavy pails of ice, but somehow graduated to the higher-priced Red Hots where I spent most of my time. To start the day I hefted a metal container against my tummy, straps high over the shoulders, and was sent out to one of several commissaries under the stands. I often got D Commissary, way out behind the upper deck in right field. The counterman there would lift a sack of weiners out of a tub of water, hold it over the biggest compartment in my box, cut the netting, and tumble in the weiners. Then came packages of rolls, cups with mustard and catsup, and napkins. I charged out into the stands and started yelling, "Here y'are, getcher Red Hots. Red Hots here."

And those Red Hots were never hot! They were never even warm. Every time I hollered "Get 'em while they're hot," I thought to myself, "Hell, these aren't hot at all." Customarily they were about the same temperature as the rest of the place. If the ice cream did freeze your teeth, the Red Hots wouldn't do a thing to unfreeze them. For night games, when they should have been warmest, they were just plain cold. While Bob Prince—he's still there—was telling the radio audience it was 48 degrees at Forbes Field that night, he might as well have said the hot dogs were 48 degrees right along with everything else.[4]

The only time my Red Hots were ever warm was when I got my first supply. The counterman poured in some hot water from the big vat to start me off. But that was when the gates opened, and there weren't enough fans around for the first hour to fill up the dugouts. By the time I made my first sale the steam had faded away, and it was downhill for the next nine innings. Never the ace salesman, I permitted no lousy weiners to interfere with the action on the field. The game was the thing, and the Hots had plenty of time to cool. I made sales between plays, as long as the bases weren't loaded or something, but even while glancing toward a customer I had my mind in the right place. I developed an acute sense of the pitcher's habits and the crowd sounds, so I'd know exactly when to look back to the field for the next pitch. Sometimes I was late (you get sloppy after somebody fouls off a few), but when I missed a pitch I developed an incredible ability to tell from the ring of the bat and the immediate crowd reaction just where the ball was going. Once in upper right field I heard Dick Stuart swing, and I threw my glance instantly to the scene above the scoreboard at the left field wall. A moment later the ball passed into view—beautiful!—on its way toward Honus Wagner's statue out in Schenley Park. The Red Hots, meanwhile, were turning cold and gray.

I know from personal experience that the last weiners

in each load were really cold, because I usually ate one or two of them. We got four packs of rolls on each re-load (I dodged under the stands for this between innings only), and each pack had exactly twelve rolls. But for some reason the weiner sacks had more than forty-eight, and there was nothing to do with the extras but pop them in your mouth. You could throw them at the umpire, which I have seen done, but they're so small nobody but your immediate audience will notice. If I'd had more rolls I could have sold the over-count and kept the entire sum (twenty cents, wow!), but I never had more rolls. So the only thing to do was eat those weiners, and I can tell you you haven't missed much if you've never eaten a cold dog with mustard, catsup, napkin, and no roll.

The name Red Hots is puffery because it exaggerates what you actually get—grossly! It's false, and I know it deceived people because I heard occasional complaints like "Hey, Red Hots, c'mon back here . . . ." One guy chased me under the stands with a half-eaten weiner, of which I said he couldn't get *all* his money back unless he gave me *all* the hot dog back. I got the supervisor to confirm this to him, but it made me miss half an inning. On sales after that I kept moving and tried to be at least a section away before they took their first bite.

So I know people weren't getting what they thought they'd get, yet I have to admit the whole situation tended to confirm, sort of, all the arguments mentioned above for why puffery's deception isn't important. People for the most part didn't complain about or even mention the matter—I can't deny it. Their silence doesn't disprove the existence of an annoying degree of deception, but it certainly doesn't help me prove it. It forces me into the complexities of explaining that people are bothered substantially by puffery even though they don't complain about it.

It's also true that the name "Red Hots" wasn't taken with absolute literalness. I don't know of course how the lady who thought Olde Frothingslosh's foam would be on the bottom might have responded. There's always somebody who'll believe anything. But generally speaking, nobody thought they were going to get something which was specifically red hot, and why would they want to, anyway? I believe they were deceived nonetheless, but I will have to argue the point while admitting from my own experience that puffery's deception is partial rather than absolute.

And then there's the matter of the public's own responsibility for deception. I can think of reasons why people might have known in advance that the Red Hots would be cold, the principal one being that no other kind was ever sold at Forbes Field. A promise never fulfilled bears no obligation when the person making the promise gives full evidence that he never intended to fulfill it! So goes the obvious falsity logic, and the customer is supposed to know and recognize it. Putting the matter another way, "Red Hots" was merely a label for an item which was for sale, served cold, at Forbes Field—the old literally misdescriptive name bit! Of course I don't accept that kind of logic, but I do have to acknowledge that most people at the ball park responded just as a person would who was accepting his own responsibility for what resulted—they got crummy hot dogs and they didn't complain.

The reader will have his own real-life experiences with puffery and will no doubt agree that people tend to treat it, at least overtly, as trivia. Just bring up the subject sometime, especially with sellers, and see how unaccustomed and unwilling people are to discuss the matter. I recall stopping one evening for dessert at a roadside stand I shall call Liz' Frozen Custard (the name is changed to protect the guilty). I was with my wife, my brother, his wife, and our menage of five small children. We got cones all around, and while licking mine I noticed a display sign on the glass front which showed the three sizes of frozen custard (small, medium, and large) accompanied by cones which also varied in size from small to large.

Probably I'm more sensitized than most people to this sort of thing, and so it occurred to me to glance around the family group to see whether our cones varied in size as the sign showed. With several sizes of people we had ordered all three sizes of custard, and it was evident that each of them was accompanied by the same cone—the small one. Trying to appear casual about it, I asked the countergirls if they realized they weren't dispensing cones as they appeared in the picture. No, they hadn't realized that. Well, why weren't they giving the larger cones with the larger sizes? They didn't know; they only had one size. Well, didn't they think they ought to sell their cones the way they advertised them? Maybe; don't know; tee hee; blank stare.

I was in the midst of further comment when suddenly the boss of the establishment crashed out the door and asked what it was all about. When I repeated my questions, he made it clear there was no way he was going to talk just casually about such a topic. One size of cone was good enough, he said; it would only be a bother to stock all three. Probably so, I said, because nobody would care about the cone as much as the custard. But why did he display the picture showing the three sizes? There was a pause and a grimace of disgust, so I went on to ask whether he ever thought about the fact that he was advertising three sizes. "Why should I bother to think about something so simple-minded," he grunted. It just didn't matter, he said, and as we jousted further I noticed my sister-in-law run and hide in the car because, as it turned out, she was embarrassed as hell over the whole incident.

The contrasts, I thought, were fascinating. The seller had attached no importance to a literally false representation and had probably never given it a moment's thought before our encounter. No doubt he was perfectly sincere about the picture's insignificance, and he was joined by my poor blushing sister-in-law in thinking it was quite worth forgetting. I didn't think it was worth forgetting because I believe all the problems described in this book start right there—with the seller and the buyer who take a casual attitude toward falsity. It was only a little falsity, but the little ones spawn the big ones. Accordingly, in what follows we will take issue with the arguments which conclude that puffery is trivial.

Puffery's Deception Is Trivial Because No One Discusses It

Although it's perfectly true that we hear little public comment about puffery, I believe this is for reasons which do not imply the topic is trivial. Let's begin by examining the sellers' and advertisers' silence, and then look at that of the consumers and consumerists.

No one should be surprised that the sellers keep quiet about puffery, because they have more to lose than to gain from mentioning it in public. The general social consensus that falsity is wrong is a factor strong enough to predict embarrassment if the subject comes up. We have suggested already that consumers are not likely to introduce the matter, but it is evident as well that the consumer would probably be critical of the topic if the seller introduced it.

Sellers generally would not care to enter public debate on such matters. Imagine a forum such as Face the Nation or David Susskind's public TV panel show in which representatives for sellers and consumers debated puffery. No seller would want to get into that bind; he knows he'll be hooted off the stage. Falsity may be legally OK, but ethically it seems wrong as can be. The consumerists will make the most of that.

Sellers in a public forum could not defend themselves the way they do in court. In court they state many things the public would not accept but which customarily do not reach the public's attention. The principal thing they state about puffery is that such claims are legal even though false. They argue first, naturally, that the claims aren't even false, but for safety's sake they add the claim that puffs are not illegal even if found by some unlikely chance to be false. We were only puffing, they will say, swearing their statements were only jokes not intended to induce consumer action.[5] The real joke is to think they were intended to achieve anything else, yet the FTC will accept such arguments often while the public hardly ever would. (In fairness, consumers sometimes go into court and swear they relied and had a right to rely on some claim upon which it would be ridiculous for anyone to rely.)

Sellers' explanations before the law result in many such assertions of the absurd. You should hear the defense dreamed up by the negative option people, the book and record club promotors who ship their members an item once a month unless the member specifically declines it. The phrase "negative option" means the basic choice the purchaser gets is to say "no," not to say "yes." In 1970 the FTC decided the practice might be injurious to consumers because it foisted numerous unwanted items on people who missed the option notice or forgot to return it or procrastinated until too late.

To answer these charges the Columbia Record Club hired Ernest van den Haag, a psychoanalyst, who coolly explained that such things as their own procrastination and forgetfulness were precisely why subscribers of such clubs found negative option attractive. They used the system to "outwit their own character traits," you see. People are uncomfortable when having to choose from a vast array of books or records such as might confront them at a store. They feel much better when the club makes the decision for them. With negative option the subscriber retains only a veto power, said van den Haag, which "symbolically relieves the subscriber of the burden of decision making." Yet it "does not actually deprive him of the power to make his own decisions."

In other testimony, however, Columbia estimated it would make only one sale per ten notices sent out if it switched to positive option, whereas it was pulling one out of every two under negative option. The club questioned its ability to survive if sales dropped that much. It appears that reducing the customer to nothing but veto power has an effect on his decisions which is a good bit more than "symbolic" for both himself and for the fate of the record and book clubs.[6]

A similarly startling defense arose in a case[7] where the FTC pondered the use of "corrective ads," ads in which a company must explicitly acknowledge and straighten out past claims which the Commission has found to be deceptive. The strategy behind corrective ads is that the Commission's usual remedy, stopping misrepresentations from continuing in the future, is not enough to prevent the deception of those consumers already exposed. Even though the misrepresentations appear no more, they will be remembered from past appearances and need therefore to be counteracted by the corrective message.

The Association of National Advertisers appeared before the FTC in this case[8] to make the amazing argument that the premise is wrong that ads have residual memory effects. There's no need for corrective ads, it said, because people don't remember the ads anyway. If the ANA could have put across this idea, it would have amounted to a strong case against the necessity for corrective ads. But what a blow it would have struck against the entire advertising industry! What good are ads which nobody remembers? "We hope," editorialized *Advertising Age*, "that ANA fails to prove this." It added: "One of the important rationales for the use of advertising has always been that it does have a residual effect, and that this effect is indeed substantial. A considerable amount of accumulated research has confirmed that this is in fact the case. If the ANA succeeds . . . the disenchantment of advertisers will undoubtedly inflict more pain on the advertising business than might be inflicted by the 'corrective orders' proposed by the FTC."[9]

Testifying against your own side is not ideal, but when your back's against the wall the name of the game is Try Anything. Another example of speaking out of both sides of one's mouth involves advertising man Jerry Della Femina. In his little book with the big title (*From Those Wonderful Folks Who Brought You Pearl Harbor*) he wrote

vigorously against the regulations ("censorship," he called
it) imposed on commercials by the National Association of
Broadcasters. "There is simply no reason for it," he ex-
claimed in the full righteousness of the First Amendment's
freedom of speech guarantees.[10] We then discover sometime after publication of the book that Della Femina,
Travisano, and Partners, the ad agency of which Mr. Della
Femina is president, has been alleged by the FTC to have
aided J. B. Williams Company in running the deceptive ads
for Vivarin which we examined in chapter 14.[11] No wonder our hero hates that odious censorship!

That is the way it is with sellers and the law. When
under fire they point solemnly to that ancient and friendly
body of sellerist law which is presumably as sacrosanct as
the tablets of Moses. Any attempt to accommodate these
laws to consumerism, they grimly assure the court, would
amount to a terrible distortion of their God-given rights.
They completely ignore the fact that the laws are not what
they are because they were God-given, but only because
they were twisted out of shape in earlier centuries by
judges who were just as anxious to serve sellerism then as
some consumerists are anxious to serve consumerism today.

But we were speaking of how much sellers will discuss
puffery in public. The above types of strategies may work
in court, but in public debate they wouldn't have a chance.
In debate the consumers would charge the sellers not with
illegality but with phoniness and lack of ethics. The defense of legality wouldn't work against that, because it's
irrelevant. That is why sellers are reluctant to talk about
puffery.

In 1972 a marketing class at the University of South
Carolina demonstrated this corporate reluctance when it
queried a number of companies about their advertising
claims.[12] One student asked the president of Avis Rent A
Car Systems, Winston V. Morrow, Jr., a number of questions, including "How does Avis try harder, and who do
they try harder than?" The student added, "I trust that

your company has this information at hand, since to make unsupported claims in advertising is clearly a form of deception." Mr. Morrow might have pointed out that unsupported claims are not deceptive under current law when they are puffs, but he apparently sensed such line of reasoning would not impress this particular inquirer. In a brusque and unsympathetic letter he answered only this about trying harder, "I don't propose to debate our motto with you."

Recently advertisers have begun to discuss puffery among themselves,[13] something they didn't do in earlier times. That is probably because puffery once was insignificant among the many privileges granted to sellers by a kindly law. In times past much literal falsity was legal, and a lot of the rest was allowed because the law just didn't get around to it. Literal falsity had the same immunity from the law as implied falsity, and since it had a greater potential for producing sales than implied falsity it naturally was more attractive. If a seller might puff with immunity but might also state factual falsehoods with immunity, he would choose the latter if he happened to be seeking the highest degree of persuasion and the lowest degree of liability simultaneously.

What would be the attraction in claiming "You can be sure if it's Westinghouse" if the company could legally make the false statement, "No Westinghouse appliance has ever broken down"? I have no knowledge that Westinghouse ever made the latter claim, but there was a time when companies could have made such false claims quite legally. Under such conditions puffery didn't matter as much. Its importance has developed only as the privileges for being literally false have been removed. Today these privileges are so much eliminated or reduced in scope that puffery's implied falsity has increased in importance proportionately.

Advertisers never discuss puffery among themselves as being false, of course, but only as being true. There is only one place where they will discuss it as false, and that is in court where they know it may save their necks. But false it is, and it survives in a time when the types of falsity available are being lessened. Since Westinghouse appliances do at times break down, it is illegal today to state that they don't, but it is still perfectly legal to say "You can be sure if it's Westinghouse." Such puffery is still immune from the law and is one of the most persuasive of the immune devices which remain. No wonder advertising officials are expressing more interest.

To summarize my comments in this section, the fact that sellers and advertisers don't discuss puffery publicly does not show it is a trivial matter to them. There are excellent reasons why they do not want to introduce such ideas for public consideration. Meanwhile, their increasing willingness to discuss puffery with regulators[14] and among themselves demonstrates full well that they find the topic quite the opposite of trivial.

As for consumers, consumerists, and regulators (outside of their hearings and court appearances), it is more difficult to explain the lack of public comment. Consumerists, in particular, talk *so much* about so many things these days that one would expect them to mention any topic which mattered to them in the least. Perhaps they are so busy attending to more literally false and potentially damaging representations that they have not yet found the time for the more subtle ones. Undoubtedly they are right to concentrate their efforts on those false representations which may endanger the consumer's safety or his health or even kill him. Ralph Nader's fight for automobile safety[15] and Senator Warren Magnuson's appeals for safe toys and flameproof clothing[16] come to mind. Were I a regulator or consumer activist I would spend not a minute on puffery if I thought sufficient time were not being devoted to things such as these.

It's my observation, however, that law and consumerism have now made the kind of strides in protecting against blatant literal falsity and clear physical dangers that should earn them the luxury of working on the more subtle deceptions. Attention to puffery makes sense only as long as this is true, and it now seems true. My conclusion, in other words, is that consumerists, consumers, and regulators have no excuse, particularly in the light of the sellers' obvious interest, for not digging into puffery firmly at this late date.

Perhaps it is because they are simply ignorant of how puffery deceives, thinking it to be innocent because it does not deceive blatantly. Perhaps their idea of deception is typified by the use of a claim such as "Contains no alcohol" to describe a product which contains alcohol. That sort of deception hits you right between the eyes, and that's not what puffery does. Puffery, as we will see next, is more subtle, less direct, less damaging . . . .

Puffery's Deception Is Trivial
Because It Does Not Deceive Absolutely

This claim, bluntly, is incorrect. Puffery deceives less than the maximum, but it still deceives materially and substantially. It implies false facts which affect purchasing decisions detrimentally for a substantial portion of the public. The fact that people don't complain about it does not prove otherwise.

Let's take a look at some examples we've seen earlier. If people wouldn't expect the Red Hots to be red hot, they would still expect something. Hot dogs which are at least warm are common to our experience and are what we customarily want and expect. It is only natural that a shout of "Red Hots" would give the hungry baseball fan the anticipation of getting something with a little steam rising from the bun. The claim implies that the product will be attractive, and when it's not the claim is deceptive and materially injurious to the consumer.

"Blatz is Milwaukee's finest beer" certainly deceives in the same way, even though it does not deceive absolutely. No one would think that all the world, including Blatz's competitors, universally affirms that Blatz is Milwaukee's best. But consumers, while not insisting on that ultimate literal meaning, must think the claim means something! They must think it means that more people than just the Blatz owners and employees think Blatz is the best. They must think there is some specific criterion which the product meets in order to merit the claim of "finest." The truth is that Blatz has offered no such criterion, and to the best of my knowledge none exists. Therefore the belief implied by the claim of "finest" is false and deceptive to the public, and materially so because it affects purchasing decisions negatively.

"You'll meet the nicest people on a Honda," I've already conceded, is not interpreted by people as an absolute guarantee that they'll make the greatest friends they could ever hope to make—or their money back. Of course they won't think that, and as a result the advertiser may insist there's no important element of deception in the claim. But why then does the advertiser use that sort of claim? Undoubtedly it's because he thinks the consumer will be inclined to accept *some* aspect of belief about the relationship between social satisfaction and Honda ownership. If the claim doesn't work it won't be used; if it's used it must be thought to be working. And if it works it must be because the consumer believes *to some extent* that the cycle company is guaranteeing to contribute *in some way* to his social life. His belief may be vague—he may not know exactly how he thinks the cycle will contribute—but he believes for a fact that it will.

And when the consumer believes any such thing he has been materially deceived, because the cycle company is guaranteeing no such thing whatever. There is a vast difference between an ad implying "We'll put you on the road" and one implying "We'll put you into the fun." The manufacturer can give you the physical, tangible product which he can guarantee will put you on the road. He can give you nothing which will guarantee you'll get into the fun. Yet he uses the social-psychological type of misrepresentation because the consumer will treat it to some extent as something guaranteed.

An insidious aspect of this sort of claim is that the consumer may never learn the implied guarantee is phony. If he gets on the road today but doesn't get into the fun, he figures the fun will come tomorrow. If it doesn't come tomorrow there's always another day. He never reaches the point where he knows it's not to be. Perhaps this explains why people don't complain about deception—they have to find out about it first, and the subtlety of puffery's deception helps prevent discovery. That is the magic in cosmetic advertising, which deals heavily in social guarantees yet probably plays an infinitesimal role in actual satisfactions. Cosmetics promise much, deliver nothing, and sell like hot cakes for years on end with the same customers. The public couldn't have discovered the deception if it keeps on buying like that.

Keeping the truth hidden is more critical to the cosmetics business than the motorcycle business because its sales consist of small purchases repeated frequently. If the consumer becomes disillusioned with his Honda he will already have afforded the company a good profit on an expensive item which was intended to last for quite a while. The company wouldn't have expected to make a re-sale very soon, anyway. In cosmetics, however, the initial purchase is a small matter, and profit expectations depend significantly upon a great volume of repeat purchases by the same individual. Under these conditions the falseness of the implied promise must be kept hidden through the course of its constant failures, or there will be no point in using it in the first place. The cosmetics people need that kind of concealment, and there is every reason to believe they get it.

The conclusion from such illustrations—and many more could be offered—can only be that puffery deceives the public materially and substantially and should be prohibited. If the law has not yet agreed it is probably because the regulators have not yet sufficiently adapted their thinking to encompass deception which is subtle and indirect rather than direct and absolute. The regulators are accustomed to asking what *specific* false claim is stated or implied to the consumer so that he believes it and is therefore deceived. They are accustomed to concluding that if no *specific* falsity can be definitely identified, then there is no deception in a legal sense.

In order to get action on puffery's deception, we must get the regulators out of that habit. With puffery the consumer usually does not believe some specific claim which is false, but he believe that there is *something* specific which must be true. With Blatz, for example, the consumer does not believe any precise claim about what "finest" means, but he believes it must mean something about fineness. He doesn't believe something specifically, but he specifically believes that there's something. And if in truth the term "finest" means nothing about fineness, then the implication that it means *something* should be regarded by the regulators as a specific falsity and charged as such. Admittedly it's a more vague charge than the regulator is accustomed to handling, but surely it's a sound enough criterion to work with.

Startlingly, there occurred in 1972 a solitary regulatory incident which confirms this line of thinking. The National Advertising Review Board found General Motors to be potentially deceptive in its use of a puffery claim consisting of the symbol "GM" and the phrase "Mark of Excellence" superimposed on a square resembling a small plaque.[17] The Review Board felt the claim's use would be acceptable only if restricted to employment as a company signature or trademark in the corner of a print ad or at the end of a broadcast commercial. But using the claim as a primary part of the company's sales story would be deceptive "in view of the recent spate of recalls of cars because of defects constituting possible safety hazards."

This decision amounted to an admission that "Mark of Excellence" meant something to consumers. It was considerably different from the usual ruling about a phrase so vague. For once, the regulators did not insist on knowing precisely what it would imply, but were content with knowing something it wouldn't imply. It wouldn't imply the sloppy workmanship that has resulted in recalls; it wouldn't imply the dangers to life and limb caused by defects not recalled. Whatever "Mark of Excellence" did mean, it certainly didn't mean those things.[18]

The decision was noteworthy because it used subtle means to interpret subtle deception. It's too bad it wasn't made by the FTC. The National Advertising Review Board is an industry self-regulating organization composed of fifty appointees from advertisers, ad agencies, and the public. Its decisions do not have the force of law and do not constitute legal precedents. Still the ruling was a step in a new direction and contributed strongly toward rejecting the idea that puffery's deception is trivial because it is not absolute.

Puffery's Deception Is Trivial
Because the Consumer Deceives Himself

That famous advertising executive, author, French chef, and chateau collector David Ogilvy once declared, in defiance of the motivation researchers' mounting evidence to the contrary, "The consumer isn't a moron, she is your wife."[19]

The comment was made with the realization that advertising's successes would be more respectable if its targets were more respectable. So we may be forgiven for wondering whether Ogilvy was merely performing a public relations version of a cover-up caper. "If David really believes that," said another prominent ad man, "how come he's got doves flying in and out of her windows and crowns popping onto her head . . . . I think he just believes it's what clients would like to hear."[20]

"Sometimes it seems," wrote another observer, "that the consumer is not only your wife, she's also a moron; and what's more so are you and the kids." If some advertising is moronic, he added, there's a strong suspicion that much of the public responds to it, else otherwise it would quickly disappear.[21]

I hate to agree with the latter observers, but I believe it is more correct to point out that consumers' responses are not always what the professional consumerists would like them to be. There are those who prefer to think that the bothersome effects of sales messages are exclusively produced by those who communicate them, but I simply cannot think that. I can't because I went to graduate school and had it drummed into me that communication is a two-way process. (That may seem funny, to be taught by a one-way process that communication is a two-way process, but that's what happened!) The theoretical articles and books I read were fairly complicated, but they can be summed up easily enough. They say it takes two to tango.[22]

The theory of how mass communication works didn't always say that. It once consisted solely of explaining how the communicator sent messages and got effects with a passive public which never acted but only reacted. The message content determined the recipient's response, and if that response was moronic it was no discredit to the recipient because he couldn't help what happened.

Today the theory of mass communication adds a whole opposite side to the picture, explaining how the public is active rather than passive toward communications. Citizens receiving mass media messages have their own ideas and insist on exerting them. Their responses may reflect the persuasion in the message, but they also reflect the responders' own considerable initiative. The result of such independence is exhibited frequently in the marketplace, where it upsets marketing plans right and left. You've probably read the popular criticisms about whether various products are really necessary—underarm deodorants, for example, not to mention the newer deodorants applied to more exotic bodily parts. Let's observe what happened when those deodorants were put on the market, along with the Edsel, duPont's Corfam shoes, and the midi skirt. All of these new products got lots of advertising, following which the people didn't buy the Edsel, didn't buy the Corfam shoes, and didn't buy the midi skirt.

But they did buy the deodorants! And they've shown terrific desires in recent years for things which haven't even been supported by huge ad campaigns—bicycles, for instance, ten-speed racing jobs. Could it be that people decided on their own initiative that they wanted those deodorants and those bicycles? Well, yes! And today's more sophisticated mass communication theory takes such initiative into account, explaining not only how the public reacts to messages, but also how the public's reactions and actions affect what messages the communicators send next. If the public likes something, they'll get more of the same. If the public is annoyed but doesn't complain, they'll still get more of the same. A mass media message doesn't just get effects; it's an effect itself. The evidence which proves this has piled up, and can't be denied.

And it means, alas, that puffery is caused in part by those innocent victims themselves, the consumers! They encourage it because they don't discourage it. The seller is the one who produces it, but the seller isn't entirely responsible for its existence because the consumer's tolerance and acceptance is necessary, too. It's not a popular view to offer the public, I'm afraid, but it would be absolutely unfair to claim otherwise.

My own sympathies remain with the consumer because I think the current rules allow the seller undue advantage, and because I think the current problems are largely the seller's fault. But I don't think they're *all* his fault. The blame must be placed in part upon the consumer himself. I said this once in a speech to a consumer education organization,[23] and some funny reactions occurred. All the representatives of industry thought it was great and came up afterward and enthused about how I'd said a lot that needed to be said. They mistakenly thought I was on their side just because I directed a portion of my criticism to the other side. The consumerists in the audience, meanwhile, were glum because they weren't used to going to consumer meetings and hearing consumers get blamed for anything at all. My speech was later printed in the official journal of the organization,[24] but the editor let it in only as a piece of opinion rather than a "real" article. He didn't think the notion of a two-way process of communication was very objective!

I give similar offense all the time in two courses I teach at the University of Wisconsin. In "Mass Communications for the Consumer" there are several sections of reading and discussion in which I criticize consumer communication in various ways, followed by a section in which I turn the tables and talk about the consumer's own responsibility for what goes wrong. Most of the students have come into the course with proconsumer, antibusiness attitudes, and you should see how they fuss when the accusing finger turns in their direction.

The same reaction happens in "Principles of Advertising," which I orient basically toward the industry viewpoint as part of the advertising major at the University. One of my brightest students, Mark Feiner, told me after the semester I hadn't done enough to make him enthusiastic about going into advertising. I had provided reasons for getting excited about the industry, he said, but I had also brought up criticisms which tended to deflate that excitement. I pointed out to Mark that his generation had grown up demanding us "establishment types" to "tell it like it is," yet here he was chiding me for doing exactly that. There are many excellent reasons why a student might go into advertising, but I feel on the whole it's best described as what Mark would call a mixed bag. So that's the way I tell it.

Moderate positions aren't easy to maintain within the emotionally charged setting in which the marketplace is disputed today. The atmosphere rewards advocates, not dispassionate analysts, which makes it difficult to advocate stricter regulation while conceding that the effects of sales representations could not happen without some degree of consent by consumers. I'm not really that much of a moderate, however, because I do not believe the two-way idea implies that consumers are *equally* responsible for what happens. The truth, more likely, is that they are only a little responsible and that their modest culpability should not be used to absolve the sellers from their larger share.

It is simply impossible to claim that the citizen sitting with his magazine or watching television has power in the communication chain equal to that of the seller who produces the advertisements in those media. The consuming public can have equal or greater power only in the aggregate, and there is no guarantee that any individual's purchasing decisions will ever be joined with those of other individuals so as to activate that aggregate. When it happens the effect can be strong, as when the American public spurned Detroit and made mass purchases of foreign compact cars. We have seen other examples where the public aggregated its power either to buy (deodorants, bicycles) or not to buy (Edsel, etc.). But in more typical marketplace maneuvering, the citizen's power is limited cruelly to a small voice and a few dollars against the giants. The idea that he bears some responsibility for his own actions can be understood without distortion only if it is understood within that context of pitiful inequality.

The idea that the consumer's responsibility renders puffery's deception trivial stands today as an out-dated leftover from the caveat emptor notion of equality of buyer and seller. This notion may have been sensible when it applied to two citizens trading a horse, but equality nowadays is a fiction which resides in the law only by ignoring the realities of the mass media age. The consumer's power today is only a fraction of the seller's, and his responsibility should be measured by that same fraction. If the law assesses both seller and consumer with responsibilities equivalent to power, there is no way in which the seller's responsibility for puffery's deception can be called trivial.

We cannot leave the topic of responsibility, however, without mentioning the intriguing idea that the consumer desires to be deceived. Principal advocate of this notion is Theodore Levitt,[25] who says most citizens actually crave seeing the world in a puffed-up state (a nondrug reference, although not inconsistent with some popular drug purposes): "Whether we are aware of it or not, we in effect expect and demand that advertising create these symbols for us to show us what life might be, to bring out the possibilities that we cannot see before our eyes, and screen out the stark reality in which we must live."

We positively want embellishment, Levitt says. We refuse to settle for "pure operating functionality" in products, and we reject products which reflect the drabness of life we see often enough in other things. We wish for unobtainable things, for "Why promise ourselves reality, which we already possess? What we want is what we do *not* possess."

Levitt concedes that much advertising deception is harmful, but argues that the issue is not to prevent distortion but to know which kinds of distortion we want. Eliminating puffery, presumably, would throw out the good with the bad: "The consumer suffers from an old dilemma. He wants 'truth,' but he also wants and needs the alleviating imagery and tantalizing promises of the advertiser and designer. Business is caught in the middle."

No doubt there is something to the viewpoint, but also a lot against it. Consumers want imagery which they can retain, and the consumer movement has made clear that no image will be alleviating beyond the moment when it is exploded by the deception it produces. The trouble with Levitt's comparison of advertising to poetry is that poetry is an end in itself while advertising is not. When one regards the Grecian urn of Keats (Levitt's example) one does not contemplate the image in one's mind and then go out and buy an urn on the basis of the representation.

In literature, in poetry, and in speechmaking, puffery is known as hyperbole and is understood to be the conveyor of feelings and emotions, not facts. It is intended to fill one with excitement, passion, patriotism, beauty, awe, a sense of duty. Hyperbole is the stuff of political candidates and pep rallies and love letters. It is accepted as a customary feature of such discourse with little discussion of the criticisms we have been citing of puffery. The slightest mention of such criticisms in connection with hyperbole would be awkwardly out of place, as the following "annotation" of a famous poem suggests.[26] The annotator says he did it in the manner of an FTC deceptive advertising review:

Half a league, half a league . . .
>   (Not correct; the distance of the charge was actually a mile and a half. A league is 2.4 miles—so half a league is 1.2 miles, not 1.5 miles. Statement should be changed.)

Half a league onward,
All in the valley of Death,
Rode the six hundred.
>   (Inaccurate; there were 607 men involved in the action at Balaclava. It should be so stated.)

"Forward the Light Brigade!
Charge for the guns," he said.
>   (Exact source of the quote is not precisely given. Lord Lucan, who is sometimes credited, denies authorship. Should not be quoted.)

(etc.)

The advertising man who pointed out the above added, "We'd suggest it be withdrawn from publication until such time as puffery, bordering on deception, can be eliminated. Same procedure is suggested for 'Old Ironsides,' 'Sheridan's Ride,' and other documents intended to incite patriotism without proper documentation."

But we are concerned here with puffery in the market, not hyperbole in art. When you accept the exaggerations and subjective opinions of hyperbole, the bargain you receive is not a tangible, physical object which you compare to what was claimed about it. In the marketplace you *do* get a physical object, and the factual similarity of that object to the claims made or implied becomes significant. You expect the product the seller says you will get. Sellers may say puffery is only fanciful and not intended to represent the product, but we have seen reason enough to believe that every element of reference they make to the product is put there for the purpose of representing it.

The law, therefore, should recognize the difference between puffery and hyperbole and not accept puffery as mere consumer-inspired embellishment. Some credence should be given to the notion that eliminating puffery would eliminate something desirable, but the notion should not be expanded into the belief that any deception which puffery produces will therefore be trivial. On the contrary, embellishment lovers should realize the consumer's appreciation of puffery's embellishment will be destroyed at the moment he realizes the puffery is deceptive. We can't say, therefore, that puffery's embellishment renders its deception trivial, because the reverse in fact is true. This makes getting the deception out of puffery more important rather than less, and is my final way of rejecting the idea that puffery's deception is trivial.

Conclusion

In this chapter I have aired the idea that puffery doesn't deceive enough to be important. The conclusion is that it deceives considerably despite the intriguing facts that (1) it isn't discussed much, (2) it doesn't deceive in the absolute way that literal falsity does, and (3) the consumer is responsible to some extent for his own deception.

There are other problems with puffery, too, in addition to its deceptiveness. In the final chapter we will examine these problems in order to build further the case that false puffery should be eliminated from the American marketplace.

17

Puff, Your
Magic's Draggin'

PUFFERY WOULD be bad enough if it merely deceived. I have concentrated on its deception because that is its worst offense, and possibly the only one which may be remedied by legal means.[1] But the bill of particulars contains several other ways by which puffery makes trouble. We will wind up this book by identifying these other offenses and showing how they add to the need for tighter control of false representations. They will be discussed in turn as consumers' problems, sellers' and advertisers' problems, and the law's problems. A concluding section will describe some recent modest movements of the market which have pointed it toward the reforms urged in this book.

Consumers' Problems

Puffery troubles consumers primarily by deceiving them, but also by encouraging the growth of two other characteristics of sales representations. The first is the prevalence of various nonpuffing misrepresentations which sellers feel they can get away with by utilizing the protective *loophole* which the puffery rule provides. The second is the *loss of information* which the use of puffery helps produce.

Puffery's role as a legal loophole is owed to the fact that the borderline between it and various types of nonpuffing falsity is very difficult to draw. This lets the advertiser or salesman use it as a protective umbrella to shelter practices he might not otherwise be able to defend. His message is attacked as deceptive, and he shrugs it off with "I was only puffing" and sometimes gets away with it. Without this prepared position to fall back on, the advertiser might not risk the message in the first place. But with the probability of immunity appearing high, he goes ahead with it. The puffery rule, in other words, lets him get away not only with puffery but also with misrepresentations which more vigorous enforcement would call illegal. The result can be a snowballing process in which one deception breeds another. Competitors, after all, must stay competitive.

Even when the advertiser gets caught at this he causes the public trouble which might have been avoided by withholding the temptation in the first place. The Rapid Shave promotors, for example, were probably encouraged by the puffery loophole to go ahead with their famous sandpaper demonstration.[2] In the end they failed with their puffery defense, but without the hopes it provided they might have begun more cautiously. They probably were encouraged in their false demonstration by the commonness of puffery in the numerous TV shaving commercials which preceded theirs. For years there have been ads in which the blade glides smoothly and quickly over the face and completes the job in a few swipes. Such demonstrations sorely contradict actual experience with shaving, but they have never been questioned by the regulators. The man in the scene always shaves downward with the grain, while I cannot shave closely unless I go against the grain with plenty of pressure and repeat attempts. No one shaves in a real bathroom the way people do on TV.

Whether or not they directly mislead, the quick and smooth shaving scenes undoubtedly invite the next advertiser to go a step further. No wonder Colgate thought the Rapid Shave ads would get equal leniency. Legal writer Milton Handler was unquestionably correct in saying in 1939, long before television was widely used, that the only sensible way to eliminate falsity is to eliminate *all* falsity.[3] The sandpaper mess could have been staved off by requiring earlier ads to show shaving as it really is. Maybe those ads never tricked anyone, and maybe the sacrifice of creativity would be unfortunate, but the loophole would have been closed.

The observant Handler also noted that advertisers not only defend various falsities as just puffery, but tend actually to *see* them as only puffery. "No advertiser will ever believe, no less admit," he wrote, "that his untruths rise above the plane of puffs."[4] Furthermore, "If any progress is to be made in this movement for the elimination of falsehoods in advertising, it must be realized that the nub of the problem consists of puffing. . . . [When you] legitimize puffing while forbidding downright falsehood . . . the door is open to subterfuge, litigation, and argument."

In a similar vein, Robert Choate, critic of children's food advertising, has suggested that "advertising men, afloat in a world of puffery, have lost the ability to judge when they are lying."[5] The comment referred to the creation of the National Advertising Review Board, a self-regulation unit which to Choate's dismay was to be formed mostly of industry people. Whether or not his words apply to all ad men, we may agree that in an industry where deception is normal the public cannot be assured of benefiting from a program of self-regulation.

The second unfortunate characteristic of sales messages which puffery makes possible is a severe loss of information content. That is the precise opposite of what consumerists have demanded, and it has happened, ironically, precisely because of consumerism's demands. The effort to get information of greater quality and quantity has spurred tighter laws against false advertising, but the ad industry's response to them has brought something other than the hoped-for improvements. The advertisers saw that they had to alter their use of information if they continued to use it, but this mattered, they noted, only if they continued to use it. Why not discontinue using information, they asked themselves, and substitute a type of content not subject to being called deceptive.

Other content must be available, of course, and there it was, conveniently—puffery. As a result, puffery today may often be less troublesome for its own content than for its role as a substitute for content which industry wants to avoid. One has to say something, after all, and puffery is what advertisers provide when they do not want to provide information. The law may have achieved its goal of making more information nondeceptive, but only in conjunction with the sad yet perfectly legal fact that a lesser proportion of message content now is informative.

An example of the difference this can make appeared in *The Medical Messiahs* in a comparison of British and American labels used in 1912 on a patent medicine called Swamp Root.[6] The British label had twelve falsehoods which were prohibited on American labels by the Food and Drug act of 1906. The American label contained as many claims as the British, but the lies such as "cures Bright's disease" were eliminated in favor of puffs such as "Swamp Root makes friends" and "It will be found very beneficial in cases of Debility."

Moves away from information were untypical in 1912, but a firm trend in that direction has been documented in the 1970s. William Tyler is a writer who picks top campaigns each year for *Advertising Age,* the industry newsweekly. He was surprised to find while making his 1970 selections that the ads for that year contained less information than before.[7] He had expected a greater reflection of the contemporary political atmosphere, which was demanding an increase rather than decrease of information. "The pressure was on us from Washington and consumer groups," as he put it, "to provide more information or perish." He added that official circles were making it clear to the advertising industry that "our economic justification is the product information we communicate through advertising." Trying to explain what happened, Tyler thought advertisers in 1970 were aware of these warnings and only temporarily ignoring them, due to a business recession in which the desperate need for sales could be satisfied only by "overpowering" rather than informative ads.

Another advertising man, J. R. Carpenter, observed that advertisers had not merely ignored the warnings about information but deliberately flaunted them.[8] "Information can be challenged," Carpenter wrote, and so the new strategy was simply to avoid it:

Specific claims can be argued on the basis of facts. Logic can be questioned. As a result, it is increasingly difficult to get information copy approved without a long list of legal qualifiers and disclaimers that take away the impact of the advertising. But, it is difficult to challenge image, emotion, style (whatever you want to call it). Therefore, agencies and advertisers are turning to the image approach because it is "safer." And as consumer pressure mounts, the trend to "non-challengable" image advertising will grow. Ironic, isn't it? The consumer pressure may, in the end, be self-defeating.

That trend has continued. "A number of copywriters," declared the *Wall Street Journal* in early 1972, "say they're under orders to keep virtually all specific claims out of their work, no matter how strong the supporting evidence appears."[9] Specific claims were becoming increasingly vulnerable to charges of deception by the FTC and other agencies. The zeal for finding deception appeared in the specification of many new kinds of it[10] as well as more severe prosecution of the old kinds, to the point that shell-shocked advertisers began believing that any factual claim whatever might be called deceptive in some newly defined sense. And while these pressures mounted, industry also faced the development of brand new regulatory methods such as the FTC's demands for documentation to substantiate advertising claims and the demands made for "counter ads" under the "fairness doctrine."

The substantiation program consisted of FTC requests for the facts behind a wide variety of ad claims without regard for whether they seemed deceptive.[11] With the collected information made available for public examination, the program meant a far more severe scrutiny of claims than advertisers had formerly known. The development of counter ads[12] grew out of a widening interpretation of the "fairness doctrine," imposed by law on the broadcast industry, which required stations to give time to an opposing side where issues were of a controversial nature. For advertising, this evolved into the notion that when a company's ads discussed such issues there might be free time given for counter ads prepared by persons with opposing views.

Such new developments stifled the ad industry's desires to provide consumers with information. FTC Chairman Miles Kirkpatrick, though obviously supporting his agency's substantiation program, himself conceded that the high costs absorbed by industry in complying might lead companies to "choose to adopt wholly uninformative advertising programs."[13] A vice president in Washington for CBS-TV, Richard Jencks, observed that "the uncertainty that surrounds much broadcast advertising as a result of fairness decisions forces advertisers back toward puffery, in the belief that the only safe thing is to say nothing."[14]

Les Loevinger, a former Federal Communications Commissioner and vigorous opponent of counter ads, illustrated the matter[15] by noting a variety of possible advertising lines which might be used for a soft drink:

... Drink Burpo!
... Burpo tastes good.

... Burpo makes you feel good.
... Burpo has vitamin C.
... Burpo has lots of vitamin C.
... Burpo with vitamin C is good for you.

He then pointed to the differences in these lines: "Which of these is most likely and which is least likely to incite attack in counter-advertising? The answer is obvious. The ad with the most factual information is the most vulnerable, and the ad with the least factual information is least vulnerable. . . . The net effect will surely be to diminish the amount of information now available to the average consumer, rather than to increase it."

The ultimate of ads containing no information at all may seem extreme, but it soon became part of the 1970s scene. Typical was Standard Oil's use of Johnny Cash, who talked in a homespun way about Standard's quality, ending with the phrase "You expect more from Standard and you get it." Don't try holding your breath waiting for Johnny to explain what you get, because an official of Standard Oil has admitted that "the 'charisma' of Johnny Cash is the only ingredient establishing the quality angle in people's minds."[16] Cash's image is an excellent one for such purposes, instilling trust, producing gratitude, and grinding out sales probably faster than the factual claims the company could make. As a salesman he is topped by none except possibly Arthur Godfrey among the contemporary images on TV. Folks feel the world is better with Johnny around, and if he rejoices in Standard then we must, too.

But the rise of such persons means the fall of information. When what a company means to viewers is the "feel" they get from its spokesman, then what the company means to them involves nothing in the way of product facts. *Advertising Age* dubbed these developments "The latest ad gimmick: non-advertising," and described another campaign:

Shell Oil Co.'s new ad campaign, we fear, may be a harbinger of things to come: Non-advertising. It's the first advertising we can remember that urges us to buy the product without making any direct claims or citing any advantages of the product itself. Instead, Shell talks about its engineering efforts in other fields as reasons why its gasoline is worthy of purchase. . . . If this sort of non-advertising spreads to other fields—and given the FTC's current militancy, there's good reason to believe it will—we can look forward to a barrage of meaningless jingles and generalities . . . .[17]

Companies in trouble over factual claims might wish they had offered the consumer no more than jingles and generalities or a charismatic Cash. Sterling Drug Company could feel that way after attack by the FTC for its Lysol disinfectant advertising.[18] Lysol kills flu germs on surfaces such as table tops, but the FTC alleged this claim was used misleadingly because the germs which affect people are only those floating freely in the air. If your table has flu, Lysol will cure it! But the inference that "curing" the table will aid nearby people was called deceptive, and the FTC wants future Lysol ads to confess the same by containing these "corrective" words: "Contrary to our prior advertising representations, the use of LYSOL Brand Disinfectants in the home will not have significant medical benefit in reducing the incidence or preventing the spread of colds, influenza, or other upper respiratory diseases."

Should the FTC investigation find, when completed, that the public understood the ad to be making the alleged inference, we should not be surprised in the future to see Lysol adopt Standard Oil's strategy of having a well-known figure state merely that Lysol is "the best" and that he uses it.[19] McDonald's, similarly, might adopt Burger King's strategy to avoid trouble of the sort it had with its "quarter-pound" hamburger.[20] Burger King's extra-size burger is known as the "Whopper," a puffing name which cleverly dodges any commitment to actual size. The "quarter-pounder" is held to specific performance by its name, but "Whopper" is far less informative and therefore commits Burger King to far less of a promise.

To digress briefly, may I say that while I feel the loss

of information through such practices is certainly hard on consumers, I do not feel that attacking the advertisers for wreaking these hardships is entirely justified. I am fully aware of a strong consumerist viewpoint which states that all companies have a moral and ethical obligation to supply full product information and to supply nothing else but information (i.e., no persuasion). Consumerists holding this view seem to assume that advertising exists at their convenience in the first place, and should therefore do exactly what they want. A Consumers Union official, for example, told the FTC it should require any advertisers who omit essential product information from their ads to fork over 25 percent of their ad budgets to allow other information sources to present the missing facts.[21]

Advertisers, of course, dispute this viewpoint vigorously, insisting it's their own money they're using and they have a right to use it to communicate whatever content serves their interests.[22] They have not been reticent in acknowledging that withholding of full facts has existed in selling and advertising for a long time, probably always. One of David Ogilvy's "confessions" is that he has been continuously guilty of suppressio veri, as he calls it, suppressing the truth. "Surely it is asking too much," he wrote, "to expect the advertiser to describe the shortcomings of his product? One must be forgiven for putting one's best foot forward."[23] A bit less diplomatic expression of the same philosophy was made by Ogilvy's coworker, Andrew Kershaw, who insisted that advertising "can tell the truth, can tell nothing but the truth, but should not be required to tell the whole truth."[24]

Surely the advertisers have a strong point in this, since any rule requiring them to communicate full product information would clash violently with their privilege not to communicate at all if they don't want to. And any rule requiring that their communication consist only of information would clash with their freedom to speak on other things. There are certain legal requirements governing the use of messages, the advertisers will concede. But these consist only of requiring that messages they choose to communicate must contain certain designated disclosures (i.e., the cigarette warning) and must not contain claims which are deceptive. There are no rules which govern whether they must speak in the first place, or what else they must say when they do speak.

Consumerists would quickly point out that this defense by the advertisers runs to a strict legalistic basis rather than a moral or ethical one. The advertisers as usual, they would say, are interpreting what is legal to be what is moral. But in my opinion the consumerists have not satisfactorily demonstrated the advertisers' moral obligation to provide information. It is clear that the consumer's need for information is vital; it is less clear that the need must be fulfilled by messages which are essentially voluntary on the part of the advertisers. I say "voluntary" because advertising messages are made not in response to anyone's demand, but by the initiation of the advertiser. When a consumer actively demands information from a company, I think the company is morally obligated to answer fully. But voluntary ads are a different kind of communication; I cannot see why the demand for full information and nothing but information should be applied to such messages.

Some consumerists will disagree with my viewpoint, and I acknowledge that future trends in defining morality may coincide with their position. In any event, there is at present no effective legal or ethical way to force advertisers to supply full information.[25] They have chosen to decrease the supply instead, by substituting puffery, and the public has little choice but to accept that decision.

A fascinating related question, however, is this: How can advertisers, in their own selfish interest, *not* use information? Isn't information necessary to make their advertising effective? Must they not give the consumer a reason for buying the product? Surely they are only harming themselves when they remove facts from their ads and use other content instead.

No doubt that is what consumerists and regulators have thought, but it's just not the case. Information *isn't* necessary to make advertising effective. The consumer must have a reason for buying the product, but it need not consist of information. It need not consist, that is, of what people with consumer sympathies call information, meaning true product facts.

What advertisers and sellers mean by information is something different. It is anything which makes people see values in their product which they do not see in the competitor's product.[26] This definition actually excludes true product facts in many heavily advertised fields such as gasoline, bread, margarine, cigarettes, beer, whiskey, and others where the competing brands are hard to differentiate from each other. The facts about these competing brands are insignificant to the sellers as information because they are virtually the same for each brand. They do not distinguish a brand from its competitors. Attempts have been made at advertising nonunique facts so as to imply their uniqueness, but such attempts, as we have seen, have come under FTC scrutiny.[27] Therefore it is not surprising that the advertiser is willing to give up factual statements; they were doing him little good, anyway.

An indication of this viewpoint came when ad man Alfred J. Seaman, testifying before the FTC,[28] called for restraint in the drive for more and more information in advertising. "We need the language of enthusiasm. We need the luxury of harmless puffery," he said, and added that "poeticizing is different from deceiving." But how does the advertiser use puffery to play a value-producing role in place of facts?

There are two parts to the answer, the first being that puffery implies facts, as we have seen at length already.[29] The second and equally important answer is that it attracts attention and causes the consumer to become familiar with the product. Familiarity is "information" because it acquaints the consumer with the product's values, and because it is one of those values itself.[30] Sheer familiarity is a product value because consumers are prone to avoid the strange and buy what they know. The ultimate for which every advertiser strives is to have the top score on "first brand awareness," which means that consumers who are asked to name the first brand they can think of in the product category are more likely to mention his brand than any other.

We may examine how these principles of noninformational selling work by recalling the grandiose claims about this book which I stated in its very first paragraph. Suppose those words were on the front of the book, unaccompanied by my explanation of them. You would probably recognize them as the kind of thing you see on lots of books, words to be ignored, words that mean nothing. You are familiar with such things and have learned to deflate their meaning or reject them entirely. Possibly you sense some annoyance in realizing they are false. Otherwise you are not affected, certainly not in a positive way.

Let's go back over your reaction again. I believe there probably were some subtle effects which you don't usually notice, and which might have occurred, in fact, precisely because you didn't notice them. The words did attract your attention, didn't they? I mean you saw them, and I wonder whether they might have led by chance to your looking the book over carefully and showing some interest. Just casually, of course—you're not really interested. It just caught your eye, and you can't help letting that happen every now and then. It's the same with bright colors or striking designs—the eye locks onto them, and it's only a reflex action you can't control. It lasts a second, but you pull yourself away and pay no heed.

Might it have been fifteen seconds, really, or even thirty? Did you pick the book up during your "glance"? Did you look inside while you were deciding to pay no attention? Maybe you read a little, and in fact don't you once in a while actually buy one of those books you started out paying no attention to? On a casual thirty-minute visit to a thinly stocked bookstore of only 1,800 volumes, you would have an average of one second to examine each book. It's rather significant, then, that it takes more seconds than that to recognize and reject the ridiculous puffing claims on the cover, by which time you have inadvertently made a commitment of attention and interest which far exceeds what you could give to most other books.

It's only your attention, you say, and not your interest? It was only your eye which was caught and not your mind? But your mind cannot be attracted to what your eye does not first see, and you will leave the bookstore with not even a conscious glance at most of the titles therein. The puff cannot guarantee your interest, but it helps make interest possible for this book by making it impossible for many others. It helps assure that you will not see the rival volume which has no puffery on the cover and which you might have found to be a better bargain.

Do you think this encourages book publishers to put puffs on their covers? Of course! And illustrations of provocative girls—they are puffs, too, when they suggest falsely that the contents will in large part involve sexual adventures. It's an expectation well fulfilled in many cases, but used also on books with a minimum of such content. Classics such as *Wuthering Heights* have been given this treatment. All such puffs establish book-judging criteria, items of "information," which are false because they do not truly describe the contents and their value. You may not explicitly believe them, but there is a sense in which you rely on them, whether you know it or not, to help make your purchasing decision. You rely on them and they serve therefore in place of real information, enabling the advertiser to do without that commodity which seems so precious in the public's eye, but which he has learned perfectly well to do without.

In the world of selling there are a million attention-getting devices. Among the most popular are the spoof characters such as the Marlboro man, Virginia Slims girl, the Hamms bear, Charley the Tuna, Morris the Cat, the

Pillsbury doughboy, the Jolly Green Giant, Schlitz Malt
Liquor's bull, and Mr. Clean. Then there are the spoof
situations, of which one of my favorites is the Hamms beer
wagon commercial. It opens on a residential neighborhood,
with a vehicle in the distance that looks like a Good
Humor wagon. Its bell is tinkling, and numerous people in
the area drop their activities and head toward the street.
They're not children, though, they're men, and the wagon
doesn't say Good Humor, it says Hamms. The driver stops,
gets out, and opens up a rear compartment while the gang
gathers around. There's a flurry of activity; you hear the
driver excitedly saying "Wait your turn," "Here's your
change," and so on. In a few more seconds the mob bursts
into the Hamms drinking song, and the shot cuts away to
the only chap in the neighborhood who hasn't been se-
duced out of his yard. Up on the roof nailing shingles, he
looks at the scene with amazement, and says, "They can't
do that."

It's a marvelous attention-getting device, and in fact it
relies on attention-getting alone to produce value in the
consumer's mind. Not one factual claim is made for
Hamms, yet the increased familiarity with the product
name gives Hamms all it needs to get its money back from
this ad. And it gives advertisers all the proof they need to
identify puffery as a successful substitute for real information.

Regretfully, the result of all this for the consumer is
that the facts are not as plentiful in sales talk as they might
be.

Sellers' and Advertisers' Problems

A cartoon in a 1973 issue of the *Wall Street Journal*[31]
shows a small boy sitting on his father's lap as they watch
TV. The father speaks: "No, he can't really fly . . . no, the
bad guys don't really have a ray gun . . . no, this cereal
really isn't the best food in the whole world . . . no, it
won't make you as strong as a giant . . . ."

The world of selling and advertising makes an enormous amount of trouble for itself because it treats puffery as a matter of legality rather than, as in the cartoon, a matter of credibility. It is trouble which it might just as easily avoid by skipping puffery entirely. Why does it not do so?

Habit plays a role, I suppose; salesmen have always used puffery. And the unwillingness to give up any selling device which remains legal is undoubtedly a big factor. The latter desire includes an understandably negative feeling toward abandoning anything one's competitors may keep using. As Judge Learned Hand pointed out, you engage in puffery because if you don't, while everyone else does, people will think something's wrong with you.[32] The industry acting in concert will not be hurt by abstaining, but the lone individual will. That above all probably explains why puffery continues in advertising and selling today.

Supposing the entire industry gave up these practices, what would be gained? For one thing, with no individual company put at a disadvantage, perhaps all involved could save some money as the cigarette makers did when they left radio and TV. For another thing, each advertiser would be giving up a privilege which does not belong to him exclusively anyway, and which, as Ringling Brothers-Barnum and Bailey found out, can be used just as strongly against him as for him.

The circus's painful realization of that fact came when another company successfully stole the famous line, "The greatest show on earth." Chandris America Lines was not a circus but a Caribbean cruise operator. It ran an ad headlined "The Greatest Show on Earth Isn't," implying in smaller print that the greatest show was not on earth at all, but at sea. Among various charges brought by Ringling, in an attempt to obtain damages and an injunction, was that the cruise ad amounted to malicious disparagement by inferring that Chandris's shows were better than Ringling's.

The court decision of 1971,[33] however, said such

assertion was only "a legitimate trade comparison falling well within the limits of ordinary trade puffing." The circus, in other words, was prohibited from stopping other companies from claiming to be the greatest, for the exact same reason that it itself could make the claim in the first place. If you can puff a claim about yourself, and it's false, then anyone else can puff the same claim against you, *even when it's false*. The privilege is meaningful only when you're the only one doing it. It guarantees no advantage, and doesn't even assure you'll be as well off as you were before.

These are good reasons for abandoning puffery, but the opportunity to improve credibility is an even better reason. By dropping such messages, all involved could rescue themselves from a credibility gap which some feel could have major long-term consequences: "This lack of confidence in advertising—if true—ought to be a matter of national concern. After all, advertising is the communications medium of business. In a real sense, a decline in its effectiveness can represent a danger to the nation's economic health."[34]

The decline may not be steep enough for danger yet, but the warning signs are in evidence. An advertising journalist showed some ads to a panel of "students and young marrieds" and was startled to find that they looked for the catch in every one. "That was their routine approach to advertising," he said, and gave his article the headline "To Youth, Ads Are An Upper Class Con Game."[35] *Harvard Business Review* published a survey of the attitudes business executives hold toward advertising and discovered widespread tendencies by such persons to respond negatively.[36] *Advertising Age* commented editorially that public cynicism can only be enhanced by the fact that American auto makers boast of their "Mark of Excellence" and their "better ideas" while at the same time moving vigorously to avoid stricter government controls on auto pollution.[37]

In the face of these problems the sellers continue as

they always have. They are convinced that puffery helps sell goods, and they seem unaware that the whole idea of nondeceptive falsity carries a constant and heavy risk of backfiring. Falsity is falsity, and no matter how legal puffery may be, consumers could someday develop a distaste for it for just that reason. I have argued that a substantial portion of the public will accept puffery as true, but there are always some who will not. If there are a few now, there may be many more later, and once recognizing the falsity they are not likely to remain tolerant for long of the notion that it is somehow legally nondeceptive. Such a counter-effect could even predominate some day and turn what is currently an advantage into a fearsome disadvantage. We do not know this will happen, but advertisers invite it with each puff and should not be surprised if it comes.

The irony for the advertiser is that false puffery is potentially damaging no matter how it functions and no matter what the law decides about how it functions. If it's deceptive, as I'm convinced it is, it may someday be determined so legally and outlawed. If it's deceptive but continues to escape legal action it may possibly retain its effectiveness with the public indefinitely, but there is always the chance of a credibility boomerang. Even the possibility that false puffery is actually nondeceptive gives no solace to the advertiser. Such event might seem superficially attractive to him, but would mean in fact that his puffery is not doing anything and he is foolish for using it.

That is the ad man's Catch-22. If the consumer rejects puffery, there is no reason for using it. If the consumer believes it, the law's reason for excusing it disappears. The advertiser defends false puffery because it's legal, but it can be legal only because it doesn't work. The advertiser thus is supporting it for a reason that tells him there's no point in supporting it. A sensible reason for using false puffery could only be that it works, which would then make it illegal. Whether false puffery is illegal or not may be important to the regulators, but the result seems dismal for the advertiser in either case. If it is, he's in trouble with the law. If it isn't, he is asking for trouble with the public, encouraging distrust and contributing to a potential credibility gap that could spoil the effectiveness of his true factual claims as well as his puffs.

If these credibility problems damage industry they will damage the wider society as well, and will add immensely to the catalog we are compiling of puffery's offenses.

The Law's Problems

When we earlier identified puffery as a loophole in the law, the purpose was to emphasize the deception showered upon the public by those who take advantage of the borderline similarity between puffery and illegal falsity. We return now to describe how this confusion at the borderline may cause serious embarrassment for the law as well, damaging its credibility significantly with sellers and consumers alike.

The law's task is to make precise differentiations among false claims so that everyone knows which are legal and which are not. It is a task which has not been carried out well. Witness the fuss when the FTC announced in 1971 that selected industries must reveal substantiation for their advertising claims. The Commission made the customary concession that "mere puffery" would be exempted.[38]   But then it demanded substantiation for General Electric's claim that its room air conditioner would provide "the clean freshness of clear, cool mountain air."[39] We can appreciate that a resident of, for example, Gary, Indiana, might experience difficulty in getting his G.E. device to produce clear and mountain-like air. But would he expect that on the basis of the ad? *Advertising Age* responded indignantly that the claim was only puffery, and why was the FTC being so "picayune" about it?[40]

A similar rhubarb occurred over Article 8 of the Advertising Code of American Business, a self-regulatory instrument developed by organizations representing industry.[41] Consumerist Ralph Nader charged in 1970 that many companies violate this precept, which states that "advertising shall avoid the use of exaggerated and unprovable claims."[42] Howard Bell, president of the American Advertising Federation, one of the code's sponsors, rejoined that "Mr. Nader did not always distinguish clearly between puffery and performance claims."[43] By Bell's interpretation Article 8 never included puffery, but applied only to *other kinds* of exaggerated and unprovable claims. Nader's refusal to see the distinction left the two on opposite sides of a widening gap.

That same gap, if not picayunishness, has been reflected in comments by former FTC Commissioner Philip Elman.[44] While organizing a truth-in-advertising campaign for law students he wrote, "A seller may describe his product as 'beautiful,' 'the greatest,' etc., so long as it is understood to be only an expression of his opinion, not a representation of fact." But he also wrote, "A skillful advertiser, making shrewd use of exaggeration, innuendo, ambiguity, or half truth, can mislead the consuming public without misstating a single fact."

No two sentences joined together have ever illustrated the problem better. The law's credibility is at stake when the puffery loophole is defined so that no one knows what it means. "We don't know what the rules are," wailed Andrew Kershaw, Ogilvy & Mather advertising agency chief, in 1971.[45] At the time certain ads are prepared, another observer noted, there is no way of knowing that the techniques they involve will later be defined as deceptive.[46]

When the advertiser uses a type of false representation he supposes is excusable as puffery, but which may not be, the law has a potential loss of credibility on its hands no matter which way it decides. If the message is denied the puffery label, the law has failed in the eyes of advertisers who thought they were protected. If it is called puffery the law has failed again, this time with the public. The constant bickering this invites is surely another serious consequence of the fact that puffery is called legal in American law.

Such things invite satirizing. A cartoon showed two men in the engineering department of an automobile company, glancing glumly toward an associate who was just leaving. "Our advertising department," one engineer explains, "wanted to know if it was technically correct to say our new V-8 engine was as quiet as the whisper of lovers' feet on the golden sands of the tropics."[47] The joke would be good enough if the advertising department really needed to know that, but the true situation these days is even stranger: the advertising department *doesn't know* whether it needs to know that.

The laws we respect and uphold should be those which solve problems, not produce them. Too often, with the laws we have seen in this book, the outcome has been more confusion rather than less. Some of the unhappiness is partisan, of course, because consumerists want the rules tightened and sellers want them relaxed. Consumerists want messages prohibited which sellers traditionally use and want messages required which sellers traditionally don't use. Sellers, naturally, frown on the imposition of those prohibitions and requirements. An individual's choice among such viewpoints depends a great deal upon the position he occupies in the marketplace.

But some of the dissatisfactions are bipartisan. Both sides want the laws to be founded sensibly and reasonably upon the true facts of the situations they govern. When we cannot understand why the law says what it says and cannot respect it for the reasons it gives, we may be dissatisfied no matter where we stand in the marketplace. A great deal of the ferment caused today by consumerism, and by industry's response to consumerism, is due to regulations such as those governing puffery which might just as reasonably have been written in reverse, permitting what they prohibit or prohibiting what they permit.

When this happens, all parties are disadvantaged. For

the participant, be he consumer or advertiser, who does not like a certain law, the suspicion that the law lacks any reasonable basis for existence brings the frustration of dealing in the market under conditions which seem unfair. Yet simultaneously for the other side, for the group which the law appears to benefit, the same suspicion produces an inability to act confidently because of uncertainness that so arbitrary a ruling can remain on the books as it is. The result on both sides is a decrease of efficiency and a loss of credibility for the legal process which has produced such confusion.

The principal arbitrariness, as reviewed extensively in earlier chapters,[48] is that puffery is ruled nondeceptive not merely because consumers shouldn't trust it, but because they *won't* trust it. Despite evidence to the contrary, the law rules arbitrarily that the bulk of people in the United States who act with reasonable sense and care in the marketplace simply will not trust comments such as those with which I opened this book. The law declines to evaluate the evidence and decides as a matter of law rather than of fact that people will not trust. It does this because it clings to the legal precedents developed under sellerism, which, as our historical survey has shown, are indefensible now largely because they were indefensible then. The arbitrariness which no one minded because no one recognized under sellerism is greatly recognized today—and greatly minded.

Rules are not objectionable just because they are arbitrary. Often they are perfectly acceptable despite such origins. There are rules in sports which I find foolishly inconsistent, but which no one—players, coaches, fans—seems to mind. When a football team kicks off, the ball is free and belongs to the team which recovers it, while on a punt it belongs to the receiving team no matter who recovers it. I would feel more comfortable with rules growing organically from the fundamental nature of the game, so that if one kind of kick is interpreted as giving up the ball, then both kicks would be interpreted that way.

But I am the only one I know who cares about this; it is of no concern to those affected most strongly, the players. The reason for their indifference is apparently that all of their rules apply equally to each side and so favor neither. No one is disadvantaged by an unnatural rule when the actions it regulates are shared by both parties in a competitive situation.

In the marketplace this balance does not exist because both sides do not get an equal opportunity to "run the same plays." The law of sales misrepresentations applies technically to both sellers and buyers, but most messages are transmitted by sellers and received by buyers. Rules changes thereby give a huge advantage to sellers when they make more sales messages legal, and give a corresponding advantage to buyers when they make fewer messages legal. Unreasonable arbitrariness under such circumstances has the nasty consequence of helping determine who wins the game. There is nothing neutral about changing the rules on the market gridiron.

I am not pointing out the arbitrariness of puffery rulings, however, because I think they represent any conspiracy of those who for obvious reasons continue to embrace sellerism. I prefer to avoid the conspiratorial viewpoint that sellerist tendencies remain because the law has been captured by the bad guys, the sellers, in order to take advantage of the good guys, the consumers. I think current conditions are due rather to inertia, and feel as Stanley Cohen did when he reviewed a book called *Who Put the Con in Consumer?:* "Despite its enticing title, the book identifies few 'con' artists. No honest author can. When it comes to the 'con,' the consumer has more to fear from the system than from the occasional crook."[49]

That is precisely my attitude. Though the crooks may be more than occasional, I feel that what my book describes is far more a matter of a social system of many centuries' standing[50] than of the machinations of contemporary individuals. The puffers will machinate, naturally, within the range of legality available to them, but the essential determinant of their activities is the heritage which defined that range so widely. Those holding the conspiracy theory might better focus on the forces which created sellerism in past centuries than on the sellers who take advantage of it in this one.

The law's problem, meanwhile, no matter what the reason for it, is that in choosing to distinguish puffery from deception it has created a serious credibility gap. It has lagged by clinging arbitrarily to rulings developed under sellerism when the long-term trend is to replace sellerism with consumerism. The disadvantage it faces in working under such a handicap is a final addition to the list of puffery's offenses which this chapter has set out to describe.

Some Corrections of the Problems

Should false puffery be someday eliminated, consumers will have less deception and more information, advertisers will have restored credibility with the public, and the law will have restored credibility, too. Such worthy results deserve to happen, and I will finish this tale by acknowledging that to certain small degrees they already have. Throughout the preceding chapters I have noted various events which have moved the law modestly toward the goal of eliminating puffery. I have subordinated these events to the book's principal theme, which is that nothing really substantial has been accomplished to curtail the deception which false puffery produces. But little steps where big ones are needed are better than no steps at all; we are lucky to have them. What follows are some other recent developments which indicate similar stirrings.

Late in 1971 a commercial for an aerosol antiperspirant opened with a man saying, "If you think advertising lies, this is for you." Holding a can of Stay Dry, he went on to say: "I'm the president of an ad agency with a client whose product I want you to buy: I think you will if

I simply tell you the truth. It's an anti-perspirant with two kinds of drying ingredients, and still it can't keep you dry. No anti-perspirant can. Not even ours, and that's the truth. The one thing maybe not altogether true is our name, Stay Dry. Probably it should be Stay Dryer because that's what we really help you do—stay drier. And that's the truth."[51]

The president, Bob Dolobowsky, acknowledged that he hoped the commercial would help sales as well as credibility, saying "We should make some of the other commercials on the air today look a little shopworn." He was concerned about advertising's credibility, he said, because he had been talking to youngsters in schools and found "They don't believe the ads." Mr. Dolobowsky's own credibility might have been more enhanced if he had not used the phrase "stay drier" as an open comparative. Does it mean drier than competitors, or only drier than you would be without the product? Dolobowsky should know that semantic usages such as that have been criticized often in the past. Nonetheless, his ad is remarkable for denying a claim which his competitors often have stated or implied falsely. There are many opportunities available for advertisers who want to do it, but that is the first I have ever seen it done.

Also in 1971 Hunt-Wesson Foods announced it no longer would advertise products on the basis of "minor differences which have little relevance to product value."[52] The company has many brands which are relatively undifferentiated from competitors, a spokesman said, but it has decided it would no longer take an irrelevant difference and promote it as though the difference were important. Commercials for two of Hunt's products, he said, were being abandoned for that reason even though the differences they suggested would have meant greater sales: "The decision was not to produce these commercials because the benefits suggested were not relevant to the performance of the product. It would have had no meaningful benefit to the consumer."

The decision did not mean Hunt-Wesson was ruling out

the importance of psychological benefits, he added, but it did mean that decisions would be made in individual cases as to whether these benefits were real. Though I have argued earlier that psychological benefits are false in the sense of implying more facts to the consumer than actually exist, I am glad to see that a major company has at least moved as far as restricting them in this way.

On July 1, 1972, the automobile dealers of Wisconsin took an uncharacteristic step; they eliminated puffery from their advertising.[53] The action was required under the state's new Motor Vehicle Trade Practices Code. But its inclusion in the code was proposed voluntarily by the dealers' own organization, the Wisconsin Automotive Trades Association. Statutes and voluntary codes in the past have appeared to forbid puffery, because they have outlawed false representations and even exaggerations. But in practice, through convenient interpretations, these regulations actually have protected puffs as exceptions to the general rule.[54] In contrast, the Wisconsin code forbids puffery specifically by name, stating, "Terms such as 'best,' 'less' and 'greater,' and other superlatives and comparatives indicate puffery and are prohibited unless there is detailed proof for such claim."

The dealers of course did not request this rule in the interests of consumers solely; they must have felt it was better for their own affairs as well. But that they did it selfishly makes the move even more significant than if they had done it grudgingly to placate consumers. The perception required to see that sacrificing puffery may be personally beneficial represents an improvement in sellers' insights which may be ahead of its time, but has been a long time coming. I hope other sellers will soon begin making the same discovery.

Betty Furness recently told advertisers to get up-to-date when she was asked whether it mattered that Betty Crocker and Aunt Jemima were phony persons as long as they didn't make phony claims.[55] "To begin with," said Ms. Furness, "this kind of stuff is pathetically old-fashioned." She added, "If people think she [Betty Crock- · er] exists, then she's a lie. And if she doesn't exist, why have her? It's all part of what makes young people believe that they can't even believe truthful advertising. It may not matter as much as other things, but it does matter."

John Howard and James Hulbert think it matters, too. They are professors who in 1973 published a summary and analysis of testimony given before the FTC in its marathon hearings on advertising held in 1971.[56] Advertising has contributed to an artificial rise of consumer expectations, they said, reflecting the success it has achieved with exaggerations about superiority and overstatements about performance. They commented on a growing recognition that puffery is probably deceptive: "We wonder, for example, whether 'Ford has a better idea' is not deceptive to consumers. It is an incomplete comparative." They recommended that the FTC apply the same substantiation requirements to puffery that it applies to other claims.

Oftimes in the past have such recommendations and hopes been stated. I have written this book to say that it is time they are not merely stated, but finally fulfilled.

NOTES

TABLE OF CASES

INDEX

Notes

This book is annotated in legal style, since so many of the references are to legal sources. Readers not experienced in researching the law may be well advised to consult a librarian for help in obtaining the cited materials. The following explanatory comments are offered in order to keep such consultation to a minimum.

"65 U.S. 493" or "65 *Harvard Law Review* 493" means the case or article is in Volume 65 of the specified series, beginning at p. 493. "65 U.S. 493, 506" means the reference is specifically to p. 506 of the case beginning on p. 493. "*Advertising Age,* July 2, 1 (1973)" means the article begins on p. 1.

Abbreviations used include:

U.S.: United States Supreme Court Reports.

S.C.: Supreme Court Reports (an alternate source of the reports in "U.S.").

L.Ed.: Lawyers Edition (a third source of the reports in "U.S.").

F.: Federal Reports (cases of the U.S. Circuit Courts of Appeal and the U.S. District Courts).

F.2d: Federal Reports, 2d Series.

1st Cir.: U.S. Court of Appeals for the First Circuit.

Wis.: Reports of the Wisconsin courts (same treatment for other states).

A., N.E., N.W., P., etc.: Reports for the Atlantic, Northeast, Northwest, Pacific, etc., areas (generally alternate sources for cases in state reports).

Wis.2d, A.2d: Wisconsin Reports, 2d Series; Atlantic Reports, 2d Series.

TRR: Trade Regulation Reporter.

FTC: Federal Trade Commission Decisions.

CFR: Code of Federal Regulations.

Eng. Rep.: English Reports (reprints of early English cases).

Y.B.: Yearbooks (early English law).

CHAPTER 2: FALSITY WITHOUT DECEPTION

1 I am speaking principally of the Federal Trade Commission, which has acted against deception, and in fact against the mere "capacity to deceive," since its formation in 1914. Its actions are detailed in chapter 9. In common law the term *misrepresentation* (see chapter 6) is used rather than *deception,* and it is established that misrepresentation rather than falsity per se is what is illegal. William L. Prosser, *Handbook of the Law of Torts,* 4th ed., chap. 18 (1971).

2 Hot Wheels: *Mattel,* consent order, 79 FTC 667 (1971); Johnny Lightning: *Topper,* consent order, 79 FTC 681 (1971).

3 The difficulties of this process are further detailed in chapter 9, at note 43 ff.

4 Reasons for assuming the falsity of virtually all puffery are stated in chapter 3, following note 10.

5 See full discussions in chapters 7 and 11.

6 Geritol: *J. B. Williams v. FTC,* 381 F.2d 884 (6th Cir., 1967), affirming *J. B. Williams,* 68 FTC 481 (1965); Wonder Bread: *ITT Continental,* TRR 1970-73 Transfer Binder, ¶ 20,464, FTC Dkt. 8860 (1973); Un-Burn: *Pfizer,* dismissal of charges, 81 FTC 23 (1972); Hi-C: *Coca-Cola,* dismissal of charges, TRR 1970-73 Transfer Binder, ¶ 20,470, FTC Dkt. 8839 (1973); Chevron: *Standard Oil of Cal.,* preliminary dismissal by judge, TRR 1970-73 Transfer Binder, ¶ 20,321, FTC Dkt. 8827 (1973); Zerex: *DuPont,* complaint and withdrawal of charges, TRR 1970-73 Transfer Binder, ¶ 19,849, FTC Dkt. 8870 (1971); consent order, 81 FTC 169 (1972); Lysol: *Sterling Drug,* complaint, TRR 1970-73 Transfer Binder, ¶ 19,925, FTC file no. 662 3550 (1972); Firestone: *Firestone,* 81 FTC 398 (1972); Ocean Spray: *Ocean Spray,* consent order, 80 FTC 975 (1972).

7 Readers may make a compilation of such speeches by examining *Advertising Age,* which is indexed by the *Business Periodicals Index.* Also recommended are the series of speech reprints published by the American Association of Advertising Agencies.

8 This is particularly true of the activities of the Federal Trade Commission; see detailed discussion in chapter 9, especially following note 13.

9 Traditional common law holds that injury must occur specifically because of a person's justifiable reliance upon a message, if action is to be taken against the message. *Restatement of the Law of Torts,* § 525 (1938); Prosser, *Torts,* 4th ed., § 108. The

same principle is applied in requiring the Federal Trade Commission to determine that a message has the capacity to deceive. Details follow in chapters 6 and 9.

10 See discussion of the "ignorant man" in chapter 10.

11 See chapter 13, note 1. Obvious falsity is discussed in detail in chapter 13.

12 This desire was reflected in the famous rule of caveat emptor, which is examined in detail in chapter 4 and referred to frequently in subsequent chapters.

13 *Williams v. Rank & Son Buick,* 44 Wis.2d 239, 170 N.W.2d 807 (1969).

CHAPTER 3: PUFFERY

1 Sample definitions are:

(1) "Puffing . . . is considered to be offered and understood as an expression of the seller's opinion only . . . . An opinion may take the form of a statement of quality, of more or less indefinite content. . . . The 'puffing' rule amounts to a seller's privilege to lie his head off, so long as he says nothing specific, on the theory that no reasonable man would believe him, or that no reasonable man would be influenced by such talk." William L. Prosser, *Handbook of the Law of Torts,* 4th ed., 722-23 (1971).

(2) "expressions of opinion or personal evaluations of the intangible qualities of a product." Ira M. Millstein, "The Federal Trade Commission and false advertising," 64 *Columbia Law Rev.* 439, 469 (1964).

(3) "exaggeration . . . rather than misrepresentations of fact." 2 TRR, ¶ 6533.

(4) "Puffery . . . is permissible, if only because it seldom can be challenged by any objective measure of truth." Donald M. Gillmor and Jerome A. Barron, *Mass Communication Law* 592 (1969).

(5) "When the seller praises in general terms, without specific content or reference to facts, buyers are expected to and do understand that they are not entitled to rely literally upon the words." *Restatement of the Law of Torts (Second),* §542, Tentative Draft No. 10 (1964).

(6) "[Puffing] ceases to be such if the defendant intends it to

be taken seriously and literally and is successful in inducing the vendor so to take it." F. V. Harper and M. C. McNeely, "A synthesis of the law of misrepresentation," 22 *Minnesota Law Rev.* 939, 1006 (1938).

See also statements in the many cases cited in chapters 7 and 11.

2 *U.S. v. New South Farm*, 241 U.S. 64 (1916). This case has been cited in Federal Trade Commission actions against companies defending their misrepresentations as puffery; see chapter 7, at note 28, and chapter 11, at notes 27-28. Other such statements are:

(1) " 'Puffing' does not embrace misstatements of material fact." *Colgate*, 59 FTC 1452, 1469 (1961).

(2) "Puffing refers, generally, to an expression of opinion not made as a representation of fact. . . . While a seller has some latitude in 'puffing' his goods, he is not authorized to misrepresent them or to assign to them benefits or virtues they do not possess." *Gulf Oil v. FTC*, 150 F.2d 106, 109 (1945).

3 Note from the several beer examples that competitors don't fight puffery; they join it. And the conflicting claims thus produced are held noncontradictory by the law—because they are held not to be facts.

4 Puffery includes the comparative *better* as well as the superlative *best*, since in advertising the comparative typically implies the superlative. "Ford gives you better ideas" hardly means better than just one competitor.

The Ford slogan is of interest in light of a statement by a Ford executive, John J. Morrissey, that "we don't make unsubstantiated claims in our advertising, and we never have." "Auto makers seem unperturbed over FTC ad substantiation plan," *Advertising Age*, June 21, 3 (1971). See also "Ford's better idea: collapsing front wheels," *Consumer Reports*, November, 657 (1970).

5 These two examples are interesting for their restraint; they make comparisons only with previous products of the same company.

6 Inability to measure is one of the keys to successful puffery.

7 A comment from "Is it or isn't it?," *Wall Street Journal*, February 25, 13 (1971): "The *Chicago Tribune* bars advertisers from using such superlatives as 'lowest prices,' but it bills itself as 'the

world's greatest newspaper.' Is it? 'In a journalistic sense we definitely are,' declares H. F. Grumhaus, president and publisher. 'Of course we aren't,' says editor Clayton Kirkpatrick. 'It's not a literal statement, any more than the *New York Times* actually prints all the news that's fit to print, or the *Atlanta Journal* covers Dixie like the dew. It's a poetic phrase that attempts to set some objectives.' "

8 I do not mean that the Federal Trade Commission has explicitly called each of these claims puffery. But it has tolerated them, which amounts to the same thing.

9 Some of the key presentations in general semantics are: *ETC.: A Review of General Semantics*, a quarterly periodical; S. I. Hayakawa, *Language in Thought and Action* (1949); Wendell Johnson, *People in Quandaries* (1946); Alfred Korzybski, *Science and Sanity: An Introduction to Non-Aristotelian System and General Semantics* (1933); Irving J. Lee, *Language Habits in Human Affairs* (1941).

10 Ray L. Birdwhistell, *Kinesics and Context,* 227 (1970). See similar comment by a Federal Trade Commissioner, chapter 11, at note 43.

11 *Gourmet,* December, 112 (1972).

12 See details in chapter 6, at note 8 ff.

13 This is my conviction. It is not accepted by the law, but it seems thoroughly reasonable. See the argument developed on this point in chapter 7.

14 See chapter 2, at note 13.

15 Relying on a belief which the hypothetical "reasonable man" would not believe generally spoils one's chances to press a misrepresentation charge successfully. Federal Trade Commission practice, however, is to approve such reliance when it is thought to be typical of a considerable number of people. See chapter 10.

16 See definitions in note 1. It is conceded that stray persons may be deceived, but that fact is given no significance; see discussions in chapters 10 and 11.

17 Sid Bernstein, "Puffery wins a smallish victory," *Advertising Age,* October 23, 16 (1972). Through a generous editorial policy, I was permitted a rejoinder to Mr. Bernstein in his own publication: "Challenges stand that puffery may be low-priority problem," November 27, 47 (1972).

18 "FTC hits puffery claims at ad hearings," ibid., October 25, 1 (1971); "Overholzer tackles the nuts and bolts of advertising," ibid., November 1, 181 (1971).
19 Pamphlet, American Association of Advertising Agencies (1970).
20 *The Bruskin Report,* no. 40 (New Brunswick, N.J., 1971).

CHAPTER 4: THE ROOTS OF SELLERISM

1 Anthony Fitzherbert, *Boke of Husbandrie,* §118 (1534).
2 Under Sweden's Marketing Act of 1971 an advertiser may say nothing he can't prove. "You can't say a product is 'best,' for instance," according to a Swedish advertising executive. "It takes away a lot of cliches and stupid things. You have to talk about important things, not artificial things." Kathryn Sederberg, "Consumer ombudsman is feature of Swedish law," *Advertising Age,* May 22, 98 (1972).

  Canada's Competition Act of 1971 prevents even harmless puffery and obvious exaggeration. A Canadian official stated that the courts would, should an appeal be taken, interpret the sections of the act dealing with misleading advertising as applying to the "credulous man" (called in this book the "ignorant man"; see chapter 10), thus eliminating the advertisers' defense that a reasonable man would not have believed the exaggeration. "Canadian law will prevent puffery claims," ibid., October 4, 77 (1971).

  In Germany puffery has been curtailed considerably, though not so outrightly as in Sweden or Canada. Highly subjective assertions, such as a florist's claim to have "the most beautiful flowers in the world," are still permitted. But the claim that "Wiscoat is the world's best coat," the sort of assertion which runs rampant in the United States, has been found deceptive. Warren S. Grimes, "Control of advertising in the United States and Germany: Volkswagen has a better idea," 84 *Harvard Law Rev.* 1769, 1794 (1971).
3 Walton H. Hamilton, "The ancient maxim caveat emptor," 40 *Yale Law Journal* 1133 (1931).
4 Ibid., 1156. "No Roman author whose works survive seems to have scribbled the two words down."
5 "Grolier ads tell consumer he's 'entitled to protection,' " *Advertising Age,* June 28, 56 (1971).

6 Hamilton, "Caveat emptor," 1157, note 166.
7 Ibid., 1136-63. Henri Pirenne, *Economic and Social History of Medieval Europe,* 176-88 (1937).
8 Hamilton, "Caveat emptor," 1138.
9 Ibid., 1137.
10 Ibid., 1141.
11 Ibid., 1141 ff.
12 Pirenne, *Medieval Europe,* 180; W. J. Ashley, *An Introduction to English Economic History and Theory,* 90 (1919).
13 Hamilton, "Caveat emptor," 1153.
14 Ibid., 1158-59.
15 Ibid., 1162.
16 Ibid., 1163.
17 Ibid.
18 Ibid., 1153.
19 Ibid., 1169 ff.
20 Ibid., 1163-69.
21 This exception was not set down explicitly in earlier times when buyers' normal distrustfulness usually made them decline items which were not available to examine. Later, when trust developed, the requirement of opportunity to examine was made specific: *Barnard v. Kellogg,* 77 U.S. 383 (1870); *Way v. Ryther,* 165 Mass. 226, 42 N.E. 1128 (1896); *Kell v. Trenchard,* 142 F. 16 (4th Cir., 1905).
22 Hamilton, "Caveat emptor," 1166-69, 1173.
23 Samuel Williston, *The Law Governing Sales of Goods,* § 194 ff (1948); William L. Prosser, *Handbook of the Law of Torts,* 4th ed., §97 (1971); *Uniform Laws Annotated,* 1 *Uniform Commercial Code, Master ed.* (1968; 1970). For broader discussion of warranty, see chapter 5.
24 Often shortened to "fraud." Also called, especially in early law, "deceit." Prosser, *Torts,* 4th ed., chap. 18. For broader discussion see chapter 6.
25 Hamilton, "Caveat emptor," 1138.
26 Y.B. 42 Ass. 259, pl. 8 (1367). This case was acknowledged as a precedent in the later *Dale's Case* and *Chandelor v. Lopus,* being identified in both cases as "42. Ass. 8" (see notes 27 and 33 below).
27 Cro. Eliz. 44, 78 Eng. Rep. 308 (1585).
28 Samuel Williston, "Liability for honest misrepresentation," 24 *Harvard Law Rev.* 415, 417 (1911). See the discussion of *Dale's Case* in chapter 5, at notes 3 and 28.

29 See detailed discussion in chapter 6.
30 Anthony Fitzherbert, *Fitzherbert's Abridgment,* Monstrauns de Faits [A showing of deeds] , pl. 16 (1577).
31 Anthony Fitzherbert, *Natura Brevium,* 94c (1534).
32 Hamilton, "caveat emptor," 1138.
33 Cro. Jac. 4, 79 Eng. Rep. 3 (1603); Hamilton, "caveat emptor," 1166 ff.
34 Sir James A. H. Murray, ed., *The Oxford English Dictionary* (1933).
35 Credit for unearthing these facts is owed to Grant Gilmore, "Products liability: a commentary," 38 *U. of Chicago Law Rev.* 103, 107 (1970).
36 *The Random House Dictionary of the English Language,* unabridged ed. (1966).
37 Gilmore, "Products liability," 108.
38 Prosser, *Torts,* 4th ed., § 97.
39 Hamilton, "Caveat emptor," 1169 ff.
40 No indication is available that this original case was published; the sole reference made to it occurs in the Exchequer case. See note 33 above.
41 *Southern v. Howard,* Cro. Jac. 468, 79 Eng. Rep. 400 (1618).
42 "Chandelor v. Lopus," 8 *Harvard Law Rev.* 282 (1894). A footnote mention of this missing third case was made in 73 Eng. Rep. 160, but the editor's notation identified it as a reference to the second case—further bad luck. See R. C. McMurtrie, "Chandelor v. Lopus," 1 *Harvard Law Rev.* 191 (1887); and Emlin McClain, "Implied warranties in sales," 7 *Harvard Law Rev.* 213 (1893).
43 Hamilton, "Caveat emptor," 1169.
44 Ibid., 1169 ff.
45 See note 47.
46 Hamilton, "Caveat emptor," 1186.
47 2 Caines (N.Y.) 48 (1804).
48 Coke's statement is quoted by Kent from *Co. Litt.,* 102a (1633).
49 *Barnard v. Kellogg;* see note 21 above.
50 Karl N. Llewellyn, *Cases and Materials on the Law of Sales,* 210 (1930).
51 *Burns v. Lane,* 138 Mass. 350 (1885).
52 "The central purpose of the provisions of the Federal Trade Commission Act . . . is in effect to abolish the rule of caveat emptor which traditionally defined rights and responsibilities in the world of commerce. That rule can no longer be relied upon

as a means of rewarding fraud and deception." *FTC v. Sterling Drug,* 317 F.2d 669, 674 (2d Cir., 1963). The case cites similar statements made by the Supreme Court in *FTC v. Standard Education Society,* 302 U.S. 112, 58 S.C. 113 (1937) (see chapter 10, at note 23), and by the court of appeals in *Goodman v. FTC,* 244 F.2d 584 (9th Cir., 1957) (see chapter 11, at note 33). George J. Alexander wrote that "Caveat emptor is dead" in his *Honesty and Competition,* 226 (1967).

CHAPTER 5: WARRANTY

1 See chapter 4, at note 33 ff.
2 Carthew 90, 90 Eng. Rep. 656 (1689); Holt, K.B. 5, 90 Eng. Rep. 900 (1689); also *Cross v. Garnet* (same case), 3 Mod. 261, 87 Eng. Rep. 172 (1689).
3 See chapter 4, at note 27.
4 1 Salk. 210, 91 Eng. Rep. 188 (1700); 1 Lord Raym. 593, 91 Eng. Rep. 1297 (1700); Holt, K.B. 208, 90 Eng. Rep. 1014 (1700).
5 Samuel Williston, *The Law Governing Sales of Goods,* § 196 (1948).
6 3 T.R. 51, 3 D. & E. 51, 100 Eng. Rep. 450 (1789).
7 Williston, *Sales,* § 198.
8 See chapter 4, note 47.
9 13 Mass. 139 (1816).
10 *Budd v. Fairmaner,* 8 Bing. 48, 131 Eng. Rep. 318 (1831).
11 *Borrekins v. Bevan,* 3 Rawle (Pa.) 23 (1831).
12 9 Watts (Pa.) 55 (1839).
13 Thomas A. Street, 1 *Foundations of Legal Liability,* 391 (1906).
14 Williston, *Sales,* § 199.
15 James Kent, 2 *Commentaries on American Law,* 11th ed., (George Comstock, ed.), 633 (1867).
16 51 N.Y. 198 (1872).
17 See also *White v. Miller,* 71 N.Y. 118 (1877). For a discussion of the New York and Pennsylvania warranty cases, see K. N Llewellyn, "On warranty of quality, and society," 36 *Columbia Law Rev.* 699 (1936), and 37 *Columbia Law Rev.* 341 (1937).
18 1 *Uniform Laws Annotated (Sales)* (1950; 1967), hereafter cited as USA.
19 56 and 57 Victoria, c. 71 (1894).

20 *Heilbut v. Buckleton,* A. C. 30 (1913).
21 *Walker v. Kirk,* 72 Pa. Super. Ct. 534 (1919); *Michelin Tire v. Schulz,* 295 Pa. 140, 145 A. 67 (1929); *Pritchard v. Liggett & Myers,* 350 F.2d 479 (3d. Cir., 1965).
22 *Pritchard v. Liggett & Myers;* see note 21 above.
23 *Uniform Laws Annotated,* 1 *Uniform Commercial Code, Master Ed.* (1968; 1970), hereafter cited as UCC. Section 2-313 states: "(1) Express warranties by the seller are created as follows: (a) Any affirmation of fact or promise made by the seller to the buyer which relates to the goods and becomes part of the basis of the bargain shall conform to the affirmation or promise. (b) Any description of the goods which is made part of the basis of the bargain creates an express warranty that the goods shall conform to the description. (c) Any sample or model which is made part of the basis of the bargain creates an express warranty that the whole of the goods shall conform to the sample or model."
    The Uniform Sales Act had contained what it described as "implied" warranties on descriptions and samples in its sections 14 and 16. Williston has explained, "It is customary to call the warranty in a sale by description an implied warranty, and for that reason this nomenclature has been preserved . . . in the Sales Act. The warranty might more properly, however, be called express, since it is based on the language of the parties" (Williston, *Sales,* § 233, and the same point is stated for samples in § 249). In the Uniform Commercial Code, therefore, these warranties have been called express. See distinction between express and implied warranties in the text following this note.
24 The idea was firmly established *prior* to sellerist times as well, although not using the terminology of "implied warranty." See chapter 4, at note 7 ff.
25 When Coke (as quoted in *Seixas,* chapter 4, at note 48) declared that "the common law bindeth him not, unless there be a warranty in deed, or law," this was the warranty in law to which he referred (an implied warranty, in modern terms, though he called it "express"). See Street, 1 *Foundations of Legal Liability,* 379.
26 See Lord Holt's cases, at notes 2 and 4 above.
27 See chapter 4, note 26.
28 See chapter 4, note 27.
29 2 *Blackstone's Commentaries* 451 (1771). That was not the last

word in England. As late as 1849 a court ruled there was no
implied warranty of title: *Morley v. Attenborough*, 3 Exch. 500.
But by 1864 it was established for good: *Eichholz v. Bannister*,
17 C.B.N.S. 708, 112 E.C.L. 708. In America the argument was
settled earlier: "If the seller has possession of the article, and he
sells it as his own, and not as agent for another, and for a fair price,
he is understood to warrant the title": James Kent, 2 *Commentaries on American Law*, 1st ed., 478 (1827). Also see Arthur
Biddle, *Law of Warranty in the Sale of Chattels*, 212 ff (1884).

30 USA, § 13.

31 UCC, § 2-312. The warranty of title in the UCC is not called
"implied," though not called "express" either. This appears to
be a technicality, to exempt section 2-312 from certain qualifications imposed on implied warranties by section 2-316. Still, the
warranty of title is based on the sale itself and not on words of
the seller.

32 Williston, *Sales*, § 228.

33 2 East 314, 102 Eng. Rep. 389 (1802).

34 The matter was aired in *Stuart v. Wilkins*, 1 Doug. 18, 99 Eng.
Rep. 15 (1778), but the warranty idea was actually quashed in
that case, the justice said, although the record might give the
opposite impression.

35 4 Camp. 144, 171 Eng. Rep. 46 (1815).

36 *Gardiner* may seem to have involved an express rather than
implied warranty, since it was based on the words "waste silk" in
the sale note. But Ellenborough felt the buyer deserved to
receive a commodity which would be not merely *describable* as
waste silk, but also *salable* (merchantable) as such, the latter not
being expressly stated. The implied warranty concept therefore
was invoked to quash the seller's defense that the goods were
called waste silk and therefore fulfilled the bargain.

37 William Prosser has written an authoritative article on the subject, but he cites no leading case: see "The implied warranty of
merchantable quality," 27 *Minnesota Law Rev.* 117 (1943).
Some relevant New York cases are discussed in Llewellyn, "On
warranty of quality."

38 USA, §15(2).

39 UCC, §2-314: "(1) Unless excluded or modified (Section
2-316), a warranty that the goods shall be merchantable is
implied in a contract for their sale if the seller is a merchant with
respect to the goods of that kind."

40 Prosser, "Implied warranty," says the earliest case was *Jones v. Bright,* 5 Bing. 531, 130 Eng. Rep. 1167 (1829). But *Hoe v. Sanborn,* 21 N.Y. 552 (1860), which contains a long discussion of the history and rationale behind implied warranties, says it was *Bluett v. Osborne,* 1 Stark. 384, 171 Eng. Rep. 504 (1816).

41 110 U.S. 108, 3 S.C. 537 (1884).

42 USA, § 15(1).

43 UCC, § 2-315: "Where the seller at the time of contracting has reason to know any particular purpose for which the goods are required and that the buyer is relying on the seller's skill or judgment to select or furnish suitable goods, there is unless excluded or modified under the next section an implied warranty that the goods shall be fit for such purpose."

44 Ibid., §§ 2-314, 2-315, 2-316.

45 Williston, *Sales,* § 234.

46 UCC, § 2-316.

47 Ibid.

48 William L. Prosser, "The fall of the citadel," 50 *Minnesota Law Rev.* 791 (1966).

49 168 Wash. 456, 12 P.2d 409 (1932).

50 William L. Prosser, *Handbook of the Law of Torts,* 4th ed., 652 (1971).

51 32 N.J. 358, 161 A.2d 69 (1960).

52 A prominent earlier case which attacked the "privity of contract" requirement was *MacPherson v. Buick,* 217 N.Y. 382, 111 N.E. 1050 (1916). It did not involve a sales representation express or implied, however; it was concerned with strict liability for negligence in manufacturing, a topic beyond the scope of this book. Although negligent misrepresentation is discussed in chapter 6, negligence in manufacturing is a separate concept: see Prosser, *Torts,* 4th ed., chap. 17; and Charles O. Gregory and Harry Kalven, Jr., *Cases and Materials on Torts,* 2d ed., chap. 8 (1969). Neither *Baxter* nor *Henningsen* (which cited *Baxter*) discussed *MacPherson* as a precedent, but both *Baxter and Mac-Pherson* relied upon *Thomas v. Winchester,* 6 N.Y. 397 (1852), the case which first established limited conditions under which negligence might be charged beyond the bounds of a contract.

53 3 TRR, ¶ 10,377, Report on Automobile Warranties (1970). Stanley Cohen, "Pollution threat may do more for consumers than laws, regulations," *Advertising Age,* March 2, 72 (1970).

54 Michael G. West, "Disclaimer of warranties—its curse and possible cure," 5 *Journal of Consumer Affairs* 154 (1971).

55 UCC, § 2-313.
56 Ibid., § 2-316.
57 Prosser, *Torts*, 4th ed., 656; and see articles and cases cited therein.
58 16 CFR 239, 4 TRR, ¶ 39,013, adopted April 26 (1960).

CHAPTER 6: MISREPRESENTATION

1 See chapter 4, at note 33 ff.
2 1 Lev. 102, 83 Eng. Rep. 318 (1663).
3 See chapter 5, at notes 2 and 4.
4 In *Bree v. Holbech*, 2 Doug. 654, 99 Eng. Rep. 415 (1781), we see the more usual result when an aggrieved party wanted a court to find fraud without proving knowledge of falsity. The claimant Bree was receiver of a document called genuine but in reality forged. The supplier Holbech was an apparently innocent party who believed the paper was good security and stated without qualification that it was. The receiver acknowledged the supplier "might not know of the falsehood," but argued for fraud because of the firm nature of the representation. The notion was far ahead of its time; it would be another century before intent to deceive would be defined to include "knowledge of lack of knowledge of truth" as well as "knowledge of falsity." See remainder of this chapter.
5 See chapter 5, note 6.
6 See chapter 4, note 47.
7 2 East 92, 102 Eng. Rep. 303 (1801).
8 What would this have accomplished in *Seixas*, (see chapter 4, at note 47), where the agent was presumed innocent because he did not know the wood was not brazilletto? He did not know it *was*, either, yet he stated so firmly.
9 11 M. & W. 401, 152 Eng. Rep. 860 (1843): "It is not necessary to show that the defendants knew the facts to be untrue; if they stated a fact which was true for a fraudulent purpose, they at the same time not believing that fact to be true, in that case it would be both a legal and moral fraud."
10 *Restatement of the Law of Torts*, § 526 (1938).
11 William L. Prosser, *Handbook of the Law of Torts*, 4th ed., 701 (1971).
12 L. R. 1 H. L., Sc. 145 (1867).

13 14 A.C. 337, 58 L. J. Ch. 864 (1889).

14 Some writers say this finding of fact was not reasonable, which is a point of evidence rather than of law. Samuel Williston, "Liability for honest misrepresentation," 24 *Harvard Law Rev.* 415, 439 (1911).

15 The fraud rule therefore, said Herschell, was as follows: "Fraud is proved when it is shown that a false representation has been made (1) knowingly, or (2) without belief in its truth, or (3) recklessly, careless whether it be true or false. . . . The third is but an instance of the second, for one who makes a statement under such circumstances can have no real belief in the truth of what he states. To prevent a false statement being fraudulent, there must, I think, always be an honest belief in its truth. And this probably covers the whole ground, for one who knowingly alleges that which is false, has obviously no such belief."

16 Williston, "Liability for honest misrepresentation," 439.

17 Prosser, *Torts,* 4th ed., 699, 705.

18 Ibid., 705.

19 Ibid., 699.

20 Ibid., 3d ed., 720.

21 See chapter 4, note 23, and chapter 5, note 18.

22 See chapter 5, at note 48.

23 See chapter 5, following note 51.

24 Prosser, *Torts,* 4th ed., 710.

25 Or "strict responsibility." Ibid.

26 See chapter 7, note 30.

27 See detailed discussion in chapter 9.

28 Prosser, *Torts,* 4th ed., 686.

CHAPTER 7: OPINION AND VALUE STATEMENTS AND PUFFERY

1 For warranty, see definitions in chapter 5, following note 18 and in note 23. For misrepresentation, see William L. Prosser, *Handbook of the Law of Torts,* 4th ed., 685 (1971).

2 See detailed discussion in chapter 2.

3 It did not begin with *Chandelor v. Lopus;* see chapter 4, note 33. Earl W. Kintner, as quoted although not cited in Frank Thayer, *Legal Control of the Press,* 4th ed., 647 (1962), has identified *Chandelor* as an exponent of the puffing privilege: "The court

went on to say that the seller's simple declaration that the stone was a Bezor stone was mere legitimate puffing of the article for sale." The court did not, of course, say that, although it did say that "every one in selling his wares will affirm that his wares are good." The affirmation about the stone, however, was treated as one of fact rather than of value, although some due must be given to the consideration that whether a thing was or wasn't a bezar-stone was a point on which men might have differed. In any event, *Chandelor* has never been cited as a precedent for opinion or puffery statements by any source prior to Kintner, who was FTC chairman from 1959 to 1961.

4 Yelv. 21, 80 Eng. Rep. 15 (1602).

5 Yelverton's report, dated Mich. 44 and 45 Eliz., was brief probably because it was merely a description by counsel of an earlier case, from Mich. 39 Eliz. This was noted by Justice Buller in *Pasley v. Freeman;* see note 10 below.

6 3 Bulst. 94, 81 Eng. Rep. 81 (1615); Cro. Jac. 386, 79 Eng. Rep. 331 (1615).

7 Ibid., Cro. Jac. 387: "and it was a matter which lay in his own view and conusance; and if he doubted of the weight thereof, he might have weighed it; and was not bound to give credence to another's speech; and being his own negligence, he is without remedy: as where one buys an horse upon warranting him to have both his eyes, and he hath but one eye, he is remediless; . . . The whole Court was of that opinion: although it was said, that there was apparent fraud here in him who affirmed." The ruling was based on Brian's decision; see chapter 13, at note 1.

8 See chapter 6, at note 2.

9 This other report was labeled "*Leakins v. Clissel,*" but is the same case: 1 Sid. 146, 82 Eng. Rep. 1022 (1663). "Land or jewels," the court explained further, "have more value to one man than to another, but otherwise is rent or other things certain, because the value is knowable and measurable to all."

10 3 T.R. 51, 3 D. & E. 51, 100 Eng. Rep. 450 (1789). See chapter 5, at note 6, and chapter 6, at note 5.

11 See chapter 8, at note 3; there is detailed discussion of this rule in chapter 8.

12 *Vernon v. Keys,* 12 East 632, 637, 104 Eng. Rep. 246, 249 (1810).

13 In *Seixas* (see chapter 4, note 47) Kent stated: "To make an affirmation at the time of sale a warranty, it must appear by

evidence to be so intended; (Buller, J., 3 D. & E. 57; Carth. 90; Salk. 210;) and not to have been a mere matter of judgment and opinion, and of which the defendant had no particular knowledge." The portion prior to the parentheses referred to Buller's references to *Crosse v. Gardner* and *Medina v. Stoughton*, in which Lord Holt had helped establish the warranty concept; see chapter 5, at notes 2 and 4. The portion following the parentheses was drawn from Buller's reference to *Harvey v. Young*. *Harvey* and *Pasley* involved fraud, not warranty, and Buller did not discuss the exemption of opinion statements from warranty considerations. Kent's statement, nonetheless, appears to have brought the opinion exemption into warranty law in America.

14 *Cochrane v. Cummings,* 4 U.S. (Pa.) 250, 1 L.Ed. 820 (1802), tended to disavow the opinion rule by describing as facts what were usually called opinions.

In *Gimblin v. Harrison,* 2 Ky. 315 (1804), a buyer charged a misrepresentation of land as "second-rate," the land actually being inferior to that description. However, the seller had reported what a third party had said, thus he was excused without a discussion of the possible status of "second-rate" as an opinion statement. "Second-rate" is a "superlative" rarely encountered in American advertising, but used successfully by Avis to help capture business from the third, fourth, etc., car rental companies rather than from number one Hertz.

In *Sherwood v. Salmon,* 2 Day (Conn.) 128 (1805), discussed in detail in chapter 13, at note 4, Sherwood's counsel argued on behalf of the misrepresentations that "the assertions of the defendant amount to no more than the expression of an opinion." He also argued that the defects were "discoverable by the exercise of due care" and therefore caveat emptor applied. The court decided for Sherwood on the second argument, therefore the first was not discussed. Later review at chancery (equity) rather than at law, 5 Day (Conn.) 439 (1813), determined that the seller's misrepresentations were of material facts, citing *Cochrane v. Cummings,* but the earlier decision was not voided.

15 5 Johns. (N.Y.) 354 (1810).

16 The decision stated: "Per Curiam. There was no express warranty or fraud proved in this case. The plaintiff below purchased the wagon, on sight, and the assertion of the defendant that it was worth more than its real value, furnishes no ground of action (1 Johns. Rep. 97. 274. 414. 4 Johns. Rep. 228. 4 Johns.

Rep. 421.) The judgment below must be reversed." The ruling appears to have been based on the authority of *Seixas* (see chapter 4, note 47), since three of the five cases cited found a basis in that case.

In 1827 Kent cited *Davis* along with *Harvey* and *Baily* in support of a similar rule: "A mere false assertion of value, when no warranty is intended, is no ground of relief to a purchaser, because the assertion is a matter of opinion, which does not imply knowledge, and in which men may differ. Every person reposes at his own peril in the opinion of others, when he has equal opportunity to form and exercise his own judgment." 2 *Commentaries on American Law,* 1st ed., 381 (1827). In his second edition, 2 *Commentaries* 485 (1832), Kent added to the above the following: "Simplex commendatio non obligat [Mere recommendation does not bind] ." No source was cited.

Kent apparently sided with Buller (*Pasley;* see note 10 above) in feeling the opinion exemption should not apply when the opinion was stated falsely. His statement above is reminiscent of Buller, and the comment directly following it is even more so: "If the seller represents what he himself believes as to the qualities or value of an article, and leaves the determination to the judgment of the buyer, there is no fraud or warranty in the case." In support of this statement Kent cited *Jendwine v. Slade,* 2 Esp. Rep. 572, 170 Eng. Rep. 459 (1797).

17 6 Metcalf (Mass.) 246 (1843).

18 This was dictum applying to statements between sellers and buyers; the actual decision went against the misrepresentor because he was a third party. See chapter 8, note 18.

19 3 Allen (Mass.) 380 (1862).

20 Walton H. Hamilton, "The ancient maxim caveat emptor," 40 *Yale Law Journal* 1133, 1186 (1931).

21 11 Cush. (Mass.) 348 (1853). The decision continued: "And there are other cases, in which it is held that an action will not lie, when he who sustains damage from a false affirmation might, by ordinary vigilance and attention, have ascertained that the statement on which he acted was false. See Harvey v. Young, Yelv. 21; Baily v. Merrell . . . ."

22 *Kimball v. Bangs,* 144 Mass. 321, 11 N.E. 113 (1887). See also *Gordon v. Parmelee,* 2 Allen (84 Mass.) 212 (1861); *Parker v. Moulton,* 114 Mass. 99 (1873); *Bishop v. Small,* 63 Me. 12 (1874). *Bishop* included this twist on the usual explanation as to

why value statements should be exempt: "It is not so much that such representations are not enough to amount to fraud and imposition, but that they are, so to speak, too much for that purpose. Most of them are too preposterous to believe."

23 148 Mass. 504, 20 N.E. 107 (1889).

24 *Vulcan Metals v. Simmons,* 248 F. 853 (2d Cir., 1918).

25 *Gordon v. Butler,* 105 U.S. 553 (1881).

26 Another Supreme Court case, *Southern Development v. Silva,* 125 U.S. 247, 8 S.C. 881 (1888), was similar in topic and result.

27 *American School of Magnetic Healing v. McAnnulty,* 187 U.S. 94, 23 S.C. 33 (1902).

28 241 U.S. 64 (1916).

29 *Uniform Laws Annotated,* 1 *Uniform Commercial Code, Master Ed.* (1968; 1970), § 2-313(2), hereafter cited as UCC. This result has been called "out of accord" with common law holdings that value statements under some conditions were held to be warranties: George Bogert, "Express warranties in sales of goods," 33 *Yale Law Journal* 14, 32 (1923).

30 This analysis involves misrepresentation law only; it is virtually impossible to designate a statement of opinion or value as a warranty on the ground that it implies a fact. It is possible in warranty law to obtain a ruling that an alleged opinion statement is in reality a factual statement, provided it makes a positive and unequivocal assertion of a fact. But warranty rulings favoring buyers are not made on the basis of what a statement implies (UCC, § 2-313). This is one of the areas in which warranty law has not supplanted misrepresentation law in offering protection to the consumer in modern times.

31 *Stebbins v. Eddy,* 4 Mason 414, 22 Fed. Cas. 1192 (1827).

32 *Edgington v. Fitzmaurice,* L. R. 29 Ch. D. 459 (1885). Among American cases applying this rule, Samuel Williston, *The Law Governing Sales of Goods,* § 628b (1948), gives strong credit to *Spead v. Tomlinson,* 73 N.H. 46, 59 A. 376 (1904).

33 "A representation of the state of mind . . . is a misrepresentation if the state of mind in question is otherwise than as represented. Thus, a statement that a particular person . . . is of a particular opinion or has a particular intention is a misrepresentation if the person in question does not hold the opinion or have the intention asserted." *Restatement of the Law of Torts,* § 525, comment b (1938).

34 L. R. 28 Ch. D. 7, 51 L.T.N.S. 718, 49 J. P. 182 (1884).

35 See cases cited by *Restatement of the Law of Torts (Second)*, Tentative Draft No. 10 (1964), as authority for section 539. One of them, *Andrews v. Jackson*, 168 Mass. 266, 47 N.E. 412 (1897), is noteworthy for being distinguished from *Deming v. Darling*. Both were decided in Massachusetts and dealt with vague claims about securities. In *Andrews* it was held that statements that certain notes were "as good as gold" could be intended to represent facts not knowable to the buyer, such as that the notes are known to be valid or that their maker is of known integrity and financial ability. The same holding would have been reasonable in *Deming*.

36 *Restatement of Torts (Second)*, Tentative Draft No. 10. The developments indicated by section 539 are due in part to the widening of the definition of fraud to include lack of knowledge of truth as well as knowledge of falsity, as discussed in chapter 6.

37 Ibid.

38 11 Mich. 68 (1862).

39 *Picard* was based largely on summaries of the law by Joseph Story, *Equity Jurisprudence*, § 198 (1836); William W. Story, *Sales*, § 170 (1847); and Kent, 2 *Commentaries on American Law*, 1st ed., 382, which suggest that the decision represents a natural development of Ellenborough's rule (see above, at note 12). In other words, while Ellenborough's rule was used at first to eliminate opinions from liability, the same principle was now being used to make them liable.

40 *Restatement of Torts (Second)*, Tentative Draft No. 10, § 542, comment on clause (b). For cases on which the clause is based see *Restatement of the Law of Torts*, Tentative Draft No. 13 (1936).

41 *Restatement of Torts (Second)*, Tentative Draft No. 10, § 542, comment on clause (c).

42 *Mattauch v. Walsh Bros.*, 136 Iowa 225, 113 N.W. 818 (1907).

43 *Restatement of Torts (Second)*, Tentative Draft No. 10, § 542, comment on clause (d).

44 Ibid., § 538A.

45 Little has been said about the buyer's role, but the assumption at law apparently is that the buyer will just as routinely make counterstatements which "blow down" the object which the seller is blowing up. No name has been given to this process of deflating.

46 See chapter 4, at note 51.

47 See chapter 4, at note 47.
48 Ivan L. Preston, "Why use false puffery?" *The New York Times,* February 25, business section, 17 (1973).
49 H. Ross Ford, Jr., April 17, 1973. Mr. Ford pointed out that I had incorrectly implied that all the new personnel had moved from Philadelphia. Only some had done so.
50 The comments were not, of course, freely offered. They were solicited.
51 "ANA, 4 A's, hit FTC's proposed drug ad rules," *Advertising Age,* July 7, 1 (1969).

CHAPTER 8: FACTUAL PUFFERY

1 The earliest legal reference to such statements as "puffs" was in *Picard v. McCormick* (1862) (see chapter 7, note 38). "Puffing" had been used earlier in legal parlance to refer to bids entered at auctions for the purpose of driving up prices artificially.
2 "Developments in the law: deceptive advertising," 80 *Harvard Law Rev.* 1005, 1054 (1967).
3 Vol. 1, 101, pl. 16 (1668). The phrase "M. 40 and 41 Eliz. B.R." is the citation for the 1598 case.
4 1 Sid. 146, 82 Eng. Rep. 1022 (1663); see chapter 7, note 9.
5 1 Lev. 102, 83 Eng. Rep. 318 (1663); see chapter 7, note 8, chapter 6, note 2.
6 The *Rol. Ab.* rule was not explicitly cited, but there is no doubt it was that rule. In a report of the same case labeled *Leakins v. Clizard,* 1 Keb. 510, 83 Eng. Rep. 1082 (1663), a citation is made to "Mich. 40 Eliz., pl 31." And in *Leakins v. Clizard,* 1 Keb. 522, 83 Eng. Rep. 1090 (1663), the rule is stated and attributed to 33 Eliz. *Leakins v. Clizard* is also reported at 1 Keb. 519, 83 Eng. Rep. 1088 (1663).
7 See chapter 7, note 10.
8 Possibly Grose arrived at this interpretation by improperly combining the results of *Leakins* and *Ekins.* The *Leakins* report showed the court accepting the *Rol. Ab.* rule on the grounds that it involved matters of uncertain value; it said nothing about whether such matters could be investigated independently. The *Ekins* report did not mention the rule, but showed the court stating that rent statements were subject to liability for falsity

because they could not be investigated independently. Grose concluded that the *Rol. Ab.* rule involved figures which could be investigated independently.

9 See chapter 7, note 12.
10 Mis-cited in the report as "1 Rol. Abr. 801, pl. 16."
11 This result reflected the confusion produced by existence of both the *Leakins* and *Ekins* reports. One was used by the plaintiff and the other was used by the defendant, each thinking the case would support his position.
12 On a further appeal to the Exchequer, *Vernon v. Keys*, 4 Taunt. 488, 128 Eng. Rep. 419 (1812), the luckless Vernon received this brief and curt opinion from Chief Justice Mansfield: "The question is, whether the defendant is bound to discuss the highest price he chuses to give, or whether he be not at liberty to do that as a purchaser, which every seller in this town does every day, who tells every falsehood he can, to induce a buyer to purchase. Judgment affirmed."
13 See chapter 7, note 15.
14 In 1827 Kent accepted for American law the explanations of Grose and Ellenborough for the *Rol. Ab.* rule: "The cases have gone so far as to hold, that if the seller should ever falsely affirm, that a particular sum had been bid by others for the property . . . no relief was to be afforded, for the buyer should have informed himself from proper sources of the value." James Kent, 2 *Commentaries on American Law*, 1st ed., 318 (1827). In a footnote to this comment Kent reflected Grose's authority by similarly blending together elements of *Leakins* and *Ekins* as though they were the same report: "1 *Rol. Abr.* 101, pl. 16. In the case of *Leakins v. Clissel*, 1 Sid. 146, 1 Lev. 102, the same law was declared [actually only in 1 Sid. 146], but a distinction was there taken between . . . value . . . and . . . rent, for the rent was a matter of fact resting in the private knowledge of the landlord and his tenants [actually only in 1 Lev. 102]."
15 See chapter 7, note 17.
16 *Cowen's Treatise* discussed and approved such statements, citing some of the same cases plus others, none of which appear to have been legitimate precedents for the particular point.
17 The court acknowledged the lesson of *Ekins* that rent could not be determined by the buyer, and that "fraudulent misrepresentations of particulars in relation to the estate, which the buyer has not equal means of knowing" (an obvious, though uncited,

quotation from Ellenborough, chapter 7, at note 12) are not allowed. It then declared that price paid was not one of those particulars. The fiction was maintained that the buyer could examine for himself.

18 The representor actually was found guilty—because he was a third party rather than the seller. Thus we are certain that the *Medbury* court held the price-paid affirmation to have been false and used with intent to defraud. The rules discussed in this chapter seem especially fictional when we realize that they applied only when the misstatements came from buyer or seller. See a complaint about this arbitrariness in a dissenting opinion in *Holbrook v. Connor,* 60 Me. 578, 589 (1872).

19 See chapter 7, note 21.

20 8 Allen (Mass.) 334 (1864): "The representations of a vendor of real estate to the vendee, as to the price paid for it, are to be regarded in the same light as representations respecting its value. A purchaser ought not to rely upon them; for it is settled that, even when they are false, and uttered with a view to deceive, they furnish no ground of action." See also *Poland v. Brownell,* 131 Mass. 138 (1881), and *Boles v. Merrill,* 173 Mass. 491, 53 N.E. 894 (1899).

21 60 Me. 578 (1872).

22 *Bishop v. Small,* 63 Me. 12 (1874); see chapter 7, note 22.

23 In *Dorr v. Cary,* 108 Iowa 725, 78 N.W. 682 (1899), a defense of such statements on the grounds that they were merely opinion, citing *Holbrook* as precedent, was soundly rejected.

24 Samuel Williston, *The Law Governing Sales of Goods,* § 628a (1948).

25 139 N.Y. 290, 34 N.E. 779 (1893).

26 A definition of materiality reflecting such decisions is given in § 538(2), *Restatement of the Law of Torts (Second),* Tentative Draft No. 10 (1964).

27 Williston, *Sales,* § 628a.

28 328 Mass. 341, 103 N.E.2d 692 (1952).

29 Tentative Draft No. 10, § 538.

30 See chapter 7, note 22.

31 Quoting a similarly worded statement from Melville M. Bigelow, 1 *Fraud* 13 (1877).

32 43 Ind. 38 (1873).

33 The fault apparently belongs with Bigelow, *Fraud.* I have seen his book cited as "1 Big. Fraud."

34 26 *Corpus Juris* 1097-98 (1922).

35 In *Holloway v. Forsyth,* 115 Mass. 358, 115 N.E. 483 (1917), statements similar to those in *Kimball* were held not to be dealer's talk but rather "statements of past or existent facts which a prudent person might regard as important elements . . . ." In *Corpus Juris Secundum* the rule was downgraded considerably: 37 *CJS* 241 (1943).

CHAPTER 9: THE FEDERAL TRADE COMMISSION

1 Federal Trade Commission Act, 38 Stat. 719 (1914), hereafter cited as FTC Act.
2 Ira M. Millstein, "The Federal Trade Commission and false advertising," 64 *Columbia Law Rev.* 439, 450 (1964).
3 FTC Act.
4 Millstein, "The FTC and false advertising," 450 ff; Earl W. Kintner, *A Primer on the Law of Deceptive Practices,* 16-17 (1971); Milton Handler, "Jurisdiction of the Federal Trade Commission over false advertising," 31 *Columbia Law Rev.* 527, 539 (1931); FTC Annual Report 6 (1916).
5 *Sears, Roebuck v. FTC,* 258 F. 307 (7th Cir., 1919).
6 253 U.S. 421, 40 S.C. 572 (1920).
7 *FTC v. Raladam,* 283 U.S. 643, 51 S.C. 587 (1931).
8 52 Stat. 114, 115 (1938).
9 See detailed discussion in chapter 6.
10 *Sears, Roebuck v. FTC.* See note 5.
11 FTC Act, § 5(b).
12 Even the violation of an order had no effective penalty apart from unattractive publicity until the Wheeler-Lea Amendments provided for a $5,000 fine; § 14, 52 Stat. 115 (1938).
13 Edward F. Cox, Robert C. Fellmuth, and John E. Schulz, *Nader's Raiders: Report on the Federal Trade Commission* (1969); *Report of the American Bar Association Commission to Study the Federal Trade Commission* (1969).
14 *Printers' Ink,* November 23, 68 (1911), and several other 1911 issues beginning with November 16, 2; "Untrue advertising," 36 *Yale Law Journal* 1155 (1927); Milton Handler, "False and misleading advertising," 39 *Yale Law Journal* 22 (1929); "Developments in the law: deceptive advertising," 80 *Harvard Law Rev.* 1005, 1018 (1967).
15 A survey reported in 1956 showed that most states had never

used the statute, and only a few had used it more than a handful of times. "Note: The regulation of advertising," 56 *Columbia Law Rev.* 1018, 1063 (1956).

16 "Deceptive advertising," 1123.

17 "Untrue advertising," 1157-60; Handler, "False and misleading advertising," 32.

18 *State v. Shaengold,* 13 Ohio Law Reporter 130 (1915).

19 It was also implied in *FTC v. Winsted,* 258 U.S. 483, 42 S.C. 384 (1922). See detailed discussion in chapter 15, at note 3.

20 291 U.S. 67, 54 S.C. 315 (1934). See chapter 15, at note 5.

21 See chapter 6, at note 13.

22 127 F.2d 792 (2d Cir., 1942).

23 The Commissioners might be wrong, of course, and therefore are subject to appeals court review. Review is limited, however, to matters of law and to the interpretation of the facts upon which the assessment of capacity to deceive has been based. Section 5(c) of the FTC Act provides that "the findings of the Commission as to the facts, if supported by evidence, shall be conclusive." The Commission has been reversed at times when a court found no evidence for the stated findings of fact. But given particular facts, the courts have generally declined to interfere with the Commission's interpretation that capacity to deceive exists.

24 *Sears, Roebuck v. FTC;* see text at note 10 above.

25 See note 8.

26 125 F.2d 679 (7th Cir., 1942).

27 Henry Bernstein, "New group asked rule on ads for 'identical' brands," *Advertising Age,* January 18, 1, and "We are what we are," January 25, 12 (1971).

28 Stanley Cohen, "Attack on nutrition-thwarting TV ads intensifies: food folk befuddled," ibid., February 22, 10 (1971).

29 *ITT Continental,* proposed complaint, TRR 1970-73 Transfer Binder, ¶ 19,539 (1971); complaint, TRR 1970-73 Transfer Binder, ¶ 19,779, FTC Dkt. 8860 (1971).

30 John Revett, "ITT strongly counters FTC charges, but execs split on Wonder ad claims," *Advertising Age,* July 17, 1 (1972). See also comments by Professor Yale Brozen in "Prof. Brozen, Pitofsky clash in Wonder case," ibid., May 22, 2 (1972).

31 *ITT Continental;* see chapter 2, note 6. The Commission soft-pedaled its charges against "uniqueness" in this final order. Still, it ordered that Wonder Bread should not be represented as an essential source of a nutritional value, where there are other

sources of the same or similar values, unless the claim can be substantiated. Meanwhile, another advertiser has agreed to FTC demands that it stop calling its Domino sugar unique: *Amstar,* consent order, TRR 1970-73 Transfer Binder, ¶ 20,356, FTC Dkt. No. 8887 (1973); "FTC hits Amstar for testimonials in its ads," *Advertising Age,* July 19, 3 (1971), and "Amstar okays corrective ads on sugar," June 18, 8 (1973).

32 *Pfizer;* see chapter 2, note 6.

33 FTC Act: "In determining whether any advertising is misleading, there shall be taken into account (among other things) not only representations made or suggested ... but also the extent to which the advertisement fails to reveal facts material in the light of such representations or material with respect to consequences which may result...."

34 132 F.2d 165 (7th Cir., 1942).

35 186 F.2d 52 (4th Cir., 1950).

36 See also *Charles of the Ritz v. FTC,* 143 F.2d 676 (2d Cir., 1944); and *Kalwajtys v. FTC,* 237 F.2d 654 (7th Cir., 1956).

37 127 F.2d 765 (7th Cir., 1942).

38 *J. B. Williams v. FTC;* see chapter 2, note 6.

39 *American Brands et al,* consent orders, 80 FTC 455 (1972).

40 Trade Regulation Rule for the Incandescent Lamp (Light Bulb) Industry, 2 TRR, ¶ 7972 (1970).

41 Trade Regulation Rule on Posting of Minimum Octane Numbers, 16 CFR 422, 4 TRR, ¶ 38,023 (1972).

42 36 FTC 563 (1943). Reversed by the Supreme Court, *Siegel v. FTC,* 327 U.S. 608, 66 S.C. 758 (1946), but not on this point.

43 *Gelb,* 33 FTC 1450 (1941), and *Gelb v. FTC,* 144 F.2d 580 (2d Cir., 1944). See chapter 10, at note 30.

44 *ITT Continental; Pfizer; DuPont;* see chapter 2, note 6.

45 "Howard's research will draw debate until substantiated," *Advertising Age,* June 19, 16 (1972).

46 Ernest Gellhorn, "Proof of consumer deception before the Federal Trade Commission," 17 *Kansas Law Rev.* 559 (1969); "Does ad mislead consumers?," *Advertising Age,* November 13, 56 (1972).

47 *Sun Oil,* proposed complaint, TRR 1970-73 Transfer Binder, ¶ 19,856 (1971); complaint, TRR 1970-73 Transfer Binder, ¶ 20,033, FTC Dkt. 8889 (1972).

48 289 F. 985 (6th Cir., 1923), modifying *L. B. Silver,* 4 FTC 73 (1921).

49 The court cited the decision in *McAnnulty* (see chapter 7, note

27) as controlling, and also cited *Harrison v. U.S.*, 200 F. 662 (6th Cir., 1912), as determining that a scheme to defraud "can not be found in any mere expression of honest opinion."

50 *Raladam v. FTC*, 42 F.2d 430 (6th Cir., 1930), reversing *Raladam*, 12 FTC 363 (1929).

51 *FTC v. Raladam;* see note 7 above. The case is known primarily for its questioning of the FTC's jurisdiction over advertising, as discussed at note 7.

52 *Raladam*, 24 FTC 475 (1937).

53 *FTC v. Raladam*, 316 U.S. 149, 62 S.C. 966 (1942), following *Raladam v. FTC*, 123 F.2d 34 (6th Cir., 1941). A somewhat related case, *Scientific Manufacturing v. FTC*, 124 F.2d 640 (3rd Cir., 1941), setting aside *Scientific Manufacturing*, 32 FTC 493 (1941), involved a person engaged not in trade but in voicing opinions about a matter of trade. For this reason alone the FTC's jurisdiction was voided, and the court stated, "Surely Congress did not intend to authorize the Federal Trade Commission to foreclose expression of honest opinion in the course of one's business of voicing opinion." The opinions, describing harmful effects on food of cooking utensils made of aluminum, were found false but also honestly held.

54 *Justin Haynes v. FTC*, 105 F.2d 988 (2d Cir., 1939). For other cases see "Note: Proving the falsity of advertising: the McAnnulty rule and expert evidence," 32 *Indiana Law Journal* 350 (1957).

55 The *Standard Brands* case completed in 1973, consent order, TRR 1970-73 Transfer Binder, ¶ 20,316, FTC Dkt. C-2377, suggests that the Commission may be mellowing to the point of allowing claims based on minority expert opinions. The FTC apparently has been concerned with the First Amendment implications of a policy which denied minority views based on evidence which was substantial but not preponderant. "Margarine case reveals FTC shift in minority scientific opinion view," *Advertising Age*, January 8, 1 (1973).

56 Hearing before Administrative Law Judge Harry Hinkes, September 10 (1973). See note 47 above.

57 Actually one of the classes saw an alternate ad in which a car pulls two boxcars and a caboose along a railroad track. The claims made in that ad were virtually identical to those in the "Coliseum" version, so I discuss the project here as though it involved only one ad.

58 *Sun Oil* complaint; note 47 above. The alleged misrepresentations are paraphrased here for simplification. The "Coliseum" ad was only one of several ads alleged to contain these misrepresentations.

59 David Ogilvy, *Confessions of an Advertising Man,* 140 (1963).

60 The case resulted in a cease and desist order against the advertising: *Sun Oil,* 3 TRR, ¶ 20,704, FTC Dkt. 8889 (1974).

61 The hearings resulted in a new regulation: Price Comparison Advertising, Ch. Ag 124, Department of Agriculture, State of Wisconsin, June 18 (1973).

62 " 'Corrective advertising' orders of the Federal Trade Commmission," 85 *Harvard Law Rev.* 477 (1971); "Corrective advertising and the FTC," 70 *Michigan Law Rev.* 374 (1971); "Corrective advertising—the new response to consumer deception," 72 *Columbia Law Rev.* 415 (1972).

63 The substantiation program began on June 10, 1971. 2 TRR, ¶ ¶ 7573, 7996 (1971). The FTC selects industries from time to time and demands detailed documentation from all or most of the firms therein. The program is intended to continue indefinitely. Stanley Cohen, "FTC to demand substantiation of ads, supply it to consumerists," *Advertising Age,* June 14, 1 (1971).

64 Brief filed by FTC with FCC, January 6, 1972, *CCH Newsletter* No. 2, January 12, (1972); "FTC tells FCC it supports 'counter' ads," *Advertising Age,* January 10, 2 (1972).

CHAPTER 10: REASONABLE CONSUMER OR IGNORANT CONSUMER?

1 "Ignorant man standard" is my own term, which I feel is correctly blunt. The terms "credulous man standard" and "lowest standard of intelligence," which lack semantic punch, have been used elsewhere; see *Truth in Advertising: A Symposium of the Toronto School of Theology,* 2-3, 30-34 (1972); Ira M. Millstein, "The Federal Trade Commission and false advertising," 64 *Columbia Law Rev.* 439, 458-62 (1964).

2 FTC Act, § 5(b); see chapter 9, note 1; Millstein, "False advertising," 483-87; "Developments in the law—deceptive advertising," 80 *Harvard Law Rev.* 1005, 1023-25 (1967).

3 See chapter 2, at note 13.

4 "Deceptive advertising," 1082; Millstein, "False advertising," 494; Edward F. Cox, Robert C. Fellmuth, and John E. Schulz,

Nader's Raiders: Report on the Federal Trade Commission (1969).

5 Millstein, "False advertising," 462-65; "Deceptive advertising," 1027-38; Peter B. Turk, "Justice Hugo Black and advertising: the stepchild of the First Amendment," in *For Freedom of Expression: Essays in Honor of Hugo L. Black*, ed. Dwight L. Teeter and David Grey (in press).

6 *Restatement of the Law of Torts (Second)*, § 283 (1965). Section 283A adds that a child must act as would a reasonable person of like age, intelligence, and experience under like circumstances.

7 *Vaughan v. Menlove*, 3 Bing. N.C. 468, 132 Eng. Rep. 490 (1837). For other cases and references see Reporter's Notes to § 283 of *Restatement of Torts (Second)*.

8 See chapter 6, following note 10.

9 The term *contributory negligence* is not always used, but the idea of denying recovery for unreasonable reliance on misrepresentations is based on that concept; William L. Prosser, *Handbook of the Law of Torts*, 4th ed., 717 (1971).

10 Prosser, ibid., 716.

11 See extended discussions in chapters 3, 7, and 11.

12 FTC Act, §5(b); see chapter 9, note 1.

13 *FTC v. Universal Battery*, 2 FTC 95 (1919).

14 See also *FTC v. A. A. Berry*, 2 FTC 427 (1920); *FTC v. Alben-Harley*, 4 FTC 31 (1921); *FTC v. Williams Soap*, 6 FTC 107 (1923); *Alfred Peats*, 8 FTC 366 (1925).

15 See discussion above at note 6 ff.

16 *Restatement of Torts (Second)*, § 283, comment c.

17 Francis H. Bohlen, "Mixed questions of law and fact," 72 *Univ. of Pennsylvania Law Rev.* 111, 113 (1923).

18 8 FTC 177 (1924).

19 *John C. Winston v. FTC*, 3 F.2d 961 (3rd Cir., 1925).

20 *Nugrape*, 9 FTC 20 (1925); *Ostermoor*, 10 FTC 45 (1926), but set aside in *Ostermoor v. FTC*, 16 F.2d 962 (2d Cir., 1927); *William F. Schied*, 10 FTC 85 (1926); *Good Grape*, 10 FTC 99 (1926); *Hobart Bradstreet*, 11 FTC 174 (1927); *Frank P. Snyder*, 11 FTC 390 (1927); *Dr. Eagan*, 11 FTC 436 (1927); *Berkey & Gay Furniture*, 12 FTC 227 (1928), but set aside in *Berkey & Gay Furniture v. FTC*, 42 F.2d 427 (6th Cir., 1930); *Northam-Warren*, 15 FTC 389 (1931), but set aside in *Northam-Warren v. FTC*, 59 F.2d 196 (2d Cir., 1932); *Fairyfoot Products* 20 FTC

40 (1934), affirmed in *Fairyfoot v. FTC*, 80 F.2d 684 (7th Cir., 1935).

21 *Standard Education Society*, 16 FTC 1 (1931).

22 *FTC v. Standard Education Society*, 86 F.2d 692 (2d Cir., 1936).

23 302 U.S. 112, 58 S.C. 113 (1937).

24 Ibid., 116: "It was clearly the practice of respondents through their agents, in accordance with a well matured plan, to mislead customers . . . ."

25 114 F.2d 33 (2d Cir., 1940).

26 *Moretrench v. FTC*, 127 F.2d 792 (2d Cir., 1942). This was the same judge who once had rejected similar claims on the grounds that "there are some kinds of talk which no man takes seriously . . ."; *Vulcan Metals v. Simmons;* see chapter 7, note 24.

27 See notes 29 and 30 below.

28 *D.D.D. v. FTC* (1942); see chapter 9, note 26; *Aronberg v. FTC* (1942), see chapter 9, note 34; *Gulf Oil v. FTC*, 150 F.2d 106 (5th Cir., 1945); *Parker Pen v. FTC*, 159 F.2d 509 (7th Cir., 1946). In the latter case the FTC's role was said to be to "protect the casual, one might say the negligent, reader, as well as the vigilant and more intelligent . . . ." A much-used quotation, cited in *Aronberg, Gulf Oil,* and *Gelb* (see note 30 below), stated, "The law is not made for the protection of experts, but for the public—that vast multitude which includes the ignorant, the unthinking, and the credulous, who, in making purchases, do not stop to analyze, but are governed by appearances and general impressions"; *Florence v. Dowd*, 178 F. 73 (2d. Cir., 1910). This was a pre-FTC case with evidence of deliberate deception.

29 *Charles of the Ritz v. FTC*, 143 F.2d 676 (2d Cir., 1944), following *Charles of the Ritz*, 34 FTC 1203 (1942).

30 *Gelb v. FTC*, 144 F.2d 580 (2d Cir., 1944), following *Gelb*, 33 FTC 1450 (1941).

31 39 FTC 357 (1944).

32 *Carlay v. FTC*, 153 F.2d 493 (1946).

33 *Allen B. Wrisley v. FTC*, 113 F.2d 437 (7th Cir., 1940); also later in *Buchsbaum v. FTC*, 160 F.2d 121 (7th Cir., 1947).

34 See detailed discussion of such cases in chapter 7.

35 *Lorillard v. FTC* (1950), see chapter 9, note 35; *Independent Directory*, 47 FTC 13 (1950) (but see dissent by Commissioner Mason); *Goodman v. FTC*, 244 F.2d 584 (9th Cir., 1957); *FTC v. Sewell*, 353 U.S. 969, 77 S.C. 1055 (1957) (see chapter 11, at

note 32); *Bantam Books v. FTC*, 275 F.2d 680 (2d Cir., 1960) (but see questions raised by Judge Moore); *Exposition Press v. FTC*, 295 F.2d 869 (2d Cir., 1961); *Giant Food v. FTC*, 322 F.2d 977 (D.C. Cir., 1963); *FTC v. Colgate*, 380 U.S. 374, 85 S.C. 1035 (1965) (see chapter 15, at notes 38-42).

36 63 FTC 1282 (1963).

37 In *Papercraft*, 63 FTC 1965, 1997 (1963), Commissioner MacIntyre protested that the retreat from the extreme ignorant man position was unfortunate. The majority opinion had withdrawn from protecting the "foolish or feeble-minded," and MacIntyre dissented: "Should this observation be construed as a retreat from our long-held position that the public as a whole is entitled to protection, including even 'the ignorant, the unthinking, and the credulous,' then the result may well be confusion."

38 *Truth in Advertising*, 31.

39 "It might be said that the test of consumer competence generally employed by the Commission appears to approximate the least sophisticated level of understanding possessed by any substantial portion of the class of persons to whom the advertisement is addressed." Personal correspondence to Peter B. Turk from Gale T. Miller, law clerk, Bureau of Consumer Protection, Federal Trade Commission, December 6, 1971. The "class of persons" assumed generally consists of adults. Special consideration for representations made to children (see note 6) was recognized in *FTC v. Keppel*, 291 U.S. 304, 54 S.C. 423 (1934). As for other groups, Miller wrote: "It is the position of the staff that advertising geared towards other special audiences, such as the ghetto dweller, the elderly, and the handicapped, might also be subjected to a more rigorous test than is applied to advertisements addressed to the public at large."

CHAPTER 11: THE FTC AND PUFFERY

1 The ill-fated Printers' Ink Statute (see chapter 9, at note 14) experienced the first two of these trends. Undoubtedly its authors wanted to control those opinion or value statements which might deceive. But the criminal sanctions made it unlikely that the courts would use the statute to prohibit anything but literal-

ly false facts. In *People v. Clarke,* 252 App. Div. (N.Y.) 122 (1937), the court said the statute prohibited "representations of fact," and found that some of the statements involved were only opinion. Conscious untruth was not found to exist in the case. Factual misrepresentations would have been liable even if not made with conscious knowledge of their untruth, but the court would not hold opinion statements liable unless that requirement were met.

2 *FTC v. Universal Battery;* see chapter 10, note 13.

3 See cases in chapter 10, note 14; also *Nugrape, Schied, Good Grape, Bradstreet, Snyder,* and *Eagan,* chapter 10, note 20. These decisions ran parallel to the type of analysis offered by § 539, *Restatement of the Law of Torts (Second),* Tentative Draft No. 10 (1964). See chapter 7, at note 36.

4 *Electric Appliance,* 2 FTC 335 (1920).

5 *Vulcan Metals v. Simmons;* see chapter 7, at note 24, chapter 10, note 26.

6 *Ostermoor,* 10 FTC 45 (1926).

7 *Ostermoor v. FTC,* 16 F.2d 962 (2d Cir., 1927).

8 *Fairyfoot Products,* 20 FTC 40 (1934).

9 *Fairyfoot v. FTC,* 80 F.2d 684 (7th Cir., 1935).

10 *Kidder Oil,* 29 FTC 987 (1939).

11 *Kidder Oil v. FTC,* 117 F.2d 892 (7th Cir., 1941).

12 52 Stat. 114, 115 (1938); see chapter 9, at note 8.

13 *Cong. Record,* 74th Cong., 2d sess., vol. 80, pt. 6, 6592, May 4 (1936).

14 *Moretrench,* 28 FTC 297 (1939).

15 *Moretrench v. FTC;* see chapter 10, note 26.

16 See chapter 10, at note 23.

17 See chapter 10, note 28. The court also provided this definition: "Puffing refers, generally, to an expression of opinion not made as a representation of fact."

18 Some other cases which attacked elements of puffery, though not labeling it as that: *David V. Bush,* 14 FTC 90 (1930); *Tarbell,* 14 FTC 442 (1931); *Howe v. FTC,* 148 F.2d 561 (9th Cir., 1945), affirming *Howe,* 36 FTC 685 (1943).

19 *Carlay v. FTC,* 153 F.2d 493 (7th Cir., 1946), setting aside *Carlay,* 39 FTC 357 (1944).

20 *Langendorf,* 43 FTC 132 (1946), may appear to contradict this point, since it involved FTC action against a company's claim to

have "the bread that baking experts judged America's finest."
What was called deceptive, however, was not the opinion claim
about "finest" but the factual representation that experts had
made such a judgment. The Commission's findings stated, "No
tests have been made by qualified experts."

21 46 FTC 162 (1949). The record of the decision includes a report
of the complaint.

22 If the *Carlay* court reversal convinced the FTC while the *Ostermoor* and *Kidder* reversals did not, the reason perhaps was that
Carlay cited common law precedents favoring puffery while the
other decisions did not.

23 *Washington Mushroom*, 53 FTC 368 (1956).

24 *Postal Life and Casualty Insurance*, 54 FTC 494 (1957).

25 *Necchi*, 53 FTC 1040 (1957).

26 *Tanners Shoe*, 53 FTC 1137 (1957).

27 See chapter 7, note 28.

28 *Gulf Oil v. FTC*, discussed at note 17 above, said something
similar, though without citing *New South Farm* (see chapter 3,
note 2). For similar cases see *Dobbs Truss*, 48 FTC 1090 (1952);
C. H. Stuart, 53 FTC 1127 (1957); *Unicorn Press*, 47 FTC 258
(1950). But did the FTC temporarily flaunt the *New South
Farm* rule when it allowed as puffery the claim that Celanese was
"different from any type of fiber ever made" although there was
no evidence of difference between this fiber and other syn-
thetics? *Celanese*, 50 FTC 170 (1953).

29 *Steelco*, 46 FTC 643 (1950), affirmed in *Steelco v. FTC*, 187
F.2d 693 (7th Cir., 1951).

30 *National Health Aids*, 49 FTC 1661 (1952), affirmed in *FTC v.
National Health Aids*, 108 F.Supp. 340 (1952).

31 See note 26.

32 *Sewell*, 50 FTC 806 (1954), reversed in *Sewell v. FTC*, 240 F.2d
228 (9th Cir., 1956), but affirmed in *FTC v. Sewell*, 353 U.S.
969, 77 S.C. 1055 (1957), citing *Standard Education* and *Algoma*.

33 *Goodman*, 52 FTC 982 (1956), affirmed in *Goodman v. FTC*,
244 F.2d 584 (9th Cir., 1957).

34 55 FTC 354 (1958).

35 The hearing examiner, now called administrative law judge, is the
FTC official who conducts the preliminary hearing, collects the
testimony of witnesses and other evidence, and renders a deci-

sion for the Commissioners' consideration. The Commissioners may agree or disagree with the judge in rendering their official decision.

36 59 FTC 1231 (1961).
37 61 FTC 840 (1962).
38 59 FTC 1452 (1961). The case has a history of appeals on matters other than puffery; see chapter 15, at notes 38-42.
39 Cases discussed at notes 6, 10, and 19 above.
40 *Western Radio*, 63 FTC 882 (1963), modified by *Western Radio v. FTC*, 339 F.2d 937 (7th Cir., 1964); *Wilmington Chemical*, 69 FTC 828 (1966); *Waltham Watch*, 60 FTC 1692 (1962); *Heinz W. Kirchner*, see chapter 10, note 36. In *Kirchner* the FTC refused to admit Swim-Ezy's "unsinkability" as puffery; the refusal was upheld on appeal in *Heinz W. Kirchner v. FTC*, 337 F.2d 751 (9th Cir., 1964). However, in accepting the term *invisible* the FTC appears to have treated it as puffery, although not calling it that. The Commissioners compared it to "inconspicuousness," and invisibility is the maximum degree of that. Thus they were treating "invisible" perhaps over-generously as an exaggeration of an actual quality. They passed up the chance to argue on the grounds of the *New South Farm* definition, at notes 27-28 above, that invisibility was a characteristic not literally present and thus not eligible to be called puffery. Also in *Kirchner* the FTC consented to regard two other matters as puffery.
41 *Carnation*, consent order, 77 FTC 1547 (1970). Stanley Cohen, "FTC hits loaded comparisons and 'deception' in food ads," *Advertising Age*, November 1, 21, 76 (1971).
42 Trade Regulation Rule; see chapter 9, note 40.
43 Speech before New York State Bar Association, food, drug, and cosmetics law section, January 1971; "Advertising needs 'fundamental attitude change': FTC's Jones," *Advertising Age*, February 1, 68 (1971). A similar comment has been made by Milton Handler: "The advertiser should be credited with sufficient business acumen not to waste valuable space on statements which serve no function"; *Trade Regulations*, 3d ed., 981 (1960). Very likely it should be found as a matter of law that every element of an advertising message is material, i.e., affects the buyer's purchasing decision; see chapter 9, at note 25. See also chapter 3, at note 10.

44 In a 1971 interview, Robert Pitofsky, chief of FTC's bureau of consumer protection, mentioned three cases where the puffery defense would apply: (1) where the assertion is immaterial, (2) where the exaggeration is insubstantial, (3) where the exaggeration is of a type that can't be measured ("amazing," "perfect," "better," "great"). The article reporting the interview suggested that puffery's limits were being greatly reduced. Stanley Cohen, "This week in Washington," *Advertising Age,* March 29, 121 (1971). Words, however, such as "immaterial," "insubstantial," and "can't be measured" are vague concepts open to widely varying interpretations. Clues to such interpretations are best obtained from the Commission's actual cases.

45 See chapter 7, note 4.

46 2 TRR, ¶ 7899, effective February 19 (1967).

47 "Philco-Ford wonders if FTC plays favorites with ad data," *Advertising Age,* March 13, 2 (1972). In a case involving a self-regulating body rather than the FTC, the Missouri Public Interest Research Group asked the National Advertising Review Board for a ruling against Schlitz advertising which said a better beer than Schlitz is in the area of unexplored territory. The response was that the claim was a matter of taste and there was no way to invalidate such opinions. MoPIRG cited the Advertising Code of American Business, Article 8, which says "Advertising shall avoid the use of exaggerated or unprovable claims." This rule would seem to prohibit the Schlitz advertising, but the self-regulators refused to enforce it. See similar comment regarding Article 8 in chapter 17, at note 41.

48 *Coca-Cola,* complaint, TRR 1970-73 Transfer Binder, ¶ 19,351 (1970).

49 See chapter 2, note 6, and discussion of literally misdescriptive names in chapter 15.

50 *Standard Oil of California,* complaint, TRR 1970-73 Transfer Binder, ¶ 19,352 (1970).

51 See chapter 2, note 6.

CHAPTER 12: SOME ADDITIONAL KINDS OF PUFFERY

1 See detailed discussion in chapter 3.

2 See chapter 2, at note 13.

CHAPTER 13: THE BALLOONING OF OBVIOUS

1 Y.B. 11 Edw. IV, 6, 10 (1471). Note that warranty and misrepresentation (deceit) are combined in a confusing way. That was typical in early times, before the two concepts were established as separate legal actions; William L. Prosser, *Handbook of the Law of Torts*, 4th ed., 685-87 (1971). Establishment of Brian's rule was aided considerably by its mention in *Ekins v. Tresham;* see chapter 6, note 2.

2 See chapter 7, notes 6-7.

3 Brian's rule was stated in *Baily*, Cro. Jac. 387, and it was cited in *Baily*, 3 Bulst. 94, 95, as "11 E. 4."

4 2 Day (Conn.) 128 (1805). See chapter 7, note 14.

5 See chapter 7, note 22.

6 80 U.S. 379 (1871).

7 153 Mass. 60, 26 N.E. 416 (1891).

8 215 Mo. 312, 114 S.W. 979 (1908).

9 But for a strong opposing view just one year later, see *Mabardy v. McHugh*, 202 Mass. 148, 88 N.E. 894 (1909).

10 See chapter 10, at note 23.

11 *Uniform Laws Annotated*, 1 *Uniform Commercial Code, Master Ed.* (1968; 1970), § 2-313, hereafter cited as UCC.

12 Samuel Williston, *The Law Governing Sales of Goods*, § 207 (1948). The same source notes, however, that a general warranty of soundness is not intended to cover any obvious defects. To warrant a blind horse as "sound" is to mean "sound except as to his eyes."

13 *Restatement of the Law of Torts (Second)*, Tentative Draft No. 10 (1964). Curiously, the attached comment refers to the horse example in note 12, causing one to wonder whether section 541 means precisely what it says.

14 *Restatement of the Law of Torts* (1938). The 1964 re-draft was rejected; see note 15.

15 Francis Bohlen, 13 *American Law Institute Proceedings* 342 (1936). This historical trend was emphasized in 1964 when William Prosser proposed a new version of section 540, to read: "The recipient of a fraudulent misrepresentation is justified in relying upon its truth without investigation, unless he knows or has reason to know of facts which make his reliance unreasonable." Certain ALI members thought this was a return to the notion that the buyer's contributory negligence would negate an action for fraudulent misrepresentation. Prosser said it con-

cerned the issue of "notice," not negligence. Professor R. E. Keeton observed that the developments since the first drafting of the *Restatement* "have all been in the line of giving the fool somewhat greater protection against the defrauder than he had in those days." 4 *ALI* 509 (1964). In a heated discussion, adjourned for one year and renewed, ALI members voted 67-39 to retain the original wording of section 540, which thoroughly negated the buyer's obligation to inspect. 42 *ALI* 322 (1965).

16 Remaining are rulings, regarding both warranties and misrepresentations, covering the situation where the buyer chooses to inspect and his inspection successfully detects the truth about a defect. UCC, § § 2-313, 2-316; *Restatement of Torts (Second)*, § 541. If the buyer buys the object anyway, he must rely upon anything he happens to know. Similarly, if he happens to indicate that he will rely on his own inspection, then it, whether successful or not, supersedes the seller's liability. But these are not serious impediments to consumerism because they are matters of volunteering to inspect rather than being obligated to inspect.

17 *Williams v. Rank & Son Buick;* see chapter 2, note 13.

18 The dissenting opinion in the 4-3 decision, ibid., stated: "At a time when there is so much emphasis on consumer protection, the majority, in effect, revitalizes the old caveat emptor doctrine without specifically mentioning it."

19 Some of the FTC's recent actions toward children's advertising are noted in *Advertising Age,* August 6, 1, August 13, 1, 62, August 27, 6, and September 10, 36 (1973).

20 For FTC, see chapter 9, at note 25; for common law, see *Restatement of Torts,* § § 525, 538 (1938).

21 *Lever Bros.,* affadavit of voluntary compliance, TRR 1967-70, Transfer Binder, ¶ 18,711 (1969). The company claimed it was a spoof; "Case talks to FTC," *Advertising Age,* November 8, 148 (1971).

22 "Case talks to FTC," 148.

CHAPTER 14: WISHING IN THE MARKET

1 See chapter 3 at note 17 ff, and chapter 17, following note 37.
2 See chapter 3, at notes 1-2.

3 The analysis which follows owes much to David Potter, "The institution of abundance: advertising," chap. 8 of his *People of Plenty* (1954).

4 Leigh R. Isaacs, "Psychological advertising: a new area of FTC regulation," 1972 *Wisconsin Law Rev.* 1097 (1972).

5 See chapter 2, note 6, and chapter 9, at note 29 ff.

6 In the final decision, ibid., this portion of the complaint was decided in Wonder Bread's favor. This means that the "new area of FTC regulation" is defined by only a single case.

7 *J. B. Williams,* consent order, 81 FTC 238 (1972). The advertising agency, Della Femina, Travisano, and Partners, was also a party to the order.

8 The FTC has given some indication that it may attack social-psychological misrepresentations on grounds of unfairness rather than (or in addition to) deception. Unfairness in advertising, as contrasted to unfairness in competition, has only recently been given consideration, despite the fact that the Commission has been mandated since 1938 to prohibit "unfair or deceptive acts or practices"; see chapter 9, at note 8. Conceivably it could become commonplace to rule that sellers' messages are unfair and therefore illegal even though not deceptive. Gerald J. Thain, "Consumer protection: advertising—the FTC response," 26 *Food, Drug and Cosmetic Law Journal* 609, 621 (1971); *FTC v. Sperry & Hutchinson,* 405 U.S. 233, 92 S.C. 898 (1972); James A. Carney, "Section 5 of the Federal Trade Commission Act—unfairness to consumers," 1972 *Wisconsin Law Rev.* 1071 (1972); Isaacs, "Psychological advertising."

CHAPTER 15: STILL MORE KINDS OF PUFFERY, BUT CONTROLLED

1 These decisions have not been made by specific regulatory actions, but merely by the lack of such actions. To suggest that lack of action amounts to a deliberate decision in such cases seems reasonable in the light of other cases we will see in which action *was* taken. While I am here discussing designations conceded to be literally false and the consequent fear that the FTC might err in failing to identify those among them which are deceptive, George J. Alexander discusses designations which are literally true, and indicates that the FTC may systematically fail

to identify those among them which are *not* deceptive. *Honesty and Competition,* chap. 2 (1967). I agree fully. The matter, however, is beyond the topic set out for this book.

2 Stone China: *Harker China,* consent order, 62 FTC 1382 (1963); Plyhide: *Sales Development Corp.,* consent order, 62 FTC 1461 (1963); Six Month Floor Wax: *Continental Wax v. FTC,* 330 F.2d 475 (2d Cir., 1964); Made in USA: I swear I saw a citation to this once, but I can't find it now. Caveat reader. There's no question, though, that goods made in Japan have been so mislabeled: *Giant Plastics,* consent order, 61 FTC 179 (1962), among others; *National Laboratories of St. Louis,* 63 FTC 948 (1963).

3 258 U.S. 483, 42 S.C. 384 (1922).

4 288 U.S. 212, 53 S.C. 335 (1933).

5 291 U.S. 67, 54 S.C. 315 (1934). See chapter 9, at note 20.

6 Earl W. Kintner, *A Primer on the Law of Deceptive Practices,* 118 (1971).

7 *Institute of Hydraulic Jack Repair,* 63 FTC 127 (1963).

8 *Ship 'n Shore,* consent order, 58 FTC 757 (1961); modified order, 70 FTC 631 (1966). FTC statement on use of the term *Madras; FTC Advertising Alert,* No. 6, June 30 (1965).

9 *United Garment,* 66 FTC 711 (1964).

10 *Pan American Cigar,* consent order, 72 FTC 752 (1967).

11 *County Tweeds,* 50 FTC 470 (1953).

12 *Elliott Knitwear v. FTC,* 266 F.2d 787 (2d Cir., 1959).

13 *Carter Products v. FTC,* 268 F.2d 461 (9th Cir., 1959).

14 *Grand Rapids Furniture v. FTC,* 134 F.2d 332 (3rd Cir., 1943).

15 *Virginia Products,* 29 FTC 451 (1939).

16 *United States Testing Co.,* consent order, 61 FTC 1312 (1962).

17 *FTC v. Army and Navy Trading Co.,* 88 F.2d 776 (D.C. Cir., 1937).

18 Fed. Alcohol Admin. Act, § 5.22, 27 CFR 12 (1973); "Brandies," *Consumer Reports,* November, 603 (1967).

19 FAAA, § 5.22, 27 CFR 34 (1973); "Scotch whiskies," *Consumer Reports,* November, 622 (1968).

20 FAAA, § 4, 27 CFR 12 (1973); "Champagne," *Consumer Reports,* November, 638 (1969).

21 FAAA, § 4, 27 CFR 12 (1973); "Ports," *Consumer Reports,* August, 434 (1968).

22 FAAA, § 4, 27 CFR 12 (1973); "Sherries," *Consumer Reports,* June, 314 (1968).

23 "Sherries," *Consumer Reports,* June, 314 (1968).

24 Felix Kessler, "A territorial question brings strife to home of Roquefort cheese," *Wall Street Journal,* November 13, 1 (1972).

25 It backfired because the FTC Act entitled the Commission to go beyond common law without attention to past limitations, which meant its decisions on misdescription amounted to the setting rather than the following of precedent. No precedent existed that misdescription was unfair to the public, but none said it was fair, either. *Winsted;* see note 3 above.

26 311 F.2d 358 (1st Cir.), following *Korber Hats,* 60 FTC 642 (1962).

27 "FDA moves to bar deceptive locale advertising," *Advertising Age,* June 22, 3 (1970).

28 Dismissal of charges, 63 FTC 2017 (1963).

29 See detailed discussion in chapter 4, at note 7 ff.

30 "Some McDonald's patties cited for short weight," *New York Times,* July 25, 46 (1973). Perhaps McDonald's should have said "approximately." The FTC once stopped the selling of rugs by the description "9′ x 12′" when they were actually 103″ x 139″. The statement "All sizes approximate" had been used, but was adjudged impermissible for describing such a difference. The Commission said, however, "The word 'approximate' will perhaps cover an inch or two departure from the norm." *Gimbel Bros.,* 61 FTC 1051 (1962). Re the issue of where one draws the line, see the discussion of permissible puffing versus impermissible exaggeration in chapter 7, following note 45.

31 Charlotte Montgomery, "Consumerism today: where it's at," *Context,* Du Pont Company, No. 1 (1973).

32 Details below, particularly following note 42, on the legality of such actions.

33 *Aluminum Company of America,* 58 FTC 265 (1961).

34 *Colgate,* 58 FTC 422 (1961).

35 *Standard Brands,* 56 FTC 1491 (1960).

36 *Libby-Owens-Ford v. FTC,* 352 F.2d 415 (6th Cir., 1965).

37 *Carter Products v. FTC,* 323 F.2d 523 (5th Cir., 1963).

38 *Colgate,* 59 FTC 1452 (1961); see also chapter 11, at note 38, and Daniel Seligman, "The great sandpaper shave: a real-life story of truth in advertising," *Fortune,* December, 131 (1964).

39 310 F.2d 89 (1st Cir., 1962).

40 *Colgate,* 62 FTC 1269 (1963).

41 *Colgate v. FTC,* 326 F.2d 517 (1st Cir., 1963).

42 380 U.S. 374, 85 S.C. 1035 (1965).

43 "Johnny Carson hits 'dishonest' ads on his show," *Advertising Age,* October 31, 167 (1966).
44 Maurine Christopher, "Creative folk say they don't dig FTC rules," ibid., March 16, 3 (1970).
45 *Philadelphia Inquirer,* July 10, 1-B (1973).
46 *Campbell Soup,* consent order, 77 FTC 664 (1970). Another result was the development of Students Opposing Unfair Practices (SOUP), a law students' organization which participated in the case and urged the FTC to make Campbell's not only stop using marbles but admit in future ads that it had practiced deception in doing so. The latter request was denied on a 3-2 vote in which one of the dissenters noted that the Campbell's violation was particularly flagrant since it was committed in the face of the Supreme Court's decision about mock-ups in *Colgate.*
47 *Borden,* consent order, 78 FTC 686 (1971).
48 *American Home Products,* consent order, 81 FTC 579 (1972).
49 Ibid.
50 Ibid.
51 *Bishop Industries,* consent order, 77 FTC 380 (1970).
52 See chapter 2, note 2.
53 Ibid.
54 "Did Lever use bootlegged lather in '64 for Lifebuoy tv commercial?," *Advertising Age,* August 16, 6 (1971).
55 *DuPont:* see chapter 2, note 6.

CHAPTER 16: AND IT'S NOT TRIVIAL

1 See chapter 9, at note 25.
2 See chapter 9, following note 42.
3 Myron Cope had a similar experience and described it wonderfully in "The immaculate reception and other miracles," *Sports Illustrated,* August 23, 28 (1973).
4 In a 1973 story about the San Diego Padres being sold, the new owner explained how he was going to shape things up. He was an official with a food chain and he said, "We're going to have hot hot dogs and cold cold beer." Well, good luck, Charley. Sam Goldaper, "Padres are sold to a Washington group," *The New York Times,* May 29, 43 (1973).
5 The sandpaper case, for example; see chapter 11, at note 38.

6 Henry Bernstein, "Negative option lets consumer 'outwit his own character traits,' FTC is told," *Advertising Age,* November 23, 1 (1970). The eventual result was passage by the FTC of a Trade Regulation Rule on Negative Option Sales Plans, 4 TRR, ¶ 38,032 (1973).

7 *Firestone;* see chapter 2, note 6.

8 Ibid. Also Stanley Cohen, "ANA seeks to intervene in FTC 'corrective ad' case," *Advertising Age,* December 7, 1, 71 (1970).

9 "A vital move on those "corrective ads,' " *Advertising Age,* December 14, 12 (1970).

10 Jerry Della Femina, *From Those Wonderful Folks Who Brought You Pearl Harbor,* 182 (1970).

11 See chapter 14, at note 7.

12 Arch G. Woodside, "Will advertisers back their claims? Not very often, students discover," *Advertising Age,* February 12, 40 (1973).

13 See chapter 17, at note 8 ff.

14 For example, *Colgate;* see chapter 11, at note 38.

15 Ralph Nader, *Unsafe at Any Speed* (1965).

16 Warren Magnuson and Jean Carper, *The Dark Side of the Marketplace* (1968).

17 "NARB upholds GM's use of 'Mark of Excellence' slogan," *Advertising Age,* September 25, 1 (1972); Ivan L. Preston, "Challenges stand that puffery may be low-priority problem," ibid., November 27, 47 (1972).

18 The NARB has since reinforced this viewpoint with a ruling that Schick's "King of Beards" claim implied superiority over all other shavers and thus "cannot be excused as mere trade puffery." A Schick executive protested to no avail that Budweiser is permitted to call itself the "King of Beers." "NARB rules against Schick shaver ads, cites 'implications,' " ibid., December 31, 1, 25 (1973). In a ruling against Fram oil filter advertising the NARB also restricted puffery and exaggeration "in connection with advertising claims concerning quantitative or qualitative measurement." Nancy Giges, "Guidelines emerge as NARB rules out Fram ad 'puffery,' " ibid., February 18, 1 (1974).

19 David Ogilvy, *Confessions of an Advertising Man,* 84 (1963).

20 "Kurnit blasts 'anti-creative' forces within the industry," *Advertising Age,* May 10, 2 (1971).

21 Sid Bernstein, " 'The public is not a moron' ... but??," ibid, July 16, 14 (1973).

22 See discussion and citations to theoretical literature in my article, "Some observations on the consumer's use of the mass media," *Journal of Consumer Affairs,* Summer, 59 (1969).

23 Ibid. The article was given first as a speech to the Council on Consumer Information, annual convention, Pennsylvania State University (1968).

24 See note 22.

25 Theodore Levitt, "The morality (?) of advertising," *Harvard Business Rev.,* July-August (1970).

26 Kensinger Jones, as noted in letter to editor by Harry E. Collins, *Advertising Age,* October 18, 58 (1971).

CHAPTER 17: PUFF, YOUR MAGIC'S DRAGGIN'

1 Puffery may be vulnerable on the grounds of unfairness as well; see chapter 14, note 8. But that possibility is highly speculative at this time.

2 See chapter 11, at note 38; chapter 15, at notes 38-42.

3 Milton Handler, "The control of false advertising under the Wheeler-Lea Act," 6 *Law and Contemporary Problems* 91, 99 (1939).

4 Milton Handler, "False and misleading advertising," 39 *Yale Law Journal* 22, 30 (1929).

5 "Choate raises some eyebrows at FTC hearing," *Advertising Age,* November 15, 86 (1971).

6 James Harvey Young, *The Medical Messiahs,* plate opposite 204 (1967).

7 William D. Tyler, "Two trends in '70 campaigns: more shockers, less information," *Advertising Age,* March 22, 33 (1971).

8 Letter to editor, ibid., April 19, 57 (1971).

9 James MacGregor, "Skeptical consumers, tough regulators spur a new candor in ads," *Wall Street Journal,* January 12, 1 (1972).

10 See detailed discussion in chapter 9.

11 See chapter 9, at note 63.

12 See chapter 9, at note 64.

13 "FTC opposes 'truth' bill; Moss seeks consumer unit," *Advertising Age,* October 11, 2 (1971).

14 "Extensions of 'fairness' doctrine endanger informative ads: Jencks," ibid., December 13, 3 (1971).

15 Lee Loevinger, "The politics of advertising," pamphlet, Television Information Office (1973).
16 "Gas ads avoid big claims," *Advertising Age,* March 6, 58 (1972).
17 Ibid., 18.
18 See chapter 2, note 6.
19 "Corrective advertising and the FTC," 70 *Michigan Law Rev.* 374 (1971), contends that corrective ads will produce nothing but a "stream of drivel."
20 See chapter 15, at note 30.
21 James V. O'Gara, "Hearings ambience projects advertising as winsome, warty," *Advertising Age,* October 25, 90 (1971).
22 Stanley Cohen, "Voluntary cigaret label move may signal easing of attitude to consumer," ibid., September 21, 10 (1970).
23 *Confessions of an Advertising Man,* 140 (1963).
24 "Advertising inquiry will stir hysteria: O & M's Kershaw," *Advertising Age,* August 2, 1 (1971).
25 Nor is there a good way for consumers to feed their own information (or persuasion!) back to industry, since, as the FTC has said, "Advertising may well be the only important forum of public discussion where there exists no concomitant public debate." Stanley Cohen, "This Week in Washington," ibid., January 17, 26 (1972).
26 Raymond A. Bauer and Stephen A. Greyser, "The dialogue that never happens," *Harvard Business Rev.,* November-December, 2 (1967).
27 See chapter 9 at note 27 ff.
28 "FTC questions puffery claims during opening of ad hearing," *Advertising Age,* October 25, 96 (1971).
29 See detailed discussions in chapter 3 and 7.
30 Among those who have argued this is Philip J. Nelson, as reported in "FTC enforcement hinders ad information, Nelson says," *Advertising Age,* May 7, 78 (1973).
31 *Wall Street Journal,* August 13, 8 (1973).
32 See chapter 7, at note 24.
33 *Ringling Bros.-Barnum & Bailey v. Chandris America Lines,* 321 F. Supp. 707 (S.D.N.Y., 1971).
34 Stanley Cohen, "This week in Washington," *Advertising Age,* June 7, 4 (1971).
35 William D. Tyler, "To Youth, Ads Are An Upper Class Con Game," ibid., June 1, 45 (1970).
36 Stephen A. Greyser and Bonnie B. Reece, "Businessmen look

hard at advertising," *Harvard Business Rev.,* May-June (1971).

37 "Polluting an image," *Advertising Age,* April 23, 16 (1973).

38 See note 11 above; and chapter 9, at note 63; "FTC stops short of requiring 'adequate' ad proof: Kirkpatrick," *Advertising Age,* June 28, 2 (1971).

39 John Revett, "Comparison, qualities, semantics pique FTC in data bank info quest," *Advertising Age,* August 30, 3 (1971).

40 "What next?," ibid., September 13, 12 (1971). Other examples of such apparent inconsistency are mentioned in chapter 11, following note 46.

41 The code was a joint development of the American Advertising Federation and the Council of Better Business Bureaus. It is still operative, although it may be overshadowed by the principles promulgated and applied by the National Advertising Review Board, a more recent venture in industry self-regulation: Stanley Cohen, "AAF self rule gets down to the nitty gritty," *Advertising Age,* February 8, 2 (1971). For another flap over Article 8, see chapter 11, note 47.

42 Stanley Cohen, "Force advertiser to substantiate his ad claims, Nader urges FTC," *Advertising Age,* December 14, 1 (1970).

43 Stanley Cohen, "Nader demand for info to back up ads may spur alternative policing devices," ibid., December 21, 14 (1970).

44 "Elman creates student 'FTC'; offers ad manual," ibid., November 16, 16 (1970).

45 "Advertising inquiry will stir hysteria: O & M's Kershaw," ibid., August 2, 1 (1971).

46 "Tough to battle bad ads without guides: Riess," ibid., November 15, 8 (1971).

47 Ibid., August 13, 16 (1973).

48 Particularly in chapters 7 and 11.

49 *The New York Times Book Review,* February 25, 20 (1973). The author was David Sanford (1972).

50 Stanley Cohen has written that real regulation is contrary to American tradition; "This Week in Washington," *Advertising Age,* November 16, 78 (1970).

51 "Dolobowsky makes tv pitch for 5 Day Labs' Stay Dry," ibid., October 4, 35 (1971). For a follow-up story: "5-Day to rename brand Stay Dryer," ibid., September 3, 42 (1973).

52 Kathryn Sederberg, "Hunt-Wesson won't push goods on basis of minor differences," ibid., May 10, 1 (1971).

53 Ivan L. Preston, "Is ad puffery doomed?," ibid., July 3, 21 (1972).

54 See text at note 41 above.
55 See chapter 15, note 45.
56 John Howard and James Hulbert, *Advertising and the Public Interest* (1973). 4 TRR, ¶ 50,168. Discussed in "Book based on FTC study skeptical of brand managers, market research,"*Advertising Age,* March 19, 4 (1973).

Table of Cases

References to page numbers in this book are in italics

Alfred Peats, 8 FTC 366 (1925), *328*

Allen B. Wrisley v. FTC, 113 F.2d 437 (7th Cir., 1940), *329*

Aluminum Company of America, 58 FTC 265 (1961), *233, 339*

American Brands et al, 80 FTC 455 (1972), *325*

American Home Products, 81 FTC 579 (1972), *340*

American School of Magnetic Healing v. McAnnulty, 187 U.S. 94, 23 S.C. 33 (1902), *107, 318, 325*

Amstar, TRR 1970–73 Transfer Binder, ¶20,356, FTC Dkt. No. 8887 (1973), *325*

Andrews v. Jackson, 168 Mass. 266, 47 N.E. 412 (1897), *319*

Aronberg v. FTC, 132 F.2d 165 (7th Cir., 1942), *143, 329*

Baily v. Merrell, 3 Bulst. 94, 81 Eng. Rep. 81; Cro. Jac. 386, 79 Eng. Rep. 331 (1615), *93–95, 97–98, 103, 125, 196–200, 317, 335*

Bantam Books v. FTC, 275 F.2d 680 (2d Cir., 1960), *330*

Barnard v. Kellogg, 77 U.S. 383 (1870), *307, 308*

Baxter v. Ford Motor, 168 Wash. 456, 12 P.2d 409 (1932), *75–76, 312*

Berkey & Gay Furniture, 12 FTC 227 (1928), *328*

Berkey & Gay Furniture v. FTC, 42 F.2d 427 (6th Cir., 1930), *328*

Bishop v. Small, 63 Me. 12 (1874), *317, 322*

Bishop Industries, 77 FTC 380 (1970), *340*

Bluett v. Osborne, 1 Stark. 384, 171 Eng. Rep. 504 (1816), *312*

Boles v. Merrill, 173 Mass. 491, 53 N.E. 894 (1899), *322*

Borden, 78 FTC 686 (1971), *242, 340*

Borrekins v. Bevan, 3 Rawle (Pa.) 23 (1831), *309*

Bradford v. Manly, 13 Mass. 139 (1816), *61–64, 309*

Bree v. Holbech, 2 Doug. 654, 99 Eng. Rep. 415 (1781), *313*

Bristol-Myers, 46 FTC 162 (1949), *180–82, 332*

Brown v. Castles, 11 Cush. (Mass.) 348 (1853), *102–5, 125, 127, 317*

Buchsbaum v. FTC, 160 F.2d 121 (7th Cir., 1947), *329*

Budd v. Fairmaner, 8 Bing. 48, 131 Eng. Rep. 318 (1831), *309*

Burns v. Lane, 138 Mass. 350 (1885), *308*

Campbell Soup, 77 FTC 664 (1970), *241–42, 340*

Carlay, 39 FTC 357 (1944), *172, 180, 331*

Carlay v. FTC, 153 F.2d 493 (7th Cir., 1946), *180, 182, 186, 189, 329, 331–32*

Carnation, 77 FTC 1547 (1970), *333*

Carter Products v. FTC (Liver Pills), 268 F.2d 461 (9th Cir., 1959), *338*

Carter Products v. FTC (Rise), 323 F.2d 523 (5th Cir., 1963), *235, 339*

Celanese, 50 FTC 170 (1953), *332*

Chandelor v. Lopus, Cro. Jac. 4, 79 Eng. Rep. 3 (1603), *37–38, 42–50, 53, 56, 58–65, 68, 77, 81, 111, 307–8, 314–15*

Charles of the Ritz, 34 FTC 1203 (1942), *329*

Charles of the Ritz v. FTC, 143 F.2d 676 (2d Cir., 1944), *170, 325, 329*

C. H. Stuart, 53 FTC 1127 (1957), *332*

Coca-Cola, TRR 1970–73 Transfer Binder, ¶20,470, FTC Dkt. 8839 (1973), *302, 334*

Cochrane v. Cummings, 4 U.S. (Pa.) 250, 1 L.Ed. 820 (1802), *316*

Colgate (Dental Cream), 58 FTC 422 (1961), *234, 339*

Colgate (Rapid Shave), 59 FTC 1452 (1961), *185–86, 236, 304, 339, 341*

Colgate (Rapid Shave), 62 FTC 1269 (1963), *237, 339*

Colgate v. FTC, 310 F.2d 89 (1st Cir., 1962), *237, 339*

Colgate v. FTC, 326 F.2d 517 (1st Cir., 1963), *339*

Continental Wax v. FTC, 330 F.2d 475 (2d Cir., 1964), *338*

County Tweeds, 50 FTC 470 (1953), *338*

Cross v. Garnet, 3 Mod. 261, 87 Eng. Rep. 172 (1689), *309*

Cross v. Peters, 1 Greenl. (Me.) 389 (1821), *125*

Crosse v. Gardner, Carthew 90, 90 Eng. Rep. 656; Holt, K.B. 5, 90 Eng. Rep. 900 (1689), *59–60, 309, 316*

Dale's Case, Cro. Eliz. 44, 78 Eng. Rep. 308 (1585), *40, 48, 59, 65, 68, 307*

Dannon, 61 FTC 840 (1962), *185, 333*

David V. Bush, 14 FTC 90 (1930), *331*

Davis v. Meeker, 5 Johns. (N.Y.) 354 (1810), *99–100, 125, 317*

D.D.D. v. FTC, 125 F.2d 679 (7th Cir., 1942), *140, 329*

Deming v. Darling, 148 Mass. 504, 20 N.E. 107 (1889), *104, 319*

Derry v. Peek, 14 A.C. 337, 58 L.J. Ch. 864 (1889), *85–87, 139, 314*

Dobbs Truss, 48 FTC 1090 (1952), *332*

Dorr v. Cary, 108 Iowa 725, 78 N.W. 682 (1899), *322*

Dr. Eagan, 11 FTC 436 (1927), *328, 331*

DuPont, 81 FTC 169 (1972), *302, 325, 340*

Edgington v. Fitzmaurice, L.R. 29 Ch.D. 459 (1885), *318*
Eichholz v. Bannister, 17 C.B.N.S. 708, 112 E.C.L. 708 (1864), *311*
Ekins v. Tresham, 1 Lev. 102, 83 Eng. Rep. 318 (1663), *82, 94–96,*
  98, 122–24, 127, 320–21, 335
Electric Appliance, 2 FTC 335 (1920), *331*
Elliott Knitwear v. FTC, 266 F.2d 787 (2d Cir., 1959), *338*
Exposition Press v. FTC, 295 F.2d 869 (2d Cir., 1961), *330*
Fairchild v. McMahon, 139 N.Y. 290, 34 N.E. 779 (1893), *127, 322*
Fairyfoot Products, 20 FTC 40 (1934), *178, 328, 331*
Fairyfoot Products v. FTC, 80 F.2d 684 (7th Cir., 1935), *178, 329,*
  331
Firestone, 81 FTC 398 (1972), *9, 302, 341*
Florence v. Dowd, 178 F. 73 (2d Cir., 1910), *329*
Frank P. Snyder, 11 FTC 390 (1927), *328, 331*
FTC v. A. A. Berry, 4 FTC 427 (1920), *328*
FTC v. Alben-Harley, 4 FTC 31 (1921), *328*
FTC v. Algoma, 291 U.S. 67, 54 S.C. 315 (1934), *138, 222, 332*
FTC v. Army and Navy Trading Co., 88 F.2d 776 (D.C. Cir., 1937),
  338
FTC v. Colgate, 380 U.S. 374, 85 S.C. 1035 (1965), *238, 330, 340*
FTC v. Gratz, 253 U.S. 421, 40 S.C. 572 (1920), *132, 323*
FTC v. Keppel, 291 U.S. 304, 54 S.C. 423 (1934), *330*
FTC v. National Health Aids, 108 F. Supp. 340 (1952), *332*
FTC v. Raladam, 283 U.S. 643, 51 S.C. 587 (1931), *323, 326*
FTC v. Raladam, 316 U.S. 149, 62 S.C. 966 (1942), *150, 326*
FTC v. Royal Milling Co., 288 U.S. 212, 53 S.C. 335 (1933), *222,*
  338
FTC v. Sewell, 353 U.S. 969, 77 S.C. 1055 (1957), *329, 332*
FTC v. Sperry & Hutchinson, 405 U.S. 233, 92 S.C. 898 (1972), *xii,*
  337
FTC v. Standard Education Society, 86 F.2d 692 (2d Cir., 1936),
  329
FTC v. Standard Education Society, 302 U.S. 112, 58 S.C. 113
  (1937), *168–72, 180, 182, 203, 309, 332*
FTC v. Sterling Drug, 317 F.2d 669 (2d Cir., 1963), *309*
FTC v. Universal Battery, 2 FTC 95 (1919), *328, 331*
FTC v. Williams Soap, 6 FTC 107 (1923), *328*
FTC v. Winsted Hosiery, 258 U.S. 483, 42 S.C. 384 (1922), *221,*
  226, 324, 339
Gardiner v. Gray, 4 Camp. 144, 171 Eng. Rep. 46 (1815), *71–72,*
  311

Gelb, 33 FTC 1450 (1941), *325, 329*
Gelb v. FTC, 144 F.2d 580 (2d Cir., 1944), *325, 329*
General Motors v. FTC, 114 F.2d 33 (2d Cir., 1940), *169, 329*
Giant Food v. FTC, 322 F.2d 977 (D.C. Cir., 1963), *330*
Giant Plastics, 61 FTC 179 (1962), *338*
Gimbel Bros., 61 FTC 1051 (1962), *339*
Gimblin v. Harrison, 2 Ky. 315 (1804), *316*
Good Grape, 10 FTC 99 (1926), *328, 331*
Goodman, 52 FTC 982 (1956), *332*
Goodman v. FTC, 244 F.2d 584 (9th Cir., 1957), *309, 329, 332*
Gordon v. Butler, 105 U.S. 553 (1881), *318*
Gordon v. Parmelee, 2 Allen (84 Mass.) 212 (1861), *199–201, 317*
Grand Rapids Furniture v. FTC, 134 F.2d 332 (3d Cir., 1943), *224, 338*
Gulf Oil v. FTC, 150 F.2d 106 (5th Cir., 1945), *180, 304, 329, 332*
Harker China, 62 FTC 1382 (1963), *338*
Harrison v. U.S., 200 F. 662 (6th Cir., 1912), *326*
Harvey v. Young, Yelv. 21, 80 Eng. Rep. 15 (1602), *93–96, 98, 100–101, 122, 125, 189, 316–17*
Haskelite v. FTC, 127 F.2d 765 (7th Cir., 1942), *145, 325*
Hawkins v. Pemberton, 51 N.Y. 198 (1872), *64–65, 309*
Haycraft v. Creasey, 2 East 92, 102 Eng. Rep. 303 (1801), *83, 313*
Heilbut v. Buckleton, A.C. 30 (1913), *310*
Heinz W. Kirchner, 63 FTC 1282 (1963), *173, 333*
Heinz W. Kirchner v. FTC, 337 F.2d 751 (9th Cir., 1964), *333*
Hemmer v. Cooper, 8 Allen (Mass.) 334 (1864), *126, 322*
Henningsen v. Bloomfield Motors, 32 N.J. 358, 161 A.2d 69 (1960), *76, 78, 312*
Hobart Bradstreet, 11 FTC 174 (1927), *328, 331*
Hoe v. Sanborn, 21 N.Y. 552 (1860), *312*
Holbrook v. Connor, 60 Me. 578 (1872), *126, 322*
Holloway v. Forsyth, 115 Mass. 358, 115 N.E. 483 (1917), *323*
Howe, 36 FTC 685 (1943), *331*
Howe v. FTC, 148 F.2d 561 (9th Cir., 1945), *331*
Hunter v. McLaughlin, 43 Ind. 38 (1873), *128–29, 322*
Independent Directory, 47 FTC 13 (1950), *329*
Institute of Hydraulic Jack Repair, 63 FTC 127 (1963), *223, 338*
ITT-Continental, TRR 1970–73 Transfer Binder, ¶ 20,464, FTC Dkt. 8860 (1973), *302, 324–25*
J. B. Williams (Geritol), 68 FTC 481 (1965), *9, 302*
J. B. Williams (Vivarin), 81 FTC 238 (1972), *258, 337*

J. B. Williams v. FTC, 381 F.2d 884 (6th Cir., 1967), *302, 325*

Jendwine v. Slade, 2 Esp. Rep. 572, 170 Eng. Rep. 459 (1797), *317*

John C. Winston, 8 FTC 177 (1924), *167, 328*

John C. Winston v. FTC, 3 F.2d 961 (3d Cir., 1925), *328*

Jones v. Bright, 5 Bing. 531, 130 Eng. Rep. 1167 (1829), *312*

Judd v. Walker, 215 Mo. 312, 114 S.W. 979 (1908), *202–3, 335*

Justin Haynes v. FTC, 105 F.2d 988 (2d Cir., 1939), *326*

Kabatchnik v. Hanover-Elm, 328 Mass. 341, 103 N.E.2d 692 (1952), *127, 322*

Kalwajtys v. FTC, 237 F.2d 654 (7th Cir., 1956), *325*

Kell v. Trenchard, 142 F. 16 (4th Cir., 1905), *307*

Kellogg Bridge v. Hamilton, 110 U.S. 108, 3 S.C. 537 (1884), *72–73, 312*

Kidder Oil, 29 FTC 987 (1939), *178–79, 331*

Kidder Oil v. FTC, 117 F.2d 892 (7th Cir., 1941), *178, 186, 189, 331–32*

Kimball v. Bangs, 144 Mass. 321, 11 N.E. 113 (1887), *128–29, 317, 323*

Korber Hats, 60 FTC 642 (1962), *339*

Korber Hats v. FTC, 311 F.2d 358 (1st Cir., 1962), *227–28, 339*

Langendorf, 43 FTC 132 (1946), *331*

L. B. Silver, 4 FTC 73 (1921), *325*

L. B. Silver v. FTC, 289 F. 985 (6th Cir., 1923), *148–50, 325*

Leakins v. Clissel, 1 Sid. 146, 82 Eng. Rep. 1022 (1663), *95, 122–23, 315, 320–21*

Leakins v. Clizard, 1 Keb. 510, 83 Eng. Rep. 1082; 1 Keb. 519, 83 Eng. Rep. 1088; 1 Keb. 522, 83 Eng. Rep. 1090 (1663), *320*

Lever Bros., TRR 1967–70 Transfer Binder, ¶ 18,711 (1969), *336*

Libby-Owens-Ford v. FTC, 352 F.2d 415 (6th Cir., 1965), *235, 339*

Lifetime, 59 FTC 1231 (1961), *185, 333*

Liggett & Myers, 55 FTC 354 (1958), *185, 332*

Lorillard v. FTC, 186 F.2d 52 (4th Cir., 1950), *143–46, 329*

Mabardy v. McHugh, 202 Mass. 148, 88 N.E. 894 (1909), *335*

MacPherson v. Buick, 217 N.Y. 382, 111 N.E. 1050 (1916), *312*

Mattauch v. Walsh Bros., 136 Iowa 225, 113 N.W 818 (1907), *319*

Mattel, 79 FTC 667 (1971), *302*

McFarland v. Newman, 9 Watts (Pa.) 55 (1839), *63, 66, 68, 309*

Medbury v. Watson, 6 Metcalf (Mass.) 246 (1843), *100–101, 104, 125, 317*

Medina v. Stoughton, 1 Salk. 210, 91 Eng. Rep. 188; 1 Lord Raym. 593, 91 Eng. Rep. 1297; Holt, K.B. 208, 90 Eng. Rep. 1014 (1700), *59–60, 316*

Michelin Tire v. Schulz, 295 Pa. 140, 145 A. 67 (1929), *310*

Monstrauns de Faits, pl. 16 (1577), *308*

Moretrench, 28 FTC 297 (1939), *180, 331*

Moretrench v. FTC, 127 F.2d 792 (2d Cir., 1942), *139, 170, 172, 180, 182, 329, 331*

Morley v. Attenborough, 3 Exch. 500 (1849), *311*

National Health Aids, 49 FTC 1661 (1952), *332*

National Laboratories of St. Louis, 63 FTC 948 (1963), *219–20, 338*

Necchi, 53 FTC 1040 (1957), *332*

Northam-Warren, 15 FTC 389 (1931), *328*

Northam-Warren v. FTC, 59 F.2d 196 (2d Cir., 1932), *328*

Nugrape, 9 FTC 20 (1925), *328, 331*

Ocean Spray, 80 FTC 975 (1972), *9, 302*

Ostermoor, 10 FTC 45 (1926), *177–78, 328, 331*

Ostermoor v. FTC, 16 F.2d 962 (2d Cir., 1927), *177–78, 186, 189, 328, 331–32*

Pan American Cigar, 72 FTC 752 (1967), *338*

Papercraft, 63 FTC 1965 (1963), *330*

Parker v. Moulton, 114 Mass. 99 (1873), *317*

Parker Pen v. FTC, 159 F.2d 509 (7th Cir., 1946), *329*

Parkinson v. Lee, 2 East 314, 102 Eng. Rep. 389 (1802), *69–73, 77, 311*

Pasley v. Freeman, 3 T.R. 51, 3 D.&E. 51, 100 Eng. Rep. 450 (1789), *60, 82, 95–100, 123–24, 315–17*

People v. Clarke, 252 App. Div. (N.Y.) 122 (1937), *330*

People v. Williams, 4 Hill (N.Y.) 1 (1842), *125*

Pfizer, 81 FTC 23 (1972), *302, 325*

Picard v. McCormick, 11 Mich. 68 (1862), *110–11, 114, 319–20*

Pike v. Fay, 101 Mass. 134 (1869), *104*

Poland v. Brownell, 131 Mass. 138 (1881), *322*

Postal Life and Casualty Insurance, 54 FTC 494 (1957), *332*

Pritchard v. Liggett & Myers, 350 F.2d 479 (3d Cir., 1965), *310*

Quaker Oats, 63 FTC 2017 (1963), *228–29, 339*

Raladam, 12 FTC 363 (1929), *326*

Raladam, 24 FTC 475 (1937), *326*

Raladam v. FTC, 42 F.2d 430 (6th Cir., 1930), *326*

Raladam v. FTC, 123 F.2d 34 (6th Cir., 1941), *326*

Ringling Bros.-Barnum & Bailey v. Chandris America Lines, 321 F. Supp. 707 (S.D.N.Y. 1971), *287–88, 343*

Roberts v. French, 153 Mass. 60, 26 N.E. 416 (1891), *201, 335*

Sales Development Corp., 62 FTC 1461 (1963), *338*

Scientific Manufacturing, 32 FTC 493 (1941), *326*
Scientific Manufacturing v. FTC, 124 F.2d 640 (3d Cir., 1941), *326*
Sears, Roebuck v. FTC, 258 F. 307 (7th Cir., 1919), *131, 135,
    138–39, 323–24*
Seixas and Seixas v. Woods, 2 Caines (N.Y.) 48 (1804), *52–54,
    60–62, 64–65, 68–69, 77, 82, 117, 310, 313, 315, 317*
Sewell, 50 FTC 806 (1954), *332*
Sewell v. FTC, 240 F.2d 228 (9th Cir., 1956), *332*
Sherwood v. Salmon, 2 Day (Conn.) 128 (1805), *198–99, 316*
Sherwood v. Salmon, 5 Day (Conn.) 439 (1813), *316*
Ship 'n Shore, 58 FTC 757 (1961), *338*
Ship 'n Shore, 70 FTC 631 (1966), *338*
Siegel, 36 FTC 563 (1943), *146, 325*
Siegel v. FTC, 327 U.S. 608, 66 S.C. 758 (1946), *325*
Slaughter's Administrator v. Gerson, 80 U.S. 379 (1871), *200–201,
    335*
Smith v. Land and House, L.R. 28 Ch.D. 7, 51 L.T.N.S. 718, 49 J.P.
    182 (1884), *109, 116, 318*
Southern v. Howard, Cro. Jac. 468, 79 Eng. Rep. 400 (1618), *308*
Southern Development v. Silva, 125 U.S. 247, 8 S.C. 881 (1888),
    318
Spead v. Tomlinson, 73 N.H. 46, 59 A. 376 (1904), *318*
Standard Brands (Blue Bonnet), 56 FTC 1491 (1960), *339*
Standard Brands (Fleischmann's), TRR 1970–73 Transfer Binder,
    ¶ 20,316, FTC Dkt. C-2377 (1973), *326*
Standard Education Society, 16 FTC 1 (1931), *329*
Standard Oil of California, TRR 1970–73 Transfer Binder, ¶ 20,321,
    FTC Dkt. 8827 (1973), *302, 334*
State v. Shaengold, 13 Ohio Law Reporter 130 (1915), *324*
Stebbins v. Eddy, 4 Mason 414, 22 Fed. Cas. 1192 (1827), *318*
Steelco, 46 FTC 643 (1950), *332*
Steelco v. FTC, 187 F.2d 693 (7th Cir., 1951), *332*
Sterling Drug, TRR 1970–73 Transfer Binder, ¶ 19,925 FTC File no.
    662 3550 (1972), *280, 302*
Stuart v. Wilkins, 1 Doug. 18, 99 Eng. Rep. 15 (1778), *311*
Sun Oil, 3 TRR, ¶ 20,704, FTC Dkt. 8889 (1974), *325, 327*
Tanners Shoe, 53 FTC 1137 (1957), *183–84, 332*
Tarbell, 14 FTC 442 (1931), *331*
Taylor v. Ashton, 11 M.&W. 401, 152 Eng. Rep. 860 (1843), *84,
    313*
Thomas v. Winchester, 6 N.Y. 397 (1852), *312*
Topper, 79 FTC 681 (1971), *302*

Unicorn Press, 47 FTC 258 (1950), *332*
United Garment, 66 FTC 711 (1964), *338*
United States Testing Co., 61 FTC 1312 (1962), *224, 338*
U.S. v. New South Farm, 241 U.S. 64 (1916), *107, 183, 304, 332–33*
Vaughan v. Menlove, 3 Bing. N.C. 468, 132 Eng. Rep. 490 (1837), *328*
Veasey v. Doton, 3 Allen (Mass.) 380 (1862), *100–101, 317*
Vernon v. Keys, 12 East 632, 104 Eng. Rep. 246 (1810), *123, 125, 315*
Vernon v. Keys, 4 Taunt. 488, 128 Eng. Rep. 419 (1812), *321*
Virginia Products, 29 FTC 451 (1939), *338*
Vulcan Metals v. Simmons, 248 F. 853 (2d Cir., 1918), *318, 329, 331*
Walker v. Kirk, 72 Pa. Super. Ct. 534 (1919), *310*
Waltham Watch, 60 FTC 1692 (1962), *333*
Washington Mushroom, 53 FTC 368 (1956), *332*
Way v. Ryther, 165 Mass. 226, 42 N.E. 1128 (1896), *307*
Western Bank of Scotland v. Addie, L.R. 1 H.L., Sc. 145 (1867), *84–86, 313*
Western Radio, 63 FTC 882 (1963), *333*
Western Radio v. FTC, 339 F.2d 937 (7th Cir., 1964), *333*
White v. Miller, 71 N.Y. 118 (1877), *309*
William F. Schied, 10 FTC 85 (1926), *328, 331*
Williams v. Rank & Son Buick, 44 Wis. 2d 239, 170 N.W. 2d 807 (1969), *13–14, 25–26, 303, 336*
Wilmington Chemical, 69 FTC 828 (1966), *333*
Y.B. 42 Ass. 259, pl. 8 (1367), *39, 307, 335*

Index

Accidental events: as cause of legal decisions, 46–49, 58, 97–103, 123, 125, 129
Administrative law judge, 332
Advertiser: *See* Seller
Advertising: public credibility of, 287–90; lacking forum for debate, 343
Advertising Age, xii, 26, 147, 257, 276, 279, 288, 290, 302, 304–6, 312, 320, 324–27, 333–34, 336, 339–45
Advertising Code of American Business, Article 8, 290–91, 334
Affirmative disclosure, 145–46, 187
Air-conditioner claims, 13–14, 25–26, 190, 193, 196, 205, 290
Alcoa claims, 29, 234
Alexander, George J.: *Honesty and Competition,* 309, 337–38
Alka Seltzer claim, 208
All detergent claim, 207–8
Allied Van Lines claim, 19
Alpacuna claim, 146
Amana claim, 19
American Advertising Federation, 291, 344
American Association of Advertising Agencies, 302, 306
American Bar Association: report on FTC, 323
American Dairy Association claim, 20
American Dental Association, 24
American Gas Association, 19
American law: as derived from English law, 53, 86
American Law Institute, 110, 335–36
American University, xii

Andeker claim, 18
Anderson, Justice, 40, 48, 59, 68
Aquinas, St. Thomas, 34, 38, 42
Army and Navy Trading Co., 224
Ashley, W. J.: *An Introduction to English Economic History and Theory,* 307
Association of National Advertisers, 257
Atlanta Journal claim, 305
Attachment of goods, 55–56
Aunt Jemima, 241, 297
Automobile Dealers of Wisconsin, 297
Avis claims, 4, 18, 258, 316
Ayds claim, 172, 184

Baily, 93–94, 103, 197, 199, 205
Baker's dozen, 230
Bare (naked, nude) assertions, 93–95, 98, 100
Barnum, P. T., 17
Barnum & Bailey, 19, 287–88, 343
Barron, Jerome: *Mass Communication Law,* 303
Bathtub ring claim, 240–41
Battery claims, 166, 175–76
Bauer, Raymond A.: article of, 343
Bayer claims, 4, 18, 141
Bell, Howard, 291
Bernstein, Henry: articles of, 324, 341
Bernstein, Sid: articles of, 305, 341
Bezar-stone: claim, 37–38, 42, 44–45, 49, 58, 60, 62–63, 77, 315; influence of, ended, 66
Bicycles: demand for, 267, 269
Biddle, Arthur: *Law of Warranty in the Sale of Chattels,* 311
Bigelow, Melville M.: *Fraud,* 322

Biltmore Hotel claim, 19
Birdwhistell, Ray L.: *Kinesics and Context,* 305
Black, Hugo, Justice, 168, 173, 182, 203, 328
Black Flag claim, 242
Blackstone, Sir William: *Commentaries,* 68, 310
Blatz claims, 4, 17, 18, 21, 26, 261–62, 264
Blue Bonnet claim, 234–35
Blue vitriol claim, 64
Board of Trade, 85
Boat draught claim, 200–201
Bogert, George: article of, 318
Bohlen, Francis, 204: article of, 328
Borden claim, 4, 19
Bounty claim, 207–8
Bowen, Lord, 109
Brandeis, Judge Louis, 132
Brazilletto claim, 52–53, 60, 62, 70, 77, 313
Breeder's claim, 148–49
Brian, Judge, 12, 195, 197, 315
Brozen, Yale, 324
Bruskin, R. H., Associates, 28; *The Bruskin Report,* 306
Buc Wheats claim, 20
Budd, Mr., 62
Budweiser claim, 18, 341
Building materials claim, 185
Buller, Justice, 60, 66, 82, 96, 98–100, 317
Bunion plaster claim, 178
Burger King "Whopper" claim, 280
Business Periodicals Index, 302
Buyer: responsiblity of, for deception caused by puffery, 247, 253, 265–72; desire of, to be deceived, 247, 269–70
—, and inspection of his purchase: obligation of, to inspect, and assumption he can, 12–14, 32–34, 37, 43, 53–54, 67, 70–74, 82, 94–95, 97, 105, 114–15, 122–24, 126, 128, 193, 197–204, 231, 316–17,

336; obligation of, prior to sellerism, 34; where not obligated to inspect, 37; lack of opportunity of, to inspect, 50–54, 59, 61–62, 69–73, 76, 94–95, 99, 102–3, 106, 110–11, 114, 117–18, 120, 122–24, 126–28, 202, 319, 321; obligation of, contrasted to rules outside marketplace, 54–56, 114–119; failure of, to take existing opportunity, 74, 112, 196–201; volunteering of, to inspect, 336
—, equality of, with seller: questioned, 43, 52, 54, 71, 111–12, 117–18, 265–72; assumed, 50–52, 99, 111; affected by false claim, 54. *See also* Buyer, and inspection of his purchase

Cadillac claim, 18
Canada: effects of Competition Act of 1971 on puffery, 306
Canadian Club claim, 18
Carnation claim, 187, 190
Carney, James A.: article of, xii, 337
Carpenter, J. R., 277
Carper, Jean: *The Dark Side of the Marketplace,* 341
Carraccas cocoa claim, 62
Carson, Johnny, 239
Carter's Little Liver Pills claim, 224
Case, Eugene, 208–9
Cash, Johnny, 279–80
Cashmora sweater claim, 224
Cattle claims, 39, 68
Caveat emptor, 41, 43, 51, 53, 57, 93, 226, 230, 244–45, 316; defined, 32, 37, 44; inaccurately attributed to Romans, 32–34; as legalized lying, 33, 121; why and how created, 33–37, 49–50; development of, in king's common law, 36–37; inapplicability of, with warranty or misrepresentation, 37–38; as foundation of sellerism, 38; superficiality of, as a protection for

buyers, 38, 42, 44; support by courts of, as good doctrine, 52, 54, 56; contrasted to rules outside marketplace, 54–56, 114–19, 199; modern rejection of, 57, 66–68, 80, 168; persistance of, in today's law though called "dead," 57, 114, 116, 269, 336; leading case of, in America, 60; most unfair aspect of, 70; "Super" version of, 195–205. *See also* Accidental events; Sellerism
Caveat reader, 92, 338
Caveat venditor, 51
CBS-TV, 278
Cease and desist order, 136, 161
Champion claim, 20
Chandelor, 42, 44–45, 48–49, 77, 111
Chandris America Lines, 287
"Charcoal" briquets claim, 228
Charge of the Light Brigade, 271
Charley the Tuna, 285
Chemical Bank claim, 20
Chesterfield claim, 185
Chevrolet claim, 18
Chevron claim, 9, 19, 191, 302
Chicago Tribune claim, 4, 20
Children: claims made to, 7, 206, 216, 330, 336
Choate, Robert, 275
Christopher, Maurine: article of, 340
Church. *See* Roman Catholic Church
Cigar claim, 224
Cigarette package warning, 146
Civil law (Roman), 35–36, 39, 53
Clairol claim, 147, 171–72
Clark, Judge, 171
Clorox, 141
Cloves claim, 61
Coca-Cola claims, 20, 28
Cohen, Stanley: book review of, 294; articles of, 312, 324, 327, 333–34, 341
Coke, Lord, 53, 310
Colgate claims, 20, 185–86, 234–38, 240, 274–75

"Coliseum" commercial, 326–27
Colt, four-year-old, claim, 62–63
Colt 45 claim, 18
Columbia Law Review: advertising articles in, 324, 327
Columbia Record Club, 256
Commodore Hotel claim, 19
Common law: of the English kings, 36, 38–39, 41, 53, 67; of cases (not statutes), 54, 65, 89, 92, 108, 121, 132–34, 136–38, 140, 164–65, 169, 175–77, 184, 205, 310, 318
Communication: as a two-way process, 266–68
Comstock, George, 64, 309
Cones, frozen custard, claim: 253–54
Congressional Record, 331
Consumer. *See* Buyer
Consumerism, 35, 292, 336; modern trend toward, 5, 30–31, 46–47, 56–58, 66, 73–74, 78, 80–81, 85, 87, 89–92, 97, 108, 130, 133–36, 138, 140–41, 146, 160–61, 203–5, 226, 244, 258, 295; defined, 30; appearance of, but not substance, 38, 78; early tendency toward, 59–60, 82; moderate position toward, 268; effect of, on information in ads, 276; demand of, for information, 281
Consumer Reports, 225, 304, 338
Cope, Myron: article of, 340
Copeland, Senator, 179
Corfam shoes: demand for, 266
Corpus Juris, 322; *Secundum,* 323
Corrective ads, 161, 257, 280
Cosmetics claims, 263
Council of Better Business Bureaus, 344
Council on Consumer Information, 342
Counter ads, 161, 278–79
Courts of Appeal, U.S.: First Circuit, 237–38; Second Circuit, 105, 169–73, 180; Third Circuit, 66; Fourth

Circuit, 144; Seventh Circuit, 172–73; inconsistency of, 172
Cox, Edward F.: *Nader's Raiders*, 323, 327–28
Cowen's Treatise, 125, 321
Craft guilds, 35–36, 230
Credibility problems: of seller and advertiser, 71, 136, 287–90, 295–96; of the law, 290–95
Credit claims, 83, 95, 123–24
Crest toothpaste claim, 24
Crocker, Betty, 241, 297–98

Damages, 134–35, 139, 168
Dancerina doll claim, 243
Danish pastry, 219–23
Davis, Justice, 54
D.D.D. Prescription claim, 140
Dealer's talk, 120, 126, 128–29, 172, 323. *See also* Seller's talk
Deceit (fraudulent misrepresentation), 12, 39, 48, 68, 84, 94, 99–100, 104, 111, 125, 302, 335
Deception: improper identification of, by law, 4, 9, 15, 29; once legally permissible, 4, 33; soft-core, 5; appeals for elimination of, 5, 263–64; illegality of, because injurious, 6–7; not necessarily accompanying falsity, 6–15, 140; legally possible without falsity, 6–15, 140–145; difficult to identify, 7–11, 15, 146–48, 158–60; how identified, 8; identification of, dependent on personal position, 10, 158–59; whether buyer or seller responsible for, 11–13, 159; expanding the definition of, 140–46, 277–78; whether based on specific falsity, 263–64. *See also* Federal Trade Commission; Misrepresentation; Puffery, effects of; Obvious falsity; Social-psychological misrepresentations
DeCoux, John, 163
Delco claim, 19

Della Femina, Jerry, 257–58; *From Those Wonderful Folks Who Brought You Pearl Harbor*, 257; agency of, 258, 337
Deodorants: demand for, 266–67, 269
Dicta, 84, 125, 317
Diet claims, 149, 172, 180
Disney claim, 18
Distrust. *See* Trust and distrust by buyers
Dolobowsky, Bob, 296
Domino sugar claim, 325
Dougherty, Phil, x
Dove soap, 243
Dr. Scholl's claim, 206–7
Drug advertisers' claim, 119
DuPont: claim, 9, 243; Corfam shoes, demand for, 266

Easy-Off: oven cleaner, claim, 20, 190; window cleaner, claim, 243
Easy-On starch claim, 243
Edison Electric Institute claim, 19
Edsel: demand for, 266, 269
Electric belts and insoles claim, 176
Eli Lilly claim, 19, 27–28
Ellenborough, Lord, 72, 99, 124, 126–27, 311, 319, 321–22
Elman, Philip, 291
Encyclopedia claims, 167–68
English law: as source of American law, 53, 86
Equality of buyer and seller. *See* Buyer, equality of, with seller
Esso (Exxon) claim, 7
ETC: A Review of General Semantics, 305
Excavating machine claim, 128

Face cream claim, 170
Factual claims. *See* Opinion claims, legal treatment of
Factual puffery. *See* Puffery, definition and types of
Fairness doctrine, 278

Falch: claim by, 95, 123–24
Falsity: not illegal if not deceptive, 6–7, 11; not necessarily deceptive, 6–16, 21, 31, 93, 95, 140, 160; easy to identify, 8; illegal when fraudulent, 25; criteria for acceptable, 206–9; not always ethical when legal, 255; reduction in types of, now legal, 259–60. *See also* Fraudulent misrepresentation; Mock-ups
Federal Alcohol Administration Act, 338
Federal Communications Commission, 161
Federal Trade Commission, x, xi, xiv, 7, 9, 57, 77, 108, 121, 258, 265, 271, 277, 280, 308
—, dealing with puffery claims: resisting puffery, 170, 172–73, 175–87; accepting concept of nondeceptive puffery, 184–87, 189, 191, 256, 305; assessment of FTC puffery policy, 187–91; how FTC could eliminate puffery, 188–89, 244; inconsistencies in puffery policy, 189–92, 290; spoofs (obvious falsity), 205–9, 336; social-psychological misrepresentations, 215–17; literally misdescriptive names, 220–23, 226–29; mock-ups, 233–38, 241–43
—, dealing with selling claims generally, 130–91; involving substantial segment of population (public interest requirement), 26, 139, 146, 162–74, 221, 223, 246, 330; relation to warranty law, 77, 79; determining misrepresentations by new criterion of capacity to deceive, 79, 88–89, 134–35, 138–47, 208; attacking unfair methods of selling, 130–34, 139, 221, 226, 337; relation to common law, 132–35, 138, 140, 164–65, 175–77, 339; elimination of fraud and negligence re-

quirements, 135, 138–39, 157–59, 169; meaning of "false advertisement," 139–40; uniqueness claims, 141–42, 283, 324–25; substantiation required, 143, 298; errors and problems in recognizing capacity to deceive, 146–47, 160, 226–29, 243, 256; use of reasonable and ignorant man standards, 162–74, 180–82; requirement of materialness, 246; negative option selling, 256–57. *See also* Children
—, procedures and actions of: hearings on modern advertising practices, xi, 27, 208–9, 298; against selling claims, 135–38, 161, 257, 277, 280; affirmative disclosure, 145–46, 187; guides and rules, 146, 187, 189, 325, 341; consumer testimony and surveys, 147, 150–60; use of expert opinion by, 147–58, 326; substantiation program, 161, 278, 290; complaint, 181; hearing examiner, 185, 332; subject to court review, 324
—, purpose and contributions of: preventive and not remedial, 79, 133, 135–39, 160; original, 130–31; to consumerism trend, 130–31, 133–34, 136, 138, 140–41, 146, 160–61, 175–77, 244
Federal Trade Commission Act: section 5, x, xii, 130, 133, 143, 324, 327–28; Wheeler-Lea Amendments, 133, 139, 140, 179, 323; section 12, 139; section 15, 143
Feiner, Mark, 268
Fellmuth, Robert C.: *Nader's Raiders*, 323, 327
First Amendment guarantee, 164, 258, 326
First-brand awareness, 284
Fitzherbert, Anthony, 32, 36–37, 41, 50; *Boke of Husbandrie*, 306; *Fitzherbert's Abridgment*, 308; *Natura Brevium*, 308

Fonblanque, 53
Food and Drug Administration, 228; Act, 276
Ford, H. Ross, Jr., 320
Ford claims, 4, 18, 28, 75, 298
Fram claim, 341
Fraud. *See* Fraudulent misrepresentation
Fraudulent misrepresentation: as awareness of incompatible facts, 25; as knowledge of falsity, 25, 38–40, 81, 83–86, 313–14; as lack of knowledge of truth, 25, 83–86, 118–19, 313–14, 319; contribution of rule of, to sellerism, 40, 49, 81–82; modern easing of the rule of, 81–89; difficulty of proving, 82, 86, 97, 169; leading case of, 82, 95, 100; and obvious falsity, 195, 198, 200, 204–5, mentioned, 14, 37, 41, 48, 53, 56, 66, 68, 87, 134–35, 137, 165, 169, 171, 188, 316, 335. *See also* Deceit; Puffery, definition and types of; Opinion claims
"Free" offer, 167–68
Furness, Betty, 297

Galbreath, John, & Co., 118–19
Gary, Indiana, 290
Gasoline octane disclosure, 146
Geer, Peter, 27–29
Gellhorn, Ernest: article of: 325
General Electric claim, 290
General Mills claim, 241
General Motors claims, 18, 264–65
General Refractories claim, 118
General semantics, 22
General Tramway Act, 85
George Washington University, 141
Georgia claim, 19
Geritol claims, 9, 145, 176, 302
Germany: puffery in, 179, 306
Gibson, Chief Justice, 63, 66, 68
Giges, Nancy: article of, 341
Gillmor, Donald M.: *Mass Communication Law*, 303

Gilmore, Grant: article of, 45, 308
Godfrey, Arthur, 279
Goldaper, Sam: article of, 340
Goldfinger, 206
Gourmet, 24
Grain claim, 69–70
Gregory, Charles O.: *Cases and Materials on Torts*, 312
Grey, David: *For Freedom of Expression*, 328
Greyser, Stephen A.: articles of, 343
Grimes, Warren S.: article of, 306
Grolier claim, 33–34
Grose, Justice, 70, 95–98, 100, 123, 321
Grumhaus, H. F., 305

Hai Karate claim, 19, 206
Hamilton, Walton H.: article of, 33–36, 50, 52, 101, 306–8, 317
Hamms commercial, 286
Hand, Augustus, Judge, 169–71
Hand, Learned, Judge, 105, 168, 170, 176, 180, 182, 287
Handler, Milton, 246, 275, 333; articles of, 323–24, 342; *Trade Regulations*, 333
Harper, M. C.: article of, 304
Harvard Business Review: article in, 288
Harvard Law Review: deceptive advertising article in, 320, 323–24, 327–28; corrective advertising article in, 327
Havana Florida Co. claim, 224
Hayakawa, S. I.: *Language in Thought and Action*, 305
Hearing examiner, 185, 332
Herschell, Lord, 85–86, 314
Hi-C fruit drink claim, 9, 190, 302
Hidden defects. *See* Latent defects
Hinkes, Harry R.: administrative law judge, 326
Hockey claim, 22
Holmes, Oliver W., Justice, 55–56, 104–5, 117, 119

Holt, Lord, 59–60, 62, 66, 82, 310, 316
Honda claim, 193, 211–12, 247, 262–63
Hops claim, 69–70, 72
Horse claims, 32, 41, 63
Hot Wheels claim, 7, 243, 302
House of Lords, 66
Howard, John: *Advertising and the Public Interest,* 298, 345
Hubbard, Justice, 100
Hulbert, James: *Advertising and the Public Interest,* 298, 345
Humphreys, William E., Commissioner, 177
Hunt-Wesson Foods claims, 296
Hush Puppies claim, 215
Hyperbole, 270–72

Ignorant (unreasonable) persons and the "ignorant man standard," ix, 4, 11, 112, 117, 162–74, 180–82, 206, 247, 253, 306, 330
Image advertising, 277
Implications of messages, 21–22, 92, 134, 140, 142–44, 151–60, 188–89, 208, 211, 213, 234, 237, 259, 262–64. See also Opinion claims, meaning of; Puffery, meaning of
Incompatible facts. *See* Opinion claims, meaning of and response to
Indiana Law Journal: article in, 326
Individualism: philosophy of, 50
Information: omission of, in much advertising, xi, xiv, 24, 43, 119, 274–80, 282; demanded in advertising by consumerists and regulators, xi, 276–77, 281–82; obligation of sellers to supply, questioned, 281–82; sellers' need for, questioned, 282–83; sellers' definition of, 283; familiarity as, 283–84
Innocent misrepresentation. *See* Misrepresentation
Inspection. *See* Buyer, and inspection of his purchase

Insurance claim, 183
Ipana claim, 180–82
Iron City beer, 163
Isaacs, Leigh R.: article of, xii, 215, 337
ITT-Continental Baking Co., 142

J&B claims, 18
Jello claim, 20
Jencks, Richard, 278
Jewelry claims, 110, 114–17
Johnny Lightning claim, 7, 243, 302
Johnson, Wendell: *People in Quandaries,* 305
Jolly Green Giant, 286
Jones, Kensinger, 342
Jones, Mary Gardiner, Commissioner, 27, 188, 208–9, 246

Kalven, Harry, Jr.: *Cases and Materials on Torts,* 312
Kashmoor sweater claim, 224
Kava coffee claim, 242
KDKA claim, 19
Keebler claim, 19
Keeton, R. E., 336
Kellogg's claim, 19
Kent, James, Justice, 53, 60, 99, 315–16; *Commentaries,* 64, 309, 311, 317, 319, 321
Kent claim, 19
Kershaw, Andrew, 281, 291
Kessler, Felix: article of, 339
Kessler claim, 18
King's Bench, 48–49
King's common law. *See* Common law
Kintner, Earl W., 314–15; *A Primer on the Law of Deceptive Practices,* 323, 338
Kirkpatrick, Clayton, 305
Kirkpatrick, Miles, FTC chairman, 278
Kleenex, 214
Knauer, Virginia, 231
Kool claim, 18

Korzybski, Alfred: *Science and Sanity*, 305
Kraft claim, 18

Laches, 96
Laissez faire, 50
Lamm, Judge, 202–3
Latent (hidden) defects, 34, 53, 69–70, 72–73
Law, matters of: contrasted to matters of fact, 13–14, 194, 196, 205, 216, 293, 333
Lawless traders, 35–36
Law merchant, 35, 39
Lawrence, Justice, 70
Lee, Irving J.: *Language Habits in Human Affairs*, 305
Legalized lying. *See* Caveat emptor; Puffery, legal treatment of
Lenin, xii
Lestoil claim, 20
Levitt, Theodore: article of, 269–70, 342
Lifebuoy claim, 243
Light bulb disclosures, 146, 187
Liquor names: protected, 224
Literally misdescriptive names, 16, 139, 218–32, 235, 244, 253, 339
Literal meaning of claims, x, 92, 108, 120, 129, 134, 140–41, 151, 155–58, 170, 176, 180, 193, 206, 211, 218–32, 234, 247, 259–60, 262, 337; contrasted to secondary meanings, 219–24, 227–30
Liz' Frozen Custard claim, 253–54
Llewellyn, Karl N.: *Cases and Materials on the Law of Sales*, 308; article of, 309, 311
Loevinger, Lee, Commissioner: article of, 278
Lopus, 42–45, 48–50
Lord Calvert claim, 19
Lottery tickets claim, 59
Louisville claim, 19
"Lumberyard explanation," 230
Lysol claims, 9, 19, 280, 302

MacGregor, James: article of, 342
MacIntyre, Commissioner, 330
"Made in USA" claim, 219–20
Madras claim, 223
Magnuson, Warren, Senator: *The Dark Side of the Marketplace*, 260, 341
Mail statute, 107
Mansfield, Chief Justice, 321
Manufacturer: obligations of. *See* Seller, obligations and responsibilities of
Market towns, 35
"Mark of Excellence" claim, 264–65, 288
Marlboro: claim, 19; man, 285
Marmola claims, 149
Marquisat claim, 24–25
Mars claim, 19
Mason, Commissioner, 329
Massachusetts: Supreme Judicial Court, 55, 104; law of, supporting exemption of opinion and puffery claims, 100–102, 104, 116, 125–28, 319
Mass communication: theory of, 266
Material nature of claims, 110–11, 124–28, 140, 145, 207, 246–47, 261–63, 322, 325, 333
Mattress claim, 177
McClain, Emlin: article of, 308
McDonald's claim, 230–31, 280
McMahon, Ed, 239
McMurtrie, R. C.: article of, 308
McNeely, M. C.: article of, 304
Meat: retaining color of, mock-up, 239–40
Medical Messiahs, The, 276, 342
Michigan Law Review: article in, 327, 343
Middle Ages, 33–35, 38–39, 50, 67
Midi skirt: demand for, 266
Milan hats claim, 227–28
Miller, Gale T., 330
Millstein, Ira M.: article of, 303, 323, 327–28

Milwaukee Journal, 14
Minute Rice claim, 20, 28
"Miracle ingredient" claim, 119
Misrepresentation: innocent (strict liability), 39, 41, 48, 87–88, 134–135, 159–60; leading cases of, 60, 85; relation of, to warranty law, 79–80; contribution of, to consumerism, 81, 87–88, 90; negligent, 84–87, 134–35, 137, 164–65, 312; rule of, applied to opinion claims, 88, 90, 92–109, 318; requirements for, in common law cases, 88, 134–35, 137; relation of, to FTC actions, 88–89, 108; common law penalties for, 136–37; as intended by seller to be taken as false, 206–7. *See also* Deception; Federal Trade Commission; Fraudulent misrepresentation
Missouri Public Interest Research Group, 334
Mock-ups, 16, 185–86, 218, 232–44
Model statutes, 65
Montgomery, Charlotte: article of, 339
Moore, Judge, 330
Morrissey, John J., 304
Morris the Cat, 285
Morrow, Winston V., Jr., 258–59
Mr. Clean, 286
Multa fidem promissa levant, 102
Murray, Sir James A. H.: *The Oxford English Dictionary,* 308
Mushroom-growing claim, 182–83

Nader, Ralph, 141, 260, 291; *Unsafe at Any Speed,* 341
Names. *See* Literally misdescriptive names
National Advertising Review Board, 264–65, 275, 334, 341, 344
Negative option selling, 256–57
Negligence, 13, 54, 312; contributory, by recipient of message, 95–96, 100, 103, 111, 164–65, 167, 203, 315, 335–36

Negligent misrepresentation. *See* Misrepresentation
Nelson, Philip J., 343
Nestlé's claim, 4, 18, 21
New York: Supreme Court of, 53–54
New York Times, x, 305, 320, 339, 340; *Book Review,* 344
NHA complex claim, 184
Norelco claim, 19
Nude assertions. *See* Bare assertions

Obvious falsity, 10, 12–16, 26, 34, 56, 168, 193, 195–209, 212–13, 219–20, 253, 315
Octane disclosure, 146
Oddjob commercial, 206–7
Offer to seller by third party: claim of, 98–99, 102, 121–28
Ogara, James V.: article of, 343
Ogilvy, David, 265, 281; *Confessions of an Advertising Man,* 327, 341, 343
Oil converter claim, 128–29
Olde Frothingslosh claims, 163, 172, 174, 205, 252
Old Golds claim, 143
Old Grand Dad claim, 18
Oldsmobile claim, 18
Opinion claims. *See also* Puffery
—, legal treatment of: lagging in consumerism trend, 92, 112–19, 330; exempted from fraud rule applying to factual claims, 92–104, 107, 111, 175, 316–18, 330–31; assumption that buyer can inspect, 94–97, 99–100, 105; first case to refer to, 95; accidental precedents for, 97–99; first American case, 99; by Supreme Court, 106–7; by FTC, 108, 148–50, 172–73; restrictions imposed on, 108–13, 316; in warranty law, 318. *See also* Massachusetts; Puffery, legal treatment of
—, meaning of and response to: implying facts, 25, 88, 92, 108–13, 116–19, 319; speaker's lack of be-

lief in, 25, 97; alleged to imply no factual knowledge, 96, 98, 108–9, 115; replacing factual claims, 97. *See also* Puffery, effects of; Puffery, meaning of, to public
—, types of: special, 112–19; opinions-as-to-fact, 113, 148; majority, 113–14; claim of "second-rate," 316
Opportunity to inspect. *See* Buyer, and inspection of his purchase
Oral misrepresentations: control of, 225
Origin, claim misstating, 221–22
Overholzer, Charles, 306
Ownership. *See* Title
Oxen claim, 59
Oxford Dictionary, 42

Pan American claim, 20, 28
Parker, Chief Judge, 144
Parker, Chief Justice, 61–62
Parker Pen claim, 20
Parliament, 85
Peachum wood, 52, 69–70
Pennsylvania: Supreme Court of, 63; law of, 63, 65–66
Pepto-Bismol claim, 20
Philadelphia Inquirer, 340
Philco-Ford claim, 190
Pie size claim, 231
Pillsbury doughboy, 286
Pine, California white, claim, 222
Pirenne, Henri: *Economic and Social History of Medieval Europe*, 307
Pitofsky, Robert F., 333
Pittsburgh Brewing Co., 163
Pittsburgh Pirates, 248
Placebos, 45, 176
Playboy claim, 211
Plyhide claim, 219–20
Polaroid claim, 23–24
Potter, David: *People of Plenty*, 337
"Premium beer" claim, 18, 189–90
"Premium tires" claim, 189–90
Preston, Albert W., Jr., 248–50, 253

Preston, Ivan L.: as FTC witness, 147–48, 150–58; as Wisconsin hearing witness, 159; experiences of, with puffing claims, 225, 229, 232, 248–54; children of, 253–54; speech of, on consumer responsibility, 267; university courses of, 268; articles of, 305, 320, 341–42, 344
Preston, Jane A., 253–54
Preston, Kathryn L., 17, 249
Preston, Roberta W., 253
Preston, Thomas A., 248–50
Price claims: price information in advertising, xiv; price paid by seller, 125–28; price comparisons, 159, 189. *See also* Offer to seller by third party
Prince, Bob, 251
Printers' Ink: model statute, 137–38, 330; articles in, 323
Procter and Gamble claim, 24
Prosser, William L., 46, 86, 335; *Torts*, 302–3, 307–8, 312–14, 328, 335; articles of, 311–12
Protestantism, 50
Prudential claim, 20
Puffery. *See also* Opinion claims
—, definition and types of: defined, ix–x, 3, 16–18, 21–22, 107, 120–21, 183, 192, 213, 218, 303–4, 331, 333–34; usually false, 9, 16, 23–25, 176, 188–89, 252, 259, 289; stating no explicit facts, 17, 115, 303; list of examples of, 18–20; sometimes true, 23–24; factual, 98–99, 120–29; problem of identifying the puffing part of an opinion, 114–15, 339; expanded definition, 192–244; counter-statements which "de-puff," 319
—, effects of: on humor, xiii; allegedly trivial, xiii, 119, 245–72; on competition and the economy, xiii–xiv; apparent widespread effectiveness, 26–29, 119, 212, 262,

289; not discussed publicly, 246, 252, 254–61, 263; deception not absolute, 247, 252–53, 261–65; consumers' responsibility for, 247–48, 253, 265–72; attractive aspects of, 270–72; contrasted to hyperbole's effects, 270–72; effects and problems beyond deception, 273–95; not exclusive to one seller, 287–88; potential for damaging sellers' credibility, 287–90; Catch-22 for sellers, 289; potential for damaging law's credibility, 290–95 —, elimination of: how FTC could eliminate, 188–89; moves toward, 295–98; voluntary, by seller, 297 —, legal treatment of: as permissible lying, ix, x, xii, 3–4, 16, 26, 33, 57, 93, 107, 114–15, 170, 193, 259–60, 289; rooted in ancient sellerism and caveat emptor, xii–xiii, 5, 30–31, 33, 57, 105, 119, 172, 189, 194, 294–95; should assume deception of substantial numbers, 26, 28–29, 103; more severe in other countries, 33, 306; in common law, 90–119; assumption of distrust questioned, 102–3, 105, 289, 293; assumption that buyer will distrust, 102–5, 114–15, 176, 196, 289, 293, 303; by Supreme Court, 107; by FTC, 108, 175–91, 334; exempted from rules applying to other types of opinion claims, 112–19; not applied outside marketplace, 113–19; assumption that seller will puff, 114–16; objection to using term *puffery*, 120–21; related to ignorant man standard, 172–73, 180–82; related to affirmative disclosure, 187; inconsistency in treatment of, 290–95; related to *Chandelor v. Lopus*, 314; earliest occurrence of term *puffery*, 320; as unfair practice, 342. *See also* Massachusetts

—, meaning of, to public: defended as meaningless and nondeceptive, xi, xiii, 4, 15, 23, 25–27, 29, 179, 182–83, 188, 191, 193, 220, 255, 259–60, 271–72, 304; attacked as meaningful and deceptive, 9, 15, 27, 172, 180, 188, 193, 245, 261–65, 273, 298, 333, 341; implying facts, 21–23, 25, 121, 181, 188–89, 283, 341; as kind of "information," 283–86. *See also* Opinion claims, meaning of and response to
—, sellers' uses of: as loophole or sanctuary, ix–xi, 31, 186, 260, 274–75; as substitute for information, xi, xiv, 24, 274–80, 284–86; insincere, 25; wide, 26–29, 119, 212; once insignificant to sellers, 259; as attention-getting device, 284–86

Quarry claim, 106

Raid roach killer, 242
Railroad bond claim, 104
Raladam claim, 150
Random House Dictionary of the English Language, The, 308
Rank & Son Buick, Inc., claim, 13
Rapid Shave claims, 20, 185–86, 235–38, 240, 274–75
RCA claim, 18
Reader's Digest, 143–44
Real estate claims, 118–19, 198–203
Reasonable persons and the "reasonable man standard," 4, 25–26, 103–6, 110, 116, 162–74, 180, 203, 305
Red Hots claim, 248–53, 261
Reece, Bonnie B.: article of, 343
Reformation, 50
Rejuvenescence claim, 170
Reliance by buyer on representations, 14, 26, 28–29, 55, 73–74, 91, 93–95, 100, 104–6, 110–17, 123–24, 134–35, 139, 164–66,

183, 193, 197, 200–201, 203–4, 285, 312, 335–36
Remington Rand claim, 190
Rent claims, 82, 94–95, 122–24, 127, 321
Restatement of the Law of Torts: section 283, 328; section 283A, 328; section 525, 302, 318, 336; section 526, 313; section 538, 128, 322, 336; section 539, 110, 116–18, 319, 331; section 540, 204, 335–36; section 541, 204, 336; section 542, 110, 114–17, 303
Revett, John: articles of, 324, 344
Reweaving claim, 184
Rise shaving cream claims, 19, 235
Robertson, Miss, 83
Rolle's Abridgement rule, 98–99, 121–26, 128, 320
Roman Catholic Church, 34–36, 50; canon law, 34–36
Romans, 33–34, 36; law of, 35–36, 39, 53
Roosevelt Hotel claim, 19
Roquefort cheese claim, 225

Sale of Goods Act. *See* Warranty
San Diego Padres, 340
Sandpaper shaving claim, 185–86, 235–38, 340
Sanford, David: *Who Put the Con in Consumer?,* 294, 344
Schick claim, 341
Schlitz claims, 18, 214–15, 286, 334
Schulz, John E.: *Nader's Raiders,* 323, 327
Schweppes claim, 215
"Scout" sleeping bags claim, 223–24
Sealtest claim, 18
Seaman, Alfred J., 283
Secondary meanings. *See* Literal meaning of claims
Secret deodorant claim, 182
Sederberg, Kathryn: articles of, 306, 344
Seligman, Daniel: article of, 339

Seller: unaware of falsity, 52–54; ability of, to judge lying, 275; right of, to use persuasion, 281; right of, not to communicate, 281–82
—, obligations and responsibilities of, 12–14, 32, 34–35, 43, 53–54, 57, 66–67, 70–71, 82, 99, 117, 134–35, 195, 202–4, 244, 267, 281–82; omitted from consideration by court, 14, 43, 54, 62–63, 70, 93; in pre-sellerist Middle Ages, 34, 38–39, 67
Sellerism, 30–57, 90, 97, 100, 102, 245; modern elimination of, 5, 30–31, 41, 46–47, 56–57, 66–67, 74–75, 81, 91–92, 108, 203–5, 295; defined, 30, 32; founded in 1534, 31–32; related events of 1534, 32; not existent in early Middle Ages, 35; contribution of *Chandelor v. Lopus* to, 44, 50; strengths which remain, 46, 92, 114–17, 121, 192, 196, 205, 210, 293; supported by sympathetic courts, 46–47, 52, 54, 56, 101, 258; defended today as ancient heritage, 47, 258; created largely by warranty rule, 49–50; assumed equality of seller and buyer, 50; sometimes utilized by buyers, 81–82, 123; related to puffery, 175, 246; support for its attitudes toward puffery, 246–48, 252; as no conspiracy of sellers, 294–95. *See also* Caveat emptor
Seller's talk, seller's statements, sales talk, 104, 115, 120
Sewing machine claims, 19, 183
Shaving commercials, 20, 185–86, 235–38, 240, 274–75
Shell Oil claims, 20, 279–80
Shoe insert and innersole claims, 183–84
Simplex commendatio non obligat, 317
Singer claim, 19

Six Month Floor Wax claim, 219–20
Smucker's: claim, 19; ice cream mock-up, 239
Social-psychological misrepresentations, xiii, 16, 193–94, 210–17, 220, 226–27, 262, 297; defined, 210–11; historical reasons for, 213–15
South Carolina, University of, 258
Spillane, Mickey, 243
Spoof claims and characters, 163, 205–9, 285–86
Standard Oil claims: California, 19; Indiana, 279–80
State Farm claims, 4, 19, 20, 28
Stay Dry deodorant claim, 295–96
Steinway claim, 20
Stone China claim, 219–20, 226–27
Story, Joseph: *Equity Jurisprudence*, 319
Story, William W.: *Sales*, 319
Strawberries claim, 159–60
Street, Thomas A.: *Foundations of Legal Liability*, 309–10
Strict liability. *See* Misrepresentation
Stuart, Dick, 251
Students Against Misleading Enterprises (SAME), 141
Students Opposed to Unfair Practices (SOUP), 340
Substantiation of claims, 118, 143, 161, 278, 290, 298, 304
Sudden Change claim, 243
Sunoco (Sun Oil) claims, 147, 150–58
Suppressio veri, 281
Supreme Court, U.S., 54, 72–73, 106–7, 132, 138, 149–50, 168–69, 173, 180, 183, 200–201, 221–23, 226, 238, 309, 318, 325, 340
Swamp Root claim, 276
Swan, Judge, 171
Sweden, Marketing Act of 1971: effects on puffery, 306
Swim-Ezy claim, 173
Swiss chocolate claims, 228

Tangible chattels. *See* Warranty
Tareyton claim, 211
Teeter, Dwight L.: *For Freedom of Expression*, 328
Tenant claim, 109
Term for years, claim, 93, 121–22
Texaco claim, 19, 28
Thain, Gerald J., xiv; article of, 337
Thayer, Frank: *Legal Control of the Press*, 314
Tiger in your tank claim, 7
Title (ownership) claims, 39, 59, 123–24
Toothpaste claims, 180, 193
Top Flite claim, 20, 190
Toronado claim, 18
Toshiba claim, 18
Tramway claim, 85
Trivial effects. *See* Puffery, effects of
Trust and distrust by buyers, 35, 56, 61–62, 93, 110–12; law's assumption that buyers distrust, 43, 102–5, 205, 293; law's assumption that buyers distrust questioned, 43–44, 102–3, 106, 168, 293; law's requirement for buyers to distrust, 44, 165, 203; law's requirement for buyers to distrust rejected, 168, 202–5. *See also* Puffery, legal treatment of
Truth in Advertising, 327, 330
Turk, Peter B., 330; article of, 328
Twelve-inch boards claim, 229, 231–32
Tyler William D.: articles of, 276–77, 343

Ultra-Brite claim, 193
Un-Burn claim, 9, 142–43, 302
Underwear claims, 221
Unfair practices, xii, 337, 342
Uniform Commercial Code. *See* Warranty
Uniform Laws Annotated, 307, 309, 310, 318, 335
Uniform Sales Act. *See* Warranty

Uniqueness claims, 141–42, 283
United Air Lines claim, 20
United States Steel Building claim, 118

Vacuum cleaner claim, 76
Value claims. *See* Opinion claims
Van den Haag, Ernest, 256
Vaseline claim, 211
Viceroy claim, 19
Vicks Formula 44 claim, 206
Virginia hams claim, 224
Virginia Slims claim, 193, 285
Vivarin claim, 216, 258
Volkswagen claim, 211

Wagon claim, 99–100, 125
Wall Street Journal, 277, 286, 304, 339
Warranty
—, definition and types of, 37–38, 41–42; express, 53, 61–63, 65–68, 70–71, 73–76, 80, 310–11; title (ownership), 59–60, 67–68, 311; implied, 66–74, 76–78, 80, 308, 310–12; fitness, 69, 72–74; merchantability, 69–74, 76, 78, 311; reach of warranty (privity), 74–75; disclaimers, 76
—, effects of legal treatment of: functioning mainly to protect sellers, 41–44, 49–50, 56, 58; contribution to consumerism today, 56, 58, 66, 80–81, 87, 90; weaknesses remaining in contribution to consumerism, 58, 318; FTC report on, 77; effects of disclaimers, 77–78, 88; factors unhelpful to buyers, 88, 134, 318
—, legal treatment of: in Middle Ages, 41–42; distinguished from affirmation of fact, 42–45, 48–49, 59–60, 62–63, 66–67, 315–17; equated with affirmation of fact, 59–64,

66, 108; by Sale of Goods Act, 65; by Uniform Sales Act, 65–66, 68, 72–74, 78, 88, 310; by Uniform Commercial Code, 66, 68, 72–74, 78, 88, 108, 318, 336; coverage extended to buyer (revoking privity rule), 74–76, 80, 88, 312; disclaimers permitted, 77–80; FTC handling of, 79; applied to tangible chattels only, 88; applied to opinion claims, 88, 90, 92–93, 108; whether represented to buyer, 91; related to obvious falsity rule, 195, 200, 203–5, 335
Waste silk claim, 71–72, 311
"Weasel" claim, 158
West, Michael: article of, 312
Westinghouse claim, 4, 19, 259–60
Wheaties claim, 19
Wheeler, Senator Burton K., 179
Wheeler-Lea Amendments. *See* Federal Trade Commission
Who Put the Con in Consumer?, 294
Williams, Herbert A., 13–14, 25–26, 163, 193, 195, 205
Williston, Samuel: 63, 86, 127; Sales, 307, 309–12, 318, 322, 335; article of, 307, 314
Wine names, protected: 224–25
Winters, Katy, 181–82
Wisconsin: Supreme Court of, 13–14; University of, 151, 268; regulatory hearing, 159; Motor Vehicle Trade Practice Code, 297; price comparison regulation, 327
Wisconsin Automotive Trades Association, 297
Wonder Bread claims, 9, 20, 141–43, 215–17, 302
Wood, load of, claim, 93–94, 97, 196, 205
Woodside, Arch G.: article of, 341
Woodward, M. Cabell, 142
Wool claims, 221
Wrigley claim, 20
Wuthering Heights, 285

Yale Law Journal: article in, 323–24
Yogurt claim, 185
Young, James Harvey: *The Medical Messiahs*, 276, 342

Zenith claim, 18
Zerex claim, 9, 243, 302

DESIGNED BY GARY GORE
COMPOSED BY THE COMPOSING ROOM, GRAND RAPIDS, MICHIGAN
MANUFACTURED BY GEORGE BANTA CO., INC., MENASHA, WISCONSIN
TEXT IS SET IN JOURNAL ROMAN, DISPLAY LINES IN TIMES ROMAN

Library of Congress Cataloging in Publication Data
Preston, Ivan L 1931–
The great American blow-up.

Includes index.
1. Advertising—United States. 2. Salesmen and
salesmanship. 3. Advertising law—United States. I. Title.
HF5813.U6P68   1975   659.1   74-27313
ISBN 0-299-06730-0